Who killed Ereminta?

God, guns and government

on the

Central Australian frontier

Peter Vallee

Restoration

R

Restoration
Canberra, Australia
restorationbooks@gmail.com

ISBN 978 0 9775312 1 9
Readers' edition (Amazon version)
with illustrations printed on text paper.
2008

CONTENTS

THE TRIAL OF THE FINKE RIVER MISSION 1890

THE TRIALS OF WILLIAM WILLSHIRE 1891

EPILOGUE

1

"ME AND ALL ABOUT BIG-FELLOW CRY"[1]

The morning twilight was the preferred time for attack in Central Australia. The Western Aranda people of the upper Finke River recognised by name eight stages in the progression from first light to sunrise. They knew precisely when there was light enough to identify a sleeping human form in the sand of the river-bed.

For this reason, when Mounted Constable William Willshire and his four Aboriginal troopers had arrived on Tempe Downs pastoral station with murder in mind they set up camp in the Walker Creek early in the evening of February 21st, 1891 several kilometres away. Willshire knew that two Aboriginal men, Ereminta and Donkey would be found there, camped in the dry sand bed of Walker Creek where it ran past the station buildings.[2]

Ereminta was a man who impressed those he met, white and black. Six years earlier, in 1885, Charles Chewings, a shareholder of the Tempe Downs Pastoral Company, had travelled widely in the country west of the station. Chewings' Aboriginal employee Jacky was not a local man and prevailed upon Ereminta to accompany Chewings. Ereminta knew no English, but he knew where all the good waters were to be found, and Jacky could interpret for him.[3] Ereminta was one of the few Aboriginal persons of the Centre whose name Charles Chewings recorded. Women also found Ereminta attractive, among them his wife Nungoolga who that night slept with Ereminta in the bed of the Walker Creek. Nungoolga was a Western Aranda woman by marriage whom Ereminta had 'stolen', according to the neighbouring missionaries, without the consent of her late husband's people. When Nungoolga followed Ereminta to Tempe Downs station she had left behind at the Finke River mission her two children from her earlier marriage, a son Rauwiraka and a daughter Sarah.

Willshire briefed his troopers before they spread their swags that night. He wanted Ereminta and Donkey dead. Troopers Aremala and Coognalthika were to shoot Donkey. The instructions to Troopers Tekua and Kwalba were, according to Aremala's later report, to shoot Ereminta if he attempted to escape. Kwalba recalled only an instruction to shoot him. Tellingly, the policeman's handcuffs and neck-chains remained in his camel pack when the party set out for Tempe Downs at 3.00 am the next morning.

It took them one and a half hours on foot to reach Tempe Downs station, a cluster of five buildings on the banks of Walker Creek. They were slowed by Willshire, one of whose feet was injured and could not be put into its boot.

The four white station workers slept outside one or other of the stone and timber buildings of the station. They were Michael Devlin and Charles Tucker, both stockmen, William Abbott, who described himself as a prospector but made his living by station work, and the station cook Denis White. Outside the kitchen building, with a ringside view of the river bed where savagery was soon to erupt, lay five Aboriginal women. Chinchewarra, Illingia, Theeanka, Lucy and Muneroo and a young Aboriginal boy, Witchetie.

Chinchewarra was a Matuntara woman, that is from the country now occupied by Tempe Downs station, and about 30 years of age. She was the mistress of the station manager, Frederick Thornton, and this, combined with strength of personality and superior command of the local pidgin English, gave her high status. Her lover and boss Thornton was not at the station that morning. Four days earlier, on February 18th, Thornton had accompanied Charles Chewings, who was again inspecting the property, past Willshire's camp at Boggy Water on the Finke River. They were on their way to inspect some of Tempe Downs' leases in the McDonnell Ranges, 150 kilometres and more to the north. [4]

Ereminta and Donkey slept separately in the sandy bed of Walker Creek, among the pale eucalypt trees. Donkey's wife Illingia was with the women sleeping outside the kitchen.

It was not to be the cleanest of raids, the kind of polished operation of which Willshire later boasted. He knew the disposition of his intended victims in the river bed before he and his troopers broke camp that morning. The two troopers who were to kill

Donkey, Aremala and Coognalthika, moved along one side of the river-bed. Tekua and Kwalba moved down the other side, to the camp of Ereminta and Nungoolga who slept a mere 100 yards from the kitchen, and 150 yards across the river-bed from Donkey.

Within sight of the sleeping forms of their targets each designated pair was to split, with one trooper approaching his victim from one direction, the other from a different direction. If either Ereminta or Donkey bolted he would run into range of at least one of the troopers' firearms.

For Aremala and Coognalthika events worked according to plan. When Aremala came to close quarters Donkey still slept. Aremala fired a single rifle shot into Donkey's chest. Donkey died where he lay.

In the silence of a desert summer morning the explosion of a rifle shot is shocking. At Tempe Downs station, facing low cliffs on two sides of Walker creek, even the echoes would have been startling. The women lying outside the kitchen wall woke immediately. Even the deepest sleeper among the white station workers must have soon realised this was not the beginning of a normal working day.

The significance of gun fire at first light was not lost on Ereminta or his wife Nungoolga. Ereminta sprang to his feet, shouting to Nungoolga, "Get up, get up, the policemen are shooting."[5] According to Illingia he also called out, "Come on Nimi my lubra we must run away."[6] Nungoolga was, of course, terrified, but she saw immediately that there was something incongruous going on here. Ereminta was employed on the station, and that gave him a higher level of protection from arbitrary violence by whites than was available to the "bush black". Nungoolga ordered Ereminta to fetch some horses, not to escape but because that was part of his job, and by asserting his status as an employee Ereminta might, for all she knew, stay Tekua's hand. Ereminta ran, but a quick shot from Tekua's rifle caught him low in the back and he fell. Kwalba approached firing two shots with his revolver from thirty yards, hitting Ereminta in the leg.

In the sixty seconds or so from the first shot to the last no words were exchanged between the troopers and their victims.

By the time Trooper Kwalba shot Ereminta, Nungoolga was sprinting the 100 yards across the sand to join the other women watching in horror from their kitchen camp. She saw no more of what happened to Ereminta.

Chinchewarra, however, was all eyes. The other women ran for the shelter of the kitchen, but Chinchewarra stood out on the river bank and saw the killing of Ereminta from a distance of 100 metres.

Willshire had not gone forward with either of the two pairs of troopers. Instead he held back near the station, limping about in excitement, shouting out, according to Chinchewarra's rendition, "Wow, wow", like white-men mustering cattle.[7]

What Willshire did next is not perfectly clear, but Chinchewarra's evidence on this point, to Postmaster Frank Gillen two months later, assured Willshire of three months of misery and the prospect of death by hanging.

Frank Gillen's evidence records Chinchewarra saying "I saw Willshire cut Roger's throat with a big knife". Gillen was appalled. Three months later Willshire's superior officer interviewed Chinchewarra and recorded that she said only that Willshire *told* the women at the station that he had cut Ereminta's throat. One way or the other, from Willshire's knife or a revolver, the mortally wounded Ereminta received his *coup de grâce*.

While Chinchewarra remained clear-eyed and observant, all the women were distraught. "Me and all about big-fellow cry" recalled Donkey's wife Illingia[8]. She had seen the troopers in the creek, when she was woken by the shot that killed her husband, but Donkey was of course motionless on the ground and out of sight.

Willshire's business was not finished. He ordered Nungoolga to remain at the station. After he and his troopers had breakfasted outside the kitchen, Kwalba and Coognalthika fetched the camels from their camp and the two bodies were carted, with Billy Abbott's assistance, to separate places within 400 metres of the station and burnt, one in the river bed, the other in sand dunes. In the several hours occupied by this work the white station workers managed, according to their evidence to Gillen, to see nothing of it. They were asleep, according to the women - frightened, according to one – and we can not know whether they feared what they knew was happening, or what they guessed must be happening.

Only Billy Abbott emerged, to help his sometime employer Willshire and the troopers with the disposal of the corpses.[9]

"Don't look for your Noona (husband) any more", Willshire told Nungoolga, and took her back with him to Boggy Water. Later she fled to the Finke River mission, thirty kilometres further up the Finke River where she was interviewed two months later, with Theeanka, by Frank Gillen.

With the departure of Willshire and his troopers relative quiet settled onto Tempe Downs station. The remaining women shared with Illingia her mourning, as best they could. Their depression can easily be imagined. Two other Aboriginal men, who were also said by Willshire to be on his wanted list and who had been sleeping in the river-bed that morning, escaped into the nearby gorges and no doubt stayed there.

The silence of the white men persisted. Billy Abbott later stated to Gillen that he had heard of the killings from Chinchewarra, but had seen nothing and "refused to listen to the lubra as I did not want to know anything about it." Michael Devlin could not even say whether or not he was there for the killings, having "no memory for dates", nor, apparently, for mayhem. Charles Tucker and Denis White heard the shots but did not bother to get up, although White, as station cook, should by that time have been busy in the kitchen.

So strong was their will not to know, that when station manager Thornton returned on March 25th they told him nothing. Even Chinchewarra, not the shrinking kind, left him ignorant.

Thornton left the homestead again on March 25th, not returning until the evening of April 22nd, at the very moment Frank Gillen arrived, with a commission from the State's Attorney-General, to tell Thornton of the ghastly events that had happened on his own premises.

It was Frank Gillen's task to find out what had happened on the morning of February 22nd 1891, and to report his findings to the South Australian Attorney-General Robert Homburg. At that point Homburg had heard only William Willshire's version. What happened thereafter was a matter for British justice, and for the politics of the democratic, self-governing British province of South Australia.

All this happened over a century ago. Nothing stands now on the banks of Walker Creek where Tempe Downs station's homestead once stood, not even ruins. Of Tempe Downs' substantial buildings, among the most substantial in Central Australia at that time, all but a few scattered stones was washed away in 1981. No-one lives within fifty kilometres today and the silence is rarely broken by the sounds of human voices or firearms. How much more can we now know of what happened in the Walker Creek over one hundred and ten years ago? Why did Tekua shoot Ereminta so cold-bloodedly? Why was it so important to William Willshire to mark Ereminta's death with such cruelty and spite? Was this normal conduct on the Central Australian frontier? Whose motives lay behind the brute deeds?

These would not be easy questions to answer had the events taken place yesterday, although there are simple answers already in print for those who want them. According to these unresearched accounts, William Willshire was responsible for "literally thousands"[10] of deaths, and he worked for a government engaged in an "unofficial policy of genocide"[11]. Fortunately for those who distrust such ready-made answers, there are tracks to follow from the silence of Walker Creek today to that event one hundred and ten years ago. The first track was followed by Nungoolga and Theeanka, at the feet of Willshire's camels, east to the Finke River and north to Boggy Water, and then to the Finke River mission at Hermannsburg. We are going to follow them. Robert Homburg, gave these women a brief moment in the public life of South Australia, but at Hermannsburg there was a longer period of illumination. What happened at Hermannsburg over the preceding thirteen years provides part of the explanation of what happened at Tempe Downs on February 22nd, 1891 and who, if anyone, should have been hanged for it.

There is no photograph of Ereminta, but can this man, photographed at Tempe Downs in 1894, three years after Ereminta's death, provide a model of his appearance? In the collection of the Museum of Victoria he is labelled as an Aranda man, but his decorations are indentical to those of other Tempe Downs men labelled Loritja, that is, Ereminta's people (MV XP14286).

Chinchewarra and Nungoolga in July 1891 (RGSSA).

"Me and all about big-fellow cry"

Coognalthika/Archie

Tekua/Thomas

Qualpa/Jack

Aremala/Larry

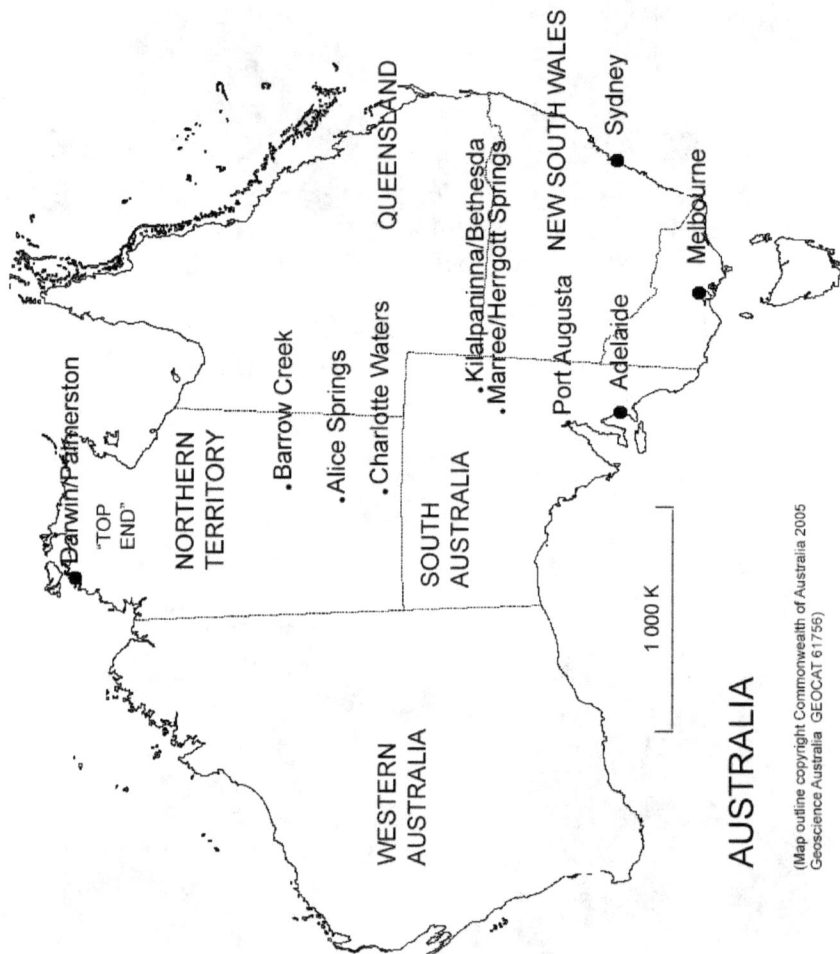

AUSTRALIA

(Map outline copyright Commonwealth of Australia 2005
Geoscience Australia GEOCAT 61756)

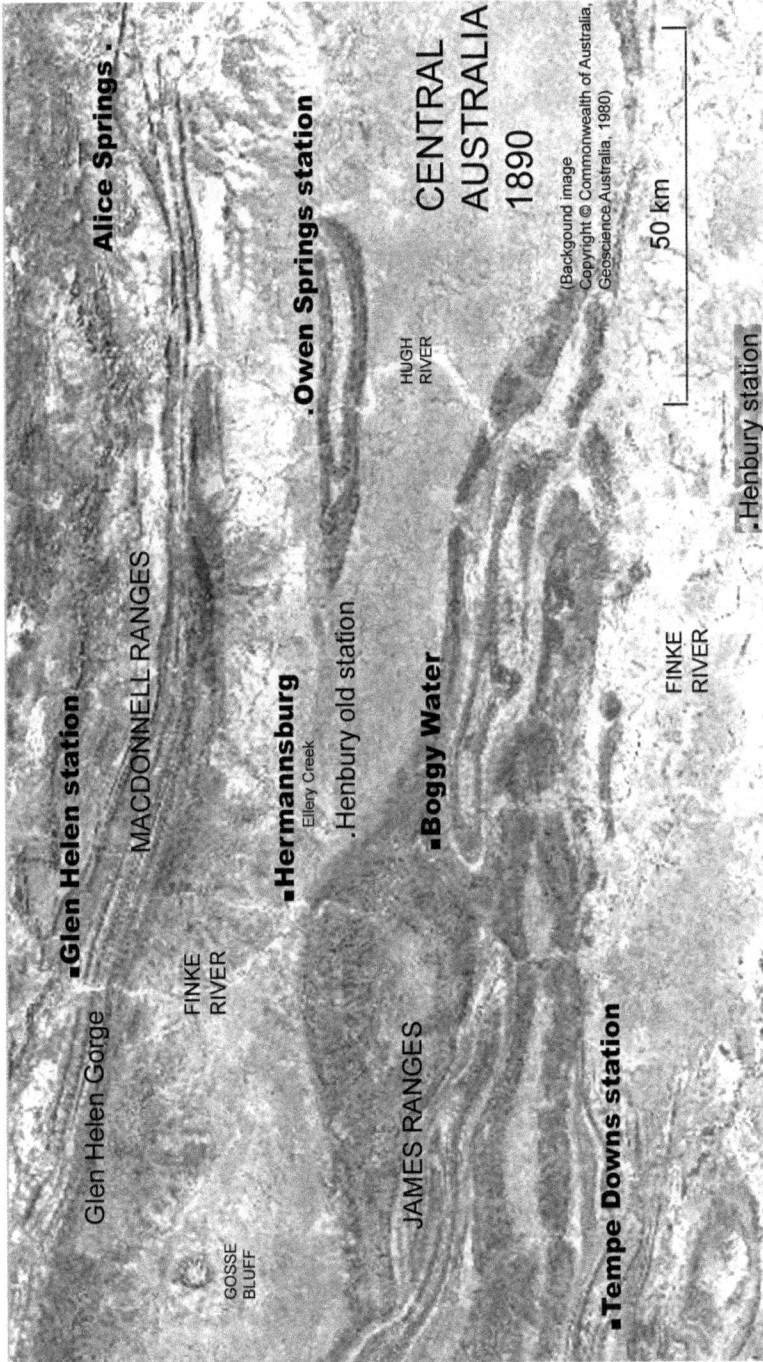

CENTRAL AUSTRALIA 1890

(Backgound image
Copyright © Commonwealth of Australia,
Geoscience Australia, 1980)

50 km

Alice Springs .

.Owen Springs station

HUGH
RIVER

.Henbury station

MACDONNELL RANGES

.Glen Helen station

Glen Helen Gorge

FINKE
RIVER

.Hermannsburg
Ellery Creek
.Henbury old station

.Boggy Water

FINKE
RIVER

JAMES RANGES

.Tempe Downs station

GOSSE
BLUFF

11

This Aranda (not Western Aranda) man photographed by Baldwin Spencer in 1894 must stand proxy for the Western Aranda men the missionaries met on the banks of the Finke in 1877, and those Western Aranda men, like Latya, who continued the old heathen ways, defying the missionaries (MV XP14301).

FAITH TO FAITH 1877-1885

2

PROPHETS TO THE DESERT

But now the righteousness of God without the law is manifested... Therefore we conclude that a man is justified by faith without the deeds of the law.[12]

Perhaps August 4th 1877, when missionaries Hermann Kempe and Wilhelm Schwarz saw two naked men approaching, was one of those Central Australian winter days, when this colourful land radiates so brightly that the land itself appears to be the source of life and energy, despite the winter drought. It is a landscape of hope and a limitless future. That was how it struck Georg Heidenreich, Superintendent of the Finke River mission when he visited the site the previous year, in August 1876, scouting ahead for the missionaries' caravan.

> *When I reached the peak and saw before me a thirty mile wide and seventeen mile long plain I was stunned with admiration, not knowing how I should extol, praise and thank the Lord. My soul was suddenly very still before the Lord... Now we saw five miles of the magnificent and mighty Finke before our eyes. It winds like a snake through our territory, from the MacDonnell Ranges to the James ranges, and has many gums trees growing along it... I have never found another spot like this.*[13]

Eventually, however, one has to address the question, "how are we to live in this place?" The Western Aranda people and their precursors had been making a hard living on the upper Finke River for many thousands of years. Their new white neighbours had begun taking up residence only six years before.

When the missionaries arrived there were solid buildings and permanent white residents at the Alice Springs telegraph station, two days ride to the north-east of the mission lease. Much closer, just seven miles to the east, on Ellery Creek, there was the head station of the Henbury pastoral lease, most of which lay south of the James Ranges. This had been stocked for almost three years. East of Ellery Creek lay Owen Springs station, and to the east of the Alice Springs telegraph station another pastoral lease, Undoolya, had been stocked since 1876 at the latest. South and north of Alice Springs, separated by hundreds of kilometers, were the Charlotte Waters and Barrow Creek telegraph stations. This was Central Australia in 1876: a couple of thousand Aboriginal souls and, at another guess, fewer than one hundred Europeans. Around the upper Finke, where the Finke River mission was soon to be established, a few hundred Western Aranda and Loritja people and a few dozen European-Australians. Only the Aborigines were not intending to leave.

On that August day in 1877 two pairs of men faced each other on the banks of the Finke River. The two white men were Hermann Kempe and Wilhelm Schwarz, missionaries of the Hermannsburg Mission Institute, a school of evangelical Lutheranism founded in 1849 on the damp plains of northern Germany. Kempe and Schwarz were both short men in their mid-thirties, strongly-built and used to hard work. They had trekked overland for eighteen months to get to the Finke, and had been waiting several weeks for this meeting to happen.

Of the two naked black men all we know from Kempe and Schwarz is that they were "imposing", the Germans' description confirmed by the photographic portraits of such senior men taken twenty years later by the ethnographers Baldwin Spencer and Frank Gillen, showing men of strong physique, their skins glowing with good health and animal fat, confident in facing powerful strangers. They were Western Aranda men of high status. They wore a record of their ceremonial life in cicatrices cut across their chests. They wore also the scars of battle wounds. Possibly their thighs were deeply cut by the spear wounds inflicted in punishments by men they had offended against, and scars on their shoulders marked the deaths of family members. They wore around their waists a string made of human hair. To Kempe and Schwarz the string appeared to be a flimsy decoration, but it was in fact an essential tool in ceremonies of power. They carried their weapons and tools of trade, spears and a woomera, possibly a boomerang, which they may have laid on the ground as a sign of peaceful intent.

What do the missionaries see? They see two men superior in dignity and appearance to the demoralised fringe-dwellers they have passed in the year and a half they have spent travelling overland from Adelaide. Perhaps they also see nakedness as a pitiable symptom of separation from God, a wanton lack of modesty, (since for a clothed person the most obvious features of another's body are the parts *their* clothes are most intended to hide), and a provocation to immorality. The missionaries certainly see people whose present way of life is doomed, as the primitive and weak must give way to the civilised and favoured of God. Unless they are saved and civilized they are also cut off from the prospect of a continuing life after the death of their bodies.

For the Western Aranda, white was the colour of the returning dead. Tjalkabota, born around the time of the missionaries' arrival, was told by his people the white men's clothes were a different skin.[14] From the point of view of men whose naked bodies were in fact the ground on which symbol and sign stood out more clearly than mere anatomy, the white men's clothing might itself be proclaiming mysterious symbols, or hide the signs they assumed were on the white bodies beneath, possibly both. Whatever they made of the missionaries' clothing - disease, deformity, magic, script or disguise, they certainly did not read into it the office of Lutheran missionary.

One item of equipment Kempe and Schwarz wore would have been known to the Western Aranda men, at least by repute. The missionaries carried revolvers onto their lease since they expected, as frontiersmen, they might have to make their own peace. We know that the missionaries wore them in 1889. If ever they wore them before that date it would surely have been for this first meeting in 1877. We can be confident that the Western Aranda men had observed fire-arms on the missionaries or their lay helpers during the several weeks of close observation that had preceded August 4th 1877. They already knew firearms were the white men's highest magic.

Although each pair of men failed to read the significance of the other's appearance each pair saw the other as visitors, and both were correct, in their own terms. The missionaries believed they had a lease from the South Australian government giving them a right to occupy this land without excluding the Western Aranda from their traditional uses, and the Western Aranda had a cosmology that linked them, above all other humans, to the same land. Neither side saw the equipment of the other's minds. And yet it is what these four men carried in their minds that was to determine, more than their joint demands on the land and its waters, the future course of the relations between them over the next fourteen years.

All four men had unshakable beliefs about how the world was constituted and the proper relationship between men and the cosmos and with each other. Ahead of them lay a period of astonishment as the missionaries presented to the Western Aranda, when they would listen, what the Lutherans thought was the key to life present and life eternal. The Western Aranda discovered that the other strange-looking humans were not humans in the same way the Western Aranda were. The Western Aranda soon began to conceal most of their cosmology and law. Hermann Kempe and Wilhelm Schwarz, on the other hand, were there to reveal their beliefs and to persuade the Western Aranda of their truth.

Kempe and Schwarz were children of hard-working and pious north-German parents, well-schooled as children of pious Lutherans should be. They graduated at fourteen through Confirmation as lay members of the Lutheran Church. While religion had done much to define them as people it was not their vocation. They entered apprenticeships, Schwarz following his father into baking, while Kempe, after some years in mining, the occupation of his father, was apprenticed to a joiner. After graduating as tradesmen they both set out to see the world, like the back-packers of today, working their way as journeymen. Before German unification in 1870 it was possible to visit foreign countries, as Kempe claimed to have done, without leaving the comfort of German-speaking populations.

Wilhelm Schwarz, an unsettled and unhappy young man, reached at least as far as Schleswig-Holstein which at the time had recently been annexed by Prussia. He was a drinker and a gambler when, according to his obituarist, "he retired to his bed one night much disquieted about his soul's salvation when the Spirit of God, who had begun His work in him, brought a verse of one of Paul Gerhardt's famous hymns into remembrance".

> *By anxious care and grieving,*
> *By self-consuming pain,*
> *God is not moved to giving;*
> *By prayer must thou obtain.*

By resigning himself into faith on this night Schwarz found release from his unease, so repeating in a less scholarly form the experience of Martin Luther himself three hundred and fifty years earlier.

He "jumped out of bed and got on his knees to call upon the Lord [and] never forgot this special time of grace, but ever loved to speak of it unto others . . . he resolved then and there to offer himself for the service of the Lord in the mission field". His first intention was to enter the Missionshaus at Basel, representing a more liberal form of Lutheranism than the Hermannsburg Mission Institute, but "He set out on his way afoot, when in a rather unexpected way his steps were guided to the 'Missionshaus' at Hermannsburg". This was a fateful re-direction towards a form of Lutheranism that rejected the inroads of science into God's domain, as that was defined by biblical text.[15]

The Bible Schwarz and Kempe were taught from was not just a moral guide-book. To evangelical Lutheran Protestants like Ludwig Harms, the founder of the Hermannsburg Mission Institute, it was the manual from which people could learn, with the right Lutheran guidance, the constitution of the universe, the origin of the world's peoples, and the future of both. For Kempe and Schwarz correct conduct sprang from their Christian cosmology logically, although many philosophers had long denied such a connection. Those striving for perfection in their personal conduct, then as now, might form themselves around charismatic leaders into communities of faith in which they expected to find the power of their faith demonstrated in their own moral improvement. They believed that living conscientiously according to their religion would also produce a just and happy community. The Hermannsburg Mission Institute was a community of those seeking the assurance of faith, and with the purpose of seeding other such communities in the broader world.

Unlike Schwarz, Kempe professed that he had been as a young journeyman "completely indifferent" to his spiritual condition. One day he was informed by an old man that "I could obtain a good midday meal at Hermannsburg without having to pay for it." He took work with a nearby blacksmith, who reprimanded him for his "dreadful habit of swearing". Kempe was impressed that "I was able to break off the habit within a short space of time, [and] I attributed this to my natural ability." An opportunity to develop further his sense of moral potency came Kempe's way when one of the Hermannsburg Mission Institute's students invited him to a private house to hear a sermon written by Ludwig Harms. It centred on the way the Holy Spirit through the preaching of the Law (in essence the Ten Commandments) "must first bring us to a knowledge of our sins" and he was possessed by a strong sense of the reference of the sermon to himself. "I was shocked, for I thought this sermon had been specially designed for me, and I grew suspicious that he [the student friend] had told the preacher all about me".

From this time Kempe's thoughts became so occupied with religion that his boss sacked him for inattention to his work. Still he had to wait three years to be admitted to the Institute, in 1870, the year work began on the Overland Telegraph from Adelaide to the Top End of Australia. At Kempe's admission ceremony Theodor Harms, the Director of the Hermannsburg Mission Institute, stressed that Jesus Christ demanded "obedience and humility above all things". Kempe found in the Institute a new home. Relations between students and staff were very close; "there was never any argument or disharmony in that home, not even a dissident tone... My term of study in the Mission House was the loveliest time of my life and passed all too quickly." He felt so stirred by the sermon presented at his ordination that "little king that I was! - I could have challenged the whole world and waged battle against it."

The Hermannsburg Mission Institute taught Kempe and Schwarz - and their colleague Louis Schulze who joined them in 1877 - that while, in an everyday sense, a sin can be a breach of some moral rule or protocol, the Christian doctrine of sin goes much further. For a breach of a rule a specified punishment can be administered and the matter settled, but Christianity was built on the idea that sin was a disease of the human spirit caused by separation from God. Original Sin is both the historical event in the Garden of Eden and a judgement that humans are in general defective. The necessary remedy for this defect was the experience of conversion into the Christian faith, a faith Kempe and Schwarz already, in an intellectual sense, shared before their evangelical conversion. That conversion into faith is, in the Christian view, an achievement of God's Grace alone, and owes nothing to human virtue or rule-keeping. That re-vivified faith, the Lutherans insisted, was also sufficient, if sincerely held, to provide the ticket to eternal life.

It is unlikely that at this early stage of their lives as missionaries Kempe or Schwarz worried themselves with the thought that on the other side of Grace lie dilemmas as difficult as those of the unredeemed life. How can the faithful be in conflict on matters of faith? How much faith is enough, and how can one have assurance that one has that quantum? If one has that much faith can one still sin, or, as the Antinomians believed, are you beyond the reach of worldly laws and common morality? Are some assured of Grace from conception, as the Pre-destinarians believed, and the rest correspondingly damned without prospect of redemption? Is Grace, then, a moral privilege whose possessors are given powers of action denied to ordinary men and women? Over this territory Christians had warred for centuries in part because, in their view, Sin, Faith and Grace were the key to life in this world, and beyond. Without experience of these forces your Christianity was a sham.

Grace is also jealous of its dignity. What do we do about backsliding? If sinning continues, and the grant of Grace needs to be repeated, is it truly God's gift and worth any more than a Priest's absolution? With frailer souls it is better perhaps to prevent backsliding by avoiding the occasions of sin. The communion of saints had better be a closed community of saints, dedicated to keeping the unregenerated at arm's length, so that Grace may be left to do its work, in its special Lutheran way.

It must have astonished Schwarz and Kempe when they found out that the Aboriginal men facing them beside the Finke River lacked completely the essential pre-condition for conversion to evangelical Christianity, a recognisable sense of sin. At least there was no sense of sin in connection with the rules the missionaries took to be fundamental. As Kempe concluded ten years later, "The only laws concerning sexual intercourse were the traditional rules of the class system, which ... permitted promiscuous intercourse within the limits of the group. That polyandry or polygamy, fornication and prostitution were sins was something so foreign to their traditions and customs that even the new converts time and again became guilty of offences against morality" Kempe was confusing an absence of shame about sexual relations with an absence of regulation. Of the way the Western Aranda regulated their society there was a great deal for the missionaries to learn, and they would do it the hard way.

On one occasion a man employed as a shepherd had taken his payment in kind, literally. He no doubt thought the payment reasonable, and the sheep's hide was found by the mission personnel not far from the shepherd. When the man had returned to the camp next door to the mission, Schwarz paid him a visit. He took hold of the man by the shoulders, as was Schwarz's style, and confronted him with his offence. The man leapt up and took to the hills, according to the missionaries, and was not seen again for some weeks. This seemed to them quaint at the time but it revealed something they really needed to understand. When asked who was responsible the other men just said, 'not me, not me'. "It never occurs to them to admit their guilt" Schulze reported, "so we have often punished a perpetrator without an admission of guilt." It never occurred to the missionaries, or to Kempe and Schulze in particular, that there was any other way to civic virtue and Christian belief but through admission of guilt.

The two imposing men on the Finke River simply thought that much of this baggage was inapplicable to their world, unnatural, undignified, unnecessary or downright cruel. As two of T. G. H. Strehlow's old informants put it in the 1930s, "Before the whites came, we were all good people. We tended the sites of our totemic ancestors. We guarded our sacred caves. We performed our ceremonies, and we had many beautiful songs to sing. We were morally blameless."[16]

They were better than blameless. For the initiated man, union with the eternal did not need to wait until death, but was achieved through correct ceremony in the midst of life. The fact that

Western Aranda men bowed down before no god or king and claimed the prerogative to share in the powers of their creator-spirits, to harness the powers that constituted the universe, this was unthinkable arrogance to the Hermannsburg Lutherans. Death, in fact, interrupted the Western Aranda man's rising trajectory of spiritual and temporal power. It meant the dissolution of the individual into the continuing flow of his particular creative force or totem, from which new men and women would find embodiment when a woman came within the influence of a powerful site. This was serial incarnation rather than re-incarnation. The affiliation of each Western Aranda man with these unseen forces was marked by a personal *tjurunga*, a board or piece of flat stone with symbolic markings. A personal *tjurunga* was allocated to each boy by the senior men of his totem. It became the key to, and the mnemonic and certificate of, the individual's life of faith.

Whatever the educated men of the British Colonial Office thought when they wrote the protocols for race relations in the Australian Colonies, the South Australian colonists themselves, after almost half a century of causing and observing the immiseration of the Aboriginal people of the Colony, were in no doubt that the hunter-gatherer life of the Aborigines was nasty, brutish and, increasingly, short. There was good evidence, in their low birth-rates, high death-rates and the racial mixing of the fringe settlements, that the Aborigines as a distinct race were facing extinction within a few generations. They also believed in a hierarchy of peoples at the top of which stood the British, while somewhere very near the bottom languished the Australian Aborigines.

Schwarz and Kempe were not discouraged from their mission by scientistic assumptions of this kind, although they must have been aware of them and of their currency among the white people who surrounded them. For the Lutherans the descent of man, provoked by Sin, led from the Garden of Eden to Central Australia in 1877, and that path could be travelled in the reverse direction. They believed, as missionary Schulze said in 1879, that "in so far as they go naked and wander around without a home, they are like cattle. But I, and every true Christian, cannot regard this condition of the natives as their greatest wretchedness which is rather that they do not know the lord Jesus...".[17] They believed that only Sin and ignorance of the Biblical Law and the Gospel separated the Western Aranda from the settled, fully-clothed life of a modern European. So, when the missionaries saw in the Western Aranda intelligence, coupled with inability to grasp what they were preaching, and capacity to learn new skills quickly, coupled with unwillingness to carry them out, they attributed all this to moral failings such as obduracy and laziness. Very judgmental of them, but closer to our modern concept of cultural difference among biologically-identical humans than was the late nineteenth Century's more educated idea of an evolutionary hierarchy of mental development, with some races shunted into dead-ends beside history's highway.[18]

Since the senior men refused to tell them, how could Kempe and Schwarz know they were talking to a people whose cosmology was as highly-developed as their material goods were simple. It had particular creator-spirits to explain the locality and its people, plants, animals and other significant phenomena, but it had no place for these invading pastoralists, their animals, foods and property, and no idea of their great, remote, patriarchal shepherd-God beyond the sky. It was not just a matter of different gods, or their number. The whole notion of a single, non-material person in whom the power of causation and moral example continued to reside was totally absent. Equally absent was the single, commanding voice of personal conscience, this role also being distributed among the spirit and human enforcers of the Western Aranda rules of conduct.

Remonstration is among the faded practices of the European past, at least so far as it might be addressed to the failures of individuals. In the first two centuries after the Protestant revolution the voice of remonstration constituted a major literary genre, usually in the form of published sermons. Remonstration was not directed only at the sinner, but also at the saved. Our three missionaries preached to each other long before they had a Western Aranda congregation to preach to. For these men of the Word the elaborated remonstration of their sermons made up the collective voice of the Protestant conscience and informed the voice of their own.

For the Western Aranda the voice of accusation was not the self-contained, the familiar voice of conscience, the voice of oneself and one's parents and one's colleagues, combining love and correction. For the western Aranda the voice of conscience was someone else's voice, and it often spoke with the spear, knife and club, or worse. It was the voice of the offended man or the revenger, who exacted the price of transgression in blood and pain, a speared thigh, broken bones, and possibly a lingering, isolated death. Your enemy might also attack you with evil magic. Any mature man had played himself the role of avenger often enough to know what kind of misery lay in store for him if another revenger caught up with him. When a person transgressed the fundamental rules of Western Aranda society, the voice of accusation was that of the old men assembled in council, whose judgement was expressed by the severest means, often fatal, and could only be avoided by placing a large distance between yourself and the men within the groups you were affiliated with. It meant leaving your family, your people and your livelihood for the dangerous life of a stranger in other people's country. To insist on Western Aranda people taking all this jeopardy onto and within themselves, as the missionaries did again, later, when the boys Tekua and Kalimalla were baptised, was to impose on them too heavy a burden.[19]

It was very unsatisfactory, but the more the missionaries looked at their neighbours the more they realised that the basis of sin lay deeper than the Gospel, deeper even than the Law of the Ten Commandments. These people might appear happy and harmless, but they were idle. Once their needs were satisfied it was time to sleep, or to party late into the night; an approach to life that shocked these industrious north Germans. It was in this sense that Kempe, Schwarz and Schulze knew their goals of civilising and Christianising their neighbours were really one goal. The path to Sin, and on to Grace, would be made through a German village.[20]

It took Kempe, Schulze and Schwarz more than ten years to grasp the simple but important fact that the Western Aranda addressed themselves with more than one voice. For the missionaries the voice of God and conscience were metaphors for what lay behind the familiar inner voice of themselves. Those who claimed more literally to have audience with God, devil or spirit were unlikely to be good Lutherans. Not so their new neighbours. At times they heard the voices of their spirit-double, and their spirit-child, and more. Many of their descendants still do.

Deeper than the ritualised expressions of magic is the magical way each person's thoughts and feelings may interact with the wider world, giving a person effect in the material world and making the individual vulnerable to the world, and to distant people. The feeling of anger, for example, might pass directly from person to person and cause harm. It could charge places and objects with the same menace. Speaking from another place and time entirely, an Aboriginal man has said "Country can get wild too".[21] Magic was the energy that drove the Western Aranda economy, as they saw it. It was to the Western Aranda, among other things, what property and labour were to the intruding South Australians.

Spirits and magic were all tied to place, and they helped make the universe of the Western Aranda intimately knowable. Our modern universe is in comparison remote, intensively measured but still, at its core, more mysterious than the world of the Western Aranda.

Kempe and Schwarz were to find that the other white men of Central Australia offered little support for the mission's purposes. In 1880 Kempe reported, "I asked a young [white] man to what denomination he belonged. He replied: I do not know by what name my denomination goes. To my question how many Sacraments his church teaches, he answered: I do not know; no one has ever asked me such a ridiculous question." [22] They soon concluded that the Centre's Aboriginal and European populations were equally heathen.

The curriculum of the Hermannsburg Mission Institute was of little help either. It comprised of the knowledge needed to equip Pastors for Lutheran congregations: Biblical texts and their Lutheran explication, German, Greek, Latin, Hebrew, music, and the liturgy and practices of Lutheranism. By 1914 the curriculum included some practical studies in arithmetic, geometry - as it could be applied to agriculture - stenography, book-keeping and nature study. The closest it came to a study of other cultures, apart from those met in the Bible, was to be found in some elementary geography. This subject and the other broader areas of the curriculum were possibly added long after Kempe and Schwarz graduated.[23]

Far more than the lay-people of South Australia, Kempe and Schwarz were men of the Word. For Lutherans the Law that demonstrated the sinfulness of men, and the recipe of Grace, were contained in the written texts of the Bible, from which the faithful Christian could extract them. Regard for the text, not the way it was interpreted by Church authority, was the blade that cut them from the main trunk of the Roman Church, and neither good works nor a good soul could make up for doctrine that diverged from God's word. And so, inevitably, a Lutheran conversion to Christianity would involve an education in literacy, and the converts' confession of faith could only be accepted as in good faith if they had first demonstrated a knowledge of Lutheran understandings of the Bible, freely accepted, and, by the missionaries' preference, in German.[24] It was the policy of the Hermannsburg Institute that the missionaries should gain enough of the language of the Western Aranda to enable them to preach in Aranda and to translate the core texts of the Bible, and a basic liturgy and catechism. These would form the basis of education on the mission.

As Heidenreich put it in the Lutheran *Church messenger* in 1885, by which time the absence of Western Aranda converts was causing some discussion among the mission's supporters, "they [the missionaries] are not seeking the fame of having baptised many souls, but the honour of faithfulness in instructing".[25]

The missionaries knew their stay would be a long one. They were still there in March 1891 when the two women Nungoolga and Theeanka walked out of the Finke Gorge. Missionary Hermann Kempe knew Nungoolga as Naomi because she had taken that name when he had baptised her three years earlier. Naomi was an Aranda-Christian, an Aranda-Lutheran to be precise. What, now, was going to happen to the shocking story she brought with her? That was up to Hermann Kempe, and what he did owed more to the way Central Australia had been governed between August 1887 and March 1891 than it owed to the Word.

Georg Heidenreich, Superintendent of the Finke
River mission, around 1870, with his wife Anna
and the first of their six children (LA).

Wilhelm Schwarz's was a mission of service. He had greater sympathy for the Western Aranda than his fellow missionaries. It led him to generalize his accusations against other frontiersmen. Hermann Kempe (below) was driven more by a sense of moral power, and could fight his political corner (1870-4; *ELM*).

3

"THERE IS NO GOVERNMENT
AMONG THEM"

You know better than I that without clear rules there can be no mission, no Church and no world. Georg Heidenreich, Mission Superintendent, 1881[26]

As Christians, Kempe and Schwarz were looking to lead the Western Aranda into Christianity with the aid of Grace, and not by exacting obedience. But they were also establishing a community of Christians, and community is both a political idea and a religious one. Communities require the exercise of power and the observance of rules.

The community Kempe and Schwarz founded on the Finke in 1877 was soon increased by several lay workers, called Colonists, who arrived with Louis Schulze. Schulze was the only one of the three intended by his parents for a missionary vocation. He was a frail man, not cut out for the bush life. The Colonists, in contrast, were practical men from the farms and villages of northern Germany, committed to the mission but not themselves missionaries. They would support the mission with their skills and labour, teaching the heathen peoples the habits of civilisation, by which the missionaries meant the life of a settled and agricultural people.

By the time the missionaries were established on the Finke most of the elements of a system of mission governance were in place. The Evangelical Lutheran Synod of South Australia had combined in 1863 with the Immanuel Synod, from which it was separated on theological grounds, for the purpose of missionary work among Aboriginal people, inviting Ludwig Harms and his Hermannsburg Mission Institute to provide missionaries for the purpose. This Harms agreed to do, on the understanding, as he saw it, that he remain in overall control while the local congregations should provide the material support of the mission work. When Hermannsburg in 1866 sent out two missionaries and a Colonist they were sent to the east side of Lake Eyre, where concentrations of Aboriginal people had been reported by pastoralists, and established the Killalpaninna mission. By January 1868 the situation at Killalpaninna had passed from hopeless to critical. It was something more fundamental than differences about governance that ended the first Killalpaninna mission. It was the prospect of imminent death from the spears and clubs of the Dieri people.[27]

But the Hermannsburg Institute's new Director Theodor Harms thought the South Australian mission committee was weak for wanting to retire the missionaries. This led to a dispute about jurisdiction. Harms wrote to the head of the South Australian mission committee, Pastor Oster, "It is self-evident that the missionaries should be subordinate to the local Board of Management and that the Directorate in Hermannsburg have the overall leadership, receiving reports and in the end determining matters in dispute. ... I must insist that our missionaries keep to the Lüneburg Church Order, *mutatis mutandis.*" [28].

The answer to Harms' determination to continue missionary work among the Australian Aborginal people lay with a graduate of Hermannsburg, Pastor Georg Heidenreich. He had arrived in 1866 with the Killalpaninna missionaries but designated to serve the Lutherans in the south, and was taken up by the congregation of Bethany in the Barossa Valley, just north of Adelaide. Harms now corresponded mostly with Heidenreich, who joined the mission committee in 1872. Heidenreich proposed a plan of management that found favour with Harms. "We must start the missionary work afresh, following your plan" Harms wrote to Heidenreich in November 1872.

The plan was a simple one. The South Australian mission work should be run directly by Hermannsburg in Germany. The Chair of the local committee, Pastor Oster, saw that for what it was, a recipe for conflict with the South Australian congregations who would provide most of the money, and to forestall it had his committee decide by a narrow majority in August 1873 to "hand over completely the leadership of and responsibility for the local mission to Director Harms". He promised full, but voluntary, support for the work, and had Hermannsburg agree to undertakings about their joint interests in the mission property and to consult on important matters of policy. The supremacy of the Hermannsburg Institute was to be expressed in the appointment of a mission Superintendent who, like the South Australian Governors in the Colonial period, would carry with him the authority of Hermannsburg while being as closely subject to control from the centre as communications would allow. The other members of the mission committee would be advisors only, critical to the continuing local support of the work, but with only the negative power to withhold cooperation.

Director Harms offered the superintendency to Pastor Oster who knew he was not the man for the job. Oster allowed the task to pass to Harms's confidant, Heidenreich, "an intelligent and far-sighted, sincere Christian, but at the same time excitable and impatient", according to official Hermannsburg historian Georg Haccius. Heidenreich knew that description to be true, but could do nothing about it. In May 1874 he wrote to Harms "I would be happy to fight tooth and nail for the sake of God's honour, if only I could do it coolly. But my passion leads me in blind enthusiasm to slash about wildly with my sword, and when I score a cut on someone's ear he goes home feeling wounded. If only the good Lord would send me the Grace to be patient. He could not have sent me to a better school to learn patience than here, but sad to say in eight years I have learnt very little of that noble art. ... Pray that I can overcome my weakness for His sake and don't spoil things for Him. I am afraid of no man, but am terribly afraid of myself."

Harms knew he had in Heidenreich the right man. In April 1875 he wrote to Heidenreich "I give a free hand to you and the other Brothers there who are loyal to Hermannsburg, provided you hold to the principle that Hermannsburg has the last word". Heidenreich had all the others. While his Mission Committee comprised several others appointed by the Hermannsburg Mission Institute, he was to be the sole signatory on the bank account for Hermannsburg's Australasian missions.[29] He remained loyal to the Hermannsburg Mission Institute, and he retained the loyalty of his local mission committee, to the bitter end.

By this time even Harms had been compelled to admit that the missionary work at Lake Eyre was hopeless, but looked forward to another attempt at missionising Aboriginal people before he would conclude that God had willed the Hermannsburg method should fail in Australia. He wrote to that effect to Oster in February 1874, and Oster, a man of diplomatic skill and patience, persuaded his Synod to agree by a large majority to pass their share of the Killalpaninna mission's assets to Hermannsburg, provided they were used for missionary purposes. Considering the needs of the southern congregations, and the dismal result at Lake Eyre, it was a tribute to their altruism and also to the central role that missionising played in the faith of these Antipodean Lutherans.

On May 6th 1875, when Hermann Kempe and Wilhelm Schwarz were ordained Pastors of the Lutheran Church in Hannover, after graduating from the Hermannsburg Mission Institute, and designated for the Australian mission field, all was in place for a new mission, bar one thing. The crucial speculation in the creation of any mission enterprise is the selection of the people who are to be, like it or not, the raw material for mission work. The pointer to Hermannsburg's goal was a thin strand of galvanised steel wire that led from Adelaide to the northern coast of Australia, the Overland Telegraph line. On its path north, near the centre of the continent, the wire crossed the Finke River. And where the Finke breached the red stone ranges of the Centre there were durable waters and some good pasture, in a good season. With these came game and with the game came people, the resident Western Aranda people. Heidenreich saw to the rest. The Finke River mission was to be his creation, and he fought tooth and nail for the next twenty years to preserve it.

Schwarz and Kempe, during the entire five years of their missionary training, had been forbidden to "court" women, even pious young women of evangelical persuasion. Indulgence of the sexual drive outside of Christian marriage was perhaps the clearest case-in-point for man's sinfulness. Having graduated, however, Kempe and Schwarz were just as firmly advised to find fiancées who could join them when they had established their mission.

"So now we quickly had to look around for a life-companion...We calculated our ... departure to be only eight weeks away...." Their first approaches were rebuffed, to Kempe's surprise, so charged was he with the importance of his mission, but they managed to equip themselves before departure with the necessary fiancees whom they were to marry two years later in the Australian desert.

After the long sea-voyage from Europe to Australia, which provided ample opportunity for Kempe to indulge his love of conversation and conviviality, he and Schwarz arrived on September 16th 1875 in the provincial metropolis of Adelaide, the anchor of the Overland Telegraph and of everything that happened in Central Australia. In a few short weeks the young men were celebrated by the local Lutheran congregations and provided with a fast-track to British citizenship through the good offices of Friedrich Krichauff, a German-born Member of the South Australian Parliament. They were then led north into the swelling wave of a desert summer by Heidenreich, who confidently expected to be back in Bethany for his Christmas services. This was wildly optimistic, even if we allow that no-one could then have predicted the drought that was to form under their feet as they moved inland. Kempe never forgave Heidenreich for so misjudging the temper of the Australian desert. He had read a book about Australia on the ship, and claimed he knew what they would face.

There was soon to be a trial that would test Kempe's spirit, as he reported himself. At Mundawadana near the bottom of Lake Eyre, where they waited to collect Heidenreich's share of the livestock from the old mission, barely a third of the way to their lease on the Finke, with more than a year of travel ahead of them, Kempe wrote: "I am sick at heart ... often our courage nearly fails us." In this Schwarz and Heidenreich concurred, but worse was soon to come in the sandhills further north. To this point Kempe had been driving the wagon which was only hauled through the sand with the help of the Mundawadana station owner's bullocks. It cost the men extraordinary effort, leaving them further exhausted. It scarred the memory of even the hardy Heidenreich, who bought some oxen at the next station. The traction for the heavy cart was now provided by "12 horses in the shafts ... and 8 oxen hitched in front of them...". The drovers pressing up ahead reported via a traveller coming down from the north that 700 of the mission's sheep had died. The party was now scattered over a long stretch of the drought-stricken country, but more supplies were needed than they could afford to buy and the new horses and oxen needed training to the cart. Heidenreich decided he must go south to raise more funds leaving Kempe and Schwarz camped in isolation at Coolong Springs. We can imagine the stress all this was placing on their morale and collegial spirit.

With Heidenreich back from Adelaide, in the middle of summer, they moved on, arriving at Finniss Springs on February 4th, 1876. Ahead lay yet more sandhills. Temperatures were rising to 130 degrees Fahrenheit and there was no shade except that of the wagon. There was little pasture or water for the horses and bullocks. The effort of getting the wagon's load across the sand pushed the three Pastors to their limits. The lay helpers Nitschke and Myers set out on foot back to Adelaide. For the missionaries there could be no withdrawal without disgrace. Kempe again sat down to write "home" (that is, to Hermannsburg in Germany) of their trials. In Scherer's paraphrase, "they were often at the point of losing both courage and reason. Many a time they had wept bitter tears, and in moments of anger and impatience had exchanged words at which they themselves were shocked." Kempe returned down the track to Finniss Springs, some six miles behind the wagon, and begged Heidenreich to relieve him of responsibility for the wagon. Heidenreich agreed and gave him the easier task of caring for the loose horses. Responsibility for sweating the wagon onwards for the remainder of the long journey was passed to Schwarz. Kempe had shown himself a weaker man than Schwarz, but he was not ashamed and his confidence remained unbroken. He had Grace enough to forgive himself and remained Heidenreich's deputy on the mission. But Schwarz was the man who could endure. His respect for Kempe, however, would not.[30]

The year before the first meeting with the Western Aranda men, in 1876, Georg Heidenreich, now Superintendent (*Propst*) of the Finke River mission, had made with Kempe a fast journey north to reconnoitre their lease on the Finke, while Schwarz and the herds were marooned by drought at Dalhousie Springs in the badlands of northern South Australia. Heidenreich climbed to the top of a nearby hill, was entranced by the view, and reported to Institute Director Harms: "I should say that we have enough – and more than enough

– in the way of heathen people, pastures, timber, water resources, fertile soil, clay, lime, sand, and stone-quarries..." for the mission colony.

A man with Heidenreich's sound biblical education might have recalled that it was the Devil who took Jesus to the top of a hill and offered him, unsuccessfully, "all the kingdoms of the world". The distinct roles of religion and government had become the subject of a highly-developed theology since Christianity graduated from marginal sect to imperial religion. Luther himself had contributed substantially to the discussion through his writing on the "two kingdoms". It is inconceivable that Heidenreich was unaware of it. But here on the Central Australian frontier secular government was vestigial and its laws reached only with difficulty. If Grace was apart from the law it was also built upon it. On the Finke there was already a different kind of law in place - Western Aranda law – a law combining regulation and morality, to which the Lutherans could not imagine submitting even if they had understood it. They considered it the work of the devil. In any case, it was to be ten years before their first two converts, Thomas and Andreas, showed the missionaries how Western Aranda law worked. Heidenreich's mission was to need much more than his sword of righteousness. It depended also on the firearms and spears of power, and the guileful words of politics that were not found in the Word.

As for the Western Aranda, in the early years of contact, before the men came to appreciate how profoundly different the Lutherans were, they could persuade themselves that their visitors would, like proper strangers, allow themselves to be assimilated to the Western Aranda social order. By the time they understood the Lutherans intended a revolution, the mission's own herds, and those of their neighbours Frederick Thornton and James McDonald, were changing irretrievably the Western Aranda economy. Of more fatal consequence to the constitution of Western Aranda society was an assault from inside, from people whose subjection the senior men took for granted.

4

WOMEN AND CHILDREN FIRST

"I longed for the important [Christian] songs." The boy Tjalkabota[31]

"I want my very own tjurunga. This is more precious." The boy Renkeraka[32]

When Tjalkabota's father allowed his son to visit the new mission station Tjalkabota was astonished above all by the buildings. He ran his hands over their walls in his attempt to understand them, as if he were blind. For the Western Aranda the new pug-walled buildings rising beside the Finke raised not only technical questions about structure and function, but the more fundamental question posed by something beyond the observers' cosmology. Nothing like this had ever risen above the ground of their territory. It was of the earth but man-made, part of the landscape but with no creator-spirit to tell its story.

On their part, Tjalkabota and the other Western Aranda children presented the missionaries with a wonder of equal significance. When Kempe and Schwarz were mere spectators of the life of Western Aranda people camping in the bed of the Finke River below the mission station they were struck by the strangeness of Aboriginal childhood. Kempe reported that "Repeatedly we had to punish the children, when we observed that they were hitting or pelting their elders from pure malice." The children's elders did not see that such a response to childish harassment was either necessary, or, in cases of vigorous corporal punishment of children, acceptable. "If ever the students got the stick, there would be such shrieking and running about you would think the place had caught fire" Schulze recalled in 1887. "One day some children stole some sugar. After school we punished the thieves, and closed the school-room door so they could not escape. But they kicked up a terrible row: the old women screamed outside as mightily as the children inside, because they thought we were beating their children to death. The men forced the door and rushed into the school to save their children. It cost us a lot of talking to convince them how necessary and useful such discipline was. To that point no child had been struck by an adult."[33] Schulze reported that the adults later accepted corporal punishment of children, and occasionally beat their children, but in 1926 the new missionary Friedrich Albrecht repeated Schulze's experience of forty-five years earlier.[34]

The missionaries raised their hands against the children not for the sake of the dozing elders, but for the sake of the children's souls. They expected to be understood by their southern co-religionists when they reported the following account of what happened after a child injured his foot: "As soon as this mishap was known, all assembled to howl and cry. It is remarkable that such parental love is found amongst our degraded heathen, a love which is so seldom requited. Unfortunately this love is merely a foolish fondness, which never corrects the children, and which returns only grief and worry, since children cannot be successfully trained without discipline."[35]

It was not until January 1878 that a group of five women and six children approached the mission station. Among the children in the vicinity were two boys about five years of age, Tekua and Kalimalla and others who were born later, shortly before or after the arrival of the missionaries. These included the boys Tjalkabota, Mototoka, Inubauka and Rauwiraka (whose mother Nungoolga we have already met). Schwarz later described Kalimalla as a vigorous, manly person, somewhat excitable[36], and Tekua as more placid and easily lead. Tekua and Kalimalla, described as "orphans", could depend on the support of the broader group of 'mothers' and 'fathers' defined for them by Aranda custom. Tekua had affiliations with people further up the Finke, in the country to the north of the MacDonnell Ranges, north-west of Hermannsburg. The attendance of Tekua and Kalimalla at the mission school was never better than patchy. They lived within the orbit of traditional Western Aranda life and as they grew older found employment on neighbouring Glen Helen cattle station.

The Western Aranda girls included Adilka, a three year old infant at the time Kempe and Schwarz arrived. Chinchewarra, the teenaged Matuntara girl, lived in the country that was later to become Tempe Downs pastoral station, ignorant of the revolution under way north of the James Ranges.

These children as they matured were to play prominent parts on the ground contested by Aborigines, pastoralists, police and missionaries.

Whatever the missionaries' wishes, the Western Aranda were their neighbours, not their prisoners. The years 1877 to 1879 were good years of above-average rainfall and the Western Aranda mostly stayed away. They moved around the country after the game animals which, liberated from the permanent waterholes, followed their food sources into a vast territory. This gave the missionaries time to study the language of the country, but they were told little about initiation, the process by which a Western Aranda boy became a man. In fact no white man or woman was allowed to see the man-making procedures, which were restricted, for the most part, to initiated men and their candidates, until Frank Gillen and Baldwin Spencer were invited to witness a special Aranda second-stage initiation festival, or *ngkura*, at the Alice Springs telegraph station in 1896. But what the missionaries complained about in Western Aranda childhood represented their greatest opportunity. In those crucial years before boys were subjected to the rigours of initiation they were taught none of the knowledge that conferred the powers, privileges and status of an initiated man. Much of what they were told, however sincerely the adults believed it, proved to be falsifiable in the new order within which the Western Aranda now lived.

While Aranda children seemed to the missionaries to suffer from uncritical adult forbearance, and to be unreasonably free from work and discipline, their life had its hazards and fears. The darkness beyond the known territory, beyond the camp-fire at night, was populated by devils, hob-goblins, spirits of malicious intent, of a kind that would have been familiar in the European villages of a century before. According to TGH Strehlow, "One religious attitude only was firmly inculcated into the young - the fear of magic and the supernatural. ... To the fear of magic and the supernatural was added [after puberty] the fear of the old men assembled in Council."[37] Western Aranda parents filled their local landscape with prohibitions supported by magical enforcers, so that the inhibitions and unease that moral training bred in the minds of European children, in connection with selfish motive or spontaneous behaviour, was replaced, to a large degree, by fear of the unseen forces that guarded the Western Aranda rules.

The country of the Western Aranda swarmed with spirits both good and evil, an invisible but potent world of cause and effect in which humans dodged and weaved like footballers finding a way through the opposing side. Here the insight, initiative and skill of the individual came into play. This was a more domestic world of faith than the cosmic scene commanded by the senior men. The cosmic may collapse while the domestic remains. [38]

Not all the monsters in the Western Aranda world were disembodied. Neighbours might be friendly or hostile, and one would generally despise them for deviating from correct language and custom, but they were known. Beyond neighbours were found strange people who were the sources of misfortunes - disease, accidental or premature death, unnatural events. The hostility of these remote strangers was often called up during inquests into deaths among the Western Aranda, and repaid whenever there was opportunity.[39]

Whatever the death rate from revenge-killing, the threat of it weighed heavily on the minds of the Western Aranda. Tjalkabota recalled this aspect of traditional Aboriginal education clearly and with implied criticism. When the children were warned off some activity, the threat raised by the parents was either supernatural retribution or the human assault of enemies bent on vengeance. Tjalkabota was told: "don't throw stones at hollow logs. They make a lot of noise. An enemy might hear this, and kill us ... don't light two fires. A revenge party might be going across, and they might see two fires burning. Then they might come towards us, and harm us or kill us. ... you must stop playing when the magpie is singing. This means that a large revenge party will be coming ... if you aren't quiet, they will hear you when they come to spy. Then in the morning they will form a circle and kill everybody.' That is how they stopped us from playing, when they wanted us to go to sleep quickly."[40]

A child was likely to witness long before puberty the bloody accounting for real or magically-inferred offences. Fifty years later, Chinchewarra recalled the horror of the revenge killing of a family member and gave it as one reason for going in to Tempe Downs station.[41]

When the Colonist Baden died in 1885 after a fall from his horse, the children were involved in the Lutheran funeral service and burial, a procedure Tjalkabota found remarkably different to the Western Aranda way. His elders were keen to correct the behaviour the children had learned from the Lutherans. "'Children, you must not look at a dead person, lest the spirit of the dead person throw something into your stomach. Don't sit in the light at night, lest a spirit comes and sees you, and throws something into you.'"[42] When the white men first arrived, the children were told the sheep and horses were devils and might kill them.

Beyond puberty, through a curtain of mystery enforced by the threat of death, lay adulthood. A boy on the threshold of manhood could see ahead of him, as all children can, the enticing prospect of adult powers, and he could hear in the sound of the bull-roarers from the ceremonial grounds, the threat of what might be done to him on the passage from child to man. The first stage of initiation involved subjecting the initiate to the power of the initiated and the physical pain of circumcision and subincision of the penis. For the boy entering adolescence the experience involved not only severe pain, but moments of absolute terror of the kind that destroys confidence and makes the candidate totally dependent on those in control. The elements of Western Aranda faith were presented in dramatic form in ceremonies that went through the nights as some of the powerful words were sung. It took several weeks, and corresponded to the Lutherans' schooling and religious confirmation, all at one time. The pain of initiation was rationalised, in part, as punishment for the child's past, ignorant breaches of Western Aranda rules.

Beyond the first stage of initiation, when the wounds had healed, with the adolescent tamed and "made quiet", began the longer process that culminated in the second stage or *ngkura* ceremony, from which he would emerge a "complete, lawful man", and be addressed as *iliara*.[43] Now we can begin to see the marvellous complexity of the system of Aranda social relations, and the way it was mapped on to the landscape. The graduate of first-stage initiation, or *erora*, was lead on a series of journeys that can be compared with the journeyings of mediaeval students through the centres of European learning, the monasteries and early universities, as they sought knowledge and insight, at a time when manuscript books, like scholars, had fixed locations. An important difference in the case of the young Aranda man was this; he was related to people throughout the known world, across barriers of language, culture, and long distances. Every person he met could be given a family relationship to himself, not just a relationship by analogy, but a relationship that had some of the qualities, including the obligations, of a blood relationship.[44] At birth you were placed in a different "section" from those of your parents. Those who share the section of your mother, for example, also share that relationship in ways that are much more than formalities. And members of that class are to be found not only among the Western Aranda clans, in the present case, but among all Aranda speaking peoples, and among neighbouring peoples speaking other languages. If the clans you meet have a different section system, correspondences are found. The vocabulary of relationship in the Aranda languages is large and to anyone not brought up in the system, thoroughly baffling.

As our *erora* travels abroad he meets no-one to whom he can not be related. From these relationships spring classes of people, those women with whom he may marry or have sexual relations, those he must not speak to or approach, and many small groups with which he can share collective personal pronouns, only translatable to us with phrases like "we who are (by classification) fathers and sons".[45] In fact, once you had established your relationship with someone you had just met, you addressed them by the name of that relationship, not by a personal name. The person is comprised of his or her relationships and status.

An equally powerful link between the Western Aranda and their neighbours was their shared cosmology. The acts of the creator spirits they shared extended vast distances across all other social and geographical divisions. When, on birth, Western Aranda children were each allocated natural phenomena as totems, the creator spirit associated with each totem joined them in a religious sense with people in other groups, even other language groups. For example, when the time came to begin the initiation of Rauwiraka, a young man from Ellery Creek on the eastern boundary of the mission lease, he was taken south to Tempe Downs by Matuntara men (one of them Numbucki, whom we have already met on the banks of Walker Creek on the morning of February 20th, 1891) and initiated among people who spoke a foreign language. Much of his higher education took place among the Eastern Aranda at Undoolya, east of Alice Springs, and the Unmatjera people of the Glen Helen area, who used the Ilpara language in their ceremonies.[46]

Both classification into sections and the allocation of totems were mapped onto the landscape, in the first case by your inheritance of a section, which drove you to other places for potential wives and husbands, who were, by *their* family relationships concentrated in particular places. It was usual for a man to have to travel fifty kilometres or more, beyond his clan's home territory, to find a woman he was eligible to marry. In the second case the powerful knowledge inherited from the creator spirits of your totem, the knowledge that through ceremony allowed the creative powers to be summoned - your *tjurunga* - was located with the senior men at significant sites. And so it is far more than metaphor to see this landscape, with the Finke River zig-zagging through the MacDonnell and James Ranges and meandering across Missionary Plain, as mapped in the Western Aranda mind. It is not surprising that we have reports of Aboriginal men in the Centre being able to draw accurate sketch maps of large areas of country at a time when no-one had flown over it, and the maps of surveyors were still wildly inaccurate. What the Western Aranda were mapping was not just places, it was cosmology, history, relationships and morality. Needless to say, the process of learning about all this took years and much travelling.

With their transition into manhood young men acquired by degrees the right to share in the life of those positive supernatural forces that had shaped the Aboriginal world – land, plants, animals, people – everything observable and much that was not. Access to the knowledge of these forces was allocated by those who already possessed it, the older men, according to the recipient's totem, age, section, personal distinction or family relationships. So emerged hierarchies of status and power among the men, and, in a much reduced form, among the women. Initiation of boys into manhood was part of the rationing of the obligations and privileges of adulthood. To put it in a somewhat modern and inappropriate way, the initiation of boys was the point at which Western Aranda society re-created in each generation its politics and its economy. Stanner writes of the Murinbata people of the Top End (who "in all essentials closely resembled the Central Australians who Spencer and Gillen described..."), almost 50 years later: "the religion was one that lent itself as easily to private as to political use" and of "the victimization of women and the self-serving way in which the cult-leaders used their power".[47]

It was not a short or easy route from childhood to the full rights, then privileges, of Western Aranda manhood, but things got better along the way. Unless you set out on the painful first steps, you got nowhere. Renkeraka, a Western Aranda youth older than Tjalkabota, had attended the mission school and was challenged by Hermann Kempe to choose the Christian way.

"'Why not? Your younger sibling Salomo has already become a Christian. So you should become a Christian, just like the boys.'

Renkeraka spoke again, "If I become a Christian, I might have to sleep at night in the dwelling with my eyes in darkness, without a fire.'

Mr Kempe said, "No they have a fire, and they also have light. Why don't you want to become a Christian?'

He said, "I want my very own tjurunga. This is more precious.'"[48]

Perhaps the greatest material benefit allocated to young men after initiation was control over the women who became their wives. Most of the calories consumed by the people were gathered by the women, in the form of small animals and plant foods.[49] By 1880, Kempe understood enough Aranda to discuss the matter. He paraphrased the men's view thus: "Well, they [the women] have to find the vegetables, we the meat. The meat supply is never plentiful, [Kempe continues] since the men are usually squatting or sleeping in the shade and the women are expected to find the daily food."[50] This does not deny the existence of strong feelings between men and women, within and outside marriage. But given the absence of any prohibition on sexual relations between men and women of the correct marrying class, marriage was defined by its economic character. A man with a wife was vastly better off than one without. A senior man with three wives lived in luxury, by the material standards of the Western Aranda.[51]

The power of men over women often expressed itself in violence when the woman offended the man in some way. So normal was the man's beating of his wives that girls in their play would model the activity, including their weeping, using Eucalypt leaves to represent the man and woman, and a small piece of bark to represent the boomerang the man used as the instrument of punishment.[52] The oppressiveness of the man's domination was reduced by the way men and women were separated during much of the day; they gathered food separately, often slept separately, and sat separately on formal occasions, such as ceremonies. Both parties to a marriage had ample opportunity to digress, even, in some cases, to live in different places.

The more regulated of the procedures by which men acquired wives, as Spencer and Gillen describe them, involved an agreement between the parents of an infant boy and an infant girl. The boy child was promised the *daughter* of the infant girl, so ensuring that a husband was usually about fourteen years older than his first wife.[53]

Girls might be allocated in infancy to men of high status, who often had two or more wives. For an older man a younger wife was not just a current benefit, but an old-age pension. Young wives brought a similar benefit to the older wives, if they could manage them. Inevitably this arrangement interfered in the natural forces of attraction between the young. An initiated man was entitled to marry.[54] If he had a promised wife, she might still be an infant. A wife might also be inherited on the death of an older brother, in the way Tekua later inherited his wife Kwabingeraka. He might also negotiate a wife from her father or guardian. Failing that, one could be stolen or seduced, but not without risking a painful, even fatal, retribution. Seduction was best left to older men of greater strength and experience, and with developed alliances among other men.

Nor were young men alone likely to prove disruptive in their pursuit of their sexual goals. Those with power and privilege are rarely satisfied, so older married men could turn to seduction. Women could manipulate. To be successful, a man's seduction magic needed a receptive object.

For a girl, her status as a possession of an older man was often determined in childhood, and she knew it. The transition to womanhood was marked by a form of circumcision, but it was more surgery than ceremony, and brought no privileges. It was simply a pre-cursor to sexual life in which she had more power than initiative.

The simplicity of the ceremony marking marriage[55] did not mean that women lacked protection when they moved to a husband's camp. Their husband took on family obligations at his initiation and could be held accountable for harsh treatment of a wife.[56] From one cause or another, these allocations of girls to men were contestable, explaining some of the violence of men towards their wives and each other. It also provides a reason to suspect that violence might increase in the presence of so many single white males. Less predictable, perhaps, but attested by good evidence, is the power of Aboriginal employees of the whites, especially the Aboriginal trackers and constables, to vault up the ranks of seniority and at a relatively young age acquire several wives. In 1887-8, William Willshire's five trackers each had at least one wife, and several had two or three, although they were all young men.[57]

Chinchewarra's experience is also instructive. She was a child of the Matuntara people, neighbours of the Western Aranda. At the time she was Frederick Thornton's mistress she also had a Aboriginal husband, Thinarrie, employed at the station. But, according to her report to Roheim in 1929, she had previously had a husband, Merilkna, whose fate is not recorded, and who had been chasing her before their marriage, although she was promised to another man. That other man, Yuna, may have been killed by police before the marriage could be consummated. She may also have evaded Yuna by her own preference.[58]

Chinkanaka's predicament was testimony to the power of both the white men and the young Western Aranda women. As Louis Schulze told the Swan-Taplin Enquiry, Chinkanaka's "two wives had been stolen by a white man. He was very angry and asked us to go and fetch his lubras back. We told him to go and get them himself. After that he said I shall go and spear the whites and beat my lubras. I advised him not to do so... I do no know if he ever got them back again. He told me the names of the white men but I have forgotten them. They were living at Mr Parker's [ie Parke's] old station on Ellery's Creek about 7 miles from here. This was end of

1879 or beginning of 1880."[59] We know from Schwarz that one of the men was Charlie Walker of Henbury station and that his common-law wife, Ilkalita, accompanied him on horseback, dressed in men's clothing. It is also significant that Chinkanaka was one of the most senior of the Western Aranda men when the missionaries arrived, the boss of the Ntaria camp adjacent to Hermannsburg.

With the arrival of the missionaries and pastoralists, two of the lowest-status groups among the Western Aranda found themselves in possession of power that they had not known before. The young men and older boys found they had services to offer the white men - as stock-men, trackers and labourers - that pride and privilege discouraged many senior men from offering.[60] In return they got access to the new goods that no senior man could magic out of the land. They might also get protection if they chose wives outside the approved classes or seduced older men's wives.

The girls and young women could also offer labour, in the homestead and with the stock. On the frontier, where white women were almost as scarce as fresh vegetables, the girls' sexual favours, when added to their labour, gave them a power that must have been intoxicating for them. Some tribal husbands, perhaps where there was a tradition of using women in diplomacy, used a wife as a means of obliging the white men to return favours. Not all white men understood the rules, or cared to obey them.

Young Aboriginal women employed by white men could find relief from the constant drudgery of hunter-gatherer life and the higher status that came from being part of the white man's world. In that world the white man with authority, the station manager or policeman for example, could claim seignurial rights in choosing women, particularly young women detached from their fathers by death and disruption. Even the missionaries of the Finke River Mission, bitterly opposed to sexual unions between white station workers and black women, had to concede that the women's circumstances were good. In 1885 Schulze reported:

The girls can not be relied on. It would be much better if there were no pastoral stations anywhere round here. The people run to them and get fattened up. Almost every white man has his black concubine. There are only three big girls here at present, although our wives would very much like to have more help. They complain most of the time of lassitude.

In his 1886 report to the South Australian government, Heidenreich reported:

The missionaries complain that some of the young men and especially the young women are enticed by all kinds of promises on to the neighbouring stations, or simply stolen. The girls are not just used for washing clothes, but also for work with the cattle, dressed in men's clothes, and are even used by white men for immoral purposes. These girls are generally better clothed and fed than those on the mission.

And yet, through all these disapproving missionary observations, as in the reports of the dominant Western Aranda men about the way things should be between men and women, we can see clearly the sense of sexual power that possessed these young women, and their determination to use it when they could escape the power of their men. The young women were making choices about their futures. Missionary Schulze made it clear in June 1889. "The girls and young women [apart from the recently baptised] take themselves off to the cattle stations hereabout and demonstrate openly their atrocious character."[61] A woman might see it differently. As Chinchewarra or one of her fellow witnesses said to a reporter in Port Augusta in 1891, "I am a whitefellow's lubra. I like white men. They don't knock you about, and give you plenty of food."[62]

It was to be another twenty years before frontier white men would confess their sexual relations with Aboriginal women to those in the south. When Kempe dismissed Theodor Schleicher, employed in the early 1880s, for his relationship with an Aboriginal woman, he gave no thought to pressing Schleicher to marry the woman. Kempe could not have married them, had Schleicher wanted it, since the woman was not a Christian.[63] Later Schleicher took responsibility for an Aboriginal woman and their children, but it made no difference to the missionaries.

Those older women who remained on the mission station seemed, to Schulze at least, equally reprehensible for their recalcitrance in the face of the Gospel. The Western Aranda were difficult to entice to, and keep at, the Sunday sermons "and the women are the worst of them", always finding more pressing tasks to do. Even the baptised and the catechumens persisted with their traditional funeral and mourning ceremonies "although they know from God's word how crazy that is, ... but they cannot abandon it, especially the women, who have received it in their flesh and blood."

It is likely that those women who came within the missionaries' influence were more likely than their sisters to choose the life offered by the heathen white men. Certainly the students at the mission school had received an education in the customs and domestic practices of the white people, although the English language was not taught in class until 1887.

For the hunter gatherer, in an arid land subject to irregular but inevitable droughts, scarcity is a powerful force behind daily life. The Western Aranda lived always one day's work away from the beginning of starvation and hard labour could not always prevent days without meals. They, of course, knew the anxiety such a life could bring, even if they were not intimidated by it. No-one who has not had to choose which child or parent to let starve in a drought (as people still must in the Sahel) can appreciate how attractive rations can be. The lesson of scarcity was sharpest for women with children, and for men and women with frail or disabled relatives.

And so, as a proportion of the eligible women along the Finke became attached to white men, a further impetus was added to the already ample causes of blood feuds between the men who competed for the remaining women. Chinkanaka, for example, had fallen to a spear by 1890.

Even the children became owners of the power to attract regular food from the missionaries just by attending classes. In their classes they gained access to the white man's magic, reading and writing, and through it to the Christian doctrines, considered by the senior men to be merely risible, but backed with the explanatory effectiveness of European cosmology, alternative force and forms of wealth the senior men could not match.

Tjalkabota's father had been helping Kempe to learn the Aranda language. For some time he kept his women and children away from the missionaries.

Then I [Tjalkabota] came back to the station in the evening. Mr Schwartz saw me with another boy and asked me, 'Boy, who are you?'

He [the other boy] said, 'This is the boy Tjalkabota'

Schwartz asked, 'Where have you been all this time?'

I said, 'I have been at Tjurkiputa all the time. My father kept me away from school.'

Schwarz said, 'Boy you are thin and covered with ashes. Come to me.'

I thought, 'He is calling me to him to give me a hiding.' But he gave me clothing. He gave me water to have a wash. I gave myself a really good wash, and then he gave me a towel to dry myself. Then he also gave me some sheep meat. Then he also gave me a blanket. Taking all this, I went back to the camp. I though[t] to myself, 'What a big present.' And I was very happy. I never gave another thought about a hiding. They also gave my father and mother a blanket. Then Schwartz said, 'Boy, you should come to school.'

And I did go.[64]

The missionaries admitted the Western Aranda children to schooling at the same age as the German children, and found them equally educable. And they gave girls the same access as boys.

The mission's schooling was far less effective heuristically than Aboriginal initiation, but it started much earlier.[65] It depended on the inducement of the food that was provided at the end of the lessons, and beatings, to encourage performance. As Schwarz reported: "The pupils are among the first to receive their portions [of the rations], since this seems to be the only way in which we can keep them here and get their attention. If they [do not]...pay attention during school hours they receive only a small portion or perhaps none at all. This method of punishment has proved itself." The missionaries handed out the food rations at the end of morning lessons, at 9.00 am. "The lessons ended, the rations are handed out and all eyes are lit up with joy that the work is done and there is something to eat." The missionaries had their breakfast at 7.00 am.

But mission school lessons offered Aboriginal boys and girls little advantage in their dealings with the white society of the Centre, and could earn the suspicion of station managers. It soon aroused the hostility of the initiated men and produced absolutely none of the privileges of Aboriginal manhood.[66]

There is no doubt, however, that Kempe was right when he reported in 1885 that "the children we are teaching from infancy on ... are learning a much broader view of the world." Their subjects of study included reading, writing, arithmetic, and the rote learning of scripture, of course, but also geography. These children were the first Western Aranda to learn that the Aranda universe was in fact part of a continent larger beyond their comprehension than the Finke and its environs, that this continent was in turn separated from others by vast tracts of water, an unimaginable green desert even larger than the red sand deserts that began where the mountain ranges of the Aranda ended. None of that was in the cosmology their parents taught.

In 1885 Kempe made a serious mistake in believing that the adults also "must also be educated like children, because in understanding they are children".[67] In fact, the Western Aranda men "once they realized why the missionaries were so eager to learn their language, ... had grown taciturn and obstinately refused to give further information on certain terms used in connection with their beliefs and superstitions. The missionaries therefore coined words to convey certain notions, e.g. 'beata' for 'happy'. The children soon learnt the meaning of such terms, but their elders were more obtuse. ...If asked at the end of a sermon whether they had understood what was preached, they would wake up as out of a dream and answer "Yes"; further questioning however left them speechless or elicited the nonchalant 'Why don't you ask the children?'"[68]

In so deflecting the missionaries' incomprehensible or inconvenient questions on religious matters, the men were deliberately, but perhaps imprudently, vacating this territory in favour of the children. But within the camps, the struggle went on.

The old men said, 'Children, you are now singing wrongly, really wrongly.'

Then we said, 'a,e,i,o,u.'

'Oh, the children are talking like crows', they said. ...'The children are speaking as though they are crying ... You are not to go to the missionaries any longer. They are teaching you wrongly.'

When the men decorated themselves and danced their ceremonies the missionaries counter-attacked.

"They pulled out the head decorations of the young men ... Mr Schwarz said ... 'You are the children of the devil ... You are heathens. This is very bad.' The men replied 'No, we are not heathens. We are iliara [fully educated men], not heathens.'" But the children went back to school. The next morning, while the children were in the school singing hymns, the men came back from the ceremonial ground. The missionaries told the children "'You are not to obey your fathers. They are leading you to what is bad. Remember God's word.'"

Schwarz told the men to put their clothes on. They protested: "'Everybody has first to see the markings of the men's tjurunga [sacred designs]. The women, the young girls, the children. All have to see it.'"

'First go and put your clothes on, then come and have something to eat.'

'...are we being called evil? We are iliara men.' Then they put their clothes on and came back. They were given food to eat. Then they went to dig in the garden.[69]

Tjalkabota was a diligent student and shepherd and grew close to the missionaries. In early 1886, while Tekua and Kalimalla were still at Bethany near Lake Eyre, waiting for the Kempes to come back from Adelaide, Tjalkabota's father wanted him to leave the school, but Tjalkabota refused. Although a boy, he was strong enough to fend for himself, and, like many Western Aranda boys, had already spent long periods away from his parents.

Father and mother said, 'Boy, if you continue here, your head will implode, and you will dry up. Then the wind will blow you away to the sand hills like a dried-up cicada, and we will be unable to find you.'

Then I said, 'No, I am better off here. I feel good. Here at the school they teach us God's word, we are happy, all of us children.' ... This scene was often repeated.

As it turned out, Tjalkabota was not baptised until 1890, three years after Tekua, Kallimalla and Adilka, and he adopted the Christian name of Moses. Afterwards he went with another newly-baptised youth, Samuel, to his father's place.

My father came out. 'Hello,' he said. 'Are you two my boys, Christians now?'

At first we did not answer.

Again he asked, 'Are you two Christians?'

'Yes, we are both Christians.'

'Yes, I saw you both at the church, when you were baptised. What, were you baptised with warm water?'

'No, with cool holy water.'

'What did you receive?'

'I had good white clothes. I had good trousers.'

'Oh?'

'And I had a good belt. I had a good handkerchief. We both had the same.'

'Yes, I saw you both being baptised with water. I saw this. You both had good clothes, for baptism.'

Then he continued, 'You were baptised with cool water. A long time ago I became a Christian, an iliara, with a lot of heat. You are recent Christians, but I am a Christian from a long time ago. All of us, all the early men, became Christians by means of that heat. You are recent Christians. We have been Christians for a long time.[70]

An ordeal by fire was the final passage in the lengthy second stage of initiation into Aranda manhood and part of the *ngkura* (Engwura) ceremony witnessed by Spencer and Gillen in 1896.

One and a half years after Tjalkabota's baptism Kempe and Schulze left the Finke for the south, defeated by disease, exhaustion and despair. The older men now asserted themselves, as they had on earlier occasions when beyond the reach of the missionaries.[71] Tjalkabota took an accommodating point of view when pressured to submit to initiation. Perhaps he recognised not only the men's threats, but their anxiety about spending a future with men who were not men as they were: "If our boys continue to be boys, they will become devils. Then they might spear us, knock us to the ground, and eat us." Or, indeed, shoot them.[72] According to Tjalkabota, while the men grew angry at his relegation of the creator-heroes and the *tjurunga* to the world of created things, they insisted only that he maintain the quiet manner appropriate to the initiand and keep the sacred secrets. More troubling for the future of the old ways, he asserts that his fellow initiands, none of them Christian, shared his rejection of the senior men's claims. He even accuses the men of hypocrisy: "They told me, 'We tell the boys this so that they will be afraid.'"

The children often disappeared to travel with their parents, or to work as shepherds with the Colonists. What they learned in one session of attendance was forgotten by the time they returned for another. "If he is taken to task for his absence, he only laughs and even questions, why this learning? Why should we always be writing or learning to read? Unfortunately they are so content with their old condition that they desire no improvement." Even in class, holding their attention was a continual struggle. "Nothing seems more strange and irksome to them than thinking" Schulze claimed in 1881. The older boys like Tekua and Kallimalla, infrequent attenders of the class-room, were more likely to ask the missionaries why they were being subjected to the burden of schooling, and to throw the Western Aranda men's jibes at them.

Nevertheless, the missionaries persisted, claiming to attract between 26 and 30 students into class each day and by the end of the first year of schooling, 1880, reported their students had made as much progress as could be expected of a class of European children.

The missionaries knew their task was difficult, but they had no idea just how powerful the Western Aranda education of their young men was until their time on the Finke had almost expired. In 1889, two years after the first baptisms, following three years of close combat with the older men over the hearts and minds of the people, Schulze recognised for the first time the way government worked among his Western Aranda neighbours.

I will now go into the so-called government of our people. In fact there is really not much to govern, since every man is his own master, and the one with the biggest mouth and the strongest body is the greatest lord. But some matters are subject to the control of the old men and the witch-doctors. ... In the past we have wondered at the respect with which the young men treat the old, but now we realise it is by the arts of magic that the men deceive the women and young people, and themselves, so that they are seen as a kind of higher being. The first stage of initiation [Beschneidung] is particularly important for implanting this perspective. If the young are disinclined to respect the old men they bring forward their initiation, so impressing the boys with their devil-learning and gradually making them into people like themselves. They don't tell them everything at the beginning, but a little more by stages as they grow older, so their understanding of their devils increases. As a result the oldest are regarded as the cleverest, and their system of control is strengthened. It follows that initiation is the principal basis of the power of their magic. I would really like to have more detailed information about it, but none of us has ever been able to see the act itself, because they keep it secret and conduct the ceremonies in private. I am sorry to say that the young Christians are not telling us everything ... Among our heathen Christians initiation with its hocus-pocus seems no longer to make an impression, and it appears to us they have completely broken away from it. Thank God they are free of these bonds because the old men's magic is Satan's main hold on these people, and the older the person the deeper he is bound and held by these sins."

Allowing for Schulze's hostility to Western Aranda ways, his analysis is close to the mark.

The Aranda men were too proud to share their knowledge with the missionaries, because it carried their status with it. The missionaries were too proud to conceive that any faith held by these "benighted heathen" could be given standing alongside the Word. Despite the ridicule the Aboriginal men heaped on the learning their children got from the missionaries, they accommodated it, up to a point, as they accommodated the weird practices and accents of their black neighbours, with whom they also shared elements of their cosmology.

Tjalkabota's father told him before the baptism "Boy, you can become a Christian, but not me." Perhaps other fathers and mothers were less accommodating, but the missionaries record only one clear case of a young convert or catechumen being killed. Mototoka, a youth who had begun his Aranda initiation and was also under instruction by the missionaries, was killed in 1888 for refusing to take part in a ceremony, probably a further stage of his initiation.[73] It is unlikely he was the only victim of such punishment.

The inheritance of Western Aranda boys through initiation was not all privilege. True, it cured the original sin of the Western Aranda boy - ignorance of the powerful ceremonial words - and led him, step by step, to share the powers of the creator-spirits. But the obligation to help repay injury and insult, real or inferred, formed a heavy element of the obligations that a boy took on through initiation into the freemasonry of Western Aranda manhood. Tekua was soon to discover this. And in case it should seem that a world in which nakedness was universal was also a world of simplicity and directness in personal relations, we should bear in mind these observations of T. G. H. Strehlow:

> But the native does not forget injuries easily. Under an outwardly calm and even friendly behaviour and a treacherous mask of effusive courtesy, he will nurse old grievances carefully but grimly, sometimes for years, until an opportunity for revenge presents itself to him. ... [there is a] strong element of snobbery and intolerance which characterizes the Central Australian native in his dealings with strangers, and in his criticisms of customs and rites and ideas which differ from his own. Differences in dialect and peculiarities of speech, too, are continually being made targets of abuse and biting ridicule. The result was inevitable: there was never any strong feeling of unity in the Aranda 'tribe' before the coming of the white man into Central Australia.[74]

While there was a profound divide between intiated men on the one hand and women and children on the other, there was another component of the Western Aranda life of faith that was shared by men, women and children. There were stories and songs that softened work and enlivened the social life of the camp. Much more than entertainment, song and story were the forms in which the Western Aranda told themselves about themselves and their world. While the sacred songs, restricted to initiated men, often employed ideas and language that were beyond the understanding of most, or all, of those singing them, these domestic songs were closely attached to the activities they accompanied - preparing food, preparing weapons, summoning up courage for a raid. They helped entrain the individual's experience to the habits of the group, raised the spirits, heightened the significance of the ordinary, diminished the daily pains of living. Song was no less than the continuing voice of the Western Aranda mind. [75]

Much of what the missionaries tried to teach their students caused their eyes to glaze. The missionaries' attempts at discipline were sometimes met by a kind of dumb insolence. Even the greatest drama of the Christianity, the Easter story, was met with a seeming indifference. "It reveals very clearly the deep corruption of the human heart that even the lesson of God's great love makes so little impression."[76] With the great songs of the Protestant reformation it was a different matter. The students, and their elders, received the Lutherans' music with enthusiasm and with an expectation of meaning that could hardly be met. The Lutherans, like the Western Aranda, and unlike the 'English' surrounding them, were a singing people. But the missionaries, blessed and burdened by the Word, failed at first to see how deep this bond was. "A happy-go-lucky people," concluded Kempe in 1880, "untroubled by the course of the world, they live their life, singing, without one thought of providing food and drink for the morrow. Fortunate for them, their thoughtlessness leaves them easily contented...".[77]

And, if the missionaries could see no form of Western Aranda government they could harness to their campaign of transformation, there was another force in Western Aranda life that found a strong echo in Lutheran practice. Like singing, pain was the accompaniment to important occasions for Western Aranda men and women, especially moving into adulthood and advancing through the degrees of male seniority. Boys and girls played games that involved enduring without complaint the pain of hot coals placed on the naked skin. Both men and women inflicted bloody wounds on themselves in grieving for their dead. Initiated men volunteered for further physical mutilation in the course of ceremonies in which a man gained further secret knowledge and could enhance his status. A willingness to endure pain was one of the ways you showed you were human, worthy, and trustworthy.

If the Western Aranda idea of law was simply incompatible with both the Christian and secular South Australian ideas of law, perhaps we can support our law with pain, and the people will appreciate the rationale in due course. This was, after all, the basis of educating children in much of Europe, certainly among these Lutherans, and the missionaries asserted frequently the moral equivalence of Aboriginal adults and European children. "'Spare the rod and spoil the child'" Kempe quoted in 1889. "If even Christians cannot do without it [corporal punishment] how can the heathen and the heathen-Christians?".[78] If it was suitable for German children it was suitable for benighted heathen. If you have the power.

Song and pain, two threads across the chasm separating these opposing faiths. But there were also more powerful forces at work. The Western Aranda, from 1870 on, had to face not only the external blows of their new neighbours – the disturbance to their economy, new violence, new diseases - but also powerful challenges to their power to recruit their young into the old ways, and to keep them there. The entire fabric of Western Aranda society was built on faith buttressing a strict system of rules that supported in turn a rigid hierarchy of status. It was enforced by magical threats and by physical punishment under the control of the old men. Now that faith was being contested by others whose faiths were as fiercely held, and whose powers were, in some respects, greater. The new opportunities brought by the whites were distributed without regard to the rigid status hierarchy of the Western Aranda, favouring women and children. In T. G. H. Strehlow's judgment, "in Central Australia, at any rate, aboriginal society was destroyed largely because the young people deliberately deserted their own people."[79] That was, no doubt, the view of the senior men.

GOVERNMENT ON THE LINE

1836-1890

5

ANIMAL SPIRITS
AND THE
WASTE-LANDS OF THE CROWN

"South Australia smokes big for very little fire."
Ernest Cowle[80]

Charles Chewings came to Tempe Downs in February 1891 for profit and for love of the country. He surveyed his pastoral leases and wrote for his fellow shareholders a prospectus for their further development. In 1885 he had also mapped the Finke River and its tributaries, following more of the river's leads than any economic purpose could justify. From his observations he published an intelligent description that was developed over the next ten years into enough geological knowledge to earn two university degrees. His father, John Chewings, had come to South Australia with the simpler and more conventional motive of getting richer, and he did this through pastoralism.

The business of the Colony of South Australia was land, pure and simple. In other Australian Colonies there were other motives as well: punishing crime, suppressing social disorder, forestalling the claims of other colonial powers, securing the marine umbilicus between the Colonies and the mother-land and providing sources of the raw materials a rising imperial power needed. The state-sponsored entrepreneurs who waded on to the beach at present-day suburban Glenelg had chosen a landing point less strategic than it was intestinal, inside Gulf St Vincent which was more lake than ocean, a sea passage leading nowhere but the terminal mangrove swamps where later Port Pirie was built. On the Adelaide Plain, however, there was land good enough for agriculture, in a good year.

And it was their agricultural potential that had made the lands of South Australia a prospective source of wealth to people from the northern hemisphere. In this post-industrial age it is worth remembering that when there is no limit to the supply of suitable land, the capital growth available from capturing the natural increase in plant and animal populations makes returns on stock-market investment appear puny in comparison. For Central Australia in the 1870s, a decade of generally favourable years, it has been estimated that cattle herds increased at a rate of 25% per annum, and sheep at more than 50%.[81] There were many other steps between land suitable for agriculture or pastoralism and the creation of wealth, but none of it worked without the land. If your land is limited - and in the 1870s the area of South Australia's better quality pastoral land was being reduced in favour of agriculture - there is always other people's. In a world of shortage, other people who fail to cultivate their land, whether from ignorance or arrogance of ownership, may be thought to be offending reason and morality, then as now. This is a view of modern Australians that can be found close to the surface of the thinking of many east Asians.

A simple formula was intended to make the privatised Colony of South Australia grow without cost to the British Treasury. In a departure from the precedent of New South Wales, South Australia's chief asset, the land, would not remain the private treasure of the British monarch, to be parcelled out to cronies of Crown and government, who could squat on it indefinitely since there were no holding costs.

Instead, by subjecting the South Australian lands to a market system at arm's length from political power, with all land having a real price or rent, and with the profits from first sale entailed to support the growth of the new Colony, the British Government hoped to build empire without risking public funds. Emigration to the new Colony could be subsidised, so increasing the demand for land and creating a virtuous cycle of increasing land values and rents, subdivision, and more emigration. As in all pyramid schemes, those investors who got in on the ground floor – including the usual cronies and friends – would pay a price but still grow rich. Large fortunes could be buttressed by grants of larger holdings on the fringes of settlement. Closer to Adelaide, a vigorous policy of subdivision would ensure there was land for the less wealthy settlers. Everyone's land values would steam ahead as each new settler made his neighbour's holding more valuable. With the passing of time small fortunes could be turned into large ones and honest toilers enter the ranks of the propertied. And so it happened, although not without political brawling between those who represented large land-owners, especially pastoralists, and those who spoke for the land-hungry. In the 1880s, the fighting continued, but few could see a future for agriculture in Central Australia. This was the domain of pastoralism, and courageous pastoralism at that.

From this marvellous machine for realising the value that lay dormant in South Australia's land grew the hero-explorers of the second half of the nineteenth Century, men like Stuart, Gosse, Tietkens, Ernest Giles, and P Egerton Warburton, whose travels were often funded by successful pastoralists. There was also a priesthood of surveyors. On their maps the intricately figured landscapes of black people's cosmologies were rubbed clear by greed, ignorance and carelessness, to become those numbered domains for white men's dreams of wealth - pastoral leases.

The source of all this was the plan of Edward Gibbon Wakefield, a schemer who, at the time he sketched the plan that became South Australia, was in prison for eloping with an heiress. It suited the spirit of the age in Britain, but the Wakefield scheme also side-lined the tender concern to accommodate aboriginal peoples that was the inheritance of the British Enlightenment. That intention was given no support in the Colony's founding legislation, the South Australia Act of 1834, which made it clear that the land was "to be open to European occupation without regard to any territorial claims the Aboriginals might have."[82]. Instead, a policy of conciliation with the aboriginal residents of the land was expressed only in the subordinate official instructions under which the first Governors operated. The 1834 Act was replaced in 1842 by the Waste Lands Act, which allowed, but did not oblige, the South Australian administration to set aside land for Aboriginal uses and to put aside up to fifteen percent of the revenues from land for the support of Aborigines. The office of Protector of Aborigines was created but was fated to have a welfare role and never to become a major holder of land or capital on behalf of Aboriginal peoples.

From the perspective of 1890 the fair conclusion is that the scheme had worked for the colonisers. Wealth, as recorded in the probated estates of departing citizens, was spread more widely than in the other British colonies of Australia. However, the dwindling groups of Aborigines in South Australia had little to show for their claim to equitable treatment. Reservation of land for Aboriginal use was unpopular and ineffectual, and much of what had been done in the south had been undone by 1890. For the Western Aranda there were, in addition to the rights and obligations they shared with all citizens of the Province, some strong words in the pastoral leases over their land protecting their rights to continue their way of life in parallel with the pastoralists.[83] The Western Aranda did not know this. There is little evidence that even their friends among the whites of the Centre placed due weight on Aboriginal rights of occupation and usage. The nearest the pro-Aboriginal lobby came to this point was to remind government how cheaply these Australian Aborigines had been dispossessed of their territories, if you compared them with the aboriginal peoples of other lands settled by Europeans. At that time, and for the next eighty years, Aboriginal land meant land leased to others for the intended benefit of the Aborigines.

The Western Aranda did not understand the rules of the British, which were very different to their own, particularly on the crucial question of property in land. For their part, the Western Aranda did not believe that merely by occupation and usage could the white intruders usurp their connection with their land, which was embedded in their cosmology and law, intertwined with their personal histories, and was the stage for their far-reaching social connections.

The Western Aranda clans certainly knew what land they considered theirs to harvest a living from.[84] It was the duty of the senior men to maintain the thread of magic that connected past creation to present subsistence. The senior men had rights and obligations to maintain the ceremonies of particular places. Despite the magical sanction of their cosmology, the boundaries of their clan estates were doubtless more porous to the travelling and harvesting of other clans than a pastoralist would have found acceptable. Not only did the erratic rainfall drive people about large areas of the Centre, but the impact of lethal epidemics, like the small-pox of 1868-70, that had left its mark on some of the people the missionaries met, must have required rapid changes in ownership as camps were wiped out or reduced to a few survivors. Communal title within an oral culture is a recipe for dispute in any case, but that fact hardly weakens the owners' sense of entitlement. Even individual ownership was understood within the estates. According to Carl Strehlow's informants, some grass placed in a tree with ripening fruit reserved the harvest for the man who placed it. Although theft of the fruit justified killing the offender, enforcing the claim was a matter for the claimant, not the council of elders.

The game harvested by the Western Aranda man had to be shared around his camp, but this was no free-for-all. The division of the carcass among his relations was prescribed with precision. Women and children got the pickings.

In 1881 and 1882, Charles Chewings explored the country of the upper Finke, to assess its potential for cattle. "The country had been leased from the Crown, and the title was good for a number of years provided one paid the rent in advance, and stocked up to a specified number per square mile within a given time. A peppercorn rental had been authorised for the first seven years...". His leases, 3,990 square miles in total, bracketed the Finke River mission's lease, with parcels of land to the north of the MacDonnell ranges proper, even to the north of Glen Helen station, and others below the James Range to the south west of Hermannsburg, land that was later to become Tempe Downs station. While he travelled in these southern parts of his estate he was accompanied by Charlie Walker who had already established Henbury station on the Finke south of the James Range. Walker's name was attached to the Creek on whose banks the Tempe Downs head station was soon to be built. Charles Chewings saw and described the land west of the Finke better than any previous explorer, marking its waters, pastures and hills. He saw no more of the Aboriginal landscape than any of the explorers who merely passed through where Chewings stayed to study, but if any white man at this time can be said to have loved the Finke, it was Charles Chewings.

In 1885 he was back on the upper Finke again. It was time to stock the leases and Chewings was there to find the best waters and pastures. He reported that over the months of his travelling he established friendly relations with the Aboriginal peoples of the country.[85] He saw his relations with the resident Aborigines as typical. "In time the natives came to know that the whites would not harm them if they behaved themselves; the younger ones were given employment and soon learned to be useful. In after years I used them to do all sorts of work ... But the natives are very primitive beings, and what seems childish to us may be very important to them."

Charles Chewings, in his other business of camel-train operator, had employed Aboriginal men exclusively. He had spent many months away from whites and out-numbered by his Aboriginal workers whose labour and skill helped his business flourish. By his own account, under his leadership Aboriginal men had demonstrated their capacity to take responsibility, repay reward with effort and trust with loyalty. In 1891 he was to give further evidence of his sense of moral responsibility when two of his Aboriginal station workers were murdered at Tempe Downs.

While Chewings spent many months on and around the Finke, he did not manage Tempe Downs on behalf of the Company formed to own the station. That task was given to Frederick Thornton, an experienced bushman, after the lease had been stocked by Robert Coulthard.

In its first decade pastoralism along the Finke was dominated by investors with large amounts of capital. Men of means pooled their venture capital in pastoral companies that owned the leases, bought the stock, and employed managers and station hands to do the exceedingly hard work of setting up the stations. It appears that most of the men they employed had bush experience gained further south, or in Queensland and New South Wales. Some were relatives of the pastoral investors, like the numerous Coulthards.[86]

One avenue for the young of South Australia to enter Central Australian pastoralism was the Overland Telegraph. Large gangs of workers moved along its track in 1870-2, and smaller gangs continued to maintain the line and its plant thereafter. We first meet Billy Abbott, as far as the public record is concerned, helping to maintain the line north of Barrow Creek. Billy's father, William H Abbott, who named his son after himself, was a senior public servant in the administration of the South Australian Post-Master General, Charles Todd. He described his profession variously as draftsman and professional clerk, but would today be regarded as a senior manager. "I look after the telegraph and telephone lines within a radius of ten miles of Adelaide [and have the] general supervision of the lines through the colony" he reported in 1890. He had responsibility for18-20 men and a salary that was close to the highest available by promotion within the public service, comparable with that of a Stipendiary Magistrate. William Abbott's career had not progressed, however. In fact, after fifteen years in the public service he had been retrenched in 1870 at a salary of £400, due, no doubt, to one of the South Australian government's recurring bouts of pending insolvency, and had not thereafter managed to improve on a temporary position in the post office, although his salary was reduced only a little. This still grieved him in 1890 when he was interviewed by the South Australian Public Service Commission, but he remained a personal friend of Charles Todd, the Post-Master General, without whose support his status may well have been a good deal lower. And now, it seemed, the Central Australian frontier was claiming his son, Billy Abbott.

It is not hard to see the attractions of the bush life to young men like Billy Abbott. You were free of direct supervision most of the time. If, like William Willshire, you found supervision irksome, and the esteem of your peers hard to win, the frontier provided both freedom from oversight and the opportunity to be master of people whose status could never challenge yours, the Aboriginal people. He might be an escapee from the authority of father and school, as Hermann Kempe suspected, but every station worker, it seems, had his Aboriginal 'boy' to fetch and carry, and to protect him from the many hazards created by his ignorance of the country and its people. And there were the Aboriginal women, whose loyalty to these bottom-of-the-pile workers was obvious. They warned their new husbands of threatened assaults by Aboriginal men, possibly their husbands under Aboriginal law, who sometimes thought the white men's claims on their women defeated their own rights.

It also irked the missionaries to find so many young women present on the stations, some of them, so they reported, openly described as "Mrs Soandso".[87] Most of the station workers were later to abandon their *de facto* wives as owners ran out of funds to pay so many white men. Some stayed on to found mixed race families whose descendants are among the leading figures in the Aboriginal communities today, although it was the women who decided whether or not these early white residents would have a posterity.

None of the early bushmen boasted of their advantage with Aboriginal women, at least not to southern audiences, but doubtless it was one of the forces that kept them in such isolation from their former families. It made their lives more comfortable than might be imagined, although it was never a gentle life.

The station managers were the government on their estates. It fell to them to protect and increase their shareholders' livestock and, willy-nilly, to control the conduct of people who might threaten the investment. As *de facto* lords over the people resident on their territory, station managers could, if they wished, claim seigneurial rights over women who had been displaced socially by death and disruption among the Aboriginal clans. Because of their high status and power, once settled into their rule they were promised young girls as future wives. James McDonald of Glen Helen made the mistake of provoking Louis Schulze by pointing out an Aboriginal boy as his. "I passed the remark that it was mine with the view of giving him something to digest as he was always preaching sermons to me on the subject of immorality".[88] Frederick Thornton suffered a similar embarrassment when an Aboriginal father sent a girl child to Tempe Downs as his wife. When Chinchewarra came in from the rocky gorges to the west of Tempe Downs station, between 1887 and 1890, Frederick Thornton locked her in a room in one of the station buildings. After she was "made quiet" by Thornton she became his mistress.

It is hard to know from their recorded statements to what extremes each man would go in opposing Aboriginal competition for their station's resources and stock. When, in their deputations to Ministers and in their statements recorded in the press of the day, they talk of what others do and might do in the absence of government protection, it is impossible to know whether they really knew what others did on other estates, or whether they were telling us what they were doing. It is always possible that they relied almost as much on rumour as their audience in Adelaide. Certainly, when Swan and Taplin questioned them directly in 1890, the managers to a man denied harsh treatment of their Aboriginal neighbours and any knowledge that others were guilty of it. They did report conflict, but most of it lay in the past.[89]

Investing in Australia's arid Centre, subject like most of the continent to the wild swings of climate now known as the El Niño-

Southern Oscillation cycle, was a risky punt. It needed a long-term perspective, time to get back money invested in buildings, stockyards, supplies, all inflated by the enormous costs of transport, never less than $20 000 a ton (in today's money) before the railway reached Quorn in 1879, and still consuming most of Hermannsburg's wool cheque in 1890.[90] Above all pastoralists needed to invest in reliable water supplies by sinking bores widely across their pastures so that stock could reach feed in the droughts. Less reasonably, pastoralists opposed percentage rentals that would cream off more of the profits they hoped to make eventually. It was unlikely the station managers would respond casually to people injuring their stock.

In 1886, as the herds on Tempe Downs were still being built up, and the Matuntara still coming to terms with their new joint tenants, Chewings reported that "Stock have increased in a way that has surpassed the expectations of the most sanguine".

Again, in April 1891, after appeals for government help against cattle-killing, in 1887, 1888 and 1890, and after a long visit to the station in 1891, Chewings wrote in a detailed report to his fellow Directors: "The cattle were very quiet, and I am well pleased with their breeding and appearance... The stock do well, grow well and fat, and increase rapidly.   There can be no two opinions as to the country being suitable for horse-breeding; the young stock on Tempe Downs are very good...".

These comments were written with two audiences in mind, Chewings' fellow shareholders and others who might buy shares. If their sincerity may be questioned, consider also that later in 1891 the Tempe Downs Pastoral Company took up the new 14-year leases available under the revised legislation, and at valuation rents; hardly a vote of no-confidence in their business.

When we find Chewings writing to the press and the Minister in November 1887 seeking help, the stocking of the lease was complete and the consequent conflict with the Matuntara probably just past its peak. In his letter Chewings acknowledged the tactical advantage the country gave the Aboriginal cattle-killers. However, "The chief difficulty has arisen through the hard & fast rules the police are bound to follow." Located in Alice Springs and Charlotte Waters, both several days ride away from Tempe Downs, police could only travel when a station manager asked for help, and could only attempt to arrest identified alleged perpetrators for whom warrants had been sworn. This meant long delays during which the perpetrators and the evidence of the deeds would both disappear.

Despite the difficult environment and the insistent lobbying, the total number of cattle killed on Tempe Downs, from the time stocking began in 1885 to August 1887, was estimated by Mounted Constable Thomas Daer, who policed the station, to be "about twelve".[91]

Chewings did not recognise another management problem that came from the country itself. Because the land was dissected by ridges of stone into numerous strips of grazing land, the stock were broken into small groups, isolated from each other and the stockmen. In these conditions they tended to go "wild", becoming less amenable to management. "A man was needed who was prepared to spend say three weeks out of every month out bush and only come into the station for a few days at a time", according to a later manager of Tempe.[92] The windows given to us onto Thornton's management style, when Frank Gillen visited in 1891 and when the Horn Expedition visited in 1894, both support the conclusion that this was just the way he worked the station. It was a way of working and a way of life that kept a manager up-to-date with the latest activity on his lease, the incidence of cattle-killing and – with the aid of Aboriginal trackers – the identity of the perpetrators. It also meant that the manager of the pastoral station, like the Aborigines who continued to be hunter-gatherers, lived a life of constant movement, with the head station a place of only occasional resort.

In August 1888 Charles Chewings was part of another delegation, this time to the political head of South Australia, the Chief Secretary. The delegation brought with them a letter from Frederick Thornton, who was not happy. "The blacks have given me no end of work; all my time is taken up after them. They have been killing cattle in the Walker Creek and the Peterman at the same time ... and after walking all night in the hills we got to their camp at 9 next morning, but they heard us coming and got out of the camp, but left most of their things behind them (spears, meat and other things). We were very thirsty, and went up the gorge to get a drink. When we got well in the blacks, who were on the top, right overhead, started throwing and rolling stones down on us, and it was with difficulty we got out. As soon as I got back I had to go after them in the Peterman to find that the cattle had been run about."[93]

Nonetheless, in 1891 the Tempe Downs Directors were as bullish in private as Chewings had earlier been in public. On March 3rd, 1891, Josiah Symon, formerly Attorney-General of South Australia and later of the new Commonwealth of Australia, told a friend that two Directors had advised him it would be "absurd" to sell at 10/- a share. Directors are not a recommended source of advice on buying and selling shares in their companies, but only a very brave South Australian businessman would try to sucker Josiah Symon. In any case he had a spy on the ground – his brother-in-law Mounted Constable Ernest Cowle, sent to Alice Springs in 1889 when Willshire was moved to Boggy Water.[94]

The seriousness of the "depredations" of Aborigines on livestock in the Centre was tested by the Swan-Taplin Enquiry when it convened at Hermannsburg in July 1890. On July 23rd, James McDonald, manager of the Glen Helen station, over the ridge of the MacDonnell Ranges north of Hermannsburg, gave his evidence. He could only cite instances involving two beasts, and buttressed his case against the Aborigines by referring to the killing of five Aboriginal men and women by a raiding party of Aborigines from 60-70 miles to the west. This kind of incident was of little concern to pastoralists, missionaries, police or the Enquiry. But, he assured the Enquiry, "Previous to the enrollment of the native force in this district cattle were killed by hundreds". Five years had passed since Willshire and Mounted Constable Wurmbrand had been provided with native constables at Alice Springs. When pressed on this point by Missionary Schulze, McDonald made this remarkable concession.

"When I state that the cattle were killed in hundreds I mean that they were sprinkled over the district and not on one particular run."[95] That is, the losses were spread over several pastoral stations, up to eight, depending on McDonald's definition of his "district", operating by the mid-1880s along the Finke and around Alice Springs. The number of livestock pastured on these runs in 1890 was greater than 20 000, going by the figures tabled at the Enquiry, and those were not complete. Nor did McDonald provide a time period for the losses he claimed. If they had occurred within a short period we may assume that he would have told the Commissioners. Since he didn't, the safest conclusion is that the losses took place over several years, perhaps the entire period since stocking had begun.

That is, McDonald was talking of total losses of about 1-5%, over a period of several years, sometime in the past.

This is hardly convincing evidence that losses to Aboriginal cattle-killing ever threatened the viability of the pastoral stations. It is certain that the stock-killing taking place in 1890, on all but the newer "outside" stations including Tempe Downs which were still receiving Aboriginal immigrants from further out, was of minor economic significance, and had been for some years before that. In particular places, at earlier times, it may have been different, but there is not convincing evidence even of that more limited claim.[96] It is equally certain that cattle-killing on the outside stations did not stop for another fifty years.

McDonald's account of stock-killing also had other meanings, however. His experience of being bailed up in a gorge with Aboriginal men throwing stones down from the cliffs was a scenario of jeopardy that foreshadowed Thornton's experience four years later and resonated with other station men's anxieties about their command of the Aborigines' respect or fear.[97] The pastoralists were a small minority of the people in the Centre, and they knew what Aboriginal warriors were capable of. If cattle-killing was an irritation, the prospect of attacks on themselves was occasionally a cause of real fear among the pastoralists, and also the missionaries.

Aboriginal attacks on cattle could be more than irritating, especially since they increased in periods of drought when losses were distressing anyway. That irritation was felt as much by the missionaries, a fact denied by Kempe in 1890 but supported by earlier evidence and also by the next master of Hermannsburg, Carl Strehlow.[98] When, at the peak of Thornton's complaints, in August 1888, a powerful delegation of pastoralists visited the Minister for the Northern Territory it included Friedrich Krichauff among its number. Krichauff represented the mission and introduced the delegation. He had "at times received communications from the missionaries there that the blacks were doing a great deal of harm. It was not the tribe that was near to the mission station, but other tribes". This was probably the nature of the cattle-killing experienced by Glen Helen and Tempe Downs too. It was this delegation that provided the political impetus leading to William Willshire's Police Patrol for the Interior, the "Queensland-style force" set up at the end of that year.[99]

The missionaries' claim that they suffered little from cattle-killing reflected poorly on the pastoralists' treatment of their resident Aboriginal populations, as it was intended to. In 1883 Hermann Kempe boasted in his report for the period November 1882 to November 1883 that "the heathen resident at the [Hermannsburg] station have given up completely stealing and killing cattle, but all our neighbours still have much to complain about in that respect."[100] Kempe ignored the fact that since their establishment Glen Helen and Tempe Downs, stocked in 1878 and 1885 respectively, had become the 'outside stations' confronting clans moving in from further west, with ready routes of escape. But as Kempe's letter of May 1884 to Mounted Constable Wurmbrand tells us, the Glen Helen cattle-killers were the same as those "rummaging" on the mission lease, although they did not, in a literal sense, reside there, and Kempe wanted to be rid of them.[101] The missionaries were more concerned that their pastoralist neighbours treated *their* resident Aborigines too well, especially the older boys and girls.

It is also true that when Aborigines hunted down stock they harassed more than they killed, leading the stock to lose condition, to become less tractable.[102] These problems threatened the pastoralists' profits, but not to the extent of the much greater damage done by drought.

There was also theft of stock by white men. It is impossible to know the scale and distribution of such losses at this time but, going by the numbers involved in the instances that are recorded, they were significant. Black men were not the only ones attracted by the sight of valuable assets standing about unattended.[103] The loss of stock to Aborigines held a special sway over the minds of the pastoralists. White thieves came and went. The Aborigines shared their land.

However great or limited their stock losses, what responses were open to the station managers? The prescription of vigilante self-help? "It is not right" Chewings argued "that Stockowners & those employed by them should be forced to protect themselves & their stock by means of the rifle. Humanity cries out against this sort of thing... Are we, as Stockowners, justified in instructing our Managers

& men to ruthlessly shoot these natives if they come and kill our Stock?" The fact that Thornton and Chewings made such frequent lobbies for more policing argues that they were not prepared, whatever their motivation, to shoot ruthlessly their neighbours, however great the irritation they caused.

Better, Chewings thought in 1887, to appoint a further mounted constable, station him on the Finke east of Tempe Downs, at Henbury station, equip him with at least six native constables, and allow one of these two squads (the other remaining at Alice Springs) to be continually on patrol. Deterrence would follow a higher probability of detection. Again, in 1888, the delegation of which Chewings was a member stressed the efficacy of police. The two members of the Legislative Council who accompanied the pastoralists, H Scott and J Warren, were particularly convinced of "the moral influence of the constable", as Scott put it, or the "great mystery connected with the policeman", in Warren's version. They were both transposing to Aboriginal people, who had no concept of an independent police force, the attitudes of the metropolitan middle classes. Frederick Thornton was saying something different.

In June and July 1888 Mounted Constable Hillier travelled to Tempe Downs in response to Thornton's complaints. He reported the situation there "all quiet and orderly", to Thornton's chagrin. "The police from the Alice were out the other day" he wrote to his Directors, "but they did no good. The party was too small, and they have not got horses to do the work."[104] Hillier reported in the Alice Springs Police Station journal that he had reprimanded Thornton for pursuing cattle-killers himself. Thornton had reported his own small punitive expedition against cattle-killers as a result of which he and his Aboriginal companion "got on their camp & gave them a start. We got about 20 spears and other things...".

Hillier's term in the Centre was soon over. Having arrived in September 1887 he was posted back south in 1889. In October and November of 1888, after the Chief Secretary had promised his assistance to the pastoralists, William Willshire also made an excursion to Tempe Downs "to try and put a stop to it, otherwise disperse the Natives which I did, & as Mr Thornton said himself he was much pleased."[105] He was not able to arrest the ringleaders, but "I managed to caution them in their own language, and while doing so, they cleared out very fast...". Willshire's language skills must have been remarkable. He had never before been in Matuntara territory. (Had he used the language of the neighbouring Western Aranda people the Matuntara might have understood him). Before imagining what Willshire might have done to the local people we should bear in mind the limitations of the camel, when compared with the horse, for use in attack. On this expedition Willshire had nothing but camels.

But the pastoralists' lobby of 1888 was successful. It helped that among the delegation were Tempe Downs' Adelaide agent W H Phillipps who was also, at the time, the President of the Chamber of Commerce, four members of the South Australian Parliament, and a leading man of wealth and influence, recently elected to Parliament, W A Horn. On the first of February 1889, Willshire was officially transferred to the portfolio of the Minister for the Northern Territory and put in charge of raising a force of Native Constables, the "proper black police force" that Thornton had been demanding.

This was no longer what Chewings wanted. In February 1890 he recommended to Minister Gordon his personal proposal for dealing with the problem. "It would be wise" he said "to have certain depots where the blacks could be got and kept." To this point Chewings and the missionaries were in accord. Both favoured a policy of protective reserves where the entry of whites and the exit of blacks would be controlled by law. But Chewings "did not mean missionary reserves, because the missionaries did not seem to have proper control over them, but reserves where they might be under the supervision of the police." His faith in the police was to be shattered one year later, but his proposed reserves were a radical departure from the opinions of his fellow pastoralists.

When Chewings dismisses the mission as a model for containment and protection of Aborigines he is drawing attention to three defects of the Hermannsburg mission that grieved its neighbours. First, not only had the mission been established on good pastoral land, at no rent, it was also provided with rations for the Aborigines. The pastoralists supported rationing of the young and the feeble. It addressed an obvious need, especially in poor seasons, and helped to discharge their obligation to the Aboriginal occupants under the terms of the pastoral leases. It discouraged that part of the cattle-killing that was aimed at fulfilling the social obligations of the able-bodied men and women to their dependents. It was, in fact, just an extension of the way pastoralists paid their workers in meat and other goods, making available to their workers' dependents the offal that would otherwise have been wasted.

But rationing stations were a magnet to Aboriginal people over a wide area during the droughts. The last thing a pastoralist needed was to have starving Aborigines trekking across his lease to reach a neighbouring ration depot. The obvious answer was to provide the rations to the pastoral stations, so strengthening their control over the Aboriginal people and intelligence about them. [106]

Second, the missionaries had no obligation to care for the aged, sick and starving from other properties, whatever the station-owners wanted. The police had no power to compel the Aborigines to go to the mission, and no power to take them back there when they left it, whatever the missionaries wanted.

There is no reason to believe that Chewings rejected Hermannsburg's enterprise for the same reason as his fellow pastoralists, that is, because it provided an alternative to the other stations, and a critical perspective in reporting back to the metropolis. Perhaps he thought that Aborigines needed regimented reserves to protect them from the temptations of cattle, grog, and the retribution of his fellow whites, and that their impoverishment could be better addressed by rationing in that context.

Most of the pastoralists of the Centre, including his manager Thornton, thought the reserves would not work. How would the police be able to keep Aborigines on rubbish country, away from their lands, and in forced association with others more foreign to them than Greeks were to Englishmen? [107] Perhaps, for most of the Directors of the Tempe Downs Pastoral Company, this lobby to Gordon was simply part of the process of negotiating lease conditions with government, and their complaints trumped up. But for Charles Chewings there was possibly also work of conscience to be done. In particular, he may have wanted to get off his conscience what he feared Frederick Thornton and his station workers might do. Did he, as an Adelaide gentleman with extensive bush experience, also fear what the police might do?

Before we follow William Willshire down from Heavitree Gap near Alice Springs to Boggy Water on the Finke, where Willshire was to establish, largely as a result of Chewings' lobbying, his own peculiar station, we need to understand more of what policing meant in Central Australia at that time.

Tempe Downs old station, 1981, shortly before it was washed down Walker Creek by flood waters (*Mrs S Crogan*).

Glen Helen station's first site, on the inner left of the bend in Ormiston Creek, middle distance, and (inset) one of the station's few remnants.

Map of the area occupied by the Hermannsburg, Glen Helen and Tempe Downs stations, based on Charles Chewings' travels (NLA RM1258)

6

LAW OR WAR? SCALING JUSTICE FOR THE FRONTIER

"... they should be made to respect the law of the Land that has been taken from them..." Ernest Cowle[108]

It was foundational doctrine of the Colony of South Australia that its Aboriginal owners were not to be treated as enemies or outlaws, but as British subjects, under the restraints and protections of British law. It was a doctrine held with a greater conviction by the British Secretaries of State for the Colonies and their appointees in the Colony, the Governors, than was felt by most of the colonists themselves. It was easier for an educated gentleman in London to believe in the nobility, or at least the shared humanity, of nomadic hunter-gatherers than it was for the colonists whose stock was being killed, whose black neighbours continued their night-long corroborees, walked naked through the town centre, showed themselves even more corruptible by grog and prostitution than the poor of London. The European settler was also confronted daily by the limits imposed on his sympathies by his presumption of superiority and by the vastly superior power of his technology and weapons.

The hope of policy-makers that Aboriginal people could be reconciled to the occupation of their land rested, in part, on confidence in the superiority of British civilization which would convince the Aborigines to adopt the economy, customs and beliefs of the newcomers. A similar doctrine and policy had applied at the foundation of the Colony of New South Wales in Sydney. The policy of conciliation had fallen apart under the pressure of competition for resources, the collapse of the indigenous population through disease, the behaviour of individuals beyond the control of government, misjudgment, mutual incomprehension, the persistence of Aboriginal culture, contempt and, finally, indifference.[109]

While the colonists of South Australia had occupied the Adelaide Plains without violent incident, within five years of the foundation of South Australia, the growing incidence of conflict was putting under pressure the assumption that Aborigines and colonists were equal before the law as citizens. By whatever combination of inducement, customary law, force and complaisance the Aboriginal peoples of the new Colony had allowed their land to be occupied, they had not acted under the concepts of the new British law. Even if we put aside this major obstacle, there were many practical problems in applying British law.

In 1839, after the murder of two shepherds near Adelaide, justice Cooper reminded the lawyers for the Aboriginal defendants that ignorance of the law was no defence. "It is not necessary in order to subject persons to punishment, that they should have a knowledge of the law by which they incur the liability." He also considered the unsworn admissions by the two Aboriginal defendants, unsupported by other evidence, sufficient grounds to convict, although they had knowledge neither of British law nor the English language. The two were hanged on the North Adelaide parklands, in front of a group of those local Aborigines who could be rounded up for the *al fresco* lesson.[110] A rough and demonstrative form of British justice was being established for Aboriginal citizens of the Colony, confirming their inferior status among the British Empire's subjects. The spread of settlement beyond the Adelaide Plains, rapid from the mid-1840s, would require a further coarsening of those standards.

Aborigines sometimes benefited from being unable to take part in the legal process. In 1848 Police Commissioner Dashwood complained that an Aboriginal man charged with murder escaped justice due to "strict adherence to legal forms and quibbles". The next year it was necessary, for similar reasons, for Anglican clergy, lawyers and other leading citizens to petition for the sentence of death passed on four Aborigines to be commuted. [111]

A critical question at this time was the role of Aboriginal evidence in court proceedings. The jurisprudence of the time thought a belief in God and the afterlife, as they were understood by Christians, was necessary for an oath to have weight in the mind of the person giving evidence. In the absence of white evidence, charges against whites or blacks could not be proceeded with. Initially under the impetus provided by Governor Grey, beginning in 1844, laws were introduced that allowed the courts discretion to hear Aboriginal evidence, provided that no conviction would be allowed to stand merely on the basis of the evidence of "uncivilised persons". This process culminated in the Aboriginal Witnesses Acts of 1848 and 1849 which remained in force until 1929. Considering its importance in a later section of this account it is worth setting out in full what this legislation provided:

"... in all proceedings ... wherein the testimony of any such uncivilized person ... may be required it shall be lawful for the Court, Judge, or Coroner, or Justice, or Justices of the Peace having jurisdiction in the matter to which the testimony relates, to receive such testimony without administering any form of oath and without any formality".

The judge or other officer in charge of the proceedings was required to explain to the witness that he or she was required to tell the truth. The next Section of the same Act provided that:

"the testimony of any such uncivilized person being reduced to writing, and being verified as hereinafter mentioned, may be lawfully received as evidence upon any trial civil or criminal, in this Province, when under the like circumstances the written affidavit, examination, or deposition upon oath of any person, might be lawfully read or received as evidence."

The following Section makes clear that an "uncivilized person" could make a "complaint" on which a Court case might be based, provided that it was properly verified by a Justice of the Peace, and signed by the complainant (an illiterate person's mark constituted a signature.)

This was, for its time, a remarkable concession to the needs of the Province's Aboriginal citizens in legal proceedings. Its implicit weakening of the part the Christian religion was taken to play in individual lives was a clear demonstration that the missionaries on the Finke were indeed occupying an outpost in more senses than one.

The 1848 Act retained, in Section 6, the power of the judge, or his equivalent, to judge the "weight and credibility" of the kind of unsworn testimony an Aborigine might give, and prevented a capital conviction being based on it. Section 6 was struck out by the amending Act of 1849. Henceforth, *any* person might be convicted of *any* offence on the sole and unsworn testimony of an Aborigine. A mighty leap forward for South Australian justice.

The 1848-9 legislation addressed not only the religious obstacle to the participation of Aboriginal people in court cases, it also spoke clearly on the language barrier.

> "... it shall be in like manner lawful for the Judge [etc] ... to receive the same by means of the interpretation of any such uncivilized person as aforesaid, without administering to him any oath ...".

Considering the other obstacles to extending British justice to Aboriginal citizens of South Australia, how far could these legislative reforms travel?

On the Adelaide Plain all the institutions of government could teach the law and apply it. On the frontiers there were in the beginning only settlers and their shepherds and other servants, often pardoned or escaped convicts who had broken British laws and experienced the rougher side of British justice. Until the arrival of police, settlers and Aborigines alike had no choice but to make their own justice.

It had also fallen to justice Cooper, in 1840, to bend British law into a shape that might allow it to serve the needs of the frontiers, beginning a work of accommodating two vastly different systems of rules that continues in the Northern Territory today. Those Aborigines living beyond the settled areas "who had never themselves been subjected to our dominion, and between whom and the colonists there has been no social intercourse" could, in effect, be treated as outlaws. Secondly, the group would be judged guilty of the offences of individuals. Officially-sanctioned violence would then be visited upon them in a measure determined by government. The first legally-sanctioned punitive expedition was mounted against the Aboriginal group considered responsible for the murder of the men, women and children who had survived the ship-wreck of the *Maria* on the Colony's south-eastern coast. Two men of the

Milmenrura clans of the Coorong coast were captured and hanged in front of their fellows. The lesson was too arbitrary to be called justice, but as retribution it showed restraint. Governor Gawler was criticised by his masters in the British Government, and advised that the action his officials had taken was technically-speaking murder. But they all knew that unconstrained revenge was the worse option.

What was developing was a doctrine of the right to self-defence against people who were legally citizens of South Australia, but effectively foreigners. The boundary between law and war was set more by policy than by law.

Some of the frontier settlers themselves thought, no doubt, they were applying these principles in taking action against Aborigines who attacked their persons and property, or even in taking action to prevent such attacks, but in practice they were extending it. Justice Cooper's principle assumed that the outlaw Aborigines were not neighours of any settlers, but as pastoralism spread its claims over large areas of the arid lands with few people, and as the passing contacts between drovers and Aboriginal groups were repeated, the defence of strangeness could hardly be continued. But, in these lands where people are alone more than they are together, where Aborigines were killed, who was to know, apart from the killers? If word got out, where were the direct witnesses? If there were any, they probably spoke no English and, since they were not Christians, could not give evidence in Court until 1849. Without witnesses, who would question a plea of self-defence? In such circumstances what rules is not law or government or politics. In their place must stand the character and moral standards of individuals.

For the police, missionaries and Telegraph officials we know, at least in part, of the powerful motivations they shared: their guiding faith, the body of rules and the superiors they were accountable to, and the colleagues to whose performance they related their own. They all reported back, and much of that reporting is still on the public record. The pastoralists in the Centre are more obscure. Few, if any, of the pastoral companies leasing land along the Finke in the 1880s have left records in the public domain. But while the average stockman of the time may have been as obscure then as he is now, his boss, the station manager, was not. They were kings of the estates they managed. Some had become public figures through exploration or by pioneering new country as drovers. They were in some cases the social equals of the shareholders of the companies they worked for and were well-connected in the metropolis. We are not entitled to assume they were indifferent to the moral shading of the scale between law and war, or that they were too callow or cowed to set limits to what others did on their estates.

On the pastoral frontier when police were available they found themselves caught between the diverging forces of law and warfare, conciliation and violence. If the climate of fear and outrage were hot enough, as it was following the attack on the Barrow Creek Telegraph Station north of Alice Springs in 1874, the police became leaders of the reprisal parties that included any white man within reach. In the south the volunteers employed in this way would be appointed Special Constables by a Magistrate employing the discretion allowed to him by law. This provided a broader legal sanction to the violence of one citizen against another. In a frontier emergency it might be possible to wire authorization from Adelaide, if authorization were sought. Where the rights of frontier citizens to act in self defence ended and the powers of police-led civilian expeditions began, and ended, are moot points, not to my knowledge ever tested in the South Australian courts. We must assume they were tested in practice.

How far could a frontier policeman refrain from violence when the settlers were roused to a rage of revenge and still keep his authority? At such times civilians also found themselves under pressure. Whatever their legal jeopardy, for a frontier white man to stand aside from such duty without very good reason would have made him a social outcast, and therefore unemployable in Central Australia. When he rode with the reprisal party, and found in his companions, and perhaps himself, a capacity for violence he would rather not have seen, he was indeed in a position of legal jeopardy, and needed the silence of his companions for protection.

As the period of sustained contact between white intruders and black residents of the Centre and Top End continued from the early 1870s to the mid 1880s, Parliament seemed unable to find answers, legislative or administrative, to the killings of the intruder by the indigenous, or vice versa. At Barrow Creek in 1874 an attack by Aborigines led to two white deaths and many more blacks killed in reprisals. The attempts of the commanders in Adelaide to enforce conformity with a lawful procedure were ineffectual, as we shall see in the next chapter. In 1878 in the Top End the murder of a white man led to reprisals against the blacks in which seventeen were thought to have died. In response government in Adelaide sought to constrain punitive violence but in terms so vague that violence was certain to continue. Police were allowed to use "severe measures" (a euphemism for shooting) not only in self-defence, but also in "the last extremity", or where it was impossible to capture the Aborigines being pursued. In such circumstances an additional pre-condition for the use of violence was to establish the collective responsibility of the people on whom the retribution was to be practised, a principle found serviceable when the survivors of the *Maria* had been killed. There must be "fair evidence that the natives belonged to the tribe criminally concerned in the outrages." The Attorney General of the time knew what he was condoning in the Top End, but could suggest nothing more regular. "It is in my opinion utterly out of the question to suppose" he wrote "that we can deal with the natives in the Northern Territory as if they were civilized. I think however the case is hardly one of 'law' but essentially one of policy".[112]

Policy allows wider scope for interpretation by officials than does a well-developed system of law. It also places officials intolerably in jeopardy when they use their discretion, unless they are sure they know where their masters' hearts lie.

In 1881, again in the Top End, the spearing of a white man 600 kilometres south-east of present-day Darwin led Inspector Paul Foelsche to advise Commissioner Peterswald that it was "perfectly useless ... to do anything lawful to stop the murders" since the Aborigines concerned were beyond the reach of his policing. "The only thing ... is to inflict severe chastisement if the Government will legalise it. If this is not done in all probability travellers will shoot the natives on the overland route which ... makes matters worse." Foelsche concluded "The whole will entail considerable expense without any good resulting unless I am empowered to punish the guilty tribe without trying to arrest the murderers which I am confident can not be accomplished." Foelsche's advice was endorsed by Edward Price the magistrate resident in Darwin, who could not in any case try murder charges. There was no judge in Palmerston - now Darwin - until October 1884.

In September 1884 the killing of four copper miners on the Daly River, much closer to Palmerston, revealed the sorry depths to which the sense of local necessity had brought British justice, and "the wide gap between southern civilized attitudes and northern frontier attitudes."[113] Parties of horsemen, one of them led by police Corporal Montagu, rode out in the district surrounding the scene of the murders, while Inspector Foelsche arrested a group of Aboriginal men suspected of including some of the killers among its number and brought them to Palmerston for trial. Foelsche's instructions to the police were, according to a policeman in Palmerston at the time, "'to call upon the natives thrice in the Queen's name to surrender, and if they did not surrender to shoot them.'"[114] According to reports, mostly oral, from the Montagu party, supported by an indiscreet reference in Montagu's written report to "the superiority of the Martini-Henry rifle both for accuracy of aim and quickness of action", it is reasonable to conclude that at least 30 Aborigines were shot by police and civilians, operating under the licence of the policy created in 1874, 1878 and 1881.

It is understandable governments should act to avoid private revenge killings by men intolerant of risk to person or property, or pre-emptive killings driven by the same motive. The trouble is, the police who were given the discretion to bend or ignore their rules were not neutral in the struggles between the intruding whites and the resident blacks. They lived among and depended on the whites. Their exercise of the life and death choices that were now placed in their hands was bound to be influenced by the attitudes of the local white communities in the cattle stations, mining settlements and droving plants they serviced. They were being asked to exercise an independence of judgement and a judicial detachment for which they received no particular training. And policing was not a favoured occupation, with frontier policing an even more unusual career choice.

In law, the authorisation for police to pursue criminals when they are not caught in the act was the arrest warrant, taken out against those accused, by name. Any Justice of the Peace could issue a warrant where there was no Magistrate. In Central Australia in 1890, Charles Gall of Owen Springs, 70 kilometres to Hermannsburg's east, and Frank Gillen at Alice Springs, were JPs. As Station Master at Alice Springs Gillen was later appointed a Special Magistrate, with the power to try cases of a less serious kind.[115] It is a matter agreed by all contemporary observers that the Aboriginal trackers and constables who assisted the frontier police could identify individuals precisely by their footprints. If an individual so identified was not known by name to the tracker, the police could allocate an alias, so at all times, when Aboriginal trackers or constables were employed soon enough after the offence, it was possible for those responsible for attacks on white property or persons to be pursued by warrant. Since the pursuit of alleged offenders may lead to violence between them and the pursuing police the practice of naming the targets of police pursuit in advance provides a valuable protection for the innocent, even when both parties are members of the same culture. Like all procedures this one may be abused, but it should not be discounted for that reason.

In the end, it remained open to the frontier settlers and police to decide when their circumstances allowed them to proceed in a lawful way and when they should, in effect, outlaw their Aboriginal neighbours indiscriminately. Their decisions might at any time be subject to the scrutiny of the South Australian press, Parliament and Courts.

With or without a warrant, the difference between a pursuit of possible black perpetrators and indiscriminate killing could be resolved into a simple matter of procedure, which I will call, as some did at the time, the "Queensland rush". This was the practice of a mounted charge at an Aboriginal camp, without forewarning, so ensuring armed resistance and attempted escapes. Either might be cited in any official report as a sufficient ground for killing. This difference of pace between a measured approach and a rush was a chasm into which all legality and even a sense of common humanity could be lost.

An especially dangerous extension of the policy of treating Aborigines as outlaws involved the use of violence, or the threat of it, to keep Aboriginal people away from the settlers' homes and other assets. As Frederick Thornton, manager of Tempe Downs station put it in 1887, "When anyone is forming a Station in

Queensland the police come out first thing", that is, to practice what was known as "dispersal".

The Queensland rush was an element of the practice of dispersal. Dispersal was the specialty of the Queensland Native Police force, in whose hands the word was made synonymous with the shooting of Aborigines although it could be, and was, practised without the assistance of armed Aboriginal people. To the men of conscience in South Australia it meant simply shooting the Aborigines, which they took to be normal Queensland practice. What was dispersal, and, since records on these events in the Centre are sparse, what might it have been?

Suppose a pastoralist arrives with his herds on the lease he is legally obliged to share with the resident Aboriginal peoples. The Aborigines drive the cattle away from their waters, or, at least, discourage them by their presence. Probably they spear a few. At the least they were unwelcome neighbours in the period of big-money pastoralism, before their cheap labour came to make the difference between profit and loss, survival and failure. The pastoralist decides he will not tolerate the losses and the inconvenience, but the nearest policeman is weeks away. He decides to take immediate action. What might he do?

At the lowest level of violence open to him he may, with his white and black stockmen, rush the Aborigines' camp and drive them away using his horses and stock-whips, his guns visible but holstered. Let us call this *dispersal in the first degree*. The Australian pastoralist J Bagot described it thus in 1888: "stockowners found that the only thing they could do [after attacks on their cattle] was to arm a large number of men to scour the country with stockwhips, and when they came upon a camp to follow it and use the whip very freely. The use of the pistol" he concluded in his submission to the Minister for the Northern Territory "ought to be discouraged."[116]

At a higher level of violence, *dispersal in the second degree*, the pastoralist may use fire-arms, aiming to miss but with a definite risk that someone will be hit, particularly if there are some in his party who do not share his policy of restraint. He can make sure the terrifying power of the fire-arms is recognised by using guns loaded with bird shot to fire directly at the Aboriginal people, intending to inflict painful but not mortal wounds.

The *third degree of dispersal* is obvious; firing to kill, using rifles at a distance and revolvers when at close quarters, so that survivors are terrified and disorganised beyond further resistance.

As to when each degree of dispersal was used, we must rely on very thin evidence, since in very few cases could it have had the protection of the law. The pastoralists knew they would need to rely on clear evidence of threat to their persons or property, against which the severity of their action could be judged. Without a threat from Aborigines in proportion to the dispersal then the dispersal was not an exercise in rough justice, but a criminal act.

The pastoralist had another option; to call in the police. It might take several weeks for the nearest policeman to respond. When he arrived he could arrest those accused of offences against the pastoralists, if they had sent him names against which warrants could be issued. He could admonish the Aborigines and warn them off. If there were an immediate risk of violence against the pastoralist, not highly likely after several weeks, the lowest level of dispersal might be justified. To act beyond that point the police relied on their right to defend themselves and to prevent the commission of an offence. If those causes were not present, any police dispersal was no more legal than it would have been if practised by a civilian.

Wilhelm Schwarz experienced the results of dispersal in the second degree in both its private and official forms. In about 1883 he was called on to remove shot pellets from the chest of a 20 year old Aboriginal man called Inubauka who was fishing at Ellery Creek lagoon, on the lease of the neighbouring Henbury station but bordering the mission block. Inubauka had failed to move quickly enough when John Breaden demanded he do so.[117] More distressing was his experience with Wodoa, a regular visitor to the mission, who arrived in the camp beside the mission the same year, accompanied by two men, all wounded by shot. Wodoa was wounded in the abdomen, so seriously she died in the bed of the Finke after three days of misery, saying nothing, in English, but "Mr Dare, Mr Dare, Mr Dare". In this latter case the dispersal was official, since Tom Daer was a Mounted Constable based at Charlotte Waters with Telegraph Station master Frank Gillen.[118]

Dispersal became the subject of public debate in South Australia in 1883 and 1884. This was the time of most intense conflict on the Central Australian frontier marking the coincidence of some large-scale stocking with several years of drought. At Anna's Reservoir station to the north-east of Alice Springs, in September 1884 and on a number of other occasions between 1884 and 1886 Aboriginal attacks were followed by punitive expeditions of police, civilians and trackers.[119]

In September 1884 the station owner W. Willoby, JP, reported using dispersal in the second degree to his partner down south, John H Gordon, Mayor of the town of Strathalbyn. "Self and party and one trooper came up with blacks on the 15th inst., near Mount Conway. It was impossible to capture the offenders owing to the inaccessible country. We fired about thirty rounds amongst them, dispersing them, and shot several dogs and broke a few weapons."[120] Willoby also reported a general sense of alarm. "The blacks also threaten to burn Owen [Springs] and Glenallan [Glen Helen] Stations. Life and property are quite unsafe here, and no one dare move about unless fully armed."

These events in the Centre coincided with a number of attacks on whites in the Top End of the Northern Territory where there was a more incendiary brew of Queensland customs and a larger Aboriginal population. The consequences gave rise to a delegation in 1884 to the Minister for the Northern Territory, R. C. Baker, asking for a force of native police. J L Parsons, the senior government official at the Top End, opposed the proposal, as did Inspector Paul Foelsche, the *de facto* Commissioner of police in the Top End. "We do not want a black police for the Queensland black force goes out and disperses and shoots natives" Parsons advised his Minister. In the end Baker was persuaded to go ahead, but had Foelsche prepare guidelines, including the clear direction that "it is to be borne in mind that the system termed 'dispersing the natives' which simply means shooting them is not to be practised and for this the officer in charge will be held strictly responsible".[121] Baker did, however, accept the advice of the Queensland Police Commissioner that the native police should be employed as a body of men, and not dispersed among the police posts.

In the hope of separating policing from Aboriginal politics the native constables intended for the Top End of the Northern Territory were recruited in Central Australia. The police of the Centre answered to Inspector Bryan Besley in Port Augusta, a provincial centre 300 kilometres north of Adelaide, at the furthest reach of the southern ocean into the interior desert, and not to Foelsche in Darwin. The central Australian policeman appointed for the task of forming and leading the new force was the self-portrayed hero of the 1884 punitive raids that followed an attack at Anna's Reservoir station, Mounted Constable William Willshire. He took the force north at the end of 1884 to begin a year "pacifying" the Aboriginal peoples of the Daly and Roper Rivers, but by May 1886 the next Minister responsible had accepted Parsons' advice and disbanded the force. Willshire was sent back to Alice Springs, where in March 1886 he took command of the police post at Alice Springs, close to the telegraph station. In April 1886 the police post was moved to Heavitree Gap, seven kilometres to the south along the track to Adelaide, where the Todd is choked to a narrow gap in the southernmost stone buttress of the MacDonnells.

Here, for the next two and a half years he formed part of the police presence in the Centre. Alice Springs was his nominal base, while Tom Daer was based at Charlotte Waters to the south, and Erwein Wurmbrand, from November 1886, had charge of the Barrow Creek post to the north. In practice they all moved about widely, including each other's territory in their travels. Certainly the Alice Springs races in December each year required the presence of at least two Mounted Constables in Alice Springs for a week.

It took four years of lobbying by the pastoral interests in the Centre before government accepted their claim that the security of their enterprises required another 'Queensland-style' native police force to supplement the work of the white police aided by Aboriginal trackers. In 1887 Charles Chewings led a group of pastoralists and supporters in a delegation, with so little effect that another was needed in August 1888. At the heart of each lobby was, of course, the loss of cattle to Aboriginal spears and disturbance, but this was closely followed by disquiet about the kinds of private dispersal that each station was obliged to practice. In fact, police presence on most stations was a rare event,[122] and certainly so on the outside stations where most of the stock killing went on. In any case it was the fire-arms carried by all white men on the stations, not their uniforms, that had a profound effect on Aboriginal morale. There is no reason, however, to doubt the metropolitan faith in the efficacy of uniforms, and no reason to doubt that more reliable law enforcement would have had a discouraging effect on stock killing. It is less clear what these city representatives of pastoralism knew of the methods of dispersal practised on the stations and how far their objection to these methods drove their lobby.

Since Aboriginal men with tracking skills were part of the plant of every drover, pastoralist and policeman on the frontier, why bother with the expense of uniforms and wages for Native Constables? In the person of the Aboriginal constable were combined the pursuit skills of the blood-hound, the licensed violence of a policeman, the killing capacity of the new Winchester and Martini-Henry rifles and an unparalleled capacity to live off the land. In the absence of good leadership the Aboriginal constable, it must be said, also brought a distinctive approach to killing, an approach formed from the obligations to continue his own vendettas and those of his kin, the callousness bred in communitarian warfare which succeeded in demonising neighbours just as effectively as war-time propaganda among nation states. The Aboriginal constable brought into the police service his community's way of explaining life's misfortunes in terms of the evil magic of others. It generated an endless supply of blame. The power of Aboriginal police – minus the cartridge-fed, breech-loading rifle - to serve justice had been demonstrated fifty years earlier in the case of the Victorian native police force. The recipe for the success of the Victorian force could well have supplied, by reversal, the principles for the murderous Queensland Native Police.[123] The heart of the matter is that the Queensland force, unlike the Victorian, was established to police only the black citizens of Queensland, and to protect only the whites. This was to become the simple charter of the native police of Central Australia. They were a security force for pastoralists. They were to be always on the move, rarely staying at settled places where they might be attached, by police accountability, to their nominal masters in the metropolis. At least this was the plan, and sometimes it was the practice. But all the Mounted Constable really *must* do was pacify the pastoralists. They were on the spot. It was their reports to the policeman's superiors down south that could make or break a career.

By early 1889, the Central Australian police patrol led by William Willshire was operating under the authority of the Minister responsible for the Northern Territory, not the Chief Secretary who had control of policing generally. Following the earlier pastoralists' lobbies, the Chief Secretary had calculated the costs of recognising that "it was undesirable that the settlers should take the law into their own hands" at £4 000 in the first year. He had worked this down to £1 400, but it wasn't until the exercise could be put on the Northern Territory's accounts that it was given the go-ahead. While Willshire reported through Inspector Besley of Port Augusta and Commissioner Peterswald, his real master was a politician whose principal concern was not justice, but economic development, and Willshire's job depended on satisfying the pastoralists whose complaints had led the Minister to create and fund his job.

A white policeman and his squad of native police constituted a group with its own powerful internal dynamic, distinguishing it from any number of policemen with their one or two Aboriginal trackers. The white officer in charge was expected to match the pace and persistence of his Aboriginal troopers or the whole exercise was pointless. In the process the white officer became dependent not only on Aboriginal tracking but Aboriginal food-gathering and, quite possibly, Aboriginal tactics of approach and attack. Unless restrained, the Aboriginal constable might well decide to use his position for personal and communal ends, to capture women or kill enemies. It is now reasonable to ask of particular events involving native police forces; who is really in charge here? It was this question, posed by Sir John Downer at Willshire's trial in 1891, that provided much of the legal pretext for saving Willshire's life.

It was not just the native-born South Australians who showed a distrust of the native police forces. We may also find the strength of the South Australian reservations reflected in the views of a man who had migrated from Queensland to the Top End and knew the advantages of native police for the pastoralists. W D'arcy Uhr had been a drover for ten to twelve years on the tracks from Queensland to South Australia, including the Northern Territory, and for eight years previously a sub-inspector of the Queensland Native Police. In that capacity he has been dis-credited with over 50 indiscriminate killings in 1868.[124] By September, 1884, a few days after a petition had been presented to the South Australian Parliament calling for the establishment of a native police force, Uhr is quoted in the Adelaide *Observer* as being "against the management there because the men often killed the blacks without cause; but it was clear to him that the natives would never be kept under properly unless they had a black force." [125]

It is not possible to know with any assurance how all these forces worked out in practice, when policemen, white and black, patrolled the stations following complaints from the managers. We can, however, look at one local case that is well documented, where a station manager was challenged by violence from resident Aboriginal men and sought to deal with it by calling in the police.

In this case, James McDonald, Hermannsburg's northern neighbour at Glen Helen, found himself facing violent death in the Glen Helen Gorge, where the Finke passes through the Macdonnell Ranges. McDonald had just taken over as manager of Glen Helen, but had worked there since it had been stocked in 1877, and had been in the Centre three years before that. He reported the incident in particular detail to the Swan-Taplin enquiry in 1890.

"On October the 4th 1884 I found 6 head of cattle side by side with their tongues cut out. On running the tracks of the blacks up I found 150 to 170 blacks camped in a narrow gorge. On [our] arriving at the entrance to the gorge they ran back over the range, we then attempted to reach home. After going down the gorge some 300 or 400 yards the blacks attacked us from both sides by throwing and rolling stones down, a stone as big as a bucket fell within two feet of where I was walking. One of the men [Theodor Schleicher] then jumped off his horse and ran back, the horse was instantly killed on the spot. After getting out of the gorge we made for another one to reach home and were again met by the blacks, consequently had to go back 30 miles to get round the range." [126]

From the unusually large number of Aborigines gathered in the gorge it is clear that a major ceremony was in progress, possibly one of the *ngkura* ceremonies held in this locality, according to the missionaries, every one or two years depending on the rainfall. McDonald's intrusion, exacerbated no doubt by the manner in which his party approached, may in itself have been the immediate cause of conflict. The group dynamics of the gathering, in which the status of the men, and the cosmic forces with which they identified, were in play, would have been inflammatory. [127] If that were not enough to turn a potential dispersal in the first degree into an attack by the Aborigines, there are three other possible contributing causes.

McDonald's cook was in dispute with some of the local Aboriginal men. The cause of the dispute was the Aboriginal women who lived in the kitchen, and the result six months after the attack in the Glen Helen Gorge was an attack on Glen Helen station itself at 3.00 am in the morning "with the intention of burning down the place and murdering the cook."[128]

Theodor Schleicher, McDonald's companion in Glen Helen Gorge, had recently been dismissed from Hermannsburg by Hermann Kempe for cohabiting with an Aboriginal woman. He may have been in dispute with the woman's Aboriginal husband and his connections. In July 1890 mission Superintendent Georg Heidenreich hinted as much.

An even more intriguing possibility: this may have been the *ngkura* ceremony that saw the confrontation between the missionaries and the senior men which Moses Tjalkabota remembered forty-five years later. This was the same event recorded by the missionaries as the setting for a confrontation between themselves and Kalimalla and Tekua when the missionaries tried in vain to prevent some of their students taking part. If so, McDonald was the second to walk onto the ants' nest.

It is what McDonald did next that makes this incident so instructive. "On reaching home got fresh horses and started for Alice Springs, I took out warrants for 9 whom I knew the names of, and left the matter in the hands of the police." From Mounted Constable Wurmbrand's report on his response we can confirm that this is indeed what McDonald did. Bear in mind that all of this is happening almost ten years after Glen Helen station had set itself down in the territory of the local clans. Some of those 150-70 men in the gorge were local to McDonald's station. Some had worked for him, or visited his station, or were related to those Aboriginal men and women who did work for him and his white station hands. So, with the help of his Aboriginal workers, he was able to provide the names for which the police took out warrants. From this it follows that a selective form of reprisal was available to McDonald, assuming that a general attack on the men at the *ngkura* was impracticable. By the established standards of reprisal killing among the local clans McDonald would not have been expected to be very selective. Yet he chose to involve police, a process that required delay and risk to his station (which was at that time located just a few kilometres from the Glen Helen Gorge). It appears that McDonald preferred law to war, a choice that is no less significant when we allow for the risks that choosing war would have brought to him and his workers, risks from South Australian as well as Western Aranda law. It is also significant that McDonald was no new-chum or eccentric in the Centre, and became one of its longest-serving pastoral managers, responsible for an 'outside station' where risks of conflict were greatest.

But the responsibility for justice which McDonald handed over to the police, Mounted Constable Wurmbrand soon brought back to him. Wurmbrand set out on 12th November 1884, following instruction from Inspector Besley in Port Augusta. He took with him two local white men and four of the Alice Springs police station's trackers and proceeded by way of Owen Springs and Hermannsburg to Glen Helen station. He failed to find any trace of the men for whom he had warrants for attempted murder and cattle-killing, but at Glen Helen homestead on November 30th he received a letter from Wilhelm Schwarz at Hermannsburg telling him that some men identified as ring-leaders had arrived at the Hermannsburg camp. Wurmbrand left that evening, with McDonald and Schleicher added to his party, to arrive at the Aborigines' camp at Hermannsburg at 4:00 am the next morning. He seized four men, although he reported only three, and released one when the missionaries vouched for his good conduct. Kempe later pointed out one of men as Latya, who had recently murdered two Aboriginal boys from Hermannsburg. In accord with universal custom in the Centre the missionaries did not consider the killing of Aborigines by Aborigines came under South Australian law, unless the victims were associates of the white people. The other two arrested were Doogoodaya and Engoordana.

Wurmbrand must have planned what he was about to do, because he had Schwarz translate into Aranda the warnings he gave the Aboriginal men against attempting to escape, so making the warnings verifiable. He then joined the three together with a neck-chain fastened with split links, took them up the Finke to the Glen Helen Gorge and shot them. When he wrote up his version of events on Boxing Day 1884 he stated that Engoordana had managed to break his split link and led the other two prisoners in a rush for one of the side gullies leading down to the Finke. Wurmbrand wounded Latya in the left shoulder but failed to halt him, and so ordered the party to open fire. "The prisoners were by that time fully 200 yards distant. Prisoners are dead. --", he concluded that section of his report.

On the face of it Wurmbrand's report raises a number of questions. Why was he taking prisoners *away* from Alice Springs? He could hardly continue his pursuit of the other accused while encumbered by three men needing constant surveillance. Why could he and eight other men not catch even the two men still joined by the neck-chain? Why were three men, shot at 200 yards range, all killed, and none brought down wounded but alive? A conscientious senior officer could hardly fail to make further enquiries. Instead Bryan Besley, one month later, on January 21st 1885, sent the report on to Commissioner Peterswald with the bland formula: "Respectfully forwarded to the Commissioner of Police for perusal". Two days later Commissioner Peterswald marked it "Seen & returned". They must have had their fingers crossed.

Wurmbrand went on to pursue more suspects, and reported shooting three near Mount Sonder. McDonald and Schleicher accompanied him again on this three week trip, but did not participate in the fatal attack, according to Wurmbrand's report. Nevertheless, after the killings in Glen Helen Gorge they knew the kind of business they were taking part in.

There the matter might have rested, but for the presence of the missionaries. The Colonist (lay worker) Jürgens was working at the sheep yards fifteen kilometres north up the Finke from Hermannsburg when Wurmbrand's party and the three securely-chained prisoners filed past. He was still there when some Aborigines coming down the Finke told him the prisoners had been shot. "We went there & convinced ourselfes from the truth of this statement. Now we expected directly the whites would say they tried to escape, & so they did, when we asked them. But who can believe it? Who can believe that the[y] broke the strong chain; who can further believe that escaping they kept together? One should think, if it happened that the[y] got unfastened the chain, they would run away in every direction, but the bodies were laying on one heap & exactly as they were chained together." But Kempe did nothing about it until April 1885 when the quoted words were written to

Protector Hamilton, in response to a letter from Hamilton on other business.[129] The incident did not become a matter of public knowledge.

Before leaving this incident, for the moment, one further observation. Wurmbrand's killing of his three prisoners was the deliberate act of an intelligent and careful man. It is reasonable to wonder whether, in choosing to shoot the men where he did, and to leave the bodies unconcealed and intact in a well-trafficked place, Wurmbrand was applying at his own initiative the kind of rough justice used, with official sanction, at the time of the massacre of the *Maria*'s survivors in 1840. If so these killings were undoubtedly murders, but they were far from indiscriminate, and their message to the local people was more informative than the sheer terror of dispersal.

The Central Australian frontier was not a frontier in the pure sense, where the only government is the do-it-yourself kind, and the only justice the kind that interested parties make with the aid of superior force. The use of the police provided the pastoralist not only with greater fire-power when he had need of it, but also with the cover of official reports that could be used against any rumours that might find their way south. Stories sourced from Aborigines could always be discounted in the south, but white witnesses were a different matter, especially those whose credibility was strong, like missionaries and station managers. But the men of the frontier were frontiersmen first, even the missionaries, who depended on each other in times of crisis and were expected to support each other by discreet silence. But only up to a point, since they were also citizens of South Australia, most continuing their personal and emotional connections to the settled south, especially the men in command who hoped for promotion to the metropolis. None of them could ever be certain that the law of the metropolis would not reach out and claim him.

Mounted Constable William Willshire. Possibly taken at
Cowell on the Eyre Peninsula, between 1892 and 1897.
(*CDHS*).

William John Peterswald, Commissioner of Police for South
Australia from 1882 to 1896. Peterswald and the other permanent
officials of the South Australian governments played decisive
roles in applying government and justice to the Central
Australian frontier. He and his Inspector Bryan Besley were
responsible for, but not completely in control of, their frontier
officers (*SLSA B 11122*).

7

COMMUNICATION, COMMAND AND CONSTITUENCY

William Willshire, we should remember, was a policeman first and a frontiersman second. He had a boss, Inspector Bryan Besley in Port Augusta who, in turn, answered to the Police Commissioner, William Peterswald, in Adelaide. The accountability of officials in the Centre - the police and staff of the Overland Telegraph – was in principle as exacting as it would have been had they been stationed in the suburbs of Adelaide.[130] The orderly flow of authority and accountability over the thousand kilometres between the metropolis of Adelaide and the Central Australian frontier was both supported and disrupted by a major force. The central Australian frontier was bound to the city by the Overland Telegraph line, only five years old when the Finke River mission was established at Hermannsburg.

Many of the posts used to carry the single strand of galvanised steel wire across the continent from Adelaide to Darwin are still standing, although the first generation of wooden poles was soon replaced by galvanised iron. There always was a mismatch between the power of the technology and its impact on human perception; a foretaste, perhaps, of the electronic age. Only in the flat, stony and treeless plains did this simple stave of poles and wire make a visual impact to match its impact on the Australian Colonies. The railway, in contrast, the noise and smoke of its locomotives fuelled by the enormous quantities of capital being shovelled into them, was still struggling northwards towards the South Australian border.

In fact, the Overland Telegraph was strung across the Centre in order to by-pass it. The whole point was to communicate with London as if Adelaide were located somewhere off the coast of

Cornwall and not half a world away, and incidentally to make governable the South Australian outpost of Palmerston at the Top End. The telegraph, in one sense, made the Centre into a less important inconvenience than it had been before 1872. While the telegraph wire could carry a signal 1000 kilometres in suitable weather, for reliable performance repeater stations were built every 250-300 kilometres, each with a staff comprising the station Master, an assistant operator and four linesmen. These were part of a skilled labour force, detached temporarily from the society of their families and friends, although they could only expect the Post Office to provide one-way passage for a visit to the south after three years' service.[131] Their presence meant, incidentally, that messages could be sent to and from the remote, otherwise unpopulated places now known as Charlotte Waters, Alice Springs to its north and Barrow Creek on the track between Alice Springs and Darwin.[132] These became stepping stones not only for the morse-coded signals but also for the people and supplies moving across the ocean of nothingness between Port Augusta and Darwin.

For the police it meant instructions could be passed from Adelaide to any of the northern police posts and brief reports returned within a day, if the officer were on station. When the pressure of circumstances demanded, a telegraphic conversation could take place over distances that made face-to-face contact impracticable more frequently than once in several years. A police Commissioner or Attorney-General might be in the position to direct action in central Australia within periods of hours or days. He might still possess only second-hand knowledge of the circumstances on the ground.

The Telegraph also made it possible for commanders in Adelaide to oversee the involvement of white civilians in the episodes of amateur law-enforcement that arose, inevitably, on the frontier. William Willoby, JP was droving cattle to Bond Springs station just north of Alice Springs in company with W B Gordon when he heard of the conflict at Anna's Reservoir in September 1884 and wired his partner John Gordon in Adelaide with an offer to join the punitive party. John Gordon passed the offer on to police Commissioner Peterswald who accepted it, but "warns all engaged to keep within the rules imposed on such expeditions by the

Government." Willoby and Gordon did not arrive in time for that particular expedition.

An energetic Minister could use the Telegraph to make enquiries directly of officials and others who were in the Centre, or passing through. There was a good chance that he would get answers before his police had taken any action that would pre-empt his own decision. This was heady stuff. Many a British Minister for the Colonies would have shed blood to have had as much control over his Colonial Governors.

However, when the police were, like the pastoralists and missionaries, well away from the telegraph line, perhaps for months, they were beyond direction by any means except their own sense of duty and the possibility that reports from third parties might eventually reach their superiors. Superior officers, especially within the police service, were obliged to trust their officers to act by the rules. Certainly Inspector Bryan Besley in Port Augusta, as we shall see later, was remarkably insensitive to telling signs in his subordinates' reports of what they were really up to. Commissioner Peterswald, being closer to the politics of policing, needed to be more careful about what he did not see in the papers arriving on his desk.

While they were subordinated by the Telegraph, police were still required to maintain journals and provide written reports. Reports from Willshire and the other Central Australian police were scrutinised by Inspector Brian Besley in Port Augusta, by Commissioner Peterswald in Adelaide and by other officials he thought should be informed or consulted. Besley, as Sub-Protector of Aborigines, copied reports involving Aborigines to the Protector of Aborigines, an office originally funded from the proceeds of land sales and occupied at this time by E L Hamilton, who was appointed in 1873 and remained in office until 1907.[133] In those days of government that was microscopic in size – by today's standards – the Commissioner of Police would forward reports and correspondence we might today regard as trivial to his Minister, either the Chief Secretary (who was in most cases also the Premier – that is, the elected head of government), or the Minister for Education and the Northern Territory who was responsible for anything to do with policing in the top half of the Northern Territory. The Minister for Education and the Northern Territory was also responsible for William Willshire after 1888.[134] Any of these officials could comment on the incoming document, usually by annotating the cover sheet.

A report from Mounted Constable Willshire sent on by Inspector Besley, or a letter from a pastoral station manager like James McDonald, destined for the police Commissioner or Minister, was covered with a foolscap-sized sheet of paper. A simple badge of the Commissioner's or Minister's office is printed in the top right-hand quadrant of this cover sheet, followed by pro-forma spaces for dating despatch and receipt. The remaining seven eighths of the two sides of the sheet are available for annotation by each official to whom the document is referred. The sheet is then placed against the back of the incoming document, printed side out, so that the printed section forms half of a front cover for what is now an official file, called a "docket", a file that could be slipped into a gentleman's coat pocket and carried thus discreetly.

Typically, Besley will endorse whatever action his men have taken in relation to Aborigines, Peterswald may comment on conformity with law and protocol, either man may refer to the need to reduce expenditure during the recurrent periods of government budget cutting, and the document is sent from the domain of the police to the Minister for his "perusal", occasionally marked with recommended action. The Minister may record a decision, after consulting his Cabinet colleagues on any significant matter, and the parcel is passed back down the chain.

A file may pass through several offices, receiving whatever attention and political treatment the office-holder thinks needed, and within two weeks be with the police officer who must act on it. Without the power-tools of word processors and copiers to generate verbage, the whole business may be accomplished within four pages, usually with space to spare.

After perhaps two months, with the possibility that telegraphed instructions have been received in the meantime, the police constable in the Centre might receive back his original report, marked with the frank comments of his Inspector, Commissioner, Minister and the Protector of Aborigines, including the decision reached, with the request to return the file in due course to the Commissioner's office for filing. However direct and intimate this communication between the top and bottom of the police force, authority was still the key. There were laws and protocols to be observed and control from the centre was the goal. The Ministers, their private secretaries and the police commanders watched the written reports that crossed their desks for signs that their remote subordinates were forgetting the rules that kept them within the law or, at least, out of public controversy.

In the case of the pastoralists and missionaries the distance separating them from the telegraph line made it impossible for their superiors to involve themselves in day-to-day business. Even in the early 1930s, for the manager of Tempe Downs station to put a question to Adelaide and receive an answer required a four-day ride each way to Horseshoe Bend plus the time taken by Adelaide to make the decision, the whole exercise costing two weeks, on top of the high cost of telegrams.[135] That was reduced to one week later in the 1930s when Hermannsburg was connected by radio. Only the introduction of the pedal radio-telephone, beginning in the 1930s but not generally available until much later, allowed Central Australian stations to be in closer contact with their directors.[136]

Pastoralists and missionaries reported back to their respective owners and constituencies. They used their connections with Ministers and the Adelaide press to promote their interests and complain about their neighbours. The pastoralists were well-connected with the South Australian Parliament and Government. Of the 250 men who were elected to the lower House of the South Australian Parliament during the 33 years between self-government in 1857 and 1890, 42 were pastoralists. Of the rest, 26 were farmers of various kinds, (no political friends of the pastoralists) and many of the other Members who were in business or the professions also depended on the pastoral industry, and those who had been made wealthy by it, for their own livelihood. From 1888 the Northern Territory returned its own Members of the Parliament. V.L. Solomon, when he was successful in the 1890 election, needed only 218 votes to be elected with a comfortable majority. Although he was a journalist, not a pastoralist, he knew the economic base of his constituency, and his newspaper would sometimes rage against the Aborigines who, of course, could not, in practice if not in law, vote. The pastoralists of Central Australia did not need to be too concerned that they contributed no more than 25 of Solomon's votes through the polling stations located in the Centre.

It would be a mistake to regard the frontiersmen of the Centre as ignorant back-country isolates. Some fitted that description; men brought up in country already remote from the cities who chose to move even further out, as drovers, stockmen and knockabout bush workers. On the other hand we have the managers, telegraph officials, missionaries, and some among the stockmen, who remained part of metropolitan life. The loadings of the camel trains to the Centre included letters, newspapers, magazines and books that were devoured eagerly by many on the frontier. Mounted Constable Cowle, who took over in 1891 Willshire's responsibility for protecting Charles Chewings' cattle, received on one occasion 40 items of correspondence at one delivery. A surprisingly large proportion of the frontier people took an informed interest in South Australian, Australian and Empire affairs. These socially- and politically-engaged people are no doubt over-represented among those who have left traces in the surviving written records. Their more silent contemporaries are better represented by descendants of mixed race who remain prominent in the Centre.

The push to federate the Australian Colonies was getting under way, based in part on a sense that Australia needed to be able to contribute more to protecting its lines of communication with Britain. Frank Gillen at Charlotte Waters and Alice Springs, as British as the next colonist, was a passionate partisan of Home Rule for Ireland. As guardian of the iron thread through which Colonies and imperial metropolis spoke to each other, he followed closely the British debates on Ireland. Most of the capital going into the Centre's pastoral properties and mines was metropolitan capital, and it focussed Adelaide's attention on this remote region.

In 1890, two decades after settlement began, the isolated white population of the Centre had a colonial culture centred on the metropolis of Adelaide. It was not a culture of isolation. Most, apart from the Aborigines, expected to move back to the settled districts when they had served their time, made their money, or sowed their wild oats.

Another result of the competing forces of isolation and connection was a frontier that lived more vividly in the mind of the metropolis than would have been the case fifty years before. The

Adelaide press carried regular reports as country further and further from the Telegraph was explored and evaluated. Most of them exaggerated the pastoral and agricultural potential of the Centre. In 1884 the Adelaide *Observer* carried thirteen lengthy reports on "The pastoral districts of the far North". Among the boosting there were also reports of the casualties among the whites and of the measures taken to enforce the law against the perpetrators.

Considering the enormous costs and discomforts of travel to the Centre a surprising number of official visitors were drawn to see for themselves this vivid landscape of heroic pioneers and exotic natives. The years 1890 and 1891 both saw Commissions of enquiry travelling around the Centre, and early in 1891 the Governor of South Australia, the Earl of Kintore, passed through Alice Springs with his retinue of officials, journalists and police, causing Frank Gillen to light celebratory fires on the summits of the hills around the Alice Springs Telegraph Station, of which he had recently been made the Master.

The Hermannsburg mission on the Finke River had three constituencies. First there was its owner the Hermannsburg Mission Institute, then those Lutheran congregations in the south of the Colony that contributed most of the funds. Last, but equally significant, was the electorate of the Colony of South Australia on whose behalf the government of the day made available the 900 square miles of land and an annual grant of cash and rations.

The Hermannsburg Mission Institute entrusted the supervision of the mission on the Finke River to Pastor Georg Heidenreich who was supported by a Mission Committee that behaved in most respects like a board of directors helping him raise support from the local congregations. But in law and by his personality and preference, Heidenreich exercised sole authority as the Institute's agent in the Colony. Like the Colonial Governors in their relations with the Colonial Secretaries in London, Heidenreich's authority was limited by his position as an agent, but in practice it was absolute until the cycle of reporting to headquarters and issuing of instructions could be completed. Heidenreich's duties were to be divided between his local congregation and his spiritual home. His heart was still in northern Germany; his convictions lay with his Australian Synod and his congregation at Bethany in the Barossa Valley near Adelaide.

The missionaries received reports from Aboriginal people passing up and down the Finke, and often received as guests individuals and officials visiting the Centre. Even the mission's critics acknowledged the warmth of its hospitality.[137] The visitors both reported Adelaide affairs to the mission and reported conditions on the mission to Adelaide.

Kempe and Schwarz, and the third missionary Schulze who arrived in 1878, continued to think of themselves as Germans in a population of "English" neighours, but they were well-connected in the metropolis. Friedrich Krichauff, a solid Member of the House of Assembly, represented, in a personal sense, that vigorous minority of German yeomen and women, tradesmen and professionals, approaching ten percent of the total population, that was rapidly assimilating into an English-speaking community that valued the Germans' talents. Krichauff's recommendation and signature had got Kempe and Schwarz their Certificates of Naturalization in less than a month, before they trekked north to the Finke. He remained close to Heidenreich, speaking for the mission in its dealings with government, presenting its annual reports to the Minister and using the information about the Western Aranda gleaned by the missionaries to boost his own standing as a man with knowledge.

The true constituency of the Hermannsburg missionaries in Australia was the broader German "mission community". Just as the Western Aranda men participated through their sacred ceremonies in the existence of their totemic forbears, these evangelists had practices that served to instil in them the sense that they were close to their God. To be in the minds of those of the mission community who stayed at home but prayed for them, donated to their work, and shared in imagination their hardships and their successes, was even more important to them since their God was, compared with the creator-spirits of the Aranda, remote from the particulars of his Creation. Heidenreich wrote to Theodor Harms two days after Christmas 1875, when the missionaries' trek north was only one-sixth completed, and when he thought he knew the hardships the journey presented, "Our unity in spirit and faith is, thank God, spiritual and deeply-felt... So pray constantly with the entire mission community for your weakest children who are undertaking the hardest and most difficult tasks in the fields of missionary work...". Harms assured him in September 1876 of "the heart-felt participation" of the entire mission community: "the most enthusiastic prayers go up to the Lord from many, many hearts, and we naturally also pray for you every Sunday. May the Lord strengthen your faith. How strongly one feels in such times the glory of our faith: I believe in the community of the saints!"[138]

The Lutheranism of the missionaries did not reach out often to the Protestant ascendancy of South Australia, but there was common ground in their revulsion at brutal treatment of Aborigines on the frontier. The focus of Protestant action on Aboriginal issues was the Aborigines Friends Association, established to support the mission of George and Martha Taplin to the Ngarrindjerri people of the lake country near the mouth of the Murray River. Its membership was tiny, but influential. Most of its members were clergy, but some were influential laymen including politicians, and others were related to men in public office. What they lacked in number they had bountifully in their conviction and their fluency in the public language of the time. What they lacked in constituency they had in lobbying skill and political access.

But the inequality of frontier Aborigines in Colonial life was increased enormously by the wall of silence between them and the Colonial metropolis. The Aborigines spoke languages exotic to the Europeans. It was often a decade or more before some of those who dealt with them regularly could claim an acquaintance with their language sufficient for doing more than issuing commands. For many groups ten years exceeded the period of their survival as a distinct group. In the meantime, Aboriginal people rapidly developed a pidgin English that served day-to-day life but could do little else. It was difficult to use when context was critical to understanding, or references to past or future were necessary, since it lacked the necessary syntax and vocabulary. Aboriginal people had few ways of communicating with the Europeans in settled society, where they had some natural allies, and therefore were not able to enlist support for their claims against the land-takers. To cement their disadvantage, the frontier settlers practised a Masonic style of secrecy about their illegal or ugly methods of dealing with Aborigines, buttressed by barefaced denial whenever outsiders questioned them directly. The private citizens who participated in reprisal attacks rarely reported publicly, and there is some evidence that even their frontier colleagues were left in ignorance. Some vigilante killers later wrote personal recollections that have survived.[139] Hermannsburg on the Finke was one of the few apertures in the wall of silence, but it was controlled by the missionaries, not the Aborigines, and sometimes, when it mattered, the missionaries failed to tell the metropolis.

At the metropolitan end of the Telegraph waited that gorilla of constituencies, the popular electorate, barely discernible most of the time, but capable of crushing careers effortlessly when it was roused, or even if it just rolled comfortably over. The popular electorate was only 30 years old in the late-1880s. From 1856 all male British subjects in South Australia were entitled to vote.[140] That included Aboriginal men, provided they enrolled. The electorate had not yet suffered a rigid division into left and right. That arose later in the 1890s when organised labour became a force and political parties became brands that overwhelmed the many other differences between those seeking election to Parliament.

Without the ossifying effect of political parties, governments during the 1880s formed around dominant individuals, dissolved under the attack of other potential leaders who had remained either in opposition or lower down the totem pole of office than they wished to be. At this time governments rarely lasted more than two Parliamentary sessions, that is, two years, and some lasted only one year. Since Parliament met only in the second half of each year, the natural life-span of a Government was from the middle of one year to the middle of the next, when Parliament resumed. An exceptional leader might hold his majority together for a further year.

Cabinets were small, a half-dozen at most, so there were always good men fretting on the back-benches. The Cabinets were correspondingly close-knit executive committees; little was done by any Minister without the involvement of his colleagues.

John Downer, a brilliant lawyer and orator, who was to defend William Willshire at his trial in 1891, experienced the vagaries of South Australian politics in 1887. His Government had lasted remarkably into a second year much of which Downer spent being lionised in London at the Colonial Conference, putting a knighthood in his baggage for the return trip to Adelaide where he found, when the House of Assembly reconvened, his majority had evaporated. He remained out of government until 1892.

Whenever governments change frequently, senior officials are empowered, especially if, as in this case, their employment was secure and continued over many years. James Bath was Secretary to successive Ministers for the Northern Territory, while Charles Cornish was another long-serving public servant who served the line of passing Attorneys General, including John Downer, until he was promoted to even higher office in the 1890s. Not all Police Commissioners served as long as these Departmental heads. They had a degree of independence of Ministers that tempted some into conflict with their governments. William Peterswald was of the other kind, a politically astute and careful man, and a disciplinarian, who held the office from 1882 until his death in 1896.

As a spectator the electorate is a sentimental beast. It applauds the hero who calls it to arms against the cruel enemy, and deserts the hero as quickly when the enemies transform into victims. If you are a victim and the electorate can share your sufferings, sympathy can become policy. An outstanding case in point is the attack on the Barrow Creek Telegraph Station in 1874, an event that shows the tracks of an electorate in motion with government trailing behind, with profound consequences for the future of justice in Central Australia.

The attack on Barrow Creek by Aboriginal warriors of the Kaititj language group was the only attack ever made on a station along the Overland Telegraph. That alone would have made it a signal event. In fact there were three attacks, the first on the evening of Sunday February 22nd, 1874 caught the station staff and visitors by surprise outside the protection of the fortress-like station building. In the first attack one man, John Franks died immediately from a spear through the chest and another, John Stapleton, was mortally wounded by a spear through the lower abdomen. The master of the Alice Springs station, Flint, who was visiting at the time, was wounded in the leg as the whites retreated to their weapons inside the station. For the immediate future the concern of the whites inside the station was survival, since their ammunition and water were limited. For the South Australian government there was also the fear that the attack represented the beginning of an organised campaign to destroy the Telegraph, and perhaps drive out the whites. Today that fear appears to be a baseless and gross exaggeration, but there is no doubt that both the frontier and the metropolis believed it in 1874. Seven hundred kilometres to the south and three days ride away from the Peake telegraph station, Alec Ross and his son John, travelling in the territory of people who knew nothing of the Kaititj, received a message advising them of the attack, and warning them to be on their guard.[141] Earlier that year Stapleton had reported the "wholesale destruction" of insulators on the telegraph line around Barrow Creek and Flint reported an attempt to pull down an iron pole. From a commercial point of view the timing could not have been worse. A huge investment had been made to construct the line. Revenues depended not only on keeping it open, but also on fulfilling the terms of the contract with the British Australia Telegraph Company, which owned the onward link through the East Indies and could claim damages for non-performance. There had also been talk of a competing line through Queensland.

As Stapleton lay dying in great discomfort the besieged party sent out their calls of alarm along the wire. To the north of Barrow Creek a party of line workers, among them Billy Abbott, had tapped into the wire, heard the calls and hurried south. [142] Police reinforcements were sent up from the Peake station. In Adelaide they soon had the attention of the police Commissioner and the Postmaster - the line's architect and builder, Charles Todd - who became the go-between for government. Within a day the fate of the men of Barrow Creek was occupying the attention of the electorate as detailed reports appeared in the press. Would there still be a station when help arrived? What were the intentions of the Kaititj?

The question of Kaititj intentions has occupied those who examine the Barrow Creek incidents ever since. At the time the favoured explanations, apart from a desire to annihilate the white presence, were black resentment over white dealings with black women, or black greed for the luxuries the whites had been doling out in return for black labour and good-will. Mounted Constable Gason, who arrived at the station shortly after the attack, advised his Commissioner on the next day that the attack was "without slightest provocation" and aimed at getting the station's supplies. Frank Gillen also favoured later this explanation, although at the time of the attack he was eighteen years old and in Adelaide, receiving and sending some of the telegrams, as it happened. "In the annals of

Native treachery there is no crueller or more unprovoked attack than that in which poor Stapleton and Frank lost their lives. Stapleton had been kind to the point of weakness to the natives giving them almost everything they asked for until their demands became wholly unreasonable and he was unable to comply with them." [143] Gillen had that version of Aboriginal motives from his Telegraph colleagues no doubt, but some of those at Barrow Creek on the day of the attack, and Charles Todd in Adelaide, knew of more substantial white provocations before the attack. Six months before, the Kaititj had experienced a dispersal at the hands of the telegraph staff. "We now know where the natives camp is & I want your authority to close the office one day so as to go out & try & disperse the whole tribe – they are about 15 miles west from station & may do much more harm if not speedily checked", J C Watson at Barrow Creek wired to Charles Todd in Adelaide on July 16th 1873. Two previous telegrams from Watson had complained of Aborigines spearing horses. There is no reply from Todd on this file, but note that the request was not for permission to conduct a dispersal, but for approval to do it at public expense.[144] Had these events been more generally known in 1874 the perceptions of Ministers, officials and electorate may well have been different.

Barrow Creek station was in no position to sustain a prolonged siege, but help was days away. Todd was compelled to hear frequent accounts of the sufferings and anxieties of his staff. He summoned Dr Gosse, and later Stapleton's wife, to the Post Office in Adelaide. On the Monday morning Flint in Barrow Creek advised Dr Gosse that Stapleton "appears much easier this morning. Has passed water freely, bowels not yet operated ... Do you advise a little opening medicine", but Stapleton's condition deteriorated rapidly during the day as blood poisoning set in from his perforated bowel. Stapleton himself reported to Gosse, and Todd, "privates shrivelled & cold, burning sensation while trying to pass water. No inclination at stool. All the muscles of the body sore. Breathing short and distressing. Can retain nothing in stomach; even a teaspoon of fluid causes an intense pain. Burning thirst. Sleep impossible. Change of position followed by intense suffering". It is unlikely that Todd passed this message to Mrs Stapleton, but to Gillen "as an operator in the Adelaide office fell the painful duty of conducting a telegraphic conversation between the dying man ... and his heartbroken wife in Adelaide." Every literate South Australian shared Mrs Stapleton's grief.

At 2.10 on Monday afternoon Flint reported "wounds are discharging blood & foecal matter. Have no carbolic acid... Most intense pain bladder with desire to pass water. His eyes looking very dull. Plse reply." Adelaide could not help. Later in the day Gason reported Stapleton's death to police Commissioner Hamilton, and Flint pointedly told Charles Todd, and those looking over Todd's shoulder, that "every mark of respect possible was shown" when Stapleton's body was buried. He had asked "that I should tell you that 'he had died doing his duty', and that he 'commended his family to your protection.'"

Commissioner Hamilton hardly needed to instruct Gason, but because of the Telegraph he did, to "not leave the station or waste any ammunition; when you fire let your shot tell. The party is safe if no one under range of your fire and beyond range of spears."

There was really nothing for Adelaide to do but wait for the reinforcements that were now nearby, and consider how justice might be done and be seen to be done. Police Commissioner Hamilton advised the Government to take prompt action to protect the Telegraph and Europeans, saying to the Chief Secretary (the Minister responsible for the police), but not to Mounted Constable Gason as far as we know, that "close adherence to legal forms should not be insisted on."[145]

In these testing circumstances, what had become of legality? Before Stapleton's death, Postmaster-General Todd had cabled Station Master Flint asking, on behalf of the Government, for the names of natives involved in the attack. It can hardly be accidental that the message went between these two, rather than from Police Commissioner Hamilton to Constable Gason. The matter of exacting justice or retribution on the Kaititj was being handled at the highest political level, by-passing the police. Flint was able to reply promptly with the names of "Harry Boy, General, Sprightly, Sink Eyes, Coonarie, Apongita, Songalla, Umpijamma, [and also] others not distinguished by name but [who] can be identified." So the attackers included men who were familiar to the station personnel, probably as occasional workers or recipients of rations, and others not familiar to the whites but identified by the more permanent Aboriginal assistants at the station. The normal processes of British justice, involving arrest warrants, could therefore be asserted by means of the Telegraph. But when Gason set out at the head of a party of volunteers, the telegraph wire proved unable to restrain them.

Within twelve days of his departure, in two separate conflicts, "several" Aborigines were killed in an attack on Gason's party and three more while they were, according to Gason, violently resisting capture. On the day following his report of this second event, Mounted Constable Gason was obliged to reply to Hamilton that "yes [those] natives shot were not mentioned in list of names given as they were not known by name but could be identified as having been at the station shortly before the attack." The thread of procedure linking offence to punishment had snapped.

Here was a declension of a standard of justice that was available to Gason, the arrest of named offenders for whom warrants had been issued, and who might as proxies for the whole group of attackers be subject to some version of exemplary punishment. It was less justice than was handed out to the group responsible for the killing of the *Maria's* survivors in 1840. What were the Government and Commissioner Hamilton to do? Could Gason and his volunteer helpers, their blood fired by fear and anger, be brought under control? If the result were to deny, or even delay, the application of rough justice to the attackers, would the Aborigines be encouraged to attack again? The Top End correspondent for the Adelaide *Register*, W T Cook, put a clear message for Adelaide on the Telegraph: "this is only commencement of attacks which has made natives bold; they now appear to be mustering in large numbers and unless thoroughly subdued ... will be dangerous." (The message cost four guineas to send, a price that made contradiction by any private citizen unlikely.) Charles Todd had confirmed in an item he wrote for the *Register* that Barrow Creek had been "a perfect hotbed of hostility" before the attack. The press in Adelaide picked up the tone of panic and anger in the reports coming down the line. The *Register's* editorial writer responded on the day of Stapleton's death by changing its previous "strictly ... neutral" line to favour a "severe lesson" while the Aborigines could be caught "red-handed", that is, still grouped for attack. "A warrant, although a formidable document in its way, is not calculated to excite dismay in the mind of an aboriginal ... It will also be necessary for them [the Government] to institute some speedier and more effective means of administering justice ... than those at present in force." The *Register* advocated a form of trial less "cumbrous" than the Supreme Court, followed by the speedy execution of the guilty "in the presence of their comrades at the place where their crime was committed" but did not specify the form of the trial it had in mind.

The *Register*'s competitor daily, the *Advertiser*, published the next Saturday a more considered response that caught nicely the paradox of frontier justice. "It is evident that the natives are bent upon the complete annihilation of the whites in that part of the country... Such a treacherous and cowardly murder of two unarmed men by savages who had received from their victims nothing but kindness may well excite a feeling of burning indignation ...It has hitherto been the unvarying policy of the South Australian Government to take the punishment of native criminals into their own hands and they cannot depart from the principle without exposing blacks and whites to mutual slaughter and reprisal. ... [therefore] retribution should fall promptly and heavily upon the murderers". Of Mounted Constable Gason's projected responses it noted "We can hardly expect that many arrests will be made... we hope Trooper Gason is not hampered by too many instructions."[146]

Would the electorate or the Parliament have tolerated restraint, having just witnessed a Victorian melodrama of suffering and death? The outcome appears to have been a lengthy campaign of dispersal in the third degree.[147] If the "Queensland rush" did not provoke the kind of violent resistance that would justify shooting the Aborigines, then the reports to Adelaide could have invented it. Those at a distance from the carnage could believe that some kind of justice was being done, tailored to the circumstances by the good men of the frontier, whose family and friends were part of the electorate in Adelaide. What bushman could refuse to take up his gun and ride when passionate anger and authority both pulled at him? None who wanted a life on the frontier. And after the blood had cooled, where could a man turn his eye without meeting the eye of another who had seen what they both had done? At best they could comfort each other with the harsh necessity that had driven them, the law of war.

It would be surprising if Billy Abbott, having returned to Barrow Creek with the northern line-workers, did not join the retribution parties.

The events at and around Barrow Creek show us how tenuous was the hold of government on the Central Australian frontier. We may imagine we are witnessing the slide from the rough justice involved in summarily punishing those identified as ringleaders to a more arbitrary form of punishment aimed at instilling a general terror among Aboriginal people. The event also demonstrates how important it was for the politics of South Australia to manage the information that came down the wire to Adelaide.

If Barrow Creek in 1874 had marked the Aborigines of Central Australia as villains in the mind of the electorate, and the whites as victims and heroes of resistance and just retribution, events in the 1880s were to create a more complex picture. Of this time it can be said, Barrow Creek notwithstanding, that "Organised attempts to drive them [the intruding whites] out of tribal lands were rare" while in the first years of the 1880s "All this was changed by the coming of the pastoralists with their herds of cattle."[148] In the period 1883-5 in particular when incoming herds and their drovers met larger aggregations of Aboriginal people, there was conflict. Most of what is recorded happened to the east of Alice Springs, such as the attack on the Anna's Reservoir homestead. William Willshire was the policeman who dealt with that event, while his colleague, Mounted Constable Erwein Wurmbrand responded to an attack on the personnel of the Glen Helen station at the head of the Finke River. We will look at both events again later. For the moment our concern is other events that were conditioning the southern electorate.

The decade of the 1880s began with the hanging in Victoria of Ned Kelly, the outlaw - to some a hero - famous throughout the Australian Colonies. Within five years of Kelly's hanging South Australia had its own outlaw-hero. His name, as far as the electorate was concerned, was Logic, and he was an Aborigine. In October 1885, Logic was five years into a fourteen year sentence at Adelaide's

Yatala prison for manslaughter of his white employer, a stockman on Tinga Tingana station in the north-east of South Australia. Logic's offence had been judged by the Supreme Court to have been severely provoked by the victim, and his petition for early release was before South Australia's Governor when Logic escaped from a work party, threw off his prison clothes and headed, naked, north towards Lake Eyre. Logic's status was to undergo a surprising shift over the next month. He left Adelaide a naked savage from the Yatala labour gang, but arrived near the town of Quorn, abeam of Port Augusta as you travel north, transformed into a popular hero by escaping a punishment that everyone thought unjust. The support of local farmers fortified Logic's natural abilities to the point that he was able to evade search parties of police and Aboriginal trackers. "From this point of his journey onwards Logic's movements were an open secret to everyone but the police. On the last day of November he visited McNeils's farm ... Two days later, ... he stopped at John Jarvis's farm near Hawker and was given a meal. On the Thursday he visited two farms ... perhaps breakfasting at the first and dining at the second." By then he had a tomahawk, boots, a butcher's knife, blankets, and wore a brown tweed suit, all given to him by the drought-stricken farmers of the district. He was well supplied with food, drink and tobacco. "There were no fear or threats in these meetings, and he was greeted as hospitably by lone women on isolated stations as by men."[149]

By the time of his recapture on December 10th, just 20 kilometres short of the copper mine of Blinman, Logic was a celebrity, his story fed to the people of Adelaide by telegraph. Crowds gathered along the progress of the train that returned him to Adelaide. The next day the pastoralists' Chamber of the Parliament, the Legislative Council, cheered a call for Logic's pardon and on December 15th the *Observer* reported a petition to Parliament of 1823 names in Logic's favour. It included landed gentry and city workers. Logic was soon pardoned and on the train again to Port Augusta where he stayed several days with Inspector of Police Bryan Besley before continuing his interrupted journey north.[150]

South Australia was experiencing an economic recession and that may have created a climate favourable to the underdog. The power of Unions was growing and no amount of harrumphing from men of property was likely to slow its progress. A hundred men on

North Terrace, shouting at the doors of Parliament, was as much disorder as the apparatus of state could handle. Police were few in number and there was no standing army, only a volunteer militia. Logic's fate also reflected the spread into popular awareness of the interest in Aboriginal culture. Beginning at the Adelaide Oval on May 31st, and continuing on the following Wednesday and Saturday, 31 000 people - one in every ten of the population of South Australia - paid sixpence each (several dollars at current values) to witness Aboriginal 'corroborees' arranged by the missionaries of Point MacLeay and Point Pearce. There was indeed a large audience for the products of the Australian frontier as it retreated further from Adelaide, although the Australian frontier was never to find its impresario. [151]

In 1884 and 1885 the readers of the Adelaide papers were also heavily engaged by reports and correspondence about the murder of white and Chinese migrants to the Top End, especially the killing of four white miners on the Daly River in September 1884. Public protests and delegations to government led to punitive expeditions that were warmly supported by southern opinion. The Adelaide *Register* joined in the spirit of retribution with few qualms, recommending that a "rough and ready process of trial and conviction must be followed by the equally primitive process of executing justice on the spot".[152]

In the course of the next year, however, the earlier calls for retribution were replaced by a deep concern about police and vigilante violence as rumours of brutal reprisal filtered down to Adelaide. The whole acrid debate was stirred along by three officials who had returned recently from the Top End after displeasing the Government Resident, the *de facto* Governor of the Top End. They included two former policemen and the former Northern Territory Protector of Aborigines Dr Robert Morice. All were articulate, determined and persuasive advocates who used the press with confidence. They provided the public with regular insider revelations and suppositions about how the police and pastoralists were conducting themselves in the tropical north. Morice claimed in the *Observer* of June 6th 1885, no doubt with inside but inadequate evidence, that 150 Aborigines had died in the reprisals for the deaths of the four miners. To cap it all, a pastoralist of impeccable credentials and a reputation for using violence against Aborigines to protect his interests, W. D'Arcy Uhr, wrote to the *Observer* with a forceful criticism of the way in which the Resident was handling the defence of several Aboriginal men on trial for their part in the Daly River murders. "This is a matter which in my opinion should be taken up and enquired into by the Aboriginals' Friends' Protection Society [Association]" he wrote. On the same day it published Uhr's letter, November 14th 1885, the *Observer* reported the tabling in Parliament of an internal report by Corporal Montagu of the Northern Territory police, and concluded its account of general slaughter, quoting Montagu, "I believe the natives have received such a lesson this time as will exercise a salutary effect over the survivors in the time to come. One result of this expedition has been to convince me of the superiority of the Martini-Henry rifle, both for accuracy of aim and quickness of action." What Montagu's account revealed above all was this; there had been no "rough-and-ready processes of trial and conviction", merely slaughter - State-sponsored terror. The South Australian government was friendless and exposed.

Southern opinion now re-discovered the virtues of due process. Even the more pastoralist-friendly *Observer* editorialised bluntly: "the cold-blooded manner in which Corporal Montague [sic] and his associates murdered these unhappy wretches is a disgrace to him, a disgrace to the community, and an outrage upon the civilization about which we boast. ... his was a butchering expedition". The voices in favour of the frontiersmen were few and feeble. Had not the government of John Colton, a pious member of the Aborigines Friends Association, already expired in the usual season, June 1885, and been replaced by the first Ministry of John Downer, it might not have lasted until the next year. As it was, Downer's Government was struggling. Its Minister in charge of the Northern Territory, John Cockburn, had to accept the advice of the Aborigines Friends Association to establish an enquiry. It was government itself, not just the Government of John Downer, which was now in disarray. [153] But government still had its usual tricks up its sleeve. An enquiry was held in secret and became a travesty.

The Daly River incidents reveal frontier policing, government and constituency confronting each other at the end of 1885. That is useful in itself, but there are two more particular matters lying within these incidents that become part of our study of events on the upper Finke River. In the first place there is one important player in the Daly River story whose name at no stage entered the public debate, William John Peterswald, Commissioner of Police. When the self-damning report of Corporal Montagu was sent south to Adelaide it must have reached as far, if no further, than Peterswald's desk. It was his responsibility to report to his Minister the Chief Secretary who was at that time also the Premier, John Colton. Colton denied receiving it, and as a prominent Methodist and promoter of Aboriginal welfare, appears to have been believed. The Chief Secretary in Downer's Government, John Bray, learned of the matter at the same time as everyone else. They were both made to look fools, or worse, when Montagu's report was leaked. If Peterswald had not held on to the hot potato, and the Ministers were not lying, the only other places to look for those responsible for suppressing Montagu's indiscretion were behind the desks of the permanent officials who ran the Ministers' offices. The Secretary to the Minister responsible for the Northern Territory was James Bath. He was "a most capable and painstaking officer" and was still in that position in 1891.[154] We would need to search among those same officials or Ministers to find the man who later leaked Montagu's report to Parliament.

The second connection to the Finke River is this. In late October or November 1885, as the demeaning pursuit of Logic continued and controversy over the Daly River incidents was reaching its climax, Hermann Kempe and Georg Heidenreich visited the Chief Secretary John Bray at his office. Police Commissioner Peterswald and the then Protector of Aborigines, Friedrich Basedow, were also there. The Lutherans had come to discuss Mounted Constable Wurmbrand's killings in Glen Helen Gorge, about which Kempe had written to the Protector of Aborigines in March of that year. "The Chief Secretary asked us if we wished to make it a criminal case we replied we did not. The Commissioner of Police thereon said he would issue instructions to the Police not to use firearms except in self defence, and asked us if we would be satisfied with that and we replied that we would." An instruction to that effect was received at the Alice Springs police station on March 29th 1886, but, more importantly, not a word appeared in the English-language press or in the files of the Chief Secretary's office. It was a narrow escape for the government, and an important one. In a political environment inflamed by controversy over the practice of frontier justice, to have a policeman charged with murder might have been the last straw for John Downer's new Government, and an impediment to the knighthood he was to receive the next year.[155]

Governments in Adelaide were pulled between the demand for protection from the Aboriginal peoples and the requirements of legality. The electorate was the arbiter of how particular governments handled the situations confronting them. When Aboriginal peoples were seen to be aggressors, the electorate demanded prompt action and was prepared to overlook the requirements of legality. When it appeared, on the other hand, that the Aboriginal peoples were victims, the demand was for legality and justice. The immediacy of the telegraph, when compounded with a free press and the popular electorate, could add to the burdens of command more than it helped enforce compliance by subordinates. It took political skill to steer governments through the hazards which resulted, and a talent for manipulation. Fortunately for South Australian governments, all that was available to them. This will become clear later in the story.

ON THE FRONTIER
OF MORAL HAZARD

1885-1890

8

THE WEIGHT OF THE WORD

"But all our pleasure in the converted heathen is mixed with trepidation."
Hermann Kempe[156]

"From our mission in the North. Seven baptised" the headlines in the *Church messenger* of September 1887 shouted - in comparison with their usual typographic reticence. It is true that between 1885 and May 1887, when the first Western Aranda were baptized, a remarkable transformation had taken place in the fortunes of the Finke River mission, but to call it success would require us to apply standards that Kempe and Schulze, at least, came not to share. But they were momentous events. Modern Western Aranda life and belief are built to a large degree on the foundations of 1887. Tekua, Kalimalla and Nungoolga were at the centre of it all.

In 1884 Louis Schulze had written what amounted to an apology for the mission's failure, published in the *Church messenger* in January 1885. "It takes longer to cultivate the spirit than the soil" he reminded his readers, who were also his principal financiers.[157] And if the missionaries were slow to produce converts, the Adelaide Lutherans should understand that it wasn't from any shortcomings in their daily practice of the pious Christian life. He recounted the daily devotions, from sunrise to sunset, the Sunday services that lasted up to three hours, the constant praying, singing and bible-reading. But among their resident heathen, it was only those who were fed by the mission, that is the school students, old people and station workers, who came to devotions, and that only occasionally. If the missionaries' preaching and practice were not at fault, what was the problem? It could not be defects in their Lutheranism, since that was of God. "So shall my word be ...: it shall not return unto me void" wrote Schulze, quoting the Prophet Isaiah.[158]

The problem lay in the "unlimited indifference of the heathen, particularly to hearing the Word of God", but also in their many other defects. "We diligently present God's word to them, as comprehensibly as possible, but there is much they can not understand." The missionaries strove not to preach over their heads, struggled to find expression in the Aranda language for the novel ideas Christianity imported to the Finke. "We spend hour upon hour, asking in every possible way, but still not finding out the words we need." In the end these were "a deeply-sunk people who are lazy and reluctant to think". Schulze conceded that this "laziness" involved also the men closing their minds against the missionaries, now that they understood they intended to drive out the old ways. "They used to be more open, but now that they know why we want such precise knowledge of their language they are holding back the meanings of many words." But, in the end, it was the fault of the Western Aranda. "Another hindrance to our success is their indifference to spiritual matters. Their minds are focussed on their stomachs. With all of their conversation, and almost all of their quarrels and fights, it comes down to how to fill their stomachs. The stomach is their god. ... If their stomach is full and stretched tight as a drum, they stroke it with both hands as if it is their greatest treasure... then they are content."

Content also to discover in their own cosmology correspondences to the missionaries', to throw back at them. According to Schulze, the Aranda did not distinguish heaven and hell, but told of a place of broad waters and plentiful food to the north, called Laiuna, where the spirits of the dead men lay in the shadow of the trees while their women brought them food. Still, they had no desire to go there, and feared death and the malevolence of the spirits and the enemies who caused it. Kempe told his Director in Germany, with some excitement, that the missionaries had found the residue of an earlier religion. The Western Aranda knew of a good God and Creator, but they did not worship him or pray to him.[159] Such stories had the opposite effect on the missionaries to that intended. It confirmed them in the view that the Western Aranda had fallen, through their deep sinning, from the higher level of knowledge Man had taken from the Garden of Eden.

Have patience, Schulze advised his readers. "Our seven years here is a long time, but short compared with some other missions that have sown in one place for 20 or 30 years." The Hermannsburgers did not have that long.

In the middle of 1885 Hermann Kempe travelled with his wife and children south to Adelaide on furlough. It was an opportunity not only to get medical treatment for one of his children, but also to escape the hardships of the Finke and experience again the convivial life he had found so enjoyable on his long sea-voyage to Australia. Kempe enjoyed talking, particularly about himself, his hardships and triumphs. For some time the opportunities for conviviality on the Finke had been few. Whatever respect Schwarz had retained for Kempe, the leader of the mission, after Kempe's collapse on the trek north, had been replaced with severe criticism. The sense of comradeship had been submerged by the irritations of their shared daily lives, and in some deeper differences the character of which awaits discovery. As a result three factions formed. Louis Schulze allied with Kempe until the bitter end in 1891 while the Colonist Jürgens became *de facto* the leader of the lay workers and contested the management of the station's economic affairs. Schwarz stood apart from his missionary colleagues, and perhaps from the Colonists. In 1882 communal meals had been abandoned, and by 1885 the common vegetable garden had been divided into three, one for each missionary. The lay Colonists, who received a pittance even smaller than the missionaries', less than £10 a year, were pressing to be allowed to run their own cattle.[160]

By 1883 morale was so low and disputation so great that Theodor Harms wrote one of several letters to the mission personnel collectively with admonition and encouragement. The missionaries were exhorted, "work on your own souls is the main task... and do not ask what is mine what belongs to the next man. ... Do not become despondent because no heathen has been converted to the Lord to date, but examine earnestly how far you are yourselves responsible".[161]

At this point Superintendent Heidenreich allowed Theodor Harms to saddle him with a decision that was, in the end, to cost him the mission. Heidenreich knew that Colonist Jürgens had more management nous than Kempe. Where a clear resolution was needed to create effective authority on the station, Heidenreich attempted instead, on Harms's direction, to impose management by committee. The management committee on the Finke comprised one missionary appointed by Heidenreich - he chose Kempe - and a Colonist selected by the other missionaries and Colonists, a position clearly intended for Jürgens. The committee would have effective control of the mission's economic affairs, while not intruding into spiritual matters.

The regulations Heidenreich wrote for this folly were presented to Kempe at Bethany in May 1886 - it may have been Heidenreich's purpose in approving the furlough in the first place - and were accepted by Kempe as "correct, Christian and appropriate", according to the words Heidenreich put in his mouth. On his return to the Finke Kempe ignored the new regulations, and the contention became progressively more severe. By mid-1887 Schwarz's disagreements with his two fellow missionaries had led to flaming rows in front of the Colonists and the Western Aranda. Heidenreich had urged both sides to reconcile, but concluded that "such reconciliation is very superficial and not based on the truth." Schwarz was asked to consider accepting a pastorate in Queensland, but he had a different idea of where his future lay. In October 1889 the Mission Committee recorded "with deep regret that the brotherly trust among the brethren there has almost completely disappeared, and in its place jealousy and selfishness, self-interest and disputatiousness have again taken root ... the main reason ... is that the regulations for the external management have been entirely neglected". Jürgens left in 1889.

In 1885, as Kempe prepared to leave Central Australia, where it seemed despair alone flourished on the banks of the Finke River, the worst of their personal strife still lay in the future. Kempe now made a fateful decision. He took to assist him on the long journey two young men, Tekua and Kalimalla. "We were pleased that Tekua and Kalimalla volunteered for the trip" Schwarz reported to Theodor Harms in 1887, "since the likelihood of their conversion was the least of any of the heathen. They left [the Finke] as true heathen, but came back with Brother Kempe after a year hungry and thirsty for righteousness."[162] Both the manly, vigorous Kalimalla and the more placid Tekua had remained within the orbit of the Aboriginal men's power and influence during the eight years of the mission's presence on the Finke. They had spent little time at the mission school since lessons began in 1880. Both had spent time working on neighbouring Glen Helen station, north up the Finke, and may well have incurred among their people the credit, and the liability, that followed a young man's participation in revenge killing expeditions. When Kalimalla on one occasion raised his spear against Schwarz, and on another threw his woomera among the personnel of the mission station, he was, no doubt, acting out the opposition of the recalcitrant faction of the more senior men among the Western Aranda. Both young men had also stood against the missionaries not long before their departure south with Kempe, when the missionaries had followed two of their school boys thirty kilometres up the Finke where the people were gathered for an initiation ceremony. Despite the missionaries' "earnest" entreaties, Tekua and Kalimalla had helped persuade the boys to submit to initiation.[163] What now brought them to the missionaries' side? We don't know. They were in the middle of three great forces, those of the senior Western Aranda men, the missionaries and the pastoralists. Each offered opportunities and posed threats. Perhaps Kalimalla, a restless, ambitious young man, had simply recognised an opportunity to explore what was on offer in the world beyond the knowledge of the senior men . If Kalimalla and Tekua had been at Glen Helen in December 1884, they would have learned from Mounted Constable Wurmbrand what could happen to those who took their opposition to the white people beyond throwing a woomera among them. It was a very discouraging lesson.

Kalimalla was not indifferent to the dangers of travelling into the distant territories of strange peoples. He insisted on the company of his friend Tekua, and carried with him "a kind of net made of human hair", protected within a bag made from the skins of marsupial rodents. At times of mortal danger it was worn around the neck for protection from the magic of strangers. Schwarz took Tekua's neck-band away from him before the party left the mission, but Kempe noticed on the journey south that Kalimalla had acquired another. [164]

Half way to Adelaide, the Kempe party visited the Bethesda mission, a residue of the two earlier missions of Killalpaninna and Kopperamanna east of Lake Eyre. It was decided that Tekua and Kalimalla should remain there until the Kempes returned from their time in Adelaide. It proved to be a critical phase of their education. They spent several months with the Dieri, a people so foreign to them that only shortly before they would have thought it reasonable to kill them on sight. These strangers, however, included young Christian converts whose accounts of their new life made a profound impact. Somewhere along the track back to the Finke Tekua and Kalimalla gave Hermann Kempe some stunning and exciting news; they wanted to be baptised. Of Tekua's and Kalimalla's reasons for this decision all Kempe recorded, and perhaps all he knew, was that they had lost their "superstitions and fears of magic and witchdoctors".[165] There were, however, more physical threats for Tekua and Kalimalla to worry about.

Kempe claimed to have left Adelaide in high spirits, looking forward to his return to the hard life on the Finke mission, his "now dear home". Although his second trip north was incomparably easier than the first, he recorded the affront of having to travel Second Class on the train while the brides of Colonists were treated to First, and took the opportunity of reminding the southern congregations of how much easier their lives were, and of how much money they wasted on luxury while the missionaries had to do without.

Having collected Tekua and Kalimalla at Lake Eyre for the wagon journey north, he had sent Tekua forward during the difficult end stages of the journey to fetch fresh horses. On August 29th 1886 as they reached the southern exit of the Hugh River from the James Ranges, three days travelling from Hermannsburg, Kempe received a message from his eastern neighbour Charles Gall, the manager of Owen Springs, that Tekua had been speared and mortally wounded by one of the Owen Springs men. Kempe abandoned his family, saddled a horse and rode on to Owen Springs "to provide physical and spiritual care, and if necessary to baptise" Tekua, although he had received little or no instruction in the Lutheran faith. Kempe bandaged Tekua's wounds and was relieved to find the next day that he was significantly improved. So Tekua completed on a makeshift stretcher on board the Germans' covered wagon this greatest journey ever undertaken by a Western Aranda person. [166]

These two young men, hungry for righteousness, now broke through the stalemate that had developed in the struggle for the hearts and minds of the Western Aranda of the Finke River Mission. They became the leaders of a revolution otherwise comprised, at first, entirely of children. Kalimalla and Tekua persuaded a small group, all young students at the mission school, to join them as catechumens, declared candidates, voluntarily undergoing instruction for baptism into the Lutheran Church.

In the preceding six years the missionaries had found among the 20-30 young people who made up the changing membership of their schools' classes a smaller group whose attendance at the mission was much more regular. In early 1887 Schulze reported as a special achievement that "there are some boys and girls who have not left the station in years, and if they have been away a few days, it is with our permission."[167] These few young people had been detached in some degree from the life of the rest of the Western Aranda, and Schulze had been instructing them in the basics of the Lutheran catechism two days every week. Of this small group nine (apart from Tekua and Kalimalla) became candidates for baptism.[168] Two boys were excluded for unspecified bad behaviour, one was considered too young, and a girl refused to renounce her designated husband. This left five, of whom four were either doubly or singly orphaned boys ranging in age from thirteen to sixteen years. Only the one girl, Adilka, thirteen years old, had a natural father, and both he and Adilka's designated husband were strong men among the Western Aranda. Nevertheless, by 1886 she had been with the missionaries for some years. She was, according to Schwarz, weak in body but strong in spirit, both characteristics contributing to her freedom to move into the missionaries' orbit.[169]

As the catechism classes proceeded in 1887 some of the candidates were housed in the simple wooden huts previously occupied by mission personnel, under the eyes of the missionaries and well away from the other Western Aranda camped in the bed of the Finke. But before the return of Tekua and Kalimalla there was among the mission's pupils, in Schwarz's perceptive account, "a fear of the future, an uncertainty and lack of clarity about the consequences [of becoming Christian] that was largely responsible for our pupils' earlier inability to declare openly that they wished to be baptised, although they lacked neither knowledge of the Truth, nor the desire to be Christian." While fear of the senior men, and of exclusion from the life of their clans must have been in the minds of these young people, Schwarz recognised, in a statement unique among the missionary accounts of this period, that "the members of our group of pupils needed one more thing, to come to their own understanding [of our ways and customs], one which makes sense to the heathen as they abandon the customs of their forefathers to become Christians."[170] That understanding, he thought, was what Tekua and Kalimalla had brought back from Killalpaninna. He was a wise man to see so far, but he could not see how far Tekua's and Kalimalla's understanding conformed to the missionaries' Lutheranism.

In that same year of the first baptisms, Schulze noted changes among the Western Aranda who were not in the baptismal group. "Many evil spirits have already been laid aside, as one can tell from their religious customs. They finish with their mourning ceremonies as simply and briefly as they can; their festivals and dances make little impact. Their monotonous singing is little heard now; instead one hears Christian songs. They have refrained from revenge expeditions for some years."[171] Perhaps more of traditional aboriginal life was now conducted at a greater distance from the mission, but the ground of Western Aranda life was moving at Hermannsburg, and not just for the young, although we must remain ignorant of how most of the Western Aranda saw it. The movement became evident at the baptism service and the celebration that followed it.

On May 30th, 1887 the seven young Western Aranda became the first of their people to be initiated as Christians. As the seven candidates entered the small church, all freshly washed and dressed in new white clothes, "not only the candidates but all the heathen present were full of expectation of what was to come. The service began at 10.00 am, and as the candidates took their place at the altar all of the heathen were present... most having to stand outside the door." Louis Schulze, their teacher, gave the sermon in Aranda, telling them they must now totally reject all the atrocious ways of the heathen and bear witness as Christians. "It was a striking sight" Kempe reported "to see these poor heathen, formerly so dirty, now sitting there so decent, clean and devout, so that it was not only we whites who could not hold back our tears, but almost all the heathen present wept." After the service everyone shared a small celebratory meal. Kalimalla now called himself Andreas, Tekua chose the name Thomas and Adilka, Maria.

On the same day a "large number" of heathen declared themselves for baptism. There was a fire burning among the Western Aranda, lit by the children. The missionaries had only one response, the Word, sin and Grace. The people were told they had much to learn, and must convince the missionaries their intention was a serious one. It is of great significance, however, that the class of catechumens being prepared for baptism in 1888 included two married couples, a man with three children, Salomo, and the widow Nungoolga with two children from her former husband, one later baptised with her mother under the name Sara. Her older child, the boy Rauwiraka/Nathanael, had been among the first group baptised in 1887. On the fringe of the group of catechumens were others who joined in the hymn singing and the festive occasions, whose intention to choose the new way may have been as clear as those of the catechumens, to themselves at least, if not to the missionaries.

It was one of the young men on the fringe of the inner circle of Christians who triggered the final defeat of the recalcitrant senior men. Mototoka had passed the first stage of initiation, was a resident of the mission and its environs for some years, and since the Christian revolution had begun, had kept much to himself, worked for the missionaries and learned incidentally the songs and prayers that were being taught to the catechumens. At Christmas 1887 he had shown his commitment to the new faith by singing before the assembled Western Aranda the hymn "Now sing and be joyful". The missionaries encouraged the Western Aranda to learn such hymns, so that they could join the baptised and the students in the singing on festive occasions. But Mototoka, according to Schwarz, was the most diligent.

After Christmas, Mototoka was persuaded by the older men, against Schwarz's strong advice, to travel up the Finke to a major ceremony being held by the northern neighbours of the Hermannsburg clans.[172] It was also the season for the sweet, black Lalitja berries, a favourite treat. "He came to me one evening and showed me four fingers, saying that was how long he would be away. ... When he had been away some time we heard that he was very ill and gaunt; he was complaining of pains in the chest and was confined to the camp. A few days later two women came here, their heads and bodies painted white, and began to sing the mourning songs. I soon learned to my horror that Mototoka had been murdered, and later we learned the real cause of his death. He had rejected several times invitations to join the heathen in their festival, and said: 'The heathen festivals are of no account, and are bad'. He could only have known and said that with the strength of God's Word. As a renegade (Abtrünniger) he incurred the penalty of death, and was foully killed the next day. His murderer is called Jola, who ... speared Mototoka's brother two years previously for similar reasons. Mototoka's death was to be a warning-shot to our natives, to hold them back from Christianity". Schwarz saw Mototoka's power to deny traditional ways as the work of the Word, expressing itself in a way that the missionaries had not provided for or expected, so he called Mototoka the Centre's first Christian martyr. Schulze saw instead the working out of yet another round of revenge-killing.

Following the news of Mototoka's murder came rumours that the northern men would soon be coming south to kill everyone at the station, missionaries and Aboriginal Christians alike. "Our heathen", reported Schwarz "did not take it as an empty boast, and had no idea what to do." Indeed, if their northern neighbours had concluded the Western Aranda of Hermannsburg were guilty of sacrilegious conduct then there lay before them the prospect of general slaughter of a Biblical savagery.[173] From Schwarz's account, the threats of the northern men had the opposite effect. "This murder exposed the cruelty of heathen belief to the open light of day, and many of our natives ... asked all the more urgently to be baptised." Perhaps the missionaries had found, by accident, a sense of Sin that lay upon Western Aranda society, their liability to violent death for offences, whether actual or supposed by magical inquest, a liability that ate at the core of the perfection conferred by Western Aranda adulthood. On April 2nd 1888 a further seventeen of the Western Aranda were baptised and, according to Schwarz, "others, particularly fathers, stood before the door of God's Kingdom and knocked." Among the third class of catechumens were, Schwarz claimed, "grey-headed men and women, and the strong ones among the people, as well as the cripples, blind and lame, down to the youngest students."[174] Be that as it may, there were no baptisms in 1889, the next year, and just five in 1890, of whom only one was older than twenty years.

Kalimalla/Andreas, whatever his motives for making his decisive move over to the Christian camp, showed every sign of sincerity, even enthusiasm, in his new faith. After seeing the impact of the Bethesda Christians on Tekua and Kalimalla, Kempe was convinced that the new Christians would be the most effective means of converting the other Western Aranda, if only they could be persuaded to assert themselves. He found the young Christians reticent. Only Kalimalla was, in the end, persuaded to stand up before his fellow Western Aranda and urge them to become Christians. "He was the first to give witness" Kempe reported "and we were pleased by it."[175] Kalimalla soon became, in Schulze's characterisation, like an old steward on the station, keeping everything in order, putting the students to bed at night, deciding who would milk the cows in the morning, driving the cart. "Andreas, the oldest of them [the newly-baptised]" Schulze wrote, "leavens his people. His manner is open, free and cheerful, and he accepts correction without making a sullen face like the others do. He asks us frequently how he should behave, even in minor matters like, for example, whether he should wear new or old trousers on Sundays. He is like a child and willing for any kind of work. He especially likes breaking in the young horses, and has become our wagon-driver. If any bad behaviour arises among the heathen or the young Christians he acts against it by word and deed. He keeps his eyes open and tells us about offences among them."[176]

After ten years of fruitless attempts to penetrate the senior men's silences the missionaries now gained new knowledge of their neighbours' beliefs and practices. "From him and those baptised with him we are getting more deeply into the horrors of the heathen life." From Andreas and the former Rauwiraka, now Nathanael, the missionaries heard for the first time of the women's practice of infanticide, (formerly such deaths were attributed to natural causes) and heard the northern and southern Loritja - the Kukatja and Matuntara - accused also of systematic cannibalism. They heard in detail of the practices of the revenge parties, their cruelty and their self-perpetuation. After two years of this education in Western Aranda ways, Schulze conceded in his quarterly report published in June 1889 that "our heathen are not at all such good-natured people as we first thought."[177] Andreas acknowledged that he had once been no better. Soon the first "idols", that is *tjurunga*, were handed in. The young men were now on dangerous ground.

Kalimalla's punctiliousness about the new Law was soon to lead to trouble. While his friend Tekua was on another journey south with the Colonists Jürgens and Koch, Kalimalla kept his eye on Tekua's wife, Kwabingeraka. Despite the pressure she was under, Kwabingeraka was not persuaded to accept baptism until 1888, when she took the name of Hanna.[178] "Just yesterday" Schulze reported from a few days before Kwabingeraka's baptism "Andreas tracked our Thomas's wife and found her committing immorality with a young heathen man. ... Andreas now wants them both to get their appropriate punishment and for that purpose I am going to entice the rascal back here. The woman is still working here, and when her husband returns from his trip the matter will be dealt with"[179] According to a later report from Schwarz both perpetrators were interrogated and confessed their deed, "the heathen man without any concern for his soul, it being completely incomprehensible to him that he had done wrong and thereby sinned. So when Brother Schulze asked him ; Is what you have done right and proper? he merely said, in all innocence, yes. ... Hanna was deeply ashamed and allowed us to reprove and punish her for her sins." Already the missionaries had adopted an Aboriginal view of how to treat moral offences. Nevertheless, when he returned immediately after the 1888 baptisms, Thomas agreed to keep his wife, after what punishment is not recorded, and they were married as Lutherans on April 6th, 1888. They "'endured each other very well", it seemed to the missionaries.[180]

Andreas's enthusiasm as a new Christian was also not without a personal cost to his prospects for personal happiness. Unlike Thomas he had no wife from his pre-Christian days and every demonstration of his zeal for the new ways could only harden the hearts of Aboriginal fathers against his case. As Louis Schulze reported in May 1889, "if a man is not popular, he can wait a long time before a wife is promised to him. This is the case with our Andreas."[181] The missionaries had, in effect, taken on a new obligation for which their training had not prepared them, the obligation to find for their young converts wives and husbands who were, or would become, Christian. For any converts they persuaded to refuse initiation into Western Aranda manhood this task was indeed difficult, even impossible. Even in Andreas's case, as a fully-qualified man, the combination of youth and defiance of the older men created a difficulty made more intractable by the effect of the marriage classes among the Western Aranda. He must find a wife far from the domain of the Lutherans, in the country of the heathen surrounding the mission's lease.

The pressure on the missionaries was increased by the young converts themselves. They did not commit the "sexual excesses" of their elders, but "it is a great struggle for them, and they enjoy talking about marriage very much. We would like to help them find a Christian spouse, although it would be better if they were to spend their youth in enjoyment of the Lord. The Lord of Lies casts upon our Christians the calumny that they fornicate with one another, but our Lord Jesus holds the field."[182]

For Andreas, a vigorous young man, doubly initiated into the ways of Aborigines and Lutherans, widely-travelled, already with command over some of his people and close to the seat of white power, the waiting must have been hard to bear. We can imagine the taunts of the heathen men and women camped in the bed of the Finke. He eventually found for himself a woman he wanted to marry. We do not know her name but she was heathen and showed no desire to learn Christianity. Andreas slept with this woman. He was, of course, reproved by the missionaries, acknowledged that this could be no Lutheran marriage, and accepted that he had sinned. Here was the other side of the marriage class system of the Western Aranda, as the missionaries saw it. It not only prevented marriage between perfectly acceptable, and rare, Christians, but also encouraged men and women of the correct classes to feel entitled to have sexual relations with each other, if there were no practical obstacles in their way. Schulze came to the conclusion, as Heidenreich summarised it for him, that the class system, and the social life that sprang from it, "were a hindrance to a proper family life, and so not compatible with Christianity".[183]

The solution the missionaries found for the dilemma they had created for Andreas was more of an offence against the law of the Western Aranda than his baptism had been. In fact, it was outrageous sacrilege. No woman Andreas fancied could satisfy the missionaries, since they were all heathen. In fact, there was only one single Christian woman in Central Australia, Adilka/Maria, but she was of the wrong marrying section. She was also younger than a girl could be decently married among the Lutherans of the south. Still, Andreas and Maria were married. Schwarz claimed that the marriage was "by his [Andreas's] desire and her acquiescence", and the evidence justifies his careful formulation, and a little more besides. Adilka's father and her promised husband, both strongly wedded to the old ways, were sufficient reason for her reluctance. Not only would this wrong marriage cut her off from her family in a decisive way, she knew that only the superior power of the missionaries, as long as it should prevail, could keep her from a savage death inflicted on the instructions of the senior men. Schulze, under cross-examination from William Willshire, told the Swan-Taplin enquiry in July 1890 "I did give a Panunga lubra to a Commara black fellow... Andreas wanted Maria for his wife but she did not want Andreas ... afterward she consented and they were married at the station according to the rites of the Lutheran Church. Her friends did not object to us... The marriage was against tribal law", he conceded, but "there was no row at our station in consequence of the marriage." If there was no row at the station it was because Maria/Adilka's entire family left the station, complaining loudly as they went down the Finke. The missionaries themselves had earlier reported this through the *Church messenger*, but only to the German-speaking Lutherans in the south.

The marriage of Andreas and Maria may have been made in the Lutherans' heaven, but it was not made to last on the Finke. "The married couple lived sometimes unhappily, sometimes happily together. At last Andreas left Maria. I do not know why", Schulze conceded to Swan-Taplin.[184] In fact whatever substance there was in the marriage had ended within a few months. The consequences of its failure were destructive for the mission, and worse for Andreas. The marriage of Thomas and Hanna did not last much longer, at least in a sense the Lutherans would understand as marriage.

By the fourth quarter of 1888 Wilhelm Schwarz was reporting "on the mission our hearts have been troubled for some months."[185] The missionaries had been given information that Andreas had offended with a married woman from outside the station. Worse, it appeared that Thomas had also offended. Some exceptional procedure was needed to drive these sins home. All the Christians on the station, black and white, were gathered together. Thomas and Andreas were sternly admonished from Biblical authority in front of the men, women and children of the congregation. They were told they must show the missionaries evidence of their sincere remorse and penitence, to serve as an example and a warning to the other Western Aranda Christians. They must pray for God's forgiveness, for it was He their behaviour had grieved. All prayed for them, and in Schwarz's account Thomas and Andreas accepted this roasting "in all humility". But it becomes clear how much this moral flagellation cost Thomas and Andreas when we learn that Andreas was unable to walk away from the gathering without assistance. This was indeed a victory too far for the doctrine of Sin and Grace, but worse was to come.[186]

In November 1888, while Andreas and Thomas were working the mission's cattle a short way from the station, rumour came back to the missionaries that heathen women had gone out to the cattle camp, and both Andreas and Thomas had slept with them. One man had followed the women's tracks out, and another woman brought the story back to the station. A row broke out on the station, between those who believed the tale-teller and those who called her a liar, and who knows what communal politics was in play. When the men came back some days later they were indignant to find their wives and the missionaries, or some of the missionaries, believed the story. Before the missionaries could conduct their own inquest into the matter they reported an event as revolutionary in Western Aranda life as any they had ever witnessed. It is hard to credit, but Schwarz recounts quite baldly that the two wives thrashed their husbands soundly, "and made quite a night of it." Thomas left the same night for Glen Helen station, where he had earlier worked and whereabouts he had relationships. The next night Andreas and Hanna followed. Schwarz regretted that the new Christians had left before they could be given the opportunity to establish their innocence or subject themselves to correction. He feared they would be spoiled at Glen Helen.

In 1889 nature was to take a hand in the dissolution of the Hermannsburg mission. It was the year of the toxic wind,[187] the hot north-westerly that in summer whips Central Australia with the tail of the tropical monsoon to save it from the Sahara's fate. In 1889 the north-west wind continued to blow through the winter, bringing only heat, an adhesive drought, foul waters and repeated bouts of disease to black and white alike.

Andreas returned to the mission in the first quarter of 1889, leaving us with one heart-breaking insight into the torment the missionaries could cause their converts. Louis Schulze had taken

Andreas to task harshly for an unspecified sin. The next morning Andreas reported that "two *iwuba* (spirits that wander about at night, according to the old men's teachings) had come to him and had wanted to sound him out, but he had answered: 'I am a Christian' and had had nothing more to do with them". Schulze had looked for tracks in the sand, without success, and put it all down to a demonstration of the Devil's power. Andreas and Thomas were now drifting between the richly-populated universe of Western Aranda spirits and relationships on the one hand and the perplexing mental landscape of the white people, with its oppressive individual conscience and its new social boundaries. Both worlds could be unforgiving to those who transgressed.

Andreas did not stay long at Hermannsburg. It was a time of comings and goings, of expulsions, excommunications and new starts, but never again could Kempe and Schulze regard Andreas as their steward at Hermannsburg. Without intending it, but with no sign of regret, the missionaries had broken the rock on which their Aboriginal congregation had been built. Whichever way Andreas walked from now on he was on dangerous ground. And Thomas, when he returned to the mission where he remained, on and off, to the end of 1889, was on his own for the first time.

One difference between the two men is the affection the missionaries, Kempe in particular, continue to have for Thomas. After leaving the mission Thomas threw his lot in with people from 70 miles west of Glen Helen - Kukatja or Western Aranda we do not know - and joined them on a raid on the Western Aranda of Missionary Plain. James McDonald claimed "from my personal knowledge" that three men and two women were killed by Thomas and his associates. McDonald reported this to Schwarz, but there is no sign that Schwarz took the matter further. Kempe and Schulze may not have known this until Swan and Taplin came to Hermannsburg, but they did know that Thomas had left their station in November 1889 "because he had been ordered by the Glen Helen Tribe to go and take revenge on another black" and that the victim had died from a spear in the eye. Thomas was welcomed back but "excommunicated" until he agreed to reconcile himself with his enemies, a dangerous enterprise he did not attempt. This was not reported to police. In fact, despite seven visits from Mounted Constables since Wurmbrand's visit in 1884, there had been no official relations between the mission and police, until Kempe and Schulze found common cause with William Willshire at the end of 1889.

From the baptisms of 1887 and 1888 there were only two converts over 30 years of age; in fact the remainder were younger than twenty. Nungoolga/Naomi was a widow of about 31 years of age. Her position was not unlike Andreas's, since most of her fellow-Christians were children, one of them her son Rauwiraka/Nathanael. She was also past the age at which young women were most attractive to the white station workers. Still, the missionaries disapproved mightily when she took up with the Matuntara man Ereminta. They claimed that Naomi's relatives also disapproved and it is likely that someone else entirely was entitled to claim Naomi by inheritance from her late husband. But Ereminta was a man strong in the old ways, who won respect among men, black and white, and loyalty from Nungoolga.

Ereminta had been noticed favourably by Charles Chewings in 1885, and was later described by Wilhelm Schwarz as one of Frederick Thornton's "most trusty blackboys". Mounted Constable Willshire, however, gave Ereminta the character of "one of the worst of the cattle-killers", a charge that may have been more exaggerated than false. Nevertheless, Ereminta continued to find employment with Frederick Thornton on Tempe Downs. Thornton seemed to appreciate that strength of character and bushmanship among Aboriginal men came with some irreducible propensity for cattle-killing. Ereminta, known as Roger to the white men, was employed on Tempe Downs when Willshire had Tekua shoot him in February 1891. In the meantime he became well known to the missionaries, and was seized by them for cattle-killing. Schwarz flogged him for it on one occasion, a response both parties understood as far safer than involving the police. It was, however, illegal. James McDonald also caught Ereminta at the end of 1889 with three others in the act of killing one of the Glen Helen cattle, but did not report what action he took against them. Three other "mission blacks" he caught out killing cattle in 1885 were still at Hermannsburg in 1890. No arrests were reported for the three visits Alice Springs police made to Glen Helen between the beginning of 1886 and the beginning of 1889. [188]

Naomi lived at Hermannsburg for a while with Ereminta-her "paramour" according to Schulze. This allowed Naomi to care for Nathanael when illness struck him down. But by the middle of September Ereminta was keen to leave, for reasons that were of no interest to the missionaries. He could hardly have felt at ease there, given the enmity between the Western Aranda and the Matuntara, dating at least as far back as the Irbmangkara massacre of 1875, and the continuing bloodshed that had followed it. But as soon as Nathanael was on his feet again Ereminta insisted on leaving, taking with him Naomi, the blind girl Martha and some others. The missionaries fetched them back, by what means we do not know but may from later evidence suppose. After a fortnight Ereminta insisted again on leaving, and a row ensued. "Brother Kempe and I showed her how unjust she [Naomi] was to her children to love her paramour more than them; the Lord would punish her and ... if she left it would show she did not love her children. The next morning they were gone... About four weeks later [on October 29th] her daughter died, surely a wake-up call for the mother. Apparently not, to date at least. We have heard and seen nothing of her."[189]

Thomas and Hanna, who had left at the end of 1888, returned to the mission, but not, as Schulze observed acidly, as repentant sinners, but because life away from Hermannsburg no longer pleased them.

One adult 'heathen-Christian' who persisted was Salomo, a father of three children on his baptism in 1888, with a boy born in the next year. His new faith was severely tested in the hot Spring of 1889. Kempe and Schulze had taken particular exception to the mourning ceremonies of the Western Aranda since their arrival on the Finke. For a start they were, of course, heathen ceremonies and seemed implicitly to deny the Christian Gospel. Death among the Western Aranda was to the Lutherans as naked as every other aspect of their lives, and even more depressing to the Lutherans. Aboriginal mourning seemed to declare the finality and hopelessness of death, as the mourners walked away from the small pile of sand in the river bed where the body lay and burned the dead person's property. They would no longer mention the person's name and feared the departing spirit. Not least, the mourning ceremonies would go on all night, with loud and heart-breaking wailing making sleep difficult, and were accompanied by a welter of self-injury on the part of the grieving relatives. And so, dissuading the people from their mourning ceremonies was to the missionaries, at least to Kempe and Schulze, one of the most telling signs that they were weakening the hold of the old, devil-driven ways on the hearts and minds of the people. Louis Schulze included the mourning ceremonies on his list of the Western Aranda's deficiencies when he reported at the end of June 1889. "They know from God's Word how crazy their funeral ceremonies are but go on with them, although not as openly as before. But they can't give them up completely, especially the women."[190]

Salomo was brought face-to-face with this demand of his new faith when his two young baptised daughters, Elizabeth and Anna, succumbed to the disease sweeping the mission in November 1889. When their younger daughter Anna died "it was difficult, very difficult, for the parents. I was worried about the father. The first thing he said was: Now I have no more children, I am going away from here. I consoled him as well as I could. We laid the child out in the church and I asked that they all now go to bed, and not make a heathen uproar. The many heathen who turned up - they have a great love of mourning - I sent to their camp. Everything remained quiet during the night. The burial took place next morning. I tried in my sermon to console the parents as much as I could ... earlier that morning Salomo handed over to me a bundle of his possessions and said he wanted to leave. I spoke to him after the burial, although he was standing as if on hot coals, and asked him:

> Why do you want to go away?
> He: To forget the suffering here.
> I: You will sooner forget that here through the preaching of God's Word.
> He: I am going.
> I: Just don't carry out any heathen mourning ceremonies.
> He: No.
> I: How long do you want to stay away?
> He: Until the next moon.
> I: That is too long; you must come back next week, to live so long without God's Word is dangerous.
> He: Perhaps (that is, I will come back then).

He then asked me for tobacco, matches and a knife, which I gave him. He then departed."

Salomo (who had, in fact, an older daughter and an infant son remaining) survived this trial of strength between the old ways and the new, and went back to his work at the station a week later.

The failure of 1889 to produce a new crop of baptisands had much to do with Wilhelm Schwarz, and with the divisions between the missionaries. Each class of catechumens was the responsibility of one missionary, who selected and instructed the students, graduated them and presided at the baptism service. The 1877 class was taken by Louis Schulze, the larger 1888 group by Hermann Kempe, and in 1888 Wilhelm Schwarz selected Tjalkabota, the girl Topatopa, Alknakulba, Solomo's heathen wife Kangitja and another Tekua who was also called Dick, and, after baptism, Samuel. The reason this class failed to proceed to baptism in 1889 is nowhere explained in the missionaries' reports to the *Church messenger*, or in Heidenreich's comments on them, or in the minutes of the Mission Committee. But one of the catechumens, Tjalkabota, has left us an account of what happened.

"He [Schwarz] wanted to baptise all of us. However, he received a letter from [the] south, calling him to come back. It was while he was teaching me; his wife brought him the letter, which had just come in the mail. Mrs Schwarz gave it to him and told him in German that they were to return. Then Mr Schwarz told us, 'Children, I am unable to teach you any longer, and I am unable to baptise you. They have called me to return.' Then after he had taught us a little more, we all went out of the school. Then all the people were very sad. ... After a few more weeks, Mr Schwarz got his horse ready. Then he got the buggy and erected a canopy on it. Then the next week he left."[191] We know from a letter of Kempe's to Heidenreich that on September 2nd 1889 Schwarz had recently left, but since it was usual for the missionaries to baptise their classes at Easter time there must be a period of several months between the letter of summons Tjalkabota reports and Schwarz's departure.

We may be sure that the events of that period between Schwarz's recall and his departure included continuing bitter disputation between Schwarz and the other two missionaries and between Kempe and Jürgens. The latter wrote on July 27th to Heidenreich complaining about Kempe's management. He concluded by resigning from his nominal position as a member of the management committee that had never met. Heidenreich thought Kempe's later reply to Jürgens's complaints "very feeble", and Schulze's defence of his colleague "a very biassed judgement".[192] It is puzzling that the Mission Committee's minutes contain no reference to any matters at issue between Schwarz and Kempe, but are limited to the generalised judgement that "brotherly trust among the brethren there has almost completely disappeared". We know from 1887 that the feelings between the two men ran deep, and it would diminish both of them to suppose that the issues between them involved nothing more than details of station management, like the best time for shearing the sheep. We can read into differences between their reports published in the Church messenger one principal difference in their approach to their Western Aranda Christians. While Schwarz's devotion to the Lutheranism they all shared was no less narrow than Kempe's and Schulze's, we do not find in Schwarz's reports from after 1877 the same blaming of the Western Aranda for their failure to live up to the missionaries' hopes. He confronts their sins, grieves over the backsliding, but retains sympathy for the gulf they have to cross and a simple, perhaps slightly manic, optimism about the future.

It may be that the best indicator we have of a major disagreement between Schwarz and the other two missionaries is found in the report Kempe writes of the first quarter of 1889, the period in which Schwarz received his summons back to Adelaide.

If we missionaries mention in our reports from time to time that we have administered corporal punishment to the heathen and the heathen-Christians, and people take that from our reports and depict us as a "flogging mission", they show they have not the slightest understanding of mission work among such deeply-sunk heathen. Not even Christians can do without it. Should evil-doers be coddled by the rest of us? Parents who want the best for their children discipline them. As has been written: 'Parents who love their children keep them constantly under the rod' ... If even Christians cannot do without it [discipline by corporal punishment] then how could the heathen and heathen-Christians? ... In our experience it is

149

better for discipline to be too strict than too weak. ... We know that no-one is converted through the discipline of the law, but it is appropriate to the education of people as they now are, thoroughly spoilt by sin.[193]

This may have been pre-emptive defence against the accusation that Schwarz had been levelling at Kempe and could be expected to take back to Adelaide. Schwarz later conceded flogging Ereminta for cattle-killing, but none of the missionaries referred to Schwarz beating a heathen-Christian as punishment for sinning.

Increasingly after Schwarz's departure the other two missionaries in their reports take refuge in what we can see as excuses for the failure of their mission, and we can hardly blame them for doing so. Schulze's refuge was ethnography mixed with criticism of Western Aranda customs and morals. His reports, after the information began to flow from the initiated baptisands, issued in a paper on the Western Aranda that is eventually translated and published in the *Proceedings* of the Royal Society of South Australia. This paper caps the ethnography Kempe had produced in 1880, which was a simpler descriptive ethnography for a simpler time.

Kempe himself took refuge in biblical interpretation, suggesting a loss of curiosity as well as of hope. Too much time had passed between the common human expulsion from Eden and the 1880s, too much time without the power of Grace. It might not be possible to recall the higher nature of the Western Aranda before their extinction would put the whole business in the hands of God. "If we take an overview of missions in Australia, the number of births and deaths proves that our task is to bring them the light of life shortly before their twilight. Unless God works wonders, one can easily calculate that by 1900 all men of reproductive age will have gone, and it is by no means certain that the young men will have children since men are now producing no children. ... The health of the natives is much weaker than ours. ... And why is that? I know of no other explanation than this: the curse of their forefather Ham rests on them and will not be lifted until they are converted."

All three missionaries shared the conviction that on the evidence before them their work with the Western Aranda did not have long to run. Soon there would be no more Western Aranda people on the Finke to receive their mission. That either made the work more urgent, or hopeless, or both, at different times.

Wilhelm Schwarz's ambition to be master of his own mission station had not died when Heidenreich would not or could not support it. On the contrary, he had fleshed out his plans, investing them with the unstoppable enthusiasm that was the character of the man. In June 1887 he had written in his report to Director Harms of the Hermannsburg Mission Institute:

Furthermore, it is our heartfelt wish that other mission stations might be set up in the interior of Australia, because there is a great need for them and the time is right if we wish to show these poorest of the heathen our Love and wish to protect them with the strength of the Gospel before they die out completely.

Moreover, Schwarz had chosen the best sites for his new stations. One site was south west of Hermannsburg on the Palmer River which ran through the Tempe Downs pastoral lease, within the country of the Matuntara whom Schwarz knew as occasional visitors. The area was receiving clans "coming in" from the sand country further west and, as a result, the home of the greatest number of 'tribal' Aboriginal people in the Centre. It was Chinchewarra's birth country. Or eastwards on the Todd River on which Alice Springs lay, probably on or near Undoolya station, one of the two oldest pastoral leases in the Centre. In neither place would Schwarz have been welcome, and there was no prospect that any South Australian Government would have forced the pastoralists to accept missionaries as even closer neighbours than they were at Hermannsburg on the Finke.[194]

Schwarz's ambition to compete with Kempe in mission management was also a threat to Heidenreich's investment on the Finke. Schwarz can have had little appreciation of what was involved in winning financial contributions from the Government and from the Lutheran congregations in the south, a place now more foreign to him than Central Australia. Schwarz was not likely to see any station he ran as second in line to Heidenreich's.

Whatever Kempe and Schulze thought of Schwarz's ambitions, or of his ability to realise them, there can be no doubt of their hostility to Schwarz the man. After he had left the Finke on his journey to Adelaide, Kempe and Schulze packed up the Schwarz family's belongings and, without consulting Schwarz, despatched them to Adelaide. He was shocked when they arrived, and was left with nothing to fall back on should his lobby for the new station fail.

The Finke River mission was now without two key people. Wilhelm Schwarz, the one counter-weight to the power of Hermann Kempe, had been withdrawn. And Andreas had been driven out, leaving Thomas alone to negotiate the rough ground between the demands of the senior Western Aranda men and the remaining two missionaries. Thomas could not go back to his former innocence as a young Western Aranda man, but living as a Western Aranda Christian was proving no easier.

9

FROLIC ON THE FRONTIER

I blow my pipes, the glad birds sing.
The fat young nymphs about me spring...
I am the lord,
I am the lord.
I am the lord of everything,
    Hugh McRae [195]

I write as I have felt, acutely. William Willshire.[196]

If the cattle stations of Owen Springs, Glen Helen, Henbury and Tempe Downs were neighbours too close for comfort, in August 1889 Hermann Kempe and Louis Schulze got a neighbour who was to present them with the frontier's most dangerous gift, the power to do what you might wish in private to do. Mounted Constable William Willshire had been instructed to establish a police post closer to Tempe Downs station than Alice Springs. Tempe Downs had been stocked four years earlier and the Government could no longer ignore Charles Chewings' complaints about cattle-killing. Willshire chose a site half way down the Finke Gorge, and a mere thirty kilometres from Hermannsburg. There is no doubt the site is strategic, in a number of senses. It sits beside but well above a large permanent lagoon in the Finke known first as Boggy Waterhole, then Boggy Water, now called Boggy Hole. All traffic along the Gorge, the Aborigines on foot, the mail contractor, Hermannsburg's Afghan cartage contractors with their camels, any other visitors to Hermannsburg, local horse traffic, all have to pass his gate. At Boggy Water an insignificant watercourse called Merrick Creek enters the

Finke. Although Merrick Creek's catchment is small, its broad sides of sandy loam near the junction provide a useful pasturage that is not available at many other places along the Finke Gorge.

It is also true that Boggy Water is a day's riding further from Tempe Downs station than other possible sites with permanent water on the south face of the James Range. Chewings himself had recommended in November 1887 that a new police post be opened on the Finke south of the James Range possibly at Henbury station which is closer to the Telegraph than Tempe Downs. Later, in 1893, the police post will be moved to such a southern site, but west of the Finke, at Illamurta Springs.

William Willshire was 37 years of age in 1889 when he moved to Boggy Water. A lightly-built man of average height, with dark wavy hair and a prominent nose, a good-looking man if you ignore the fact that his eyes visit you with a fickle attention that he prefers to direct to himself, that he changes subjects abruptly, sometimes in mid-sentence or, when he is writing, in mid-paragraph. He joined the South Australian police in 1878 at the age of 26 recording his previous occupation as drover, a reputable and responsible occupation but, unless he owned the droving plant, without the command of white men. An energetic young man, and keen to please, he was promoted from the low rank of Trooper, Third Class to the more glamorous role of a Mounted Constable, Second Class, in 1880 and had attracted favourable mention in police records by 1882. After four years of postings around the "settled" agricultural districts of South Australia, where Aboriginal de-population was well-advanced, Willshire was posted to Alice Springs at the end of 1882. If his training for the new experience of working with Aboriginal people living traditionally matched that normally provided for South Australian police moving to the Centre, he had to learn on the job at Alice Springs. By October of 1883 he had made enough impact in the challenging role of frontier policeman to be promoted to Mounted Constable, First Class.

Willshire's formal education was above average for his time, a deduction we can safely make from the fact that his father, James Willshire, once owned and ran a private school that William no doubt attended, and because Willshire senior demonstrated a close involvement in his son's later career. This was a time when most men in the Colony learned while in the workforce after a formal education that was over by the age of twelve and was concerned only to provide children with a grounding in basic literacy and numeracy. This was in the context of a proudly British culture. William Willshire was British as Hermann Kempe, Wilhelm Schwarz and Louis Schulze were Lutheran. He was also by 1888 ostentatiously a member of the Australian Natives Association, at that time growing rapidly from an association of young men aspiring vaguely to some kind of native public citizenship, to become, by 1890, the political springboard used by leaders like Alfred Deakin in Victoria to create the constituency needed before the Australian colonies could unite as the Commonwealth of Australia. South Australia was not the centre of ANA agitation, but it played a critical role when William Sowden, an Adelaide journalist and contemporary of Willshire's, initiated the ANA's Inter-Colonial Conference in January 1890. That meeting, chaired by John Bray, a former Premier of South Australia, first proposed the elements that later formed the Australian federal constitution, and, by one estimate, about forty percent of South Australian MPs were members. Willshire, according to one of his friends, delivered several "memorials" on Aboriginal subjects to the Association. Willshire's nationalism, like Frank Gillen's Irishism, was not anti-British. It sought to deepen the notion of what it meant to be British.[197]

By the measure of years spent in full-time schooling Willshire was much better educated than Justice William Bundey who was to preside at his trial in 1891 and had begun work at the age of ten, and better educated than Francis Gillen, JP, who was the master of the Overland Telegraph station at Alice Springs when he charged Willshire with wilful murder in April of the same year. Gillen had entered the service of the South Australian Post-Master General at the age of eleven, was three years younger than Willshire but by 1889 had been a Justice of the Peace for nine years and was in command of white men. As telegraph Station Master at Alice Springs he became the representative of all things official in the Centre, a Special Magistrate and later a Sub-Protector of Aborigines.

In 1883 Willshire's leadership of a search party gave him his first opportunity for notoriety in the south. The policeman replaced by Willshire at Alice Springs, Mounted Constable Shirley, was posted north to Barrow Creek. In November 1883, Shirley led a party of volunteers searching for a missing pastoralist, who was later found alive. Most members of the search party, including Shirley, were less fortunate, dying of thirst through inadequate knowledge of the local water sources. It fell to Willshire to retrieve and bury Shirley's body. Later he wrote a poem in which he imagined the experience of the dying men.

Oh, God! the hardships of that dire campaign!
Oh, God! the arid, blasted, burning plain!
Oh, God! the sweltering scrub, all waterless!
The fierce blue sky relentless overhead,
The baked earth cracking to their giddy tread,
No little cloud is seen to give them hope,
All nature one gigantic pyroscope.

Back on their tracks appalled they baffled push,
With fevered blood re-trace the trackless bush,
With cracked and swollen tongues, and throats ablaze,
And voices that a whisper scarce can raise,
With brains delirious and all infantile,
Their horses dropping lifeless every mile.
Down goes a steed, and there's a frenzied rush
To cut his throat, and drink the gory gush

until, by reaching the Telegraph, two of the party are saved.

So Giles is saved, by faithful black boy nursed,
To tell how comrades died of heat and thirst,
Oh, mourning mothers, sorrowing sisters true,
The heart of all Australia bleeds for you.[198]

Fortunately, from the point of view of this account, among Willshire's idiosyncrasies is "an inordinate love of notoriety", as one of his police colleagues in Alice Springs put it later. His early reports to his direct superior, Inspector Bryan Besley of Port Augusta – the depot town for the Centre – are introduced in the third-person: "Re Anna's Reservoir Natives & M.C. Willshire's trip to capture them", "Native Police taken to N Territory by M.C. Willshire Nov 1884", as if he is observing his own action from a distance. Police Commisioner Peterswald who has a sharp nose for tendencies to insubordination among his troops was not impressed and noted, when Besley forwarded the reports with approval, that he would have found them "a much more interesting narrative if the writer had not put himself so prominently forward." Willshire was never able to accept that the official accountability of the policeman made it prudent to stay as far out of the narratives of official reporting as possible.

Willshire's passion for contemplating himself is also expressed in a number of studio photographs in which he stars. In one, taken in Port Augusta in January 1888, he stands at the focus of a tableau formed by his native trackers and his colleague Mounted Constable Erwein Wurmbrand, all carefully arranged, Willshire with his hand raised to shade his eyes, as if from a blazing sun, staring into an imagined distance beyond the camera where his duty will take him. To be fair to Willshire, this photograph was taken, and possibly staged, by a commercial photographer with an interest in Aboriginal subjects who later used it on a post-card sold to the public. If the initiative for this photograph was not his, later photographs are less likely to have been accidents. In another, taken at another time, and captioned "the author and a boy native" Willshire sits dressed like a young dandy on regatta day, boater in his lap, in the studio's rustic log chair, while an Aboriginal boy of about eight years old, dressed like a fantasy of genteel boyhood, holds within Willshire's reach a tray of fruit. This tableau invites speculation, but Willshire's pretension to lordship is clear. Equally clear is his insensitivity to the feelings of those who are the subjects of his power, and an assumption that his audience will be impressed rather then repelled.[199]

In fact Willshire's satisfaction in his exercise of power was increased by the discomfort of his victims. In late 1885, returning from the Top End where he had delivered a party of Native Police recruited in the Centre, Willshire was accompanied by an adolescent Aboriginal boy he names "Jack Harrison". Defying the power of the old men, Willshire forced the partly-initiated boy to eat bush turkey, a delicacy strictly reserved for initiates: "to break down his superstitious fears I insisted, and stood over him while he slowly worked his jaws through the worst part of a turkey...". The boy died of a stomach complaint a few days after arriving in Alice Springs, a fact that Willshire reports twice in his account of the event, while not drawing the obvious connection.[200] In a similarly high-handed fashion Willshire led a group of Aboriginal women through Emily Gap near Alice Springs, an area forbidden to women, against the vehement opposition of some men nearby. "I cleared them [the men] out" he records, and the women "to my great astonishment, picked up some rags, bushes and grass and made coverings to their faces, and walked blindfolded, by the sound of the horse's footsteps and my black boy's voice, through the Gap...". According to a report collected recently from a man who was born ten years after this event, the women were later killed for their transgression, but there is no reason to believe that Willshire ever knew of this consequence, assuming it occurred.[201] However, Willshire's record of his pleasure in the death of Aboriginal men as a result of the attentions of his Aboriginal troopers, and possibly himself, in the years 1887-9, is as frankly sadistic as the circumstances are murky.[202] Nowhere in his writings is there a trace of remorse, or even concern, for the consequences, whether he intended them or not, of his exercise of power over Aboriginal people.

Many of the Centre's early residents and visitors engraved their names on the shaft of Chambers Pillar south of Alice Springs on the old track up from Adelaide, making it both a memorial of great historical significance and a gallery with emotional impact. Willshire was the only one to make his mark three times. In 1884 the recently-arrived Willshire inscribes "WHW 1884". By 1888 he engraves deeply, in capitals meant to last, "W H WILLSHIRE 1888".

Willshire's self-reporting falls into three distinct phases: Willshire the heroic frontier policeman, Willshire the ethnographer, frontier naturalist and reporter, and finally, after his expulsion from the Centre, Willshire the teller of frontier adventure stories. In none of these authorial roles did he succeed in winning the reputation he craved, but each of the roles he tried on represents an aspect of frontier life.

Within a year of Willshire's arrival in the Centre in 1882 the pace of pastoral occupation was reaching its climax. Large herds of livestock were being driven in drought years from the south and from Queensland to stock the leases to the south and north of Alice Springs, with colossal impacts on water supplies and pastures.

The police presence had been strengthened since the mid 1870s but Inspector Besley would not have forgotten the lesson of

1880 when Peterswald's predecessor as Police Commissioner had reprimanded Besley for not making it clear to settlers that they "must do something to protect themselves, and not ... rely only on the Police".[203] In this highly-charged atmosphere Willshire fell into the role of the heroic frontier policeman, surviving hardship, thirst and hostile Aborigines to become, in his own mind and occasionally in the minds of others, the hammer of the blacks and a pillar of white settlement.

Anna's Reservoir station north east of Alice Springs was in 1884 part of a holding of 52,000 square kilometres, nine times the size of Hermannsburg lease, stretching up to Barrow Creek. By the middle of 1884 its owners, three established businessmen in Adelaide, had stocked it with 5000 cattle and a lesser number of camels and horses. Most of the station's stockmen were working at an outstation when the two hands left at the homestead were attacked by an estimated 150 Unmatjera men. The two whites were seriously injured but escaped to join their colleagues.

Willshire was detailed to lead an expedition comprising two police, four station workers and two Aboriginal police trackers. According to his report written to Inspector Bryan Besley and dated September 17th 1884, they set out "over range after range" until on the seventh day a recently-deserted camp was discovered. Willshire stressed that although water was so short that their horses on one occasion went three days without a drink, meaning the whole party was in peril, he continued the pursuit relentlessly. The pace of the narrative increased as a sleeping Aboriginal camp was approached surreptitiously at night. At first light "we made a rush full gallop up some small hills and observed the natives running up with weapons in hand ... [I] soon had 6 bailed up and our trackers telling them to drop their spears but they said the[y] would not and sent about a dozen 10 feet spears whizzing at us one entering the trackers horse's fore arm they were then climbing on big rocks and I dismounted with a pair of handcuffs in my hand and went straight for club foot who turned smartly and struck me with his boomerang he then jumped on some rocks and was escaping when a bullet from a snider rifle brought him to the ground ... after the affray ...one of the trackers told me he had shot Slim Jim dead this was good news to me knowing that Slim Jim was the leader at the burning of the Station and also the principal ringleader of cattle killers also the native who stood throwing spears at Figg when he was being burned alive in this attack some bucks got away without being wounded I believe there were about 100 women and children around us when the fight was over all yabbering away at the same time I marched the whole lot off the range and made them show us where the water was all my party were manly fellows and treated the Lubras and piccanninnies with kindness we then discharged them". The account goes on without pause to describe the party's pursuit of suspected cattle killers through the ranges until "the notorious cattle killer Jimmy Mullins was brought down by a Spencer rifle the rest narrowly escaped the same fate...". Three lines later "another batch of niggers was seen among them was "Boko" for whom I held a warrant... my tracker was in a terrible rage at being got at by a wild nigger so he levelled his rifle and Mr Boko came toppling down from Rock to rock and landed at the trackers feet...they don't care about death a bit...I worked 30 days at the Annas Reservoir Station and believe now that party and self have done some good which ought to stop cattle killing for a time anyhow." And here he allows himself the leisure of a full-stop for only the second time since the pursuit began at Anna's Reservoir, four closely-written pages previously.

While the economy of Willshire's punctuation may be related to the fact that his report had been previously telegraphed to Adelaide, the style appears to owe more to the Western than to standard police reporting, suggesting what his leisure reading may have been. It contains, besides the overwhelming presence of the Willshire ego, a number of elements worth noting. In places there is a punctiliousness about the protocol: the Aborigines threaten him before one is shot; although the heroic Willshire is at the forefront of the action and suffers assault with a boomerang, the fatal shots are fired by others, either Aboriginal trackers or anonymous whites, possibly because Willshire's hands are occupied with the handcuffs. In another place "Mr Boko" is not shot without a warrant (although Willshire in 1891 lied about having a warrant for the men for whose killings he was arrested) but dies for no greater crime than attempting to escape arrest while under suspicion of cattle killing (and dies in a manner that suggests that the cinematic form of the Western had already been developed). Later, in total disregard of any protocol, Jimmy Mullins was summarily executed simply because Willshire believed he was guilty of cattle-killing, and other nameless "bucks" escape the same fate only by good luck.[204]

We know of Willshire's leisure reading only that he followed the Adelaide papers and admired both the [Sydney] *Bulletin* and the fiction of Rider Haggard and Ernest Favenc. It is worth bearing in mind, however, that by 1883 Buffalo Bill Cody, an army scout in the Indian wars in the United States, had achieved fame as the representative personality of their western frontier. In that same year he took his Wild West Show to Europe and soon became the most famous American, performing in private for Queen Victoria in 1887. The key to the success of Cody and of his Show was that he played himself and continued working as an army scout throughout the 1870s, performing on stage in the off-scouting seasons. His Indians also played themselves, combining reality and fiction in a way that had such strong appeal that audiences could overlook the dreadful melodramas in which they performed. If there was a voice, and an image, for a young, vain, Australian frontiersman, with his eye on the metropolitan audience, to have in his head, Bill Cody could provide it. It is unlikely the exuberant imagery of Buffalo Bill's performances had similar appeal to most other Australian frontiersmen, but Willshire was egregious, and heroic explorers and drovers weren't the only models available for imitation.[205]

Willshire's Anna's Reservoir report leaves us ignorant of what happened beyond the personal reach of Willshire. From his evidence of the 1891 killlings, it is unsafe to accept his own word even for his direct involvement in these killings, although as the policeman in charge he was accountable in a fuller sense than the other men. The punitive party consisted of six white men and Aboriginal trackers, all well armed, the whites with rifles and probably with revolvers and the trackers with rifles. Is it plausible that in that climate of fear, hatred and excitement only three Aboriginal men died and none was wounded? Is it plausible that even savages like these 'wild Aborigines' would counter-attack against a rush of armed and mounted men, and then be "bailed up" by the attackers?

As a report from a man who is admitting at least a collaborative role in multiple homicide the document would have been wildly imprudent in a climate less dominated by a generalised alarm about the security of the white people of the Centre. The climate was also influenced by recent events in the Top End where four white men had recently been murdered on the Daly River. This was a world apart from Central Australia but much closer to it in the vague geography of the southerner's imagination where both Centre and Top End seemed equally distant and dangerous. While the style of Willshire's report is unique to him, the sequence of cause and effect leading to the killing of Aborigines is found also in the reports of his police colleagues.

In fact, both Willshire's superiors knew they were reading a romance constructed to paper over the ugly reality of a punitive raid that had killed suspected offenders in order to discourage the survivors. They may well have believed that the number of victims was that implied by Willshire's account, but the editing of Willshire's report before it reached the newspapers reveals that Besley knew that the killing had gone beyond law and policy.

The *Observer* on Saturday September 20th 1884 reproduces a report attributed by Inspector Besley to Willshire. It covers the same incidents, but is not the same report. It not only leaves out much that might provide grounds for action against Willshire and his fellow raiders, but also adds authenticating detail to produce a story that is far more disciplined, and credible than Willshire's own. The word "nigger", commonly used on the frontier, by the friends of the Aborigines as well as their enemies, is deleted. The Aborigine Jimmy Mullins, whom Willshire says he killed for no greater offence than being a "notorious cattle killer" is found by Besley, or Peterswald, to be "concerned in the burning of the [Anna's Reservoir] station, and to have been "shot dead on the side of the range".

Curiously, the Besley-Peterwald re-write of Willshire adds an incident that was just as likely in 1884 to provoke outrage among the morally sensitive as it would be today. He/they write: "On the 24th August we came on a camp in which there were four lubras and some children only twenty miles from Benstead's present camp and 30 miles west of Anna's Reservoir. We took them into custody to prevent them from warning others whom we wanted. This proved to be a good plan. Through fear these old lubras gave us the information we wanted." In Willshire's report his party stumbles onto the Aborigines' camp shortly after they have abandoned it. They "found five puppies and any amount of weapons we burnt and smashed them all up and killed the dogs", and only dealt with women and children after the attack had finished. "I marched the whole lot down off the range and made them show us where the water was all my party were manly fellows and treated the Lubras and piccaninnies with kindness". It seems perverse to delete Willshire's unkindness to dogs, frequently accused of tormenting cattle, while inserting mistreatment of women.

The Besley-Peterswald revision of Willshire's account saved them all from another embarrassment. Immediately above it in the *Observer* is a report of a "private" letter from Billy Benstead, then managing Anna's Reservoir, communicated by the master of the Alice Springs Telegraph Station, Mr Flint. "They [the police party] were close up [to the Aborigines they were pursuing] when the water failed, and the party returned to station where they stayed a day getting fresh horses". This Mounted Constable Willshire of Benstead's report was the prudent Willshire who made sure of his water supplies, not the William Willshire of his own report, the one he wanted the world to see, who would risk death by thirst to get his man.

Besley and Peterswald might have justified to themselves unleashing, or, at least, condoning, an act of terror as the lesser of two evils. To them the greater evil was either uncontrolled revenge-taking by the stockmen or the collapse of pastoral enterprises in this part of the Centre, political dynamite for their governments and therefore for them. If that was their reasoning, it is hard to see in retrospect that pure vigilante justice could have been more murderous than vigilante justice under police leadership.

The accounts of Willshire the heroic frontier policeman were written to his superior officer in Port Augusta, Bryan Besley, but they found their public audience through the Adelaide newspapers. It is remarkable how soon after these reports of frontier incidents were received in the south they were published, often within a week of the incident itself. The Ministers controlled the gate between official discretion and publication, as far as police reporting was concerned, and one matter at least was marked "not for press"; the report from Mounted Constable Wurmbrand on his expeditions against the Western Aranda on Glen Helen.

Willshire won command of the new force of Native Police established by the South Australian government at the end of 1884 partly on the basis of his leadership of the punitive party that rode out from Anna's Reservoir. But he was directed to set up a squad of Native Police not because of the violence around Alice Springs, but in response to the threatening situation in the Top End where, on September 3rd, four copper miners on the Daly River had been killed in an attack that was considered by the whites to be completely unprovoked.[206] A squad of Central Australian Aboriginal men was wanted to police the Aborigines of the Top End. Most of 1885, Willshire spent either in the Top End with his squad, or travelling between the Centre and the Top End.

It was only later, in 1885, and as an afterthought, that Peterswald decided that Aboriginal trackers remaining in Alice Springs "should be classed as Native Police & you had better give them fresh names. Their own take up too much time to write..."[207] Besley's reply confirmed that "Kupannanga [was] now called Fred...".

As William Willshire leaves Alice Springs for the Top End, no longer just remote from supervision but floating between the jurisdictions of Inspectors Besley and Foelsche, it is timely to recall that the patrolling Mounted Constable of the Centre was a species of explorer. He, like the early drovers, filled in the large gaps between the tracks mapped by the earlier explorers. The possibilities of the role were not lost on William Willshire.

Settlers on the frontiers had privileged access to knowledge that was valued by people in the metropolises of the colonies, and in Europe. These members of the second rank to enter new lands could only hope to achieve a lower order of fame than the explorers, but reputations could still be built on describing what the explorers had merely passed by. A number of the independent spirits who settled the frontier were people of high intelligence, well-read and in touch with the intellectual issues of the day. From the ranks of such people came authors of diaries and pamphlets, and collectors for the professional and amateur scholars inhabiting the growing Australian universities, museums, botanical gardens and scientific societies.

It was on the knowledge he gained of Aboriginal customs while patrolling with his troopers that Willshire based his next campaign for social advancement in the Colony. Among the audience for writings on the Aboriginal peoples of the Centre were two that could be found easily, the scientific and the prurient. Only the approval of those who took a scientific interest in frontier matters could enhance an author's social standing. When Willshire returned from the Top End at the end of 1885 the Geographical Society of Australasia, South Australian Branch, had just been formed. It was a government-subsidized forum for those with a serious interest in the new lands and peoples of the Colony, and the new technologies that might be applied to them, an approach from which they expected much practical advantage. From that time to the time of his forced departure south in 1891 Willshire's target was the scientific interests of the gentlemen (and one lady) of the Society. The Society's work, like that of its less exploration-minded but older sibling, the Royal Society of South Australia, was led by the small number of tertiary-educated professional people, such as Dr Edward Stirling, the Director of the South Australian Museum. It provided a meeting ground on which those who invested successfully in knowledge might meet on equal terms with those who had invested their capital successfully or possessed the power of public office. It was the cream of the Colony's intellectual life and of Colonial society, an intersection of money, power and intelligence. James Willshire would have loved an invitation to join them. His son William came to think he was entitled to one.

The professional scholars in Australia formed close collaborations with frontiersmen and travellers who could bring them the raw material for research. Scholars could afford to spend only a limited time in the Centre. The intelligent frontiersman might be satisfied at first to feed the city scholar for payment in footnotes and species names, but long-term relationships were better founded on collaboration. Baron Ferdinand von Mueller, the leading plant taxonomist of the Colonies, was a champion collaborator. In 1880 and 1882 the work he based on missionary Kempe's collecting, totalling 287 species, was published in their joint names by the Royal Society of South Australia, although the writing was clearly von Mueller's. Kempe was elected a Corresponding Member of the Society.[208] Von Mueller also supplied Hermannsburg with seeds of vegetables for its kitchen gardens.

The ethnographer in Adelaide might correspond with the leaders of scholarship in Britain, as Stirling corresponded with the leading anthropologist J G Frazer, author of the classic *The golden bough*, but the frontiersman had the advantage of them both. The life of the Centre's Aboriginal people could not be bottled in preserving fluid and sent by camel train and rail back to Adelaide, where the scholar could describe it at his leisure. Even at the camps that sprang up at pastoral and telegraph stations and missions the life of the Aborigines had been quickly tainted by the presence of the white colonists, and much of Aboriginal thinking withheld. What the scholar saw was largely what the frontiersman arranged for him to see, or reported to him second-hand. When the Horn Expedition arrived at Tempe Downs in 1894 the corroboree it saw was not an event initiated by the local people, but a special show induced by Frederick Thornton, by then the station's owner. The very nature of ethnography demands a greater contribution in interpretation by the observer and the metropolitan expert would have been a fool not to recognise it. Professor Ralph Tate of the University of Adelaide, Fellow of the Geographical Society (of London) was such a fool. In 1880 he exhibited to a meeting of the Royal Society of South Australia two "implements" sent to him by Mr Canham of Stuart's Creek and asserted dogmatically that the "figures" found on them could not possibly have any symbolic function since they demonstrated a symmetry that was characteristic of purely decorative work. In any case "To further speculate on their meaning", he considered, "must be labour thrown away, and he very much doubted if they can be regarded as the productions of the untutored Aboriginal".[209]   Clearly, the field of enquiry remained open, but for how much longer?

In 1886, after he had spent six months leave in Adelaide, Hermann Kempe's observations on the Western Aranda were communicated to the Geographical Society by the mission's friend in Parliament, Friedrich Krichauff, and in Krichauff's name. By 1891, Louis Schulze, wrote in his own name, as did Kempe to a German audience. So William Willshire's ambition to speak in his own voice about the Aboriginal people of the Centre was ambitious but not unreasonable.

The trigger for Willshire was the publication in the Adelaide *Observer* in September 1886 of a report of a discussion at the Geographical Society, then at the apogee of its public standing. Its Council included the immensely wealthy pastoral and mining investor, Thomas Elder, Charles Todd, the hero of the Overland Telegraph and Friedrich Krichauff. Of its 79 members at the beginning of that year, three were members of the House of Assembly, including one of the Colony's occasional Premiers, J C

Bray. At the end of the year came the news that Queen Victoria had assented to the addition of "Royal" to the Society's name. Not bad for a two year-old organisation, and one in the eye for the older Royal Society of South Australia, but all was not well. The members, of whom half were in arrears with their subscriptions, showed themselves reluctant to attend general meetings, especially when the speakers were not explorers but scholars whose fascination with taxonomy and detailed description was not shared by all. Nevertheless, as long as the Government's subvention of £100 more than doubled the subscriptions of its financial members, the Society had a future. In fact it continues today, a handsome relic of nineteenth Century scientific amateurism.

Despite his willingness to countenance their violent deaths, Willshire's interest in Aboriginal people is beyond dispute. The men who deigned to pay attention to ideas and customs of the Aborigines were exceptional. In the Centre at this time we can identify Frank Gillen, the three Hermannsburg missionaries, the pastoralist and explorer Charles Chewings and Paddy Byrne of Charlotte Waters Telegraph Station. Willshire's ethnography and grasp of local languages now appear very limited, but they were based on some close observation and were valued highly at the time. Like other practical men, Willshire paid attention to the pragmatics of Aboriginal society that were not of interest to the missionaries and anthropologists, whose field was the content of the mind and their material culture. Willshire understood earlier than most the way Aboriginal religion served the social and economic interests of the men, to take one example. In 1895, after the visit of the Horn Expedition to Central Australia, and four years after Willshire's departure from the Centre, Edward Stirling, the Director of the Adelaide Museum, published in the leading British journal Willshire's ethnographic details of the Central Australian peoples as part of a survey conducted by J G Fraser[210]. This is after Frank Gillen had established his claims as ethnographer of the Central Australian peoples in the eyes of the Horn Expedition scientists, and had begun the collaboration with Baldwin Spencer that was to make both men famous. The anonymous writer on Aborigines in the 1907 *Cyclopedia of South Australia* quoted Willshire extensively, and naively, and at least one local historian of the Top End relied on Willshire's account of Aborigines of that district in a publication in the 1990s. Willshire and his contemporaries all found their capacity for understanding circumscribed by their criticism of Aboriginal ideas and behaviour, but the amateur and professional ethnographers except Willshire achieved a condescending sympathy for the position in which the Aborigines now found themselves. He was capable of strong feelings about the Aboriginal people he associated with, but rarely found room for sympathy.

The Society's was but one of a number of calls made over the years for the colonists to record the ways and the words of the Aboriginal citizens before they died out as a distinct people. It encouraged Willshire "to persevere in his researches and to arrange the materials which he had collected, with a view to their publication ... on his first return to regions of civilization."[211] By the time Willshire arrived back in Alice Springs from the Top End, the Adelaide newspapers waiting for him would have included reports of three remarkable 'corroborees' held in Adelaide.

Willshire sees, forming in the mirror he holds constantly up to his existence, the image of a new persona, that of the frontier reporter and amateur scientist, a man worthy of the educated and the wealthy gentlemen who populate the Geographical Society. He began writing his first booklet, *The Aborigines of Central Australia*, printed in 1888 in Port Augusta, while he was in his sixth year in the Centre. It records the William Willshire of the Alice Springs years in a style that is sober to the point of dullness. He can not refrain from telling the story of his part in the recovery of Mounted Constable Shirley's party, but does it without melodrama. Nor can he leave out his version of the story of the Barrow Creek conflict of 1874, but confines it to an Appendix. By the standards of his later writings, this author is on tranquillisers.

Still, while this booklet is part dry description of the pastoral stations of the frontier and part ethnography of its Aboriginal peoples, it is all the story of William Willshire. Considering the paucity of the ethnography of the Centre before the visit of the Horn Expedition in 1894, and the limited scope of the missionaries' observations from the banks of the Finke at Hermannsburg, most of it still not published in English, Willshire's scanty reporting gave him a standing among the lay public and a reputation he played for all he could extract from it. It was not enough, however, to gain him admission to the company of the gentlemen of the Geographical Society.

Perhaps Willshire also wrote too much, in another sense. He could not refrain from accounts of his work as frontier policeman, with all its baggage of worrying moral questions. He later recognised the cause of this declension in his writing, but was unable to stifle it: "...if I abandon it [his dealings with Aborigines] and its exciting incidents I cannot write enough to keep myself warm" he was to write in 1896, during his last posting to the frontier, this time at the Top End. But not even the public shame of his trial for murder at Port Augusta in 1891 was able to expunge his sense of grievance that the gentlemen of Adelaide had neglected the merits of William Willshire the frontier scholar. In his 1891 revision of *The Aborigines of Central Australia* he reveals it openly: "I do this for the good of my country - South Australia - and for the benefit of the Geographical Society and the Australian Natives Association, two admirable institutions... of the former with all my years' plodding across unknown portions of the vast Central Australia, I have not come under their notice yet. Perhaps this is because I have no influence in that direction."

But there are other ways than science to gain social distinction. There are also wealth and power.

Willshire had before him several possible ways to grow rich. He could continue the steady accumulation from the various streams of income available to the frontier policeman. Apart from his salary there were the allowances. A number of Colonial officials made the difference between the income level they shared with their peers and something notably better through allowances. Willshire's supervisor, Inspector Bryan Besley in Port Augusta, received £50 *per annum* as Sub-Protector of Aborigines, making him better off than Inspectors senior to him in rank but without significant populations of Aborigines in their domains. Tom Daer at Charlotte Waters got an allowance as a Customs Inspector. While he was at Alice Springs Willshire's allowances for travel and rations, at six shillings and six pence per day, almost matched his pay of eight shillings and eight pence. If he travelled for three quarters of the year, as he did, he could earn £204/17/6. Had money been Willshire's principal motive he might have noticed in November 1888, while he was considering

Besley's invitation to take charge of the new Police Patrol for the Interior, that his new, higher pay rate of ten shillings per day was going to leave him poorer, because he would no longer be eligible for travel allowance. Having accepted the new job he began complaining about the injustice of it. The grievance was still on a new Minister's table when Willshire was arrested two years later. "This has reached the office in an irregular manner" John Gordon's successor as Minister, David Bews, noted cryptically on the file in February 1891, a week before he died.[212]

The largest streams of gold to which a frontier policeman had access sprang from their association with Aborigines as trackers and Native Constables, or as prisoners and witnesses. The twenty one shillings to which each of Willshire's trackers or Constables were entitled each week in 1889 was paid directly into Willshire's bank account in Adelaide. Four trackers were worth 200 guineas per year in pay, plus £30 in ration allowance, all paid into Willshire's account. Since the Aboriginal assistants were equipped with police rifles and police cartridges, which were in plentiful supply, they could be expected to supplement their dry rations with game, and it was hardly necessary for Willshire to pay them all, or any, of their allowances, especially if no senior police officer ever visited the Centre to acquaint the Constables with their entitlements. The rewards of police service for Aboriginal men, in status, power, women, clothing, weapons, dignity and living conditions, already far exceeded those available to Aboriginal people from pastoral work. How much of the money paid to Willshire each year while he had four or six Native Constables went instead into his pocket? We don't know, but he did think the "half-educated black ... a scheming systematic loafer, who is not contented with food and clothing as his less instructed brother is, but begins to want money - as if it would be of any service to him away from some of the haunts of white men."[213] If the Constables or trackers didn't like it, there were others anxious to take their place, as the turnover in Willshire's Aboriginal assistants suggests.

Aboriginal prisoners and witnesses brought a double benefit. The policeman got a trip south to the bright lights of Port Augusta, even Adelaide, plus the net benefit of the allowance paid for the subsistence of the Aborigines. At the end of Willshire's trip to Port Augusta, in early 1888, a note still held between the leaves of the Police Station Journal records that Willshire was paid £12 for 240 meals for witnesses King and Jimmy, and that "we have no other records".[214]

How much might Willshire have made from all this? The enquiry of Commissioner W E Roth into conditions in the north-west of Western Australia in 1904 recorded that at a rate of "one shilling and six pence halfpenny to two shillings daily per head" Constable J Wilson received £462/2/7 between March 1902 and October 1903 from allowances for prisoners and witnesses alone. Among Wilson's police colleagues in the north-west a benefit of less than £200 per year from this trade was unusual. That is, a policeman could double his salary, before deducting what he actually spent on his prisoners. Unsurprisingly, the system of allowances created a powerful incentive to arrest more rather than fewer suspected cattle-killers (and to shoot fewer) and to shanghai as many witnesses as possible. Children made good witnesses, tractable and cheap to maintain. Young women witnesses provided also sexual benefits for the police and trackers, while benefiting from easier treatment and freedom from arrest.[215] So were Aboriginal men, women and children turned into commodities, and a frontier policeman could become significantly richer than his city comrades by trading them. The social environment in Central Australia was different. It seems that in the Centre the police trade in Court fodder was much less developed than it became later on the north west coast of Western Australia. Perhaps the police of the Centre were pioneers in this business. We can conclude that Willshire's total income was, at the least, more than double his police salary, making him richer than his immediate superior, Bryan Besley. [216]

The Police Patrol for the Interior based at Boggy Water was, in effect, an out-sourcing contract let to William Willshire. He received, by the calculus set out above, all equipment and materials, and a sum equivalent to the pay of a senior public official in the Province. In return he was expected to pacify the pastoralists of the Finke region. It was an idea before its time. Official Adelaide was uncomfortable with it. Following their experience with Willshire, the accountants in the Audit Office in Adelaide took a closer interest in how police funds were spent on the frontier, imposing procedures to make this kind of thieving more difficult, such as the direct payment of Native Constables' wages.

There were other ways to accumulate capital while in police service. Pastoralism was one. It was common practice on stations to allow a pastoral worker to run a few stock with the station herds, a kind of profit-sharing. Before arriving at Alice Springs, Mounted Constable South was fined for running his private horses on police pasture, but it is unlikely that Inspector Besley had any serious intention of stopping the practice. If you visit your subordinates but rarely it is as well to find something amiss to keep them on their toes. Years later, in 1894 when the Horn Expedition visited the Centre, South was able to lend them enough of his own horses to make a side trip that would not otherwise have been possible.[217] Whatever pasture these horses fed and bred on, it did not belong to William South. Even a missionary could take part in this interstitial capitalism. Wilhelm Schwarz offered to sell the mission Committee his blood mare and two thoroughbred foals for £65, equal to five years of his pay as a missionary. (Heidenreich offered him £50. It is not recorded whether or not the sale went through).[218]

And then, for the optimists and the grandiose, there was prospecting and investment in mining. Mining had made enormous fortunes for the fortunate few who were in on the ground floor of the great finds of the nineteenth Century. Copper exceeded gold in importance for South Australia, but South Australians were also investors in the gold rushes of the eastern Colonies, and in the colossal iceberg of silver and lead at Broken Hill, just over the border in New South Wales. In Central Australia mining made no-one rich at this time, but in this bare-boned land any observant man could turn into a prospector in an instant, and the expectation of wealth waited in every man's heart to be excited by the smallest sign of a valuable mineral. In the 1890s Frank Gillen blew enough money on speculations on the Arltunga gold field east of Alice Springs to have kept him and his widow comfortably in a retirement he did not himself live to see. Billy Abbott spent time on the Ruby field east of Alice Springs in 1888 and described himself as a "prospector" to Frank Gillen and justice Bundey in 1891, while his peers called him a knockabout station worker. He also spent time at Boggy Water, where Willshire employed him, using government funds, in building his substantial establishment there. It is possible that Willshire was also grub-staking Abbott's prospecting along the upper Finke. If so, the Minister responsible for the Northern Territory was an involuntary partner in the enterprise. We also know that Willshire was in partnership with a Dick Smith, the object of which was, more than likely, winning the gemstones or gold found east of Alice Springs.

The Ministers of government and the Police Commissioner in Adelaide could hardly complain if the men on the frontier had their eyes open for a golden opportunity, because so did their masters. In August 1887 Erwein Wurmbrand spent two weeks on the ruby fields collecting specimens, on instruction from Inspector Bryan Besley in Port Augusta. And when Mounted Constable Joseph East, a policeman stationed in Adelaide, accompanied by invitation a private expedition to the ruby and gold fields in 1888, his report to his Minister, titled *Second report on the MacDonnell Range country*, made no references whatever to matters of public order or policing. It was a geological report from a man who was transferred two years later to the South Australian School of Mines. It was not published.[219]

Travelling south down the Elder Creek, Joseph East passed the claim of the "Lindsay Co.", substantially owned by surveyor David Lindsay who was employed by the South Australian government to cut up prospective country into mineral leases. Further to the east were claims reputed to be rich in gold and "now before the public as the 'Wheal Fortune Gold Mining Co." In 1891 William Willshire reported he owned shares in Wheal Fortune, but thought he could realise no more than one shilling each for them. He should have sold while he could. All that financial investors ever reaped from the gold and 'rubies' of the Centre, at that time, was bankruptcy.[220]

By the time Willshire was faced with the expense of his trial in 1891 he had accumulated enough to acquire suburban land in Adelaide, to own 17 horses and to lend Mounted Constable William South £70.[221] That is, Willshire had enough capital to give serious thought to ways of increasing it more rapidly in future, to join the South Australian business of turning small capital into much more. And plenty to fuel fantasy. In 1891 the big-capital pastoralists of the city like the Tempe Downs Pastoral Company were two dry years away from exhausting their capital or their taste for losses, even if Charles Chewings did not recognise it in February of that year. John Gordon had already lost his money. The era of the pastoralist-manager, with little capital but sweat equity, was dawning.

Frederick Thornton moved up to ownership in 1893-4; no doubt Willshire considered it too, but 1890 was three years too soon. More to the point, cattle produce too little spiritual meat to satisfy the appetite of a man in the grip of a monstrous vanity. William Willshire needed power and he needed a spotlight.

Willshire hated subordination, but he loved the social standing of the mounted policeman and the fuel it provided for his dreams of power. On the other hand, if one could, as a policeman, be also the master of a large estate, and of a hundred or two Aboriginal people, perhaps that would be enough.

Willshire did indeed think that he possessed the formula for managing Aboriginal people on the frontier. It was simple: they needed firmness and kindness, that is to say, paternalistic authority, rations, and a reduced burden of expectations. They were not capable of understanding Christianity he thought, in the company of many including Gillen and Baldwin Spencer. He returns to this theme several times in his 1896 booklet, *The land of the dawning*, and appeals for financial support from the charitable to make such a secular mission possible.[222]

I have seen that you can make the blacks tractable and docile, but you must be firm and kind with them. ...I should like to have a depot formed, and to have them brought together and fed. ... it would be worth while getting them together and doing something for them on Christian principles. Be liberal for once and do a good turn to a lot of poor, houseless, naked creatures. Teach them to take care of their parents and children, to work in the garden and cultivate vegetables for their maintenance, and, above all, teach them not to kill and eat each other. ...I am impressed with the importance of this matter ... They [on the Victoria River] are in the full vigour of their primitive state, and all I advocate now is kindly give us the means to calm their savage nature and good results will be recorded. The details of formation, should action be taken, could be supplied by me, viz., geographical position, distances from seaport and stations, cost of transport by land and water, requisition for necessary supplies &c.

There is no evidence that he took this proposal further than written reverie, and on the evidence of his character it is hard to see him appealing successfully to any branch of metropolitan charity. But there is no reason to doubt him when he tells us that while at

Boggy Water he provided rations from his own pocket, filled from public funds (although his valuation of £300 may be an exaggeration), that he was more tolerant of Aboriginal ways than the missionaries, and that he performed a marriage ceremony for at least one couple. Willshire is here telling a part of the truth about his time at Boggy Water, and much about himself.[223] Willshire, like Wilhelm Schwarz, knew where the largest concentrations of unsettled Aboriginal people were; in the James Ranges west of Tempe Downs. When the Finke River mission's heathen-Christian women found the missionaries' discipline intolerable, it was to William Willshire's camp at Boggy Water that they turned for refuge.

This aspect of Willshire's motivation, the secular missionary or reserve manager, is easily dismissed in the light of his earlier and later activities. Considering his open advocacy of violence, his celebration of the violence and the sexual exploitation practised by his men – and by implication himself – in *The land of the dawning*, it is hard to give it weight. But the Willshire of 1896 is six years older, a survivor of a murder trial that had destroyed his hopes of advancement in the south, and now appealing in his writings not to the Adelaide gentry but to another audience altogether, the readership of the popular nationalist magazine *The Bulletin*, whose writers took the bush and its inhabitants as their subject and muse, defending both against the Anglophilic metropolis. This was the stage on which Willshire saw himself as he wrote and dreamed in 1895. William Willshire, popular teller of the stories of his own adventures, a bard of the bush, and the guide and guardian of the Aboriginal people. The evidence of Boggy Water is that Willshire's dreams of paternal authority preceded his dreams of popular literary success. Whoever said that paternal authority could not be corrupt?

A final piece of evidence supporting the conclusion that Willshire's idea of a secular mission was more than a fantasy passing through his mind in 1895. The station he set up at Boggy Water in 1889 was in two parts. His own small living area with attached, smaller rooms, presumably for storage, were built with walls of upright timbers sealed by mud, floored with flags of the local sedimentary stone, and roofed with a thatch of reeds from the lagoon. Today the stone chimney and flags remain, with some of the timbers in the last stages of decay. Four hundred metres away are the remains of an identically-constructed building with an external fireplace used for cooking. The reason for the location of this building can be inferred from the following passage: "Drastic measures are not necessary, but on the first formation of the [feeding] depot they would have to camp away from the man in charge ...".[224]   Whatever else Willshire put within this socially-distanced construction, possibly including horse and camel harness, the building was large, at seven metres by five it was bigger than his own building, which had its own store-room attached, and bigger by a factor of two or more than the store room at Illamurta Springs, where two Mounted Constables and their Aboriginal associates later lived. The fireplace shows that this second building was to serve accommodation as well as storage, although it is likely that most of Willshire's entourage preferred to sleep outside most of the time. This large building was built by Billy Abbott for £14 paid from the Northern Territory budget.[225]

While Billy Abbott was working on Willshire's new station buildings, Willshire wrote to Inspector Besley asking for Boggy Water to be made a rationing centre; "there is at present no less than seven blind and lame aboriginals at my camp besides many others aged, and more or less infirm". He wanted a ton or half a ton of rations to dole out, noting that "cattle killing on the surrounding stations is somewhat due to this that the younger of the tribes go out and kill a beast & bring it to the old ones who cannot get about... it would materially assist me in my duties as the elder natives have a wonderful influence over the younger portion of the tribe." It was a good idea, and the Protector of Aborigines supported it, provided it was paid for by the Minister for the Northern Territory. The man occupying that position at the time, John Gordon, was also paying the Finke River mission for the same purpose and was not going to pay for a second station thirty kilometres away. At that moment, February 1890, Gordon had good reason, by his own lights, to prefer a police rationing centre to the mission, but he was not yet in a position to transfer the funding. He noted on the file, "unless sick people receive shelter from the mission people no subsidy should be paid to them".[226]

Within a year of Willshire's establishment of the Boggy Water camp, in 1890, the idea of reserves to which Aboriginal people would be confined by law and under the control of police had been placed on the government agenda by the Swan-Taplin enquiry.

There were already precedents elsewhere, in stations motivated by Christian beliefs of their founder but not under the control of anyone except him. One of them, Warrangesda in New South Wales, later the Brewarrina mission, was set up by John Gribble, a compulsive creator of reserves who was even less tolerant of subordination than Willshire but was bold enough to strike out on his own.

The Mounted Constables in Central Australia at this time lived a life of constant travelling. From 1887 there were frequent shorter trips to the ruby and gold fields that had just opened up to the east of Alice Springs, and to the inside stations of Undoolya and Owen Springs, sometimes to deal with issues that had to be resolved without the aid of police on the outside stations. Most of Willshire's time was spent on the longer journeys for which, at this time, camels were employed exclusively. He was at Charlotte Waters on the border of South Australia proper three times in 1888, and in October and November spent six weeks at Tempe Downs and adjoining properties. In fact, in the whole of 1888 Willshire spent only twelve weeks at his base camp at Heavitree Gap, at the southern entrance to the present town of Alice Springs. Since the white policemen never travelled together, this meant that for three quarters of that year William Willshire was constantly in the company of his Aboriginal companions, and only them. Their visits to stations along their track rarely lasted more than one night. It was a life for men who could be content with their own company and that of people who could share little with them, who could live for months with heat, dirt, sweat, loneliness, bad food, discomfort and some danger, and then look forward to doing it again within days of returning to base. The white Mounted Constable was at least as nomadic as an Aboriginal man living a traditional lifestyle, and much further from family. It was a life beyond police training, beyond the experience of anyone in the metropolis, beyond the tolerance even of most frontier workers.

By 1887 the scale of cattle-killing, and its character, had changed from 1883-5. Tempe Downs was the newest station on the upper Finke. On the others, accommodations had been reached with the residual populations of Aboriginal peoples. Glen Helen, being, like Tempe Downs, an outside station had a more volatile mix of local, transient and immigrating groups to deal with. With the partial exception of those two stations, and Erldunda further to the south - and it is only a partial exception - the old techniques of dispersal were simply no longer relevant. A substantial part of the resident populations was dependent on station work and rations, and the stations were increasingly dependent on their labour. Those men who continued cattle-killing did so in more considered ways, knowing the risks and how to avoid them, and balancing those against the need for food and their preferred life-styles. We have already seen how Ereminta moved between station work and cattle-killing. He was not the only one.

On Owen Springs there were two notorious cattle-killers, known in the record as Billy Cloud and Melon Charlie. On August 26th 1886, Telegraph Station master Flint, who was inspecting the line south of Alice Springs, wired from Owen Springs that these two were threatening to kill tracker Wilkie, who was accompanying him at the time. Flint demanded that Willshire come and arrest them. It was, going by the date, one of these two Owen Springs men, the one called Jukutauljaka according to Moses Tjalkabota, who speared Tekua when he arrived with Hermann Kempe's family, returning from Adelaide. Willshire went to Owen Springs, but could only report that the men had escaped. While Willshire was not in the practice of making arrests, the survival of the two men is evidenced by another wire on January 22nd 1887 from Charles Gall, the manager of Owen Springs, complaining that they were killing cattle again. Again Willshire attended Owen Springs without result. In April 1888 Gall again complains about Billy Cloud and Melon Charlie, and Mounted Constable Hillier attends, again without result. These Aboriginal men challenged the reputation of the mounted police and their Aboriginal assistants. Willshire blustered that he would catch up with them, and indeed he did, in a sense. Billy Cloud was in the river bed at Hermannsburg in July 1890, when Willshire was presenting his evidence to the Swan-Taplin enquiry, in the best of health and a "reformed character", at least for the time being.

For this kind of cattle-killing dispersal of any degree was simply useless. The only answer was to arrest, punish or kill the perpetrators. It seems, from the limited evidence of Erwein Wurmbrand's reprisal killings at Glen Helen, that even threats to white lives were, after 1885, no longer answered with dispersals in the third degree. The continuing careers of Melon Charlie and Billy Cloud throughout this period also suggest that the appetite of the Mounted Constables and their Aboriginal assistants for cross-country pursuits of the kind Erwein Wurmbrand practised at Glen Helen in 1884-5 was limited. It was in fact difficult and hazardous. Wurmbrand's pursuit was only conducted with the back-up of a large party of white men and their horses and supplies, and all were pushed to the limit. It was also expensive. On the second of Wurmbrand's Glen Helen expeditions he ignored an explicit command not to hire additional horses and not to take white civilians with him. There was more political pay-off from the long-range circuits to the south by camel, showing the flag at every station in the locality. These stately progressions were no threat to cattle-killers like Ereminta, Billy Cloud and Melon Charlie.

More importantly, in 1889 the white inhabitants of the upper Finke River no longer feared for their lives as they had in earlier times, at Barrow Creek, Anna's Reservoir and Glen Helen. Many were to be driven out of the Centre by drought, but they had yet to find that out. Control of Aboriginal cattle-killing was now more local politics than police work, however much the pastoral investors in Adelaide hoped otherwise. Police attendance was never going to be frequent enough to make much difference since, as Willshire admitted, the cattle-killers knew when he was coming and kept out of his way for the few days he was around. Terrorising the Aborigines around the stations would have had no effect on their cattle-killing relatives and would disrupt the management of the stations. The Boggy Water police camp was a last desperate attempt by government in Adelaide to pacify their pastoral constituents in Adelaide. It could make little difference to the way policing worked in the Centre, except by the net addition of Mounted Constable Cowle as the third policeman in the district. To see Boggy Water as major increment in the vigour of policing in the Centre is not only to misunderstand the nature of cattle-killing in 1889 but also to misunderstand the nature of William Willshire. This was soon to become clear.

Willshire claimed to have spent the period between January 9th 1889 and April 14th of that year "in & about the Musgrave Ranges" south east of Ayers Rock, 400 kilometres as the crow flies from Alice Springs and within the border of South Australia proper. At the beginning of 1889 he was certainly sent to pursue a witness to the murder of a Chinese cook. He was in Port Augusta with the witness between the 12th and the 29th of April, and took two weeks sick leave shortly after. While the pursuit of the Aboriginal witness took at least a part of the period January - April, and he was undoubtedly occupied for some of his time in the south with arranging for the supplies he needed for Boggy Water, we have at least the three months between May 1889 and early August 1889 in which Willshire's movements remained unknown to Inspector Besley, as they would for us but for Wesley Turton, a store-keeper from Alice Springs, who happened to be in Adelaide in the middle of 1889.[227] Willshire kept no journal of the entire eight months, and his whining resistance to Besley's retrospective demand that he supply some account of them shows that whatever he was up to, the idea of reconstructing it in the usual police form irritated him intensely. Since the standard of journalising employed at Alice Springs at the time did not demand detail we are left with the impression that Willshire was less concerned to avoid work than to preserve this secret space in his life and deny his subordination as a police officer. Wesley Turton saw him twice in the central retail streets of Adelaide in the middle of the year, accompanied by two trackers and a young woman of fifteen or sixteen years of age. On one occasion Willshire and the young woman were inspecting the goods displayed in the window of J M Wendt, Jeweller, of Rundle Street, where all of Adelaide's engaged couples went to find tokens of their love.

Willshire had made no further trip to the harsh Musgrave Ranges, he was on an unapproved holiday in Adelaide, pursuing his private dreams. The young woman with Willshire was an Aboriginal woman. Mounted Constable Robert Hillier, who was posted from Alice Springs to Port Augusta from early July 1889 also met them both, at the head of the rail line as he travelled south and they north. It was an act of astonishing boldness on Willshire's part. By 1889 Aboriginal people were rare in the retail heart of Adelaide, a small city of 120,000 souls in any case, and it was likely that word of his presence would get back to his superiors. Perhaps he thought they would not care, now that he was on the payroll of another Minister. Besley eventually agreed that Willshire could begin the police journal of his new position as leader of the Police Patrol for the Interior with his arrival at Boggy Water on August 3rd 1889. This concession required the endorsement of the Minister, who must have been demanding action. Perhaps the Minister was being pressed on the matter by private reports of what Willshire was up to.

William Willshire was being foolish, but he was not the first man to be moved that way by love. To declare your love for an Aboriginal woman was, at that time, so extreme an act that it threatened exclusion from all white society, even on the frontier. The missionaries of the 1880s made themselves unpopular with their pastoralist neighbours for continuing to point out how widespread were sexual relations between white men and Aboriginal women on the frontier, and the pastoralists' denials to Swan-Taplin were unconvincing. When charges of sexual relationships between white men and black women were made in the press the usual response was silence. These relationships were certainly not illegal, but they were not respectable. Men who hoped to continue official careers down south could never admit to *de facto* Aboriginal wives. Venereal disease was general among both black and white on the frontier. Schulze thought that most of the Aboriginal people on the mission suffered from syphilis, "more ore less".[228] A southern white woman considering marriage to a repatriating frontier white man did not wish to hear that she followed his common-law Aboriginal wife or mistress. For a police officer such relationships could also be portrayed as a breach of good discipline, since they were known to create conflict between black and white men.

In his writings *after* 1891, Willshire makes insinuations of his sexual adventures central to their appeal to the new popular readership he was addressing, but not before. Willshire told Swan-Taplin that the Aboriginal women he took to Adelaide in 1888 and 1889 were his trackers' or constables' lubras, and the Enquiry's report accepted that explanation. But Swan and Taplin knew better, because they had heard a more convincing account from Mounted Constable Hillier who had spent a year with Willshire in Alice Springs in 1887-8. The Enquiry did not push Willshire on his denials, since they contrived to interview Hillier only after they had spoken to Willshire and returned to Adelaide. Hillier's evidence was specific and he held firm against Inspector Besley's cross-examination. He had seen one of Willshire's Alice Springs women, named Oticka, or Mary Ann, in Willshire's camp at Heavitree Gap. No, he hadn't actually seen them in bed together, but when Willshire took her to Port Augusta with him, dressed only in a man's shirt, neither of the two trackers accompanying Willshire was Oticka's husband. "I distinctly say" Hillier responded to Besley "the Lubra, Mary Ann or

Oticka was not a Lubra of any of the black trackers whilst I was in his Camp at Alice Springs". Oticka was later "given to Frank Stacey on the Ruby Fields". Willshire had only admitted to taking an eight-year old girl down with him, which would not have reassured the Enquiry, for other reasons, and to have left her with his brother-in-law, the South Australian Conservator of Forests, John Ednie Brown. Hillier said nothing on this, possibly because he was not asked, and possibly because it was an invention of Willshire's.

This young woman in Rundle Street was another matter. Robert Hillier did not name her, but there are two candidates. Chantoonga was an eastern Aranda woman from Emily Gap. Willshire took her with him from Alice Springs to Boggy Water, the only woman he is known to have taken there, and at some time she bore him at least one daughter later named Ruby Willshire. But perhaps the more likely candidate was Nabarong, a young woman from the west of the James Ranges. Immediately before his appointment as leader of the Police Patrol for the Interior Willshire had spent several weeks out west, his first excursion into this region of striking stone ridges and sheltered valleys, lapped on its western edge by the sand ocean that runs all the way to the Western Australian coast. The western abutment of these ranges includes the gorge now known as King's Canyon, one of the must-sees of the Central Australian tourist circuit. In the second edition of *The Aborigines of Central Australia* in 1891, and in *A thrilling tale*, published in 1895, he synthesises this trip, and possibly other trips to the same ranges. In the second edition of *The Aborigines of Central Australia* he produced a reasonably sober report, but in *A thrilling tale* we find a concoction in the style of a Rider Haggard adventure. A leaning in this direction of adventure-fantasy is already evident in the second version of *The Aborigines of central Australia*, but in *A thrilling tale* all connection with reporting has been broken, in favour of the liberty to speak frankly of his love of the power he exercises over the local people, the power of life and death, and his power to attract the devotion of one particular young woman. This young woman he calls Chillberta, the local word for rain, according to his own glossary. Chillberta may stand in Willshire's mind for what he found so loveable in both Chantoonga and Nabarong, and possibly others of the women he had in the Centre, the image they helped him create of himself, as lord and leader. Chillberta is young, innocent, beautiful and devoted to Willshire, who writes for her a dedication that is a love poem, probably the first written by a white man for an Aboriginal woman. I reproduce it in its original layout: [229]

A light-hearted girl, who loved the free air of the ranges
and the excitement of the chase. When dark clouds
overshadowed our trackless way, the sunbeams of her
heart dispelled adversity; when surrounded by scenes
of the deepest historical interest, and scenes of
desolate wildness, I was assisted to record items
of aboriginal lore that will be handed down
to posterity. When apprehensive of native
hostility by my whilom foes, in the mighty
centre of a mighty realm, she did not
desert me, but returned with my party
into civilization on the Finke River,
and died as she lived. Chaste as
the morning dew, she has now
gone to that undiscovered
country from whence
no traveller returned.

A thrilling tale is a strange book by any standard, but it is aimed at a new audience. It is the audience already captured, without the sex, by the Australian writer Ernest Favenc whose work Willshire read.[230] Into the story Willshire inserts a fantasy about a large cave within which Aboriginal elders conduct a kind of sex academy for young women. The bizarre character of this invention has led some to doubt the whole account, but it contains truthful observation and reportage, exaggerated and distorted to appeal to his audience, of which he is always the dominant member. The cave as a location for exotic events can be found in Rider Haggard's *She*, as Willshire himself notes in the 1891 version of *The Aborigines of Central Australia*. Favenc, a writer Willshire admired greatly, had used a cave in Central Australia as the location for a story of subterranean Aboriginal cannibals, although he had never been to Central Australia. The story was one of several published in *The Bulletin*, and reprinted in a booklet in 1893.[231] *A thrilling tale*, far from being a wild fantasy, reflects events that were formative in the life of the man who set about constructing his police camp at Boggy Water in August 1889. But unlike Favenc's work, Willshire's makes a very poor read unless you assume, as Willshire wants you to, that close to the strange surface of the tale lies the stranger truth. Had it been meant purely as fiction, and were we not expected to identify the author with the hero, the story's excitements could have been more explicit. It is an unusual fictional frontier hero who allows the most violent episodes to take place while he is off-stage.

Even more extraordinary, while down south with his young Aboriginal wife, Willshire staged another photographic tableau for James Taylor to print as a post-card. It is superficially similar to the one photographed the previous year in Port Augusta. The new photograph shows Willshire dressed not in the moleskins and pale shirt of the respectable bushman, but in a dark collarless shirt and trousers. Now the rifles are not ordered, with their butts on the ground, but held for firing. Willshire's posture is set for attack. His Aboriginal troopers are notably younger, two of them showing no cicatrices, or the beards that mature Aboriginal men wore. This is not a surprise. We know that when Willshire left Alice Springs all four of the experienced trackers at the station were sick, and he had to appoint novices for the trip south. But the overall impression the tableau gives is more that of a bandit gang than a police troop. There is not a recognisable item of uniform in sight. Most surprising, at the front of the group is seated a young, bare-breasted Aboriginal woman. It is unlikely this postcard could have been distributed openly without risking prosecution for obscenity. It was certainly not the impression Besley, Peterswald and their Ministers would have wanted their Police Patrol leader to make.

If Willshire was captured by a love that could not say its name, he was also incapable of not boasting of something that touched deeply a person so deserving of public attention - himself. His post-1891 writings are, as already mentioned, rich with references to the charms of young Aboriginal women and of his power over them. At places in *The land of the dawning* the author contorts himself in both celebrating the sexual appeal of a woman and at the same time insisting that the only person to benefit from it was one of his trackers. To a bush audience this would have been transparent, as is Willshire's claim of respectability for the frontier *combo,* as white men who lived with Aboriginal women were known. Willshire's support for the *combo* was not disinterested.

The standing order of the police patrol at Boggy Water was to keep on the move, to unsettle and discourage the Aboriginal cattle killers. But travelling in this region had its own attractions to Willshire. The armchair colonists of Adelaide entertained the hope that the headwaters of Lake Amadeus, a large salt lake to the north of Ayers Rock, would be found in mountainous, relatively well-watered country, just as the pastoral country of the MacDonnell and James Ranges drained south-east along the Finke River to the salt pan of Lake Eyre. Not much to go on, but fuel for dreams if you were a dreamer. On his 1888 excursion Willshire at least touched on this region, which the explorer Tietkens had entered in 1887. The western regions above Lake Amadeus provided the new matter in Willshire's revised *The Aborigines of Central Australia,* but it was as the raw material for *A thrilling tale* that this remote region found its true home in Willshire's mind.

William Willshire now had the substance of his new appointment to underpin his ambitions. As soon as his appointment was decided, the police service hastened to transfer responsibility for the expense of supporting him to the account of the Minister for the Northern Territory, as part of the deal by which the increased expenditure had been agreed to. While Inspector Besley and Commissioner Peterswald retained a responsibility for supervising Willshire's day-to-day activities, his Minister was not their Minister, the officials who had to advise Willshire's new Minister were not experienced in Central Australian affairs, and Willshire's spending was not competing with that of the other police officers in the Centre. In the Top End where the Minister for the Northern Territory was responsible for policing, along with everything else, details of administration were left to Inspector, and *de facto* Commissioner, Paul Foelsche. The Minister for the Northern Territory was, in practice, the Minister for the Top End of the Northern Territory. Willshire was now, as he knew he should be, a special case, a privileged creation of a Minister with a political problem. Peterswald and Besley had lost an incentive to look with a cold eye on this distant servant. And so they failed to notice when, in 1890, Willshire claimed twice for the cost of having Billy Abbott shoe some horses, but, in due course, the Audit Office did.

Willshire's requisitions were not modest. These Centralian officials lived entirely from imports from the south. Nothing but meat, stone and timber was produced locally. The simplest artifacts, like buckets and boots, were as good as gold-plated when the costs of transport were added. The equipment that had been accumulated at Alice Springs and Heavitree Gap over more than a decade had to be replicated at Boggy Water in short order. More than that, we find items on Willshire's list that Alice Springs had done without. The new Boggy Water station was to be equipped more like a pastoral station than a police station, a reasonable goal if we consider Boggy Water's isolation. So, in addition to the 1000 cartridges for revolvers and the 1000 for Martini-Henry rifles (to add to the 250 and 400 of each he already held), there were also sets of tools and materials for carpentry, smithying and saddlery. And 36 pounds of Epsom Salts. James Bath, the new Minister's permanent Secretary, approved it all without demur.

Willshire advised his Minister, through Besley and Peterswald, on January 3rd, 1889 that he had appointed four Native Constables. From that date three shillings a day for each constable was paid directly into Willshire's Adelaide bank account, plus one shilling and eight pence per day for food. The Audit Office was told about it in April, and about Willshire's appointment in May. While he was in Port Augusta on April 20th that year he asked for a compass, field glasses and maps of the Northern Territory from the southern border to Powell's Creek, 400 kilometres north of Boggy Water. Peterswald had seen enough of this, and wrote to James Bath "I have recommended this constable to apply to you <u>direct</u> in future". On April 30th he requested and received an additional four guineas travelling allowance for his time in the settled districts. At the end of May he was requesting money for a tin case for his maps. A year later he asked for copies of the maps of the Lake Amadeus district drawn by the explorer Tietkens and just printed, "as sometimes I am about the locality of Lake Amadeus".[232] This was also approved.

From the time of his arrival at Boggy Water in August 1889 until he was arrested almost two years later, Willshire barraged his Minister with requests and requisitions for additional payments; for his constables' clothing and uniforms, his horses and camels, for travelling expenses, for a private mail bag at Charlotte Waters. In June 1890 his Minister's office replies to Willshire's request to be appointed a receiver and destroyer of dog scalps with the sarcastic note to Besley: "The Minister however requests me to ask if that officer is aware nothing is now paid for scalps?"[233]

For much of the remaining four months of 1889 Willshire was engaged in establishing his station at Boggy Water. Towards the end of the year he made another journey, to Tempe Downs this time, returning to Boggy Water by January 9th, 1890. All up, he had spent no more time on Charles Chewings' interests in the year following his promotion than he had spent in the previous year.

Willshire was now a commander with a small platoon of heavily-armed men, their bodies, raised to nakedness, now uniformed, their heads which had known no barbering until a few years before now topped with shakos - cylindrical caps with small peaks at the front - their calloused feet softening inside Blucher boots. They were equipped with horses, camels, rifles and revolvers. A small army, but a formidable force for the scattered population of the Centre. Georg Heidenreich visited Boggy Water in July 1890, arriving in the dark after a 70 mile ride up the Finke. He thought it "gave the impression of a natural thieves' den", and Willshire "a well-educated man in his way, who did everything possible to make our stay comfortable." The next morning Willshire lined his men up in full dress uniform, with cartridge belts across their chests, revolvers on their hips and rifles in their hands, and put them through their drills, both on foot and on horse-back. "The sight of these heavily-armed men, with their black faces and red-striped white jackets, would inspire fear and horror in the mind of someone who had not seen such a thing before."[234] To this extent, at least, Willshire had achieved the purpose for which the South Australian public was paying about £1000 per year.[235]

We can now summarise the progress of William Willshire's career. He is not just the most senior policeman in the Centre, but unique in his connection to the highest level of politics and in his freedom from direct subordination or oversight. When he returns to station from his long expeditions there is no white man to ground him in his own culture. The distinctions between work and pleasure, duty and self-interest, now mean even less than they ever did for the frontier policeman. When he is on station the cycle of communication with the south has extended from hours to days. At times he is dependent on a single Aboriginal associate, Archie, but he is being paid for six. His wealth is growing faster than it had at Alice Springs and he is speculating in gold mines and suburban land. He is extending his booklet, *The Aborigines of Central Australia*, for a second edition that will cover the western James Ranges and beyond, a region he calls "Lake Amadeus and ... the Western Territory of Central Australia", because that is where the public's interest in exploration has moved. He has the means to attract aboriginal people to his domain, although he is no more able to hold them than the missionaries. And he has young women who will never claim a status equal to his, but will feed the image of himself according to which all of this is being constructed.

Boggy Hole today is in some ways more isolated now than Boggy Water was in 1890. Today only the more intrepid four-wheel drivers go down the Finke Gorge, and no one lives anywhere along it. If you spent a few weeks at Boggy Water police camp today you would not see, as Willshire did in 1889 and 1890, the mail man pass by, or the camel trains going to and from Hermannsburg, or the more frequent passing of groups of Aboriginal peoples on their endless travellings. But it is a lot quicker to get in and out of the place than it was in 1890, when the nearest white inhabitants were a day's hard riding away. There is no doubt, however, that William Willshire wanted to stay there. When public scandal erupted in January 1890, and his superiors made him answer to it, Willshire begged to be allowed to stay. On March 10th 1890 he wrote, "I can assure Inspectr Besley that I want to keep my billet by doing my duty & therefore I will not offend the missionaries if I know it, But would go a lot out of my way to please them".[236]This was no hardship posting for Willshire, despite everything that in our minds adds up to discomfort, and it was not hope of promotion to better things in the future that kept him on the Finke. He had power, growing wealth, and an extended family that included at least one child. Reflected in his mental mirror it all looked good. William Willshire was at home.

Top: Willshire with Alice Springs Native Constables (and one ring-in) and Mounted Constable Erwein Wurmbrand, Port Augusta, January 1888 (SLSA B13496). Below: Willshire with three novice Constables and girl, middle of 1889. The girl is probably Nabarong, the cause of his feud with Ereminta (*Mrs P Cole/Hesperian Press*).

Willshire at Boggy Water, July or August 1890. (SAM, AA41, AP54003)

Fireplace and flag-stone floor of Willshire's house at Boggy Water. Similar remains of a larger building for Willshire's Aboriginal associates lie some 400 metres away. (2002)

Chambers Pillar, south of Alice Springs. The last two letters of Willshire's name "RE" can be seen top left, followed by "1888". Swan, Taplin and Besley also recorded their names (2002).

10

THE LAW OF DESIRE

"Our Thomas was a mystery to us." Louis Schulze, 1889.

With Wilhelm Schwarz despatched to the south, Kempe and Schulze were relieved of a source of constant irritation. The bigger issue remained. How was Central Australian Lutheranism to be built on the already-crumbling foundations of the new 'heathen-Christians'? To what extent were Andreas, Thomas, Hanna, Naomi and Salomo Christian at all? Were they well-intentioned, but blind to the bands that still tied them to the Devil's teachings, and, like children, unable without discipline to conform to the Old Testament Law on which the Christian Gospel was built? Were they playing a double game, wanting to take what they could from both Christianity and the traditional beliefs, opportunists of a low kind? Worst of all, had they become apostates and only played Christian at meal-times? Apostate was not a word the missionaries ever used, in public, but they came close to it.

In the third quarter of 1889 Kempe lamented again Naomi's refusal to leave her heathen husband Ereminta. "Recently she has even been very refractory, enticing other catechumens and baptised Christians to leave, until finally we had to send her away. That was painful for us, but in the best interests of the others, as we have already learned. When Andreas and Thomas were still here there were constant arguments and fights, and we learned later that those two were the instigators. Things have gone much better since they left. ... It has taught us to be more careful with the adult baptisands and to take particular care that their understanding is thorough and they show themselves in their way of life to be serious Christians. We have had most joy from those baptisands of whom we expected the least." Among those who persisted was Salomo, baptised the previous year, who was an adult.

Despite Kempe's apparent resignation to the loss of Naomi, his efforts to compel the converts' compliance with the missionaries' standards were, if anything, increased. With Schwarz's departure it appears a restraining force was lifted from Kempe's and Schulze's drive to punish and constrain their back-sliding converts.

Within a few months of Willshire's arrival on the Finke he became an active player in the drama. As soon as he had set up camp at Boggy Water he attracted "A small mob of [sixteen] natives, wild blacks" by providing them with rations, paid for from his own pocket, according to his report. "In stock there were 400lbs. of flour, 2cwt [hundredweight, ie 224 pounds] of sugar, 30yds of dress material, 30 lbs. of tobacco, and other things, such as pipes, necklaces, belts, handkerchiefs, &c. These were served out and given away both to old and young. The liberality displayed to them was unlimited, for the goods distributed being the writer's private property were not disposed of under any official regulations." The only result was to prove to Willshire's satisfaction the ingratitude of these people, for "By the second week in September [six weeks after he settled at Boggy Water]... only five remained at the camp, and they seemed to be entirely oblivious of the fact that the author had given them anything." More serious was the desertion of all but one of his Native Constables, probably one he had brought from Alice Springs, Coognalthicka, or Archie, who was still with him in 1891. None of the other three Constables remaining with him in 1891 had been with the police at Alice Springs. The result was that, for "all one season" the camp was reduced to Willshire and this one Constable, a fact it is unlikely he reported to his paymasters in Adelaide. "Eventually other blacks were got to supply their places, mostly by riding to other stations and obtaining a boy here and there." It was very disappointing, and showed "how utterly destitute of any grateful feelings the aborigines ... invariably show themselves to be".

It seems that Willshire's recruiting methods could involve a degree of insistence. Sometime in the third quarter of 1889 he crossed paths with Andreas as the latter wandered between the black and white worlds of the Finke. Kempe reported "Andreas was recently here, and declared that he intended to come [back] again. He also asked for a letter to the Policeman, so that the Policeman would let him go, because he feared, not without reason, that he would detain him, as has happened, and he has been taken into the police troop.

We told him he must let go of the heathen wife he took with him and subject himself to our rules, which he promised to do."[237] We may speculate, as Kempe did not, why Willshire should have been so forceful in recruiting Andreas. Was it Andreas's grounding in the ways of the whites, his evident talent for leadership, his horsemanship? All of these possible reasons make sense. Did Willshire also count in Andreas's favour his troubled relationship with the missionaries, and see an opportunity to show himself a better leader of Aboriginal people? It grieves me to report that we are unlikely ever to know. With Kempe's reference to him quoted above, Kalimalla/Andreas disappears from the historical record of this period. He was not at Boggy Water at the beginning of 1891.

It was in the last quarter of 1889 that the toxic wind began to reap its fatal harvest among those remaining on the mission. Thomas and Hanna, who had returned to Hermannsburg earlier in 1889, remained after Naomi's departure. On the very day, October 29th, that Kempe and Schulze buried Sara, daughter of the absent Naomi, "this seed-corn, in our Field of God", another and moral infection blew in, this time from the south. The Afghan cameleers arrived with the mission's annual loading. They were to be at Hermannsburg for almost three weeks, from October 29th to November 17th, waiting for the back-loading of Hermannsburg wool to be ready. Four days before the end of their stay "Thomas and Joseph came with the news that some girls were flirting with the Afghans", according to the report in the *Church messenger*. According to Kempe's statement to Swan-Taplin, the young women committed adultery with the cameleers. Schulze's wife confirmed the bad news, but he was too busy to do anything about it, and the next day both Hanna and blind Martha had disappeared, "as we learned from others, with the idea of going after whites." The cameleers were still at Hermannsburg and remained there several days more. Schulze sent Thomas and the Colonist Eggers after them on horseback, but the women were determined not to be followed and walked over the stony ridges of the hills, not down the bed of the river. Next, Thomas and Nathanael, Naomi's baptised son, were sent on foot, carrying a letter from Kempe to Willshire:

Dear Mr Willshire

If there have come two female natives, one blind woman and one is the wife of bearer, to your camp, please deliver them to bearer if already on your camp, if not, and they come afterwards please drive them away from camp. I beg [you] to do what is in your power to help bearer to get his wife back & also the blind girl, we do not want to let them grow wild.... With kind regards, yours truly, H. Kempe.[238]

Willshire was away from Boggy Water at the time, but Billy Abbott was there to receive the letter.

Thomas and Nathanael brought the women back on the Sunday the camel train was to leave. "But", reports Schulze, "Thomas seemed to me very peculiar, totally different to the way he was before."[239]

Shortly after the missionaries were informed by Joseph - one of the married men baptised in 1888 - that the young women were again thinking about running off. So, according to Schulze's report to the *Church messenger*, "We tied them up. The next day they went about their work quite diligently. But, to our surprise, the day after they all disappeared, Thomas included. Our Thomas was a mystery to us. This time we let them go. We were past wanting to fetch them back."

Hermann Kempe introduced his account of these events to Swan-Taplin very carefully, saying "I recollect quite well what I am now going to say". By July 1890 he knew that the future of the mission depended on how Swan-Taplin chose to represent their activities to the metropolis. "These Afghans committed adultery with 3 native girls. Which these girls confessed to me. On being frightened to be punished they ran away". The third girl was Tappatappa, not baptised but under instruction. A fourth young woman, Maria, still the estranged wife of Andreas, also confessed. "Hanna, Maria & Martha being Christians, I asked what sort of punishment they wanted, whether to be excommunicated from the Church or anything else. Thereupon Thomas the husband of Hanna advised us to beat them, to which the girls Maria & Martha consented. I punished Maria with a little whip and I gave her a good hiding. Mr Schultze punished Martha and Thomas his own wife".

At this point Kempe's account varies from Schulze's earlier report to the *Church Messenger*. The young women had in fact run off again on the Sunday night with the intention of catching up with the cameleers, but were pursued and captured before they had gone far. But the crucial difference in Kempe's account is this - it seems likely from the sequence of events that the young women ran away to avoid a flogging, as much as to be with white men. These white missionaries were as ready to flog as any Aboriginal husband, and the women knew they could do better.

"Mr Schulze and I decided the best thing to do was to tie them up & prevent them following the Afghans. We kept Martha tied up till the next day after dinner and Maria till either Monday night or Tuesday, to give the Camel men time to get away. Wednesday [November 20th] all three girls disappeared and Thomas too, and went to the Police camp. ... I have not seen the girls in Willshire's camp." Martha and Tappatappa soon returned.

It is possible that Thomas's next step, joining Willshire's police troop, was prepared by Willshire's earlier recruitment of Andreas. We simply have no evidence of Andreas's whereabouts at this time. From what happened soon after we must regard as an open question the degree to which Willshire was recruiting Thomas for police purposes and Thomas was recruiting Willshire for his purposes. According to Schulze, in December 1889 Willshire and his troopers, including Thomas, passed through Hermannsburg on a "murdering expedition" against people to Hermannsburg's west. The targets of this expedition may have been the Kukatja, traditional enemies as well as ceremonial partners of the Western Aranda. It is more likely they were Matuntara, whose territory extended to the north-western extremity of the James Ranges. Wilhelm Schwarz advised Heidenreich in April 1891 that when Thomas ran away from Hermannsburg the first time, in 1888, he "roamed about in the McDonnell Ranges taking part in the murders & acts of reprisal against the Tempe Downs tribe [the Matuntara]. ... [after December 1889] Willshire knew well that the two tribes were at enmity & took delight in acts of violence against each other ... in this way ... the poor savages are shot down like wild dogs."[240] Schulze claimed in 1890: "The Aborigines in the west, Thomas's enemies, have been creating havoc among the cattle. As a consequence the mounted policeman with several natives from other regions has gone there to punish the perpetrators. As we hear it, he has already slaughtered some, and driven several to our place where they feel safer, but have no desire to hear God's word." None of this was reported by Swan-Taplin. Nor is it recorded in their evidence, whether because it was not told to them, or was excluded as hearsay, we do not know.[241]

Thomas's enemies had, in their turn, good reason for their enmity. James McDonald of Glen Helen station saw the result of one of Thomas's raids.

He joined in an expedition against some of the blacks on the Mission Run, I know this of my own knowledge; when 5 of them were killed 3 men and 2 women, those killed were belonging to the Mission Run. I reported the matter to Mr Schwarz at Glen Helen Station 6 or 8 weeks afterwards, but do no know if he reported the matter any further or not. I do not know the names of them. I saw the bodies lying dead. This took place about 25 miles from the Mission Station. ... The bodies of the dead blacks I saw were lying south of Taladooma Waterhole [Tlalaltuma], at the foot of a hill.

The missionaries watched helplessly as the second of their two first-born Christians descended further into the violent maelstrom of traditional Aboriginal enmities reinforced by police fire-power: "now many are ill-disposed towards Thomas. I believe that all too soon we will get the news: Thomas is dead. It seems to me sometimes that God has destined many of them to choose, in a perverse way, to act for the worst."

Kempe and Schulze had given up the battle to hold Thomas on the station but they were prepared to go further to hold the women. Under cross-examination by Willshire, with only Schulze's answers recorded, Schulze was pushed backwards into further confessions. Asked whether there had been other instances of chaining Aboriginal women he replied: "This was the only case we had lubras chained up during the year". He then admitted that it had happened again early the next year, 1890. When Thomas had passed through in Willshire's "murdering expedition" he had left his wife Hanna at the mission. She was kept chained "round the ankles with a piece of pump chain. The woman was hobbled but could walk about". How long was she chained like that? There was no direct answer, but the period covered Willshire's visit on February 27th 1890 and Wesley Turton's on March 4th; that is, Hanna was hobbled for at least a week.

On February 25th 1890, blind Martha again ran away down the Finke, this time in the company of Magdalene, wife of Joseph. Schulze took the opportunity to retrieve Maria also. "I went after them with a native [Nathanael] on horseback ... I tracked them to Mr Willshire's camp & found them there. I mean the natives were not at the camping place but Mr Willshire & myself sent two boys after them to bring them back from the hills. The boys brought the lubras back ... I came on a few miles and camped. I did return to your [Willshire's] camp the next morning, for Maria as she ran away again. I did not flog Martha the blind lubra at the junction of Ellery's Creek and the Finke. I did flog Martha with a whip as she would not go on. At another part of the road. I tied Hanna with a rope through the Surcingle & held the end in my hand. I tied the rope round the breast of Hanna. I led her along for about a quarter of a mile & then let her go. I did not order Joseph to flog his lubra. I cannot remember if Joseph beat his lubra. I had a horse-whip with me when I came to your camp. I had a loaded revolver with me. I cannot remember locking up any girls or women on the mission station. I have put native women in a room for the night but I cannot say whether I locked them in. I ordered the women to remain there in order to prevent them going to the whites at Ellery's Creek[,] Willshires or the Afghans."[242]

And so, step by step the painful truth was extracted from Louis Schulze. The mission had become a prison for the Aboriginal Christian women. Even worse, Kempe and Schulze were in alliance with the violence of the police and the Aboriginal men to constrain the women into a kind of conduct that they regarded as more appropriate for heathen-Christian women. "It is quite likely", Schulze conceded under cross-examination from Willshire, "I asked you to beat the blacks [women] who run away if they come to your camp. I do not remember what you said in reply." This was the imposition of morality by force. It was not a pretty picture, it was illegal and it was profoundly un-Lutheran.

Willshire was soon to feel the blow-back of the enmities he and his troopers had fostered. On January 9th, 1890, shortly after dark someone attacked one of the Aborigines' shelters at the Boggy Water police camp, spearing an older man, Namia, father of the trooper Aremala, known by Willshire as Larry. Namia died the next day. According to Willshire and his troopers, the instigator of the killing was Ereminta, and the ultimate motivation was Namia's role in the series of revenge killings originating, according to Western Aranda convention, in the Irbmangkara massacre of 1875-80. Possibly true, but it is also true that Ereminta and Willshire had other business. Willshire had stolen Ereminta's wife, one who came before Naomi/Nungoolga.

We do not know whether Ereminta regarded this as a property offence, or an alienation of his wife's affections and a disappointment of his own. Schwarz was in no doubt that the matter provoked Ereminta who "retaliated by killing cattle, & indulging in the usual acts of violence, for which he was afterwards shot by Willshire and his blacktrackers." Heidenreich confirmed, in his letter to Homburg, "I have myself seen Ereminta's former wife in Willshire's hut, & that she appeared from her deportment to be "master" of the house." This could only have been in July or August 1890.[243]

There is no evidence that the young woman Willshire took to Adelaide on his illegitimate visit in 1889 had been Ereminta's wife, but it is plausible. Ereminta took up with Naomi in 1889, after Willshire had spent several weeks in Matuntara territory and before he left on the 1889 trip south that was to end in Adelaide. Ereminta had by the middle of 1889 moved out of Matuntara territory, away from Tempe Downs where he was, according to Schwarz, Thornton's "best and most trusty blackboy", up the Finke into Western Aranda country where he could be little more than a casual shepherd and an efficient cattle-killer. We know from the missionaries that he was determined to get back to Matuntara territory, and caused Naomi to leave her daughter Sarah at Hermannsburg at the beginning of October 1889. Perhaps it was disappointment at losing his wife that detached Ereminta for a time from Tempe Downs station and set in motion the sequence of events that was to end in the bed of Walker Creek in February 1891.[244]

By the good fortune of a misunderstanding in Adelaide, the killing of old man Namia on January 9th 1890 was to boost Willshire's enterprise at Boggy Water. When he wired Besley on January 15th that "my camp attacked by blacks one of my Natives killed by spears on night of ninth instant ... badly require two more trackers", it was open to Besley and Peterswald to conclude that the "Native" referred to was one of Willshires constables and that they had a smaller-scale repetition of the 1874 Barrow Creek attack on their hands. South was wired to go immediately to Boggy Water to offer assistance, and Willshire was advised that he could add two more to his troop, making a total of six. He appointed Peter and Charley on February 1st, as far as the official record was concerned, although the two men are not heard of again. Willshire was advised "it will be necessary to obtain the signatures of the above constables to the enclosed procuration orders. The orders being in your favour some one else must sign as witness. Those forwarded by you are informal and cannot be accepted."245

We can describe Willshire's ménage at Boggy Water at the end of the first half of 1890 as comprising at least two wives, Chantoonga, the mother of his daughter Ruby and of another older girl named Lill who may also have been Willshire's, and Nabarong. There were also up to six Native Constables and their wives and children, and a variable population of Aboriginal people passing through, or attracted by rations. When the Government Geologist, H. Y. L. Brown, passed by a week or two after Swan-Taplin in July-August 1890, he stopped to take a photograph. Willshire stands, bearded, without uniform, in a banded sweater several sizes too small that may well have been knitted by his mother. Behind him is spread a long line of nine men with spears, ten women, none of them old, and five children. Only one of the men is clothed in shirt and trousers, possibly a Native Constable in mufti, but no other looks like a trooper. All but one of the women are dressed in large shirts or dresses.

Much of this lay in the future when Wilhelm Schwarz and his family passed by Boggy Water in September 1889, a month after Willshire's arrival there. Troublemakers are usually rusticated, sent to places where no-one can hear their moans. By recalling Schwarz to the metropolis Heidenreich was to set in play Schwarz's ambition, a force that, amplified by politics, could destroy Heidenreich's mission. Left on the Finke it might possibly have saved it.

THE TRIAL OF
THE FINKE RIVER MISSION

1890

11

GOD'S IMPERIALISTS
AND THE PARTY OF GOVERNMENT

On the evening of January 9th 1890, as Ereminta and Donkey were attacking Willshire's camp on the Finke, Wilhelm Schwarz spoke to a small group in the YMCA meeting room in Flinders Street in Adelaide. Schwarz had come south, arriving in the Barossa Valley near Adelaide one month earlier. The audience at the YMCA included at least one reporter for the daily *Register* and the weekly *Observer*, and next day Adelaide was alight with what Schwarz had to say about the behaviour of white police and pastoralists on the Central Australian frontier.

The South Australian Government was led by the "revolting" character of some of Schwarz's accusations, and the tactless intervention of its Minister for Education and the Northern Territory, John Gordon, to send two men on a 2,500 kilometre trek to the Centre to dampen the indignation of the frontier whites, and of the religious of Adelaide, with the balm of a Commission of Enquiry. Can Schwarz have intended all this? He was a man who shunned public attention, even favourable attention.[246] He was a brave and passionate man, but surely not a politician.

Perhaps it was Schwarz's private conversations with the South Australian Germans including Friedrich Krichauff, then a member of the upper House of the South Australian Parliament and, *de facto,* the public voice of the Mission Superintendent, Georg Heidenreich, that led to the meeting.[247] However, the person driving the event was Charles Eaton Taplin. Taplin was a son of George and Mary Taplin who had managed the Point McLeay Aboriginal reserve (now Raukkan), in the well-watered south of the Colony, from 1859 to 1879. Taplin had recently returned from a period at the Warrangesda mission near Brewarrina in New South Wales. At that time Warrengesda was run by the Anglican Bishop of Goulburn but it had been founded as a private enterprise by the redoubtable and volatile John Gribble. Since his return Taplin had been running a campaign through the correspondence columns of the Adelaide papers proposing a string of protective reserves be set up along the Telegraph for the benefit of Aboriginal people. . He cited the "atrocities" that had taken place on the New South Wales and Queensland frontiers as the warrant for government action, and foresaw annihilation for South Australia's Aborigines if nothing were done.

In looking east with fear and contempt Taplin was continuing a South Australian tradition as old as the Colony itself. Its police force had been founded in 1838, two years after the first colonists waded up the beach, for the express purpose of keeping out those undesirable whites who might be tempted to travel overland from the convict Colony of New South Wales. These escaped and ex-convicts, not the Aboriginal people of the Adelaide plains, were seen as a threat to public peace that justified spending the Colony's funds. In the years to 1890 the only larger-scale killings of white by black, and organised retributions for them, had taken place on or beyond the fringes of settlement. The city of Adelaide itself, as it grew from shanty village to Colonial metropolis, and the Colonial enterprise as a whole, never felt threatened by the Aboriginal people as they were displaced from the Adelaide Plains and, at an accelerating rate from the 1840s, from the pastoral lands beyond agricultural settlement. [248]

When Charles Eaton Taplin addressed the meeting at the YMCA he was speaking for that section of South Australian opinion that already distrusted the institution of the South Australian Native Police. In 1884, before that force was established, at the time of the 1884 killings at Anna's Reservoir in the Centre and on the Daly River in the Top End, the Aborigines Friends Association had tried to draw a line between the summary justice of the punitive party and the terror of third-degree dispersal. On October 16th, 1884 they had passed a resolution accepting that Aboriginal offenders needed to be "brought to account and punished; but at the same time desire[d]... to express their earnest hope that in the administration of justice judgment will be tempered with mercy, and the innocent natives may not be confounded with the guilty".[249] In January 1890 Taplin's small audience was, in effect, the active membership of the Associaiton.

The story that emerged from Schwarz's address and in the subsequent correspondence in the press was gruesome enough. "Very much" he said in German "has come under my notice" in fourteen years on the Finke River Mission. It was a matter of the cattle versus the blacks, he said; if a squatter wanted the country the blacks had to go. "Many of the actions that were taken against the blacks were so taken with the object of exterminating them, and especially the men." As evidence he told of an Aboriginal man peppered by shotgun pellets, of three men arrested and shot in cold blood by a Mounted Constable about three years previously. The pastoralists were happy to make use of the boys and girls, treating them fairly well. The girls were used by the whites as de facto wives, mistresses and prostitutes, as many as ten to fifteen on one station alone. Even a policeman had taken girls after shooting the men he was sent to arrest, and lived with them at the police camp at Alice Springs. As a result of the behaviour of the whites half-caste children were now common, and a "bad disease" (syphilis) was prevalent. There was debate about whether it originated with the blacks or the whites. The immorality of the whites made the work of the missionaries difficult since the Mission's girls were seduced while still young. Three of the Mission's proteges were now living with the policeman he had mentioned previously who had abducted the two women. "Very frequently blacks disappeared, and the other blacks came to the station to inform the missionaries that they had been shot." He had heard of a young aboriginal man being found with his throat cut.[250]

Those at the meeting whose comments are recorded agreed with Taplin's proposal that the matters raised should be taken to the Government, and an official enquiry called for. The meeting ended with a resolution to call on the Aborigines Friends' Association to do just that.

John Hannah Gordon was the natural target for the lobby of the Aborigines Friends Association. He occupied for the time being the seat of Minister for Education and the Northern Territory in the current version of the musical-chairs governments of South Australia. Sixteen years before, at the time of the Barrow Creek retributions against the Anmatjera people John Gordon wrote to the

Adelaide press that "defence of corporeal possessions could not justify breaking the laws of justice and humanity". He was a young man then, and son of a Presbyterian Minister. In the intervening years Gordon had become a man of property, and a pastoralist. In 1881 he had become a partner in the 22 000 square kilometres of the Crown Point and Bond Springs stations. His pastoral investments had not prospered. Crown Point in particular has been credited with driving him into insolvency two years later in 1892.[251]

While the South Australian police force in general answered to the Chief Secretary, Gordon's portfolio had also been given responsibility at the end of 1888 for the force of Native Police set up under Mounted Constable Willshire and now based at Boggy Water on the Finke River. Coincidentally, responsibility for Hermannsburg's role as the rationing centre for the western Aranda, work for which the mission had been funded since it began, came under his Education portfolio. Gordon's visitors knew just what he meant when he told them he "had had some unpleasant experiences of the Northern Territory, not only with the blacks...". He had also written on behalf of his own pastoral investments to the police, six years before, asking for more police protection in the Alice Springs district.[252]

John Gordon was, therefore, also the natural target for the response of the enraged pastoralists and a group of them were first through his door on February 19[th,] probably on an appointment made before the Schwarz bombshell. The four pastoralists, from the Tempe Downs Pastoral Company, were accompanied by a reporter from the *Register* whose sympathetic account of their lobby was carried by the paper the next day. The Company's complaints about Aboriginal cattle-killing had been on Gordon's worry list since he took responsibility for the Territory in the middle of 1889. He had already agreed to double the number of Willshire's Aboriginal troopers stationed at Boggy Water to four.

In fact Gordon had bigger problems than the complaints of the shareholders of Tempe Downs. A political tug-of-war between the Cockburn Government, of which he was a member, and the State's pastoralists was taking place through the person of Gordon for the entire period of his brief tenure of Ministerial office. The principal issue in dispute was the character of the leases through which the pastoralists held their enormous but shaky baronies. The pastoralists wanted long leases and low rentals, the Government preferred shorter terms, to ensure that any opportunities for more intensive land-use were not passed up, and somewhat higher rents.

The pastoralists had a point, but while he was Minister and bound to his colleagues in the Government, Gordon was obliged to put before the Parliament of South Australia draft laws that denied the pastoralists what they wanted. The pastoralists' friends were more numerous in the upper House of the Colonial legislature, the Legislative Council, and blocked the Bills. Immediately he lost office with the fall of the Cockburn Government in August 1890 Gordon proposed the laws the pastoralists wanted. While he remained a Minister he must have suffered as a man of populist instincts who was obliged while in power to deny his friends what he thought they deserved, and pretend that he thought it reasonable. In the cock-pit of Parliamentary debate his choice was to argue passionately for the wrong side or look like a messenger-boy for his Cabinet colleagues. In the club and the lounge room, drinking with his pastoralist peers, he had to play the victim of circumstance while trying not to look like a wimp. Such is Ministerial life.

Gordon was to be out of the political power game, a mere back-bencher, by the time the echoes of the Schwarz explosion had returned from Central Australia. Just at this moment, however, in February 1890, he needed some way to please the pastoralists.

The Tempe Downs delegation's visit was based on a letter from their station manager, Frederick Thornton, dated January 12th, three days after Schwarz's address in the YMCA meeting room. The delegation's concern was security, the security of their livestock, of their investment. In fact their problems reflected the truth recognised by the terms of their pastoral lease; their occupation of the hills and plains below the James Range was a joint occupation. The Matuntara people still thought the land theirs, and in any case had rights in law, written into the Tempe Downs pastoral leases. Now, after four years of consistently above-average rains, normal conditions had returned and Aboriginal people may have moved back in greater numbers to the durable waters of the river beds and the permanent springs of the hills, harvesting the game animals and the slower cattle that were all bound to the same waters.

Perhaps there was an increase in cattle-killing on Tempe Downs. Certainly Chewings had formed the ambition to grow blood stock, and had sent up some quality cattle for the purpose.[253] Such better cattle were kept closer in to the station, but they and their progeny would not thrive and return the big money invested in them under harassment from Aboriginal hunters.

The sharp point of the Tempe Downs lobby was a demand for Gordon to increase further from four to six the strength of the force of Native Police Mounted Constable Willshire commanded at Boggy Water. This demand they thought "reasonable beyond any thought of expense." Why five heavily-armed men, equipped with horses and camels, and using the methods established on the frontier, should have proved incapable of discouraging cattle-killing was not explained. Gordon saw the improbability of two more making the difference and pointed out that they were really talking about a further police unit, a second Willshire. Peterswald had already authorised an additional two troopers following the killing of Namia at Boggy Water, but the position was not irreversible and the Tempe Downs delegation was not told about it.

Security is the sacred cow of politics, but governments that have to feed the beast will still regulate its diet if the political weight of the electors riding it is not overwhelming. The pastoral interest was stronger than the numbers of its electors and parliamentary representatives would suggest, but it could not make or break governments on its own. The political weight of numbers lay with the population of Adelaide and the smaller land-holders who wanted more of the large holdings of good country broken up. The grand days of pastoralism in South Australia were already over. Soon it would be a subject more for nostalgia than for dreams of wealth.

Gordon had to fund Willshire's operation from his own Northern Territory budget, and it already supported another ravenous political pet, the railway that had reached Warrina, still 550 kilometres short of Alice Springs. Gordon pointed out to his pastoral colleagues that the interest bill for the line was £40,000 each year and it was not, of course, paying its way. Nor was the Telegraph, despite its reputation of success which continues to this day, unless you were prepared to sink its capital cost. If South Australia's expansion into the arid north had really been a business, the acquisition of the Northern Territory in 1863 would, by 1890, have sent that enterprise broke.[254] Then there was the delicate matter of the economics of

Tempe Downs and the other leases in the Centre. Gordon was unlikely to be unpatriotic enough to wonder out loud whether the tax-payers' losses should be cut. He did tell his visitors that the cost of Willshire's protection for Tempe Downs - he under-estimated it at £500 each year - was only slightly less than the annual rent paid by the Tempe Downs Pastoral Company - £600. Gordon was booking only the *direct* costs of Willshire's force. James Shakes, a member of the Tempe Downs delegation, cleverly asked Gordon, if protection for pastoralism in the Centre was not worth another £500, how could further investment in the railway be justified?

To no avail; it seemed that Gordon had no more money to give.[255] His decision echoed the despairing prescription of an earlier police Commissioner, George Hamilton: "something must be done by the settlers themselves".[256] What did Gordon think they had been doing these past five years? What else did he think they should do? Gordon left us all ignorant.

Gordon knew one other thing relevant to the politics of this case. The Germans of the Finke River Mission had attacked the pastoralists and police on a broad front. An experienced politician could sense that opportunities for counter-attack lay somewhere along that front. If the missionaries were also contributing to the pastoralist's security problem by protecting cattle-killers then retribution against them might be a cheap placatory gesture to Tempe Downs.

Because of the coincidence that saw Ereminta attack Willshire's camp on the same day Schwarz spoke publicly in Adelaide, January 9th, 1890, on that same day Willshire wrote a letter to Inspector Besley in Port Augusta, and through him to the Police Commissioner, Peterswald, and Minister Gordon, reporting the death of old man Namia, railing against the "depredations" of the Aborigines and labelling the mission station as the refuge of the worst of the cattle-killers.[257] Willshire meant by that accusation that his enemy Ereminta had lived at Hermannsburg on occasion. So by the time the Tempe Downs delegation came calling on Gordon, Peterswald had already sent to him the first of Willshire's responses to the Schwarz allegations. Perhaps Willshire's outburst was not all down to Ereminta. On his way south five months before, Schwarz may have brushed past Willshire at Boggy Water. At that time, if not earlier, he may with his impolitic bluntness have given forewarning of what he was later to say in Adelaide. [258]

The Government and the police Commissioner identified Willshire, alone of the police of the Centre, as the one who must respond to Schwarz's accusations. Yet Schwarz's accusations referred to a policeman who shot Aboriginal suspects and took young women back to Alice Springs. That put Mounted Constables Wurmbrand, Hillier, South and Cowle in the frame too. None was interviewed by the Enquiry except Constable Robert Hillier, and he had been nominated by the missionaries to support *their* claims.

At the time of the Wurmbrand killings Willshire was not even in the Centre. He did not return from his excursion with Native Police to the Top End until the end of 1885. Wurmbrand, who had been posted to Darwin in 1888 where he had resigned in 1889, with a clean police disciplinary record, was not even pursued with a request to assist the enquiry.[259]

However, police Commissioner Peterswald had not forgotten Wurmbrand's killing of three Aboriginal prisoners in Glen Helen Gorge in 1884. Immediately after Schwarz's public outburst, in January 1890, Commissioner Peterswald wired Inspector Besley, who held the file in Port Augusta, to send him the report Wurmbrand had written in December 1884. I doubt that Peterswald's memory needed much refreshing.

Peterswald would already have known that if public attention were allowed to fall on Wurmbrand, the police would be faced with accusations of wilful murder against one of their officers. Wurmbrand's deed had been witnessed by two white men, Theodor Schleicher and James McDonald, and McDonald was still alive. The bodies of the Aboriginal victims had been seen where they had been shot down "all on one heap" by two other white men. Of those two men, one, the Colonist Baden, had died in a fall from his horse, but the other, the Colonist Jürgens, was still alive although living in New Zealand. The whole unsavoury matter had been kept quiet by a Minister who had long since left office, and by a Police Commissioner who was still in office - William John Peterswald.

Peterswald and Besley probably knew that some at least of the accusations could reasonably be directed at Willshire. Schwarz had identified the policeman who, he said, had abducted two

Aboriginal women with the policeman who was now Hermannsburg's neighbour at Boggy Water, hosting the absconding Christian women. And here their path was smoothed by Willshire's personality. He sought the limelight where more prudent men would prefer the shadows. While he protested that he had a perfect alibi on the Glen Helen killings, Willshire never asked his superiors, Why me? Peterswald also knew that Schwarz's reference to the Glen Helen killings, the most serious of his allegations against the police, would bounce off Willshire and so be deflected from Peterswald.

It is probably incidental to Peterswald's choice of Willshire as defendant, but highly relevant to the outcome, that Willshire's approach to policing made him a good contestant. He knew that attack was the best form of defence. In pacifying Aboriginal peoples he first established authority by demonstrating his capacity for violence and the power of his weapons. He now turned this tactic of pre-emption against the mission.

Willshire wrote to Besley "I always thought that Missionaries were supposed to be kind & gentle, but these Germans up here are rude and Uncouth, They acted very friendly towards me when I was there last, that is for them because they are naturally uncourteous".[260] All other visitors found the missionaries hospitable. They shared their vegetables, when they would grow, they provided a lying-in hospital for the few white women of the Centre since their wives were trained midwives, they were the second-largest population of white people in the Centre and the only place where southern civilization had a secure home. They were also terrible nags. What Willshire resented sincerely was their German frankness, which he thought impertinent. Kempe scolded him for his drinking, possibly judging that he shared the main recreation of most frontier men, binge-drinking rum and whisky, telling him that he would be better advised to spend his money on vegetables. "Now the Revd. Gentleman never saw me drinking grog" Willshire complained, "I might be a teatotaller for all he knows." Besley knew that he had fined Willshire two years earlier for attending the Port Augusta court while drunk, but that was a minor breach of sobriety for a bush policeman on a visit to the south. Willshire descended into childish spite: "I have seen these Revd Gentlemen get up from the Verandah where Mrs Flint and their wives were sitting, & go a little way, say about 7 yards and make water, & talking all the time about, how

213

decent people ought to be". He constructed a ridiculous parody of Kempe's written English, claiming that he was quoting from a note Kempe had sent him, although when he forwarded to Besley an actual note from Kempe the English was shown to be much better. All of this infantility was incidental, and was censored from the version of Willshire's self-defence Peterswald fed to the press, another ghost-written sanitising of Willshire's ranting style.[261] In any case, Willshire had better dirt on the missionaries than that, and its potential must have been obvious to Besley and Peterswald.

Willshire knew that Kempe and Schulze had come to rely on his authority to buttress their violence against their heathen-Christians. At the end of February 1890, perhaps still ignorant of the storm brewing in Adelaide, the missionaries delivered themselves into Willshire's hands. As described in the previous section, Kempe and Schulze had asked Willshire's assistance in detaining heathen-Christian women absconding from the mission. They had asked him to beat the women when he detained them. When he returned to Boggy Water from Hermannsburg at the end of February 1890, Willshire wrote to Besley "I have been to the Mission Station & have seen both Mr Kempe & Mr Schulz[e] they treated me kindly & Mr Kempe told me he was much obliged to me for sending the children back that had run away. He is perfectly satisfied with my conduct towards aborigines & offered to take my part if ever it became necessary & he said that Schwartz mentioned things in Adelaide that had occurred long before I came in the country". Willshire had also just witnessed Hanna, Thomas's wife, shuffling about the mission station in hobbles.

It was no wonder that Willshire reciprocated the support, through the same underlying contempt. "I will not offend the missionaries if I know it, But would go a lot out of my way to please them", he told Besley.[262] The missionaries remaining on the Finke were his political allies. Both sides had secrets, ambitions that metropolitan civilization would not support and methods that were illegal. Willshire, at least, knew it. This gave him strength for the political contest that lay ahead, in which he would be pitted not against Kempe and Schulze but against metropolitan law and opinion. His task was to turn the metropolis against the missionaries without turning the missionaries against him. While Willshire's first instinct was attack, he had the cunning to know he would defend himself better in the court of official opinion if Kempe and Schulze were seen to be at his side rather than behind his back. For public consumption he was the mission's friend. In the privacy of his official reports, and in his writings published later, he attacked them as sanctimonious failures, while promising to work with them whenever possible. Unfortunately for the missionaries, their dependence on Willshire was sincere, and their strategy was not to counter-attack.

When John Gordon received the Tempe Downs delegation on Wednesday February 19th 1890 he was ready with accusations against the mission. His agent Willshire had confirmed the pastoralists' complaints that "a good deal of these depredations [cattle-killing] were committed by blacks on the mission stations. (Hear, hear.)" He quoted Willshire: "The blacks on the mission stations are the worst cattle killers in the whole district and the most knowing ... these demons seek refuge in the mission stations when pursued. These are the refuge of all the outlaws in the district" and continued with his own judgement that "This was not a time to discuss the efficacy of missions, but he was inclined to think regarding the efficacy of the missions in the Northern Territory that they were doing more harm than good. (Hear, hear)".[263] It was what the pastoralists wanted to hear, but was hardly a case that could trump Schwarz's serious and vivid accusations. It also opened Gordon to the accusation of bias, an accusation the leader writer of the *Register* proceeded to level at him: "One would imagine that Mr Gordon was a pastoralist. He certainly looks at the matter from the pastoralist standpoint. ... Mr Gordon's training as a lawyer should have taught him to wait for the case of the other side before being so uncharitable."

The other side soon responded, in a letter from Kempe and Schulze dated March 13th, 1890 addressed to Charles Eaton Taplin the chairman of the public meeting Schwarz had addressed, who forwarded it to the press, apparently after polishing its English. It was published on April 1st. The accusations that the mission harboured the worst cattle-killers were "the basest untruths". They reported a recent conversation with Willshire about a Tempe Downs man, clearly Ereminta, and claimed ignorance of his cattle-killing, promising to report his next arrival to the police, as they had earlier reported a cattle-killer to Wurmbrand. "It never enters our minds to protect those who commit outrages against the whites or their property; but what we want is to see the guilty ones punished, not the innocent, and punished justly according to the law, not, as some whites have done, to go at night into a black's camp and shoot down every one they can reach with firearms". They provided no instances of this. The fact that stock-killing on the mission was no longer carried out by the local clans, but by people from the west, and that the mission's own people kept them informed of the strangers' doings, this, the missionaries claimed, pointed to the cause of the other stations' problems, their bad treatment of their resident Aboriginal people.[264]

Kempe and Schulze added weight to Schwarz's accusations about bad treatment. "We cannot believe that natives in their original state will kill cattle for other purposes than for meat; therefore, if they do so, we think it is an act of revenge on the whites for robbing them of their wives and girls. We know how indignant they are over these acts." The trail of theft and violence led back to sexual morality. The cure they recommended was Charles Chewings'; policed reserves, a separation of the weaker from the more powerful race, but with missionaries in charge, not police.

If Gordon's accusations had aroused Kempe and Schulze, perhaps at Taplin's instigation, the missionaries' accusations enraged the pastoralists. James McDonald of Glen Helen station and his cook Ben Rogers wrote detailed defences of their position to the press, sometimes under pseudonyms. Others who can not be identified joined in. The story was building a head of steam. Murder, insecurity, immoral sexual conduct, cruelty. If it was true it was horrible and scandalous. It was also a long way away and when the story began its players were anonymous. As pastoralists, police and missionaries were dragged by their indignation from the obscurity in which they were accustomed to live it cannot be said that any of them wanted this attention of the south, but every time they sought to defend themselves from critical notice in the south they merely gave more life to the stories. A correspondent writing to the *Register* on April 2nd under the name "Old Hand", possibly the cook Ben Rogers or James McDonald himself, told the story of the attempted murder of McDonald and Schleicher in Glen Helen Gorge in some detail, making clear in a way Schwarz had not the jeopardy in which the white men found themselves. He then continued to rebut

216

Schwarz's report of an Aboriginal man being found with his throat cut. But here he relied on more distant reports and no direct knowledge at all. He argued that the alleged event was implausible on circumstantial grounds, but was less convincing. More importantly, "Old Hand" pointed directly to the Telegraph Station at Alice Springs and Owen Springs pastoral station as two places where enquiries could begin, and identified Mr Flint, the telegraph station-master, as the one who had received from some Aborigines the report on which Schwarz's more ignorant account was based. Not smart politics, but not as bad as it might have been; Ernest Flint had died in 1887.

The protagonists' friends in the south saw a simpler picture and imagined there was a victory to be won. Writing on February 17th, before Gordon's meeting with the Tempe Downs delegation, Charles Eaton Taplin feared the scandal would die because the players and their circumstances were so remote from the lives of the people of Adelaide. "In our own day" he wrote, comparing the current state of the public mind with the impulse that had led to the founding of his parents' mission at Point Macleay, "what apathy follows on the public assertion of an eye-witness, made in the Y.M.C.A. Rooms one day last month, that in the interior of our colony at the present time the blackfellow is regarded as an intruder on his native hunting-grounds; is shot down for disturbing the white man's cattle ... is shot down in chains, and his wife and daughters held in disgraceful concubinage by the "superior race". All these things may go on without disturbing the conscience of a Christian public because it is at a distance; but one poor, wretched creature brought into our midst charged with murder awakens our sympathy to its fullest extent, ...Why do not the people rise up in like manner and insist on their representatives doing something for the protection of the natives in the interior?"[265]

Taplin was referring to another case of an Aboriginal man, known as Jackey, who was brought down to Adelaide in chains on a murder charge. Missionary Flierl of Bethesda mission had written to the *Register* anonymously on December 16th 1889, complaining about the cruel treatment Jacky had experienced on the track, but the Chief Secretary had soon made him answer for his charges before a closed enquiry held by magistrate J G Russell and completed on December 24th. Jackey was not by character a suitable subject for public sympathy and the circumstances of his travel in chains not notably harsher than outback travel on camel-back inevitably was. Faced with an unsympathetic Commissioner and witnesses favourable to the policeman concerned, Flierl was made to appear a man careless with the truth and the reputations of his fellow frontiersmen. Commissioner Russell had dealt so harshly with Flierl that the *Observer*, generally regarded as a friend of the pastoralist, concluded an editorial clotted with irony that appeared on its surface to support the enquiry's findings with the harsh verdict that "we cannot regard the enquiry as much better than a sham." The *Observer*'s writer took particular exception to the way Flierl was made to bear "the whole weight of the prosecution" of a policeman experienced in court procedures. It was a taste of things to come. What the *Observer*'s editorial would have shown an astute observer from the party of government was this; a verdict that was on its face reasonable, defensible and popular, like Magistrate Russell's, can be shown to have rotten foundations if too much information about its processes, and the evidence heard, is allowed into the public domain. It also showed that in the public mind one remote German missionary was much the same as the next, describing Flierl as "one of the German missionaries stationed in the Far North". The Far North was a region of South Australia that included Central Australia.[266]

Schwarz himself made no further excursions into the world of the "English" of the south. While Taplin continued in the press his campaign for reserves, Schwarz began his own campaign among the southern Lutherans for the cause of missionizing among the Aborigines. Whose mission, his or Heidenreich's? By this time Heidenreich had left for New Zealand, to sort out the future of the Hermannsburg Mission Institute's enterprises there, and to ensure Hermannsburg remained in ownership of the New Zealand missions' properties. He had attended the meeting at the YMCA on January 9th, and had contributed to the discussion of the Wurmbrand killings in 1884, pointing out that he had raised the matter with the Chief Secretary, and also saying, incorrectly, that the matter had died because Mounted Constable Wurmbrand denied any shooting. He left the mission committee in the charge of Pastor Dorsch.

The Lutheran Church was evangelical from its foundation, and no branches of the Church were more evangelical than the South Australian congregations. There were regular Mission Festivals at which the principal target of missionising was the Lutherans themselves, since the idea of preaching to the converted - or, at least, the baptised - was not to them a pointless exercise. Rather, it was an essential means to turning those within reach of the Word into true Christians, and an aid to maintaining the faith of the congregations themselves. Wilhelm Schwarz now swung himself into the Mission Festival circuit.

On February 13th Schwarz spoke at the annual Mission Festival of the parish of Blumberg-Springton-Palmer, a well-attended event that required a tent and extra seating to be provided outside the church building itself. Speaking after lunch, Schwarz painted a "very exciting" picture of the Finke River mission. He spoke of their years of labour to implant the Word of God and of the Lord's "final victory over the Prince of Darkness" in the hearts of their baptisands. The collection raised £9.

On February 20th, when John Gordon's attack on the Hermannsburg mission was in the papers, Schwarz was the guest of the congregation at Edithburg at the foot of the Yorke Peninsula, 200 kilometres from Adelaide. He gave the opening address on the theme of God's kingdom (the German "Reich" also covers some of the senses of "empire"), a kingdom of heaven *and* earth, for all eternity. Unlike earthly empires that rose and fell, God's would continue to grow. It was into this successful enterprise that the heathen were to be introduced when they gave up their false gods. In the afternoon Schwarz preached again, reminding the congregation that Europeans had once been blind heathen, until God called them into the Christian flock. "All missionaries are mere voices in the wilderness". The festival participant who wrote this report tells us the congregation was encouraged by Schwarz's account of victory of their mission in the interior: "before these heathen were lazy and useless; now they are diligent and apply themselves to all kinds of work and ... have become obedient to the Gospel. Previously they were liars, now they love the truth; once they served their gods, now they serve the living God; before they were blind and did not know what Sin was, now they know the light of God's word, and have learned what sin is and how they can be freed from Sin. We had learned at this Festival about the gods they had given up, a victory of the Gospel over paganism. So we know that our work in the Lord has not been in vain, and we can continue it with confidence."

On March 5th he was welcomed by the Neales brass band to the Mission Festival of the congregations of Dutton-Gnadenberg-Neales. He gave a similarly up-beat presentation on the obligation of Christians to missionise. The congregation followed attentively his "very exciting news of the work of the Hermannsburg mission station", beginning with the epic trek of 1875-7. On this occasion Schwarz also praised the moral progress of the Western Aranda, "a people who had been held to be incapable of being civilized." Most remarkably, he showed the congregation at Neales a series of "gods", that is *tjurunga*, fashioned from wood and stone, "from which one can clearly recognise the deeply religious nature of these people." The collection raised £5.[267]

Wilhelm Schwarz was on a roll. In him there still lived confidence in the evangelising power of the Word and confidence that the Aboriginal people of the Finke were redeemable.

Stimulated perhaps by the missionaries' direct assertion that Aborigines had been slaughtered for cattle-killing, although Kempe and Schulze refrained from mentioning Wurmbrand's killings at Glen Helen, or perhaps by the increasing emotional temperature of public discussion, police Commissioner Peterswald now put out a detailed summary of the case against the mission as he had it, in various forms, from Willshire. The case was presented as a copy of a letter from Willshire to Besley, but no corresponding document has been found. Nor is the style Willshire's. It ended with the curiously reflexive construction "I am desirous of doing my duty and keeping my position, and I therefore wrote this to my superior officers for their perusal, and to let them know that these missionaries do not treat the blacks as they should be treated.". The police response was now broadened from the mission's supposed abetting of Aboriginal cattle-killing, an offence that grieved the pastoralists but not the electorate, to the more serious accusation of cruelty to the Aboriginal people of the Finke, the kind of matter known to provoke the electorate. John Gordon gave the "letter" to the press. It was published on May 6th 1890.

Gordon now thought he had the means to dispose of these troublesome pastors. At the end of the *Register's* story the writer added: "It is probable that the Government will order an enquiry into the allegations made by Constable Willshire."[268]

Gordon wanted to fight on the ground of his own choosing. It was reported in the *Register* that "M.C. Willshire has been asked to report specifically upon the letter of the missionaries which appeared in the *Register* of April 1", and that his reply was "with reference to the statement by the Rev. W. Schwartz". In other words, he hoped by responding only to the limited accusation put forward by Kempe and Schulze, and with a devastating attack on their own conduct, Schwarz's more serious charges might be regarded as disposed of.

The Gordon-Peterswald ploy was destined to fail because it expected too much of the Adelaide public's capacity to ignore evidence of outrageous behaviour just because it was so far away and the circumstances so indistinct. The publication of their Willshire letter was accompanied by an editorial. Under the heading "TREATMENT OF ABORIGINALS" it concluded that Willshire's reply was "chiefly of the *tu quoque* order, and in other respects unsatisfactory. Mr Willshire touches only the fringe of the question in dispute, and quite ignores the main point. Certainly his accusations against the Finke Mission Station have a grave complexion. ... If these accusations be true, the public ought to be immediately supplied with precise information upon the matter. ... But so far as the correspondence has gone the missionaries have the best of the matter."[269]

The *Register*'s leader writer went directly to the place where the South Australian police were most vulnerable, the Wurmbrand murders and the accusation against another policeman of shooting two accused Aborigines. He quoted verbatim from the report of what Schwarz had said on the Wurmbrand matter, by far the most detailed and convincing part of Schwarz's account. No-one mentioned Wurmbrand's name, or Willshire's, in connection with these killings. "But the most remarkable feature of this report from Mr. Willshire is that it leaves absolutely untouched the extraordinary charges made by Mr. Schwarz against the police. ... These statements seem almost incredible, but they are made by a man of repute, and it seems unaccountable that they have been passed by without the slightest answer, though Mr. Willshire may have had nothing to do with them." The fact that the letter attributed to Willshire makes no reference to the Wurmbrand killings is worth noting, since we know Willshire had reminded Inspector Besley that he was hundreds of kilometres away at the time. It all points to the more remarkable circumstance, that this official response to allegations of the most serious kind was coming not from the Minister, not from the Commissioner of Police, but from a police constable at the scene of the alleged events, who was a party to the matters complained of.

Of Gordon's proposed enquiry the *Register* had this to say: "It is satisfactory to see that the Government are likely to order an enquiry into their officer's strictures upon the missionaries, but that enquiry will not be complete unless it should include an investigation of the missionaries' criticisms of the police. It is unfortunate that the Minister controlling the department affected has already in an impulsive fit made himself a strong partisan in the matter".

John Gordon's partisanship had not gone unnoticed by one of his Cabinet colleagues, Robert Homburg. Like Gordon, Homburg was a lawyer destined for judicial office at the end of his political career. Now two years older than Gordon, at 42, Homburg had arrived from Saxony when he was six, just in time to avoid the burden of speaking English with a foreign accent. Like judge Bundey and Frank Gillen, Homburg's formal education ended when he was still a child, but he entered law through the usual apprenticeship at the age of nineteen and was marked out for a shining career by his native intelligence and integrity. Homburg was "not a strict Lutheran", according to his official biographer, but he remained culturally a German-South Australian, his household filled with music, literature, art and, eventually, eight children. He was not indifferent to the fate of the very German Lutherans on the Finke, and the political grape-vine had told him they were in trouble.

On the day the Gordon-Peterswald-Willshire letter appeared in the press, May 6th, Homburg wrote to Pastor Dorsch the caretaker in charge of the Mission Committee, perhaps unaware that Heidenreich had arrived back in Bethany early in April.

You will not have missed the article in today's Register concerning the Finke Mission. I have so often over the years heard in Parliament the accusation that the blacks are nothing but slaves of the missionaries that I regret that I could not refute convincingly this accusation against a distinctly German mission. In addition there were recently the complaints by the Kopperamana [Bethesda] missionary against the police. They were totally refuted and he must now pay for it in the form of counter-charges of very significant consequence. __ If this were just a matter of 'you are no better' I would not be writing this letter, but if the Government holds a private enquiry along the lines of the "Jacky Enquiry" then your missionaries and the Lutheran Mission will suffer severely.

... Do not be palmed off with a private enquiry and insist that your Mission is represented by Krichauff or other Germans who will conduct the enquiry on the spot.

Since his return from his brief trip to New Zealand Heidenreich's mind had been occupied with a grave matter of Church policy. Egmont Harms, the current Director of the Hermannsburg Mission Institute, whom Heidenreich served as supervisor of Hermannsburg's Australasian missions, had written with shocking news. The starting point of it all was Hermannsburg's acceptance of a place within the state-sponsored system of churches in the young nationalistic state of Germany. This had previously been anathema, and to many Australian Lutherans, including Heidenreich's Evangelical Lutheran Synod of Australia, it still was. It shocked Heidenreich even more deeply to hear that Hermannsburg was drawing a distinction between the African missions, which would continue to come under the Institute's direction, and the Australian mission, now funded entirely from local sources, that would need to accommodate itself to the local church's rules. If Heidenreich felt abandoned, imagine the feelings of the missionaries. They thought they were the servants, and the responsibility, of the Hermannsburg Mission Institute. Now, as their children approached the age where they needed a good German education, and they themselves were flagging from their fifteen years in the Australian wilderness, they would learn they were on their own and must find a home among the warring factions of Australian Lutheranism, where many would think they too were sell-outs.

When Dorsch passed on Homburg's letter, Heidenreich had to catch up with the consequences of Schwarz's January address, the waves of anger that were sweeping in from the Finke, meeting the politics of the metropolis and threatening to return under Gordon's direction as a consuming flood. He wrote immediately to Homburg for advice, and got this reply on May 8th: "In my opinion it is in your interests that you write yourself, or through Mr C von Bertouch, to Sir John Downer (your local Member) asking for an interview with the Education Minister.__ Mr Krichauff, I, Mr Scherk and others will accompany you in any case to protect your interests. __ You will concede that the Police report reflects poorly on your mission and it will in due course become a topic for discussion in Parliament. Before receiving your letter this morning I heard that Members of the new Parliament wish to raise the matter as soon as possible after the session opens."[270]

Gordon wanted no advice on how to carry out his enquiry. Within days Heidenreich was told by telegram that Gordon intended to appoint police Inspector Besley and Government Geologist H. Y. L. Brown (known generally as Geology Brown) to visit the mission station. Besley was an obvious choice for Willshire's Minister to make. Brown would be in the Centre in any case, in the normal course of his work. Little is known of Geology Brown the man, but all agree about his reticence and dislike of public exposure.

Heidenreich rushed to Adelaide, took counsel from Homburg and then went in Krichauff's company to see Minister Gordon. Was it true that he proposed to send the two officials on his enquiry? "Yes" was Gordon's blunt response. "I cannot concede", Heidenreich asserted, "that any enquiry should take place without my presence." "Good", Gordon retorted, "you can join them when they leave next Monday, but at your own cost."

When the shocked Heidenreich took this news back to Homburg, the latter saw that it was time to intervene openly. He took Heidenreich back into Gordon's office and negotiated on the spot a very different sort of enquiry. It would be headed by someone independent of the Government, a "judge" in Heidenreich's reporting, and that man would be joined by a nominee of the mission. It was also agreed that the mission's man would be Charles Eaton Taplin. Whether that idea was Heidenreich's or, under the pressure of this emergency, Homburg's, accepting Taplin was a major concession on Gordon's part. Taplin had already declared himself hostile to the police. Speaking publicly on January 9th he had said, "it would be very difficult to gather evidence on the spot on account of the complicity of the police". Police Commissioner Peterswald could not have been pleased.

Heidenreich took the matter to his mission committee on
May 13th. The committee decided to ask Homburg for his advice on
whether "half of its members should be German and the other half
English" and whether "these proceedings should take place in
Adelaide, and that reporters of the newspapers should be allowed to
attend." These proposals appealed to their sense of outrage, but were
unlikely to appeal to either Homburg or Gordon. In any case,
negotiations were over. It was time for action.

Another consequence of Gordon's back-down was delay. He
did not have in mind an independent man. Whatever he really
understood of events on the Finke, as an experienced politician he
knew how important his selection would be. He knew he had just
shouldered a substantial burden of risk. He had sent Heidenreich
and Homburg out the door with this unnerving promise: "If what the
police and the pastoralists have reported turns out to be true, I will
close the mission."[271] As, indeed, he could, since he was the Finke
River Mission's landlord, and they had no lease. "Those were
difficult days", Heidenreich told his fellow Lutherans later.

But Gordon was now also on the defensive. He had accepted
Taplin, but would need the acquiescence of Heidenreich in
appointing the man who was to lead the enquiry, the man whose
opinions and judgement might well decide whether it was the
mission or Gordon's career that came to a close.

Comes the hour, comes the man, but rarely can a saviour
have appeared on the scene with the timeliness demonstrated by
Henry Charles Swan. On May 8th 1890, the very day Robert
Homburg wrote the letter that shook Heidenreich to his boots,
Henry Swan wrote to the government seeking appointment to a
position of Stipendiary Magistrate, that is to say, a salaried
magistrate, which had just fallen vacant. Homburg and Heidenreich
could scarcely have left Gordon's room before Gordon's attention
was drawn to the letter. Henry Swan had form, and he had a file.[272]

Henry Swan had owned or part-owned the Angorichina
pastoral station in the arid northern Flinders Ranges of South
Australia in 1860 when a shepherd for a neighbouring pastoralist
discovered a rich lode of copper on Swan's property and became a
rich man. Henry Swan had no rights to the mineral wealth beneath
his lease, but he found something else, a taste for public authority.
He signed a petition for a magistrate to be appointed to the unruly

mining village of Blinman that rapidly formed around the mineshaft, and was himself appointed to the Special Magistracy that was created. Special Magistrates were paid on a piece-work basis, by the session of their court, and needed to keep their day-job as well. Blinman offered only the lower order of cases that arise from excessive drinking, and the sly-grogging that springs up to satisfy the miners' thirst, cases that are quickly disposed of and demand little legal reasoning.[273]

For the next quarter of a century Swan, who left pastoralism for rural contracting, hungered for a salaried government job. He applied on several occasions for appointment as a Stipendiary Magistrate, but achieved only a further term as a Special Magistrate. After Members of Parliament were granted salaries, in 1887, Swan put his name forward in 1890 for one of the two seats in the House of Assembly's vast rural electorate of Flinders. He had stood for the same seat twenty years before but failed to win it, and whatever taste he had for putting himself about the electorate was unlikely to have increased in the meantime. Like the other four candidates Swan now lived in Adelaide, in Swan's case on the esplanade at Semaphore beach, where the sea-breezes pushed back his curtains of a summer afternoon while the electors of Flinders baked. He learned on April 11th that he had not succeeded in winning a Seat in the Assembly, receiving only twelve percent of the formal votes cast, and most of those from the booths near (using "near" in its outback sense) his old station. But politics was to help him achieve his own court room and a salary of £500 per annum.[274]

It should be made clear that at a time when learning on the job was regarded more highly than it is now, Henry Swan's lack of legal training was not the disqualification it would be today. Justice Bundey, for goodness sake, had not even a school certificate to his name. In the days of his Blinman magistracy Swan had been called upon, on at least two occasions, to play a more demanding role than fining drunks. When the Moravian missionaries of Kopperamanna, east of Lake Eyre in the far north of the State, had called desperately for protection against the growing hostility of the Dieri people and their neighbours, Swan had been told off to accompany the small police party sent to rescue them, just in case conflict made it necessary to appoint Special Constables from among the white men of the district. The missionaries were extracted before a violent response became necessary.

Again, in March 1866, Swan accompanied the Protector of Aborigines to the same district, after a white man had been murdered, to advise the Minister on what action was needed to work justice. Swan reported that "two previous journeys made by [police constable] ... Gason assisted by Messrs Dean & Hacks stockmen, seem to have dispersed the natives all over the country & it will not be in the power of the police to execute the warrants entrusted to them till the natives settle". He thought the task of preventing cattle-killing hopeless since there were too many Aborigines in the district and they were too well-informed about police movements to get caught. "The only chance" he concluded " I think would be by having some half dozen native troopers armed only with swords & very frequent patrols by them of the native watering places." Such solid bush reasoning may well have recommended Swan to the Minister of the day, but tenured government employment at the level of a magistrate was too great a prize to be earned so easily. [275] Nevertheless, Henry Swan had made it clear that he belonged to the party of government, those solid citizens who understand that peace and order are the first object of governing, the necessary condition of all the other good things that grow in a well-governed society, and that government has many enemies not only among the merely self-interested or ill-disciplined but also among those who think other principles, like truth and justice, are of a higher order. Most men who held public office at this time, elected office or appointed office, can be allocated to this informal party, but until 1887 few were paid.

Swan had a lesson in identifying the enemies of government when he offered to enquire into the killing of two Aborigines by two white men near Lake Hope in 1868, but was greeted with the blunt response of the Chief Secretary Bakewell (the Minister in charge of police matters) that "I do not think that Messrs Dibney and Woodforde should be proceeded against...". Henry Swan was not discouraged. Four months later he applied for a much greater prize, the newly-created Government Resident of the Northern Territory, in effect the Governor of the Top End. "I have always been accustomed to an active life principally in the Bush" he assured the government "& having the control of a rough class of workmen... I could leave at a weeks notice if necessary". In 1868 Swan still had twenty two years to wait for his political prize.[276]

According to the 1891 Blue Book, the South Australian government's annual report to Parliament, Swan was appointed Stipendiary Magistrate for the Central District, based at Gawler, from July 23rd 1890, that is, just before the fall of the Government of Cockburn on August 19th 1890, when Henry Downer was still Attorney-General and John Gordon still in charge of the Northern Territory. This was a plum job at £500 *per annum* plus £50 travelling allowance, and led to bitter accusations in Parliament against Downer and his brother Sir John Downer. They were accused by Charles Cameron Kingston, as intemperately radical as John Downer was complacently conservative, of nepotism or, in Kingston's words, "a gross political job". A much better-qualified candidate was identified. John Downer admitted that he and his brother had political connections with Swan, and the Downers' views on Swan's political reliability were without doubt a factor in his appointment.[277] The issue was in fact raised by David Bews who, later that year, as John Gordon's successor as Minister responsible for the Northern Territory, received Henry Swan's report. Bews did not label the appointment nepotistic; he merely implied it.

By the time Henry Swan was notified of his appointment by telegram he was already on the track north to the Finke. He can have had scarcely a week's notice to pack, since he left at the end of May for the long trip north. It is beyond believing that Gordon or Henry Downer did not raise the prospect of the magistracy with Swan in the second half of May before he left Adelaide, no matter how confident they were that he would accept. If Downer and Gordon made no connection between Swan's appointment to the Finke Enquiry and the possibility he might be given the magistracy, it is inconceivable that Swan himself did not see it.

Between the second week of May, when the Gordon-Homburg deal had been agreed, and the Enquiry's departure north, there had been an exchange of correspondence between Heidenreich and Gordon's officials before Swan was, in Heidenreich's terms, "found". When Heidenreich assented, Gordon immediately wired him to come to his office in Adelaide. Heidenreich rode to Tanunda and caught the train south to Adelaide. When he arrived Heidenreich found Swan, Taplin and Besley already assembled in the Minister's ante-room, but not the Minister. They were told they could not see Gordon. Heidenreich was informed that Swan and Taplin were the Enquiry and that he and Besley were to represent the interests of the mission and police respectively. Only Swan was to be paid for his time, although Taplin received a travelling allowance. The mission would have to fund Heidenreich's costs.

On the morning of the next Saturday, May 24th, Heidenreich caught the train to Quorn where he had Church business to do before continuing further north. Before leaving he instructed Schwarz - "a loyal man in his own way", he wrote back to Germany - to stay with Heidenreich's Bethany congregation, and to make no accusations he could not support with witnesses. It had been eighteen days since Robert Homburg first wrote his urgent warning to Pastor Dorsch.

When he set off for the Central Australian desert Heidenreich knew he was in for the fight of his life. One week earlier on May 19th Heidenreich wrote a long report to Harms in Germany. "I will do everything I can to save the mission, but I don't know if I can save the missionaries. Please reserve some of your students for me."[278]

John Gordon's letter commissioning Swan and Taplin to "enquire into the charges and counter-charges which have been made as to the treatment of the aborigines of the Southern part of the Northern Territory" is dated June 13th 1890, two weeks *after* the last of the Enquiry party had left Adelaide.[279]

For Heidenreich at least there was one further surprise waiting on the railway journey north. The train stopped at Strangways Springs for twenty minutes to allow the passengers to take lunch. After fifteen minutes the train steamed off, leaving Heidenreich and Mounted Constable Chance open-mouthed at the table, with a five day wait for the next service. Heidenreich had planned to ride the mail wagon north from the rail-head, but now he had missed the post. When he arrived at the terminus, Warrina, with the rest of the Enquiry party, Heidenreich had to join them in selecting camels from Taj Jemmidar's herd of 2000. "I felt sure I lacked the strength and stamina to ride six hundred miles up and back on a camel" he said, but commended his soul to God's care, because he was sure that he needed to be at the Enquiry "from the beginning to the end". In fact it was the comradeship created between Swan, Besley and Heidenreich on the shared camel trip north that allowed them all to achieve their purposes within a few days of arriving at Hermannsburg. Heidenreich was then able to skip the Enquiry's round of interviews at the villages and stations of the Centre. Instead he spent another week with Kempe, Schulze and the Aranda-Christians, re-joining the Enquiry later for the journey south.

At the end of the first day's travelling by camel, in the course of which his first beast could not be persuaded by a severe whipping to carry him, Heidenreich reached camp so stiff from the unaccustomed exercise that he had to be lifted from the saddle by Henry Swan and Bryan Besley. "This is the first day of a new affliction" he lamented, but it was the arms of Swan and Besley that provided an apt metaphor for the way in which the arms of government were to rescue the Finke River mission from the pit that had opened beneath it. Inspector Besley suffered so much from motion sickness that he could eat nothing but flour soup. Only Henry Swan, it seems, found that his body could be tuned to the rhythm of a camel's.

Heidenreich's report of the journey did not mention Charles Eaton Taplin until the account had reached Hermannsburg. That reference was not a compliment.[280]

Henry Swan, Charles Eaton Taplin and
Bryan Besley on their Enquiry (*PRSA*).

Charles Eaton Taplin (*CSA 1;547*)

Henry Charles Swan, hungry for office but with a long wait
ahead of him, in 1864, with his wife and other members of
her family (*SLSA B18517*)

Inspector Bryan Besley, police Inspector for the Far North of South Australia, and commanding officer of the Central Australian police, date unknown. Intelligent, charming, capable of ruthlessness, Besley steered his governments between the demands for cheap frontier policing and legality. He also saved Commissioner Peterswald's reputation, and possibly his career (SAPHS).

Lutheran Mission Station

M. St. Hermannsburg April 13. 1885.

Central Australia, P.O. Charlotte waters

2

To ~~[struck out]~~ the Protector of Aborigenes.
Adelaide.

Sir

we received your letter from 2⁴/₂ wherein you say, that a police force at Alice Springs shall be established to keep both the Europeens & the Blacks in check. "Wether from this measure shall arise any good for the natives is rather doubtful, as long as there is nobody to control the actions of the police troopers. The only difference will be, the natives are now shot down by police men, whilst before that the other whites did it. One illustration for this: Some time ago a police Trooper with two black trackers & two other white men came here to punish the natives for some outrages they committed at Glen Helen, north of our Station. They captured three natives of which they thought they were guilty on our Station & Transported them with a strong trace chain fastened together round their necks to Glen Helen, but came not so far with them. They passed our sheep camp, where I was that time. The other day the natives informed us the three natives were shot down in the ranges by the whites. We went there & convinced ourselfes from the truth of this statement. Now we expected directly the whites would say they tried to escape, & so

Hermann Kempe signed this letter dated April 13, 1885, complaining about Erwein Wurmbrand's murder of three prisoners. But was someone else, possibly Colonist Jürgens, supplying his words, and why?

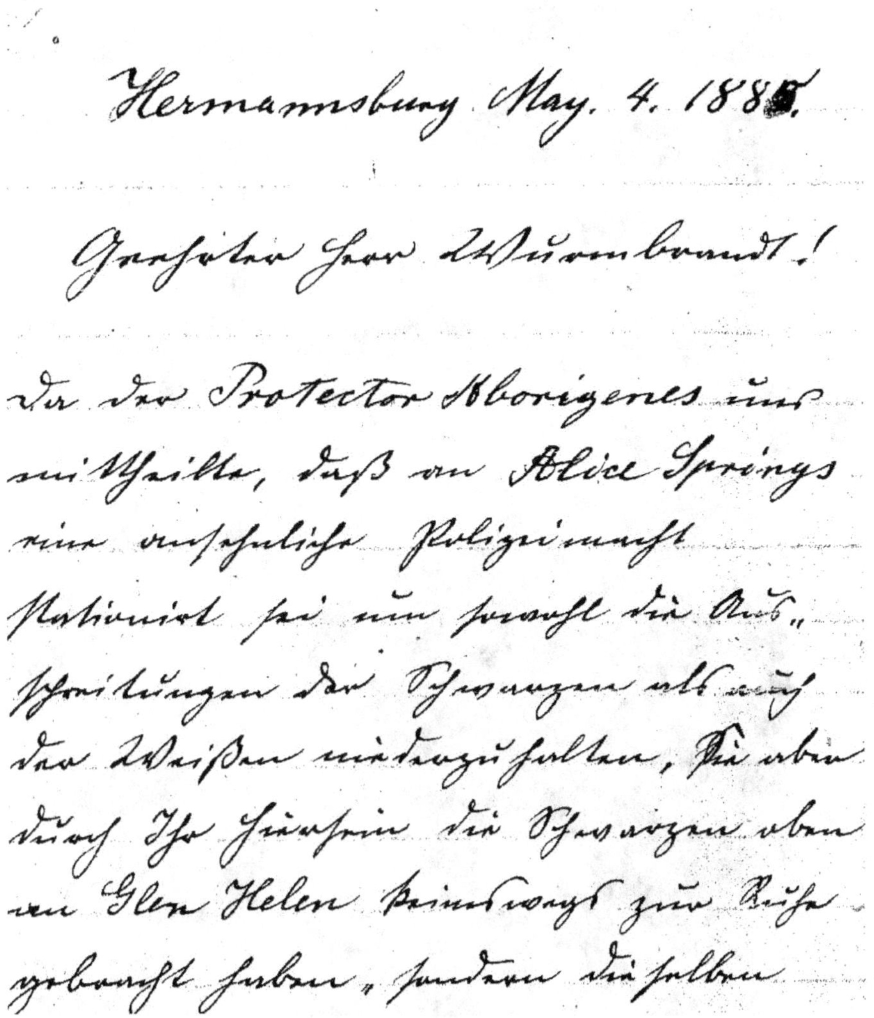

Hermannsburg May. 4. 1885.

Geehrter Herr Wurmbrandt!

Da der Protector Aborigenes uns mittheilte, daß in Alice Springs eine ansehnliche Polizeimacht stationirt sei um sowohl die Ausschreitungen der Schwarzen als auch der Weißen niederzuhalten, Sie aber durch Ihr Einschreiten die Schwarzen oben von Glen Helen keineswegs zur Ruhe gebracht haben, sondern dieselben

Hermann Kempe's letter of May 4, 1885 to Mounted Constable Wurmbrand, after the Glen Helen murders and after his letter of complaint (above), provided the police with a weapon capable of destroying the mission, and the Commissioner of Police (*PRSA GRG 52/1/1885/150;21*).

John Hannah Gordon, Presbyterian, mayor, pastoralist, Minister for the Northern Territory, and later judge. His hostility to the Finke River mission was checked by Robert Homburg's intervention, and by the agendas of the police and the missionaries (*CSA I;247*).

Some time after 1891 the three former missionaries were brought together for this group portrait. On the left, Wilhelm Schwarz, centre Louis Schulze, and Hermann Kempe. Georg Heidenreich blamed Schwarz for the near-death of the Finke River mission in 1890, but it was Hermann Kempe, his collaborator during the Enquiry, who agitated against him after Kempe fled south in 1891 (*LA7/04-2324*).

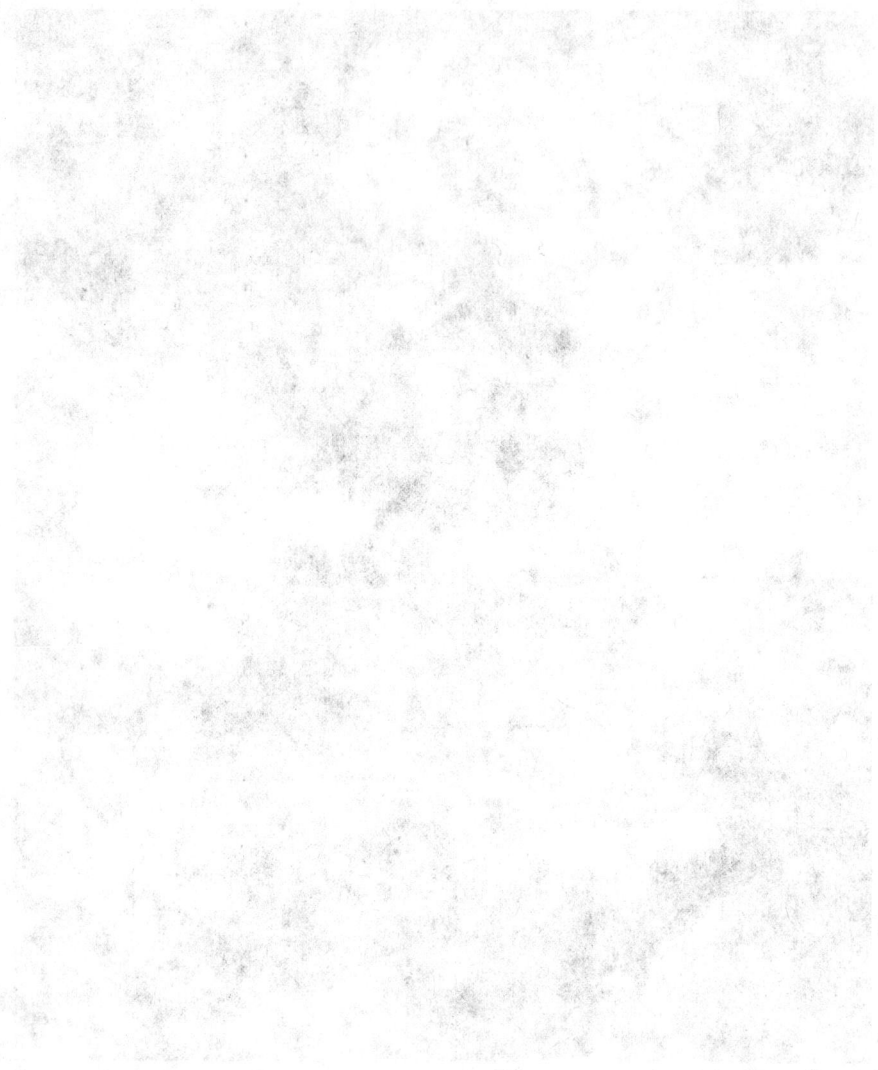

12

LISTENING IN ORDER NOT TO HEAR

On the morning of Saturday July 19th 1890 Hermann Kempe set out soap and water so that the men, women and children of the mission could wash before the arrival of the Enquiry party. The approach of the Enquiry was announced by a hullabaloo among the Western Aranda. Kempe lined his people up as the camels arrived and unloaded their riders; Henry Swan, Charles Eaton Taplin, Pastor Georg Heidenreich, Mounted Constable Tom Daer and an Aboriginal man Eriakura, known as Charlie Cooper.[281] "Watch out for P[astor] Heidenreich" Kempe told the Western Aranda, "He's the one with black cockatoo feathers stuck in his hat."[282] Kempe rushed to help the exhausted Heidenreich from his saddle and introduced him and the other visitors to the German and Aranda Christians. This was to be the only way in which the Aboriginal people of the mission were involved in the Enquiry's proceedings. The members of the party were then taken to their accommodation in the house vacated by Schwarz the previous year, where five "beautiful, clean beds" awaited them. Swan and Taplin had their own rooms. Heidenreich and Besley, who were officially-endorsed observers, had to share the one room. This was a convenient arrangement for them both. They had much to talk about.

The next day, Sunday, a strong north-westerly wind was whipping dust into clouds that drove through the doors and windows of the houses so that, according to Heidenreich, it was impossible to keep one's eyes open. Nevertheless, the morning service went ahead, with Heidenreich preaching. Before the service ended, Inspector Bryan Besley arrived on his camel after spending a further day closeted with William Willshire at Boggy Water. He was so blinded by the dust it was necessary to lead him inside to the bowl of water. He introduced himself to the Western Aranda ironically: "'I am the boss for all the people, like P[astor]

Heidenreich. But I am a bigger boss than he is.'" In the course of the afternoon William Willshire and his contingent of police arrived. They and the managers of Glen Helen and Tempe Downs stations – James McDonald and Frederick Thornton – camped in the bed of the Finke. Mounted Constable Ernest Cowle, Willshire's replacement at the Heavitree Gap police station near Alice Springs, had been called down to help with the record of proceedings and joined the white men in the river bed. Tjalkabota and the other Western Aranda were very surprised to see them all. They remained ignorant of what the white men talked about inside the mission building over the next two weeks.

It was no accident that the Enquiry heard no Aboriginal evidence. When William Willshire told Bryan Besley that "if it [the controversy arising from the missionaries' accusations] does not die out I shall bring white men & black men forward as witnesses on my behalf" he was not blustering.[283] The threat came at the end of the last of his letters in response to the missionaries' charges, dated May 5th 1890. If Peterswald and Gordon knew of this promise and threat when they constructed the Willshire letter which appeared in the press they did not reveal it. When Heidenreich met Thomas, Hanna and Maria at Boggy Water on July 18th he still had no idea. As he reported later about his time at Boggy water, "I had the blacks called together and asked those who had been baptised, Thomas, Hanna and Maria, who had been baptised by our Brothers and had run away, if they did not wish to come back with me to the station. They said, yes, they would come soon; but I did not know that they had been designated as witnesses against our Brothers." He learned soon enough after his arrival at the mission station, some time between the arrival of Besley and Willshire on Sunday morning and the start of the enquiry on Monday morning, even earlier if Willshire had warned Kempe and Schulze before the Enquiry's arrival. So it was that on the eve of the first day of the enquiry Heidenreich learned what lay behind the references Kempe and Schulze had been making to their use of corporal punishment, that the charges of Hermannsburg being a "flogging mission" were more than malicious exaggeration. He now saw the ace that John Gordon had kept up his sleeve during May. Heidenreich now knew, for the first time, just how deep was the hole the Finke River mission had dug for itself.

Heidenreich's report is silent on the negotiations that led to the Enquiry's exclusion of evidence from Thomas, Hanna and Maria. The transcript of evidence is silent on most matters of procedure. It follows logically, however, that if Willshire were to be denied his Aboriginal witnesses, then the same rule must act to exclude any Aboriginal witnesses the mission had in mind to call. It is unlikely that Kempe and Schulze intended to do so anyway, but there were two others who could have insisted: Georg Heidenreich and Charles Eaton Taplin. They clearly did not. So the Enquiry heard nothing from any Aboriginal man or woman who might have had evidence against pastoralist, policeman or missionary, or against other Aborigines. Archie was not questioned about the long patrols to the west on which he had accompanied Willshire. Chantoonga and Nabarong were not questioned about the circumstances of their joining Willshire's menage. Thomas was not questioned about the "murdering expedition" he had joined shortly after he was recruited by Willshire. The Western Aranda relatives of the woman Wodoa, who had died of her wounds at the station six or seven years earlier, were not sought and questioned. And Ereminta was not invited to tell his side of his conflict with William Willshire. It is unlikely that Swan or Taplin knew of all of these stories, but we know that Heidenreich knew most of it, for he was the conduit through which it had been transmitted in the *Church messenger* to the southern Lutherans, and he was the confidant and master of the missionaries.

The exclusion of Aboriginal witnesses, even those Aranda-Christians who could be sworn, gave Henry Swan additional licence to exclude evidence from white witnesses. Any evidence the missionaries or anyone else had "from the Blacks" could be excluded as hearsay. This is how I interpret this cryptic reference in Louis Schulze's evidence, as he is describing his return from Boggy Water with the absconding women: "I spoke to them on the road and at our place and Martha and Maria told me something." There is no elaboration. Presumably it was something too sensitive even for the secret transcript that Ernest Cowle was making, and it is highly plausible that it concerned William Willshire. Heidenreich later reported that blind Martha had complained that Willshire had made advances to her.[284]

William Willshire did not need the evidence of Thomas and Hanna to prove that the mission had been imposing illegal punishment and restraint on its Aranda Christians. He had seen Hanna hobbled at the mission, as had Wesley Turton, an Alice Springs witness called later by the missionaries on their own behalf. Willshire knew the right questions to ask and could reasonably expect to poke the truth out of Kempe and Schulze. From Inspector Besley's point of view the exclusion of Aboriginal witnesses was a very attractive deal, but it was not enough. Of greater concern to him than Willshire's morality or professionalism, or Gordon's hostility to the mission, was, as the *Register* editorialist had seen, the killings in Glen Helen Gorge in December 1884. That disgraceful event had been kept out of the press in 1885 but it had the potential to rise again to startle the people of South Australia and embarrass its government. But the fact of the Glen Helen killings was central to the mission's defence of its own conduct, and could not be ignored.

Kempe dealt with the Glen Helen killings very briefly early in his presentation on the first day of the Enquiry's hearings, Monday July 21st 1890. The point of the missionaries' defence of their conduct towards the Aboriginal people on their station was this: "How could we have any confidence in the police, because they have taken others away from here and shot them". Their only direct evidence in support of this excuse was the Wurmbrand murders. To support their generalised accusation that whites shot Aboriginal men indiscriminately (they "go at night into a black's camp and shoot down every one they can reach with firearms", as they had said in their letter to Charles Eaton Taplin) they had only Wurmbrand and the even older story of the woman Wodoa. They could not resile from the Wurmbrand story without undermining their defence. Nor could Heidenreich refrain from dealing with Wurmbrand, since some of his southern constituents had long memories. To understand their position we need to look more closely at the circumstances surrounding Wurmbrand's 1884 killings.

Despite their self-righteous claims of more friendly relations with their Abroriginal neighbours than the pastoralists, the missionaries found stock-killing an aggravation. In the 1888 pastoralists' delegation to the Minister for the Northern Territory complaining of cattle-killing, Friedrich Krichauff represented the mission, no doubt at Heidenreich's request. The mission had mostly sheep which required closer watching in any case. With fewer cattle wandering unattended they had less to lose to the Aboriginal raiders. We should not forget, either, that both cattle-killing and forceful defence of the old ways against the missionaries' preaching were led by senior men. Around the time of the Wurmbrand killings, Kempe had written to Erwein Wurmbrand, in German, with the following appeal (in Wurmbrand's own, very literal translation):

Hermannsburg May 4th 1884

Honored Mr Wurmbrand

As the Protector of Aborigines informed us that a considerable body of Police is stationed at Alice Springs to check outrages of white as well as blacks, but you by your presence by no means have quietened the blacks at Glen Helen and they still disturb the country up there and down here, as before, by rummaging now in our country and among the cattle, I would herewith request you to come up here again to take if possible the whole nest. They are now in a dense mulga scrub and therefore easy to capture.

With regards respectfully

Your

H. Kempe

Kempe's letter, on lined notepaper, is still on the police file. The last number of its date "May.4. 188[?]." is a dense blob from which the horizontal stroke of the number 5 extends to the right and upwards, like the tail from a mouse facing down the page. Wurmbrand himself tells us in a report he wrote to Inspector Bryan Besley in June 1885 that the number now obscured was a 4, and explains the matter in the following way: "The Rev: H. Kempe has evidently made a mistake by dating his letter 1884 instead of 1885, as he refers to my visit to Herman[n]sburg in November 1884." Wurmbrand is referring to the occasion on which he arrested the men he later killed in Glen Helen Gorge. We may infer that the number was changed by Besley or some other official down south, since Wurmbrand makes no reference to the superimposed 5.

But is Wurmbrand right? It was in Wurmbrand's interest to place the letter in May 1885 rather than May 1884. If Kempe had written this letter in 1884 he was offering no implicit endorsement of Wurmbrand's explanation of how he came to shoot the three Aboriginal men. But if the letter was written in May 1885 then Wurmbrand could say, as he wrote to Besley, "It is needless for me to enter into details, as the contents of the letter ... amply prove, that the assistance of the Native Police is called for again, which these Rev: gentlemen, who I am sorry to say are rather prejudiced against the Native Police, would certainly not do, if there was the least cause to complain of our conduct". And what does an 1885 dating say about Hermann Kempe?

There is evidence in the Kempe letter itself to support Wurmbrand's date of May 1885. The letter begins: " As the Protector of Aborigines informed us that a considerable body of Police is stationed at Alice Springs to check outrages of white as well as blacks ...". Kempe can only be referring to a letter from the Protector dated February 26th 1885. This letter had promised that additional police patrols would be made "with a view to keeping the Europeans, as well as the blacks, in check and preventing outrages being committed on either side." No other correspondence of the Protector's in the period 1884-5 can offer an alternative explanation of Kempe's reference, and Kempe's echoing of the Protector's phrasing, "keeping the Europeans, as well as the Blacks, in check", seems to settle the matter in Wurmbrand's favour.

Wurmbrand's translation of Kempe's May 4th letter is, if anything, generous to Kempe, whose request to Wurmbrand was that he come and "clean out the whole nest", rather than "take" it.[285] Kempe could not have known it, but on the very day he wrote that letter, Wurmbrand was up on the Glen Helen run again and shooting several Aboriginal men against whom he had warrants for attempted murder and cattle-killing. Wurmbrand had approached by a roundabout route to the north, avoiding both Hermannsburg and Glen Helen head stations.

If Wurmbrand is right, then Hermann Kempe, knowing that Wurmbrand had shot his three prisoners in Glen Helen Gorge, is asking him to come back to the mission and arrest more Aboriginal men, and what is facing the Finke River Mission, and all associated with it, is surely utter disgrace. Every German-born South Australian would have had cause for shame. Assuming, of course, that the Wurmbrand killings were wilful murder, as the missionaries had already declared them to be.

Adding to the questions raised by the Kempe-Wurmbrand letter is another curious matter of timing. Kempe signed another letter to the Protector of Aborigines on April 13th 1885, three weeks *before* his letter to Wurmbrand, responding to that same letter of February 26th from the Protector. In fact it was this earlier letter from Kempe that caused Wurmbrand to get a "please explain" from his superiors, and led Wurmbrand, in turn, to send Kempe's letter of May 4th 1884/5 down south.

The Kempe letter of April 13th makes a very different response to the Protector's assurances about police patrols. "W[h]ether from this measure shall arise any good for the nativ[e]s is rather doubtful as long as there is nobody to control the actions of the police troopers. The only difference will be, the nativ[e]s are now shot down by police men, whilst before that the other whites did it" is its terse verdict. This Kempe letter begins "*we* received your letter from 26/2..." (I have added the italics), although the Protector's letter was in fact addressed to Wilhelm Schwarz alone. Schwarz alone had written to Hamilton at the end of November 1884 complaining about the treatment of Aborigines by white *civilians.* He mentioned the sad story of Wodoa, but said she was "shot by whites" and made no reference to police or the name "Dare" (Daer) that he later reported to Swan-Taplin. But Schwarz's complaint was written a few days *before* the Wurmbrand killings, at a time when he may still have doubted that a policeman, especially a German policeman, would behave so murderously.

By now you can see that we have arrived at a startling understanding of the relationship of the mission to the police. There were two mission responses to Wurmbrand's killings. Schwarz responded with anger. Wurmbrand had not only committed murder, he had made Schwarz an accomplice when he told Wurmbrand in November 1884 that the Aboriginal victims were on the mission station. Allied to Schwarz we find the Colonist Jürgens whose gruesome task it was to inspect the bodies soon after the event, and whose first-person account – "They passed our sheep camp, where I was that time" – found its way into the letter Kempe signed on April 13th 1885. Hermann Kempe on the other hand welcomed the deaths of these trouble-making, recalcitrant men. One of them, Latya, he had pointed out to Wurmbrand on December 1st 1884 as the murderer of two young men associated with the mission. Perhaps on that day Kempe had urged Wurmbrand on, demanding severe action.

In this new interpretation of the 1884-5 events, Kempe's hand was later forced by the pressure of his colleagues' anger to write the letter of April 13th 1885 to Protector Hamilton, and when he wrote on his own account three weeks later to his fellow German Wurmbrand he was thumbing his nose at his colleagues, and re-asserting, in his own eyes at least, his authority as head of the mission. Blinded by anger he may have deluded himself into believing that Wurmbrand would treat his letter as a private matter.

To take one step further from the evidence, it may have been the impact of Kempe's dispute with his fellow missionaries on his mental state that was the precipitating cause of the Kempes' furlough in the south in the middle of 1885. Kempe may well have been, once again, near breaking point, and kind enough to himself to admit as much to Heidenreich.

When I set out to write this section I was convinced that Wurmbrand was lying about the date of Kempe's letter to him of May 4th. But once we allow ourselves to think that Hermann Kempe in his struggle with the senior men Western Aranda men and his colleagues could have endorsed willingly Wirmbrand's brutality, and the evidence points us that way, a new picture of events on the Finke starts to emerge. Here in November 1884 we may have found the key to the irreconcilable differences between Kempe and Schulze on the one hand and Schwarz and Jürgens on the other, the fracture which spread until, under the weight of their many other trials in the Centre, the mission fell apart in 1889-91. We now have to divert from this account of the Swan-Taplin enquiry to re-write also the motives of Andreas and Thomas. In doing so we are re-writing the origins of Aranda Lutheranism.

Some time shortly before the middle of 1885, when the two young men Kalimalla and Tekua accompanied Hermann Kempe on his journey to the south, they had left Glen Helen station and moved to the mission. They had been among the mission's most active opponents, and were still, according to Schwarz, considered by the missionaries to be among those least likely to seek baptism. They were only persuaded to Christianity by their months with the Dieri-Lutherans at Bethesda where they lost their fear of the old men and their magic. And it was their decision to embrace Christianity, according to the story I have told to this point, that led a children's revolution against the old Western Aranda way. Looking more closely at the limited evidence available I find reasons to think otherwise.

The Wurmbrand killings took place, as you may recall, in Glen Helen Gorge, a site of great ceremonial significance. It was also on the main road between the Western Aranda lands north and south of the MacDonnell Ranges. It must have shocked the Western Aranda even more than it shocked Schwarz and Jürgens. The victims were not chosen randomly. They were identified by the whites of Glen Helen station and their black allies, and by Kempe and Schwarz, as 'ringleaders'. That means they were senior men in positions of leadership. It was they, and a few others besides, who were in charge of the initiation ceremonies through which Kalimalla and Tekua were promoted to the status of Western Aranda manhood from the insignificance of Western Aranda childhood. These men also played leading parts in the inquests that determined who should die for magical offences against members of their clans, they arranged the revenge parties, and they ruled on matters of dispute within the clans and ordered the punishments. The most powerful Western Aranda knowledge was the private possession of these men. And then, on December 1st 1884, they are slaughtered like tethered goats in the heartland of their powers. Wurmbrand's exercise in exemplary punishment was exemplary in ways he can hardly have imagined, and who was better placed to learn the lessons than two young men, one lively and ambitious, the other a natural follower? Even before they had decided to convert to Lutheranism, Tekua and Kalimalla may have decided that the powerful knowledge and laws on which a future could be built lay with the whites. Among the whites, the men with the songs and ceremonies, with an alternative *tjurunga*, were the missionaries.

But why should it have been only Kalimalla and Tekua who learned the lesson? It seems that it wasn't. On August 30th 1886, shortly after Hermann Kempe left Adelaide for the journey back to the Finke, the mission's political patron Friedrich Krichauff read a paper to the Geographical Society in Adelaide. He began: "I have collected, arranged and translated the following particulars about the ... 'Aldolinga' [Western Aranda] .. from information forwarded by the missionary, Rev. J. Kempe, of Hermannsburg, on the Finke river, and from a letter dated July 1st, 1886, written by the missionary, L. Schulze ...". He ended with these words:

A few months ago some of the men and the elder boys who had attended the school at the Mission expressed a wish to be baptised. These receive now twice a week, in the evening, religious instruction, preparatory to their being christened.

Both of Krichauff's sources, supplemented one assumes by some face-to-face discussion while Kempe was in Adelaide, *precede* Kempe's return to the Finke with Kalimalla and Tekua. If the reference to religious instruction derives from Kempe's reports before mid-1885 it is likely that the "elder boys" undergoing instruction included Tekua and Kalimalla, who, we know from the missionaries' reports, had spent a little time at the mission school prior to their trip to Bethesda in 1885-6. We already know from the later events recounted in earlier chapters that those most likely to continue with formal instruction were the younger people. Few senior men at this time were prepared to subject themselves to the discipline and indignity of schooling.

If Tekua and Kalimalla did experience some form of conversion at Bethesda it is surprising that the head of that mission at the time, Pastor Flierl, failed to notice it. He certainly noticed their arrival, which was a significant item in his report covering that period. "It is expected that the guests, especially the two Blacks [Colonist Koch was with them], will remain for a long time with us. May the Lord grant that they take a good impression away with them when they go, and that their stay with us is a blessing to them." It would be surprising if the two young men evidenced a desire to adopt Christianity under the influence of the Dieri without Flierl drawing attention to it. In his reports over the period of Tekua and Kalimalla's stay, Flierl did notice events marking the struggle among the Dieri between the old ways and the emerging new way. These would have impressed the visitors, because nothing like them had happened on the upper Finke.

They saw the Dieri catechumens burn their weapons, "despite their fear of the blood-avengers". They shared a classroom with a girl who had shot a white man dead, apparently by accident, and had been sent to Bethesda by the Protector for want of any better idea of what to do with her. They met Dieri Christians who had survived the transition to the new way. More powerful lessons than could be found in the Lutheran catechism. Still, Tekua and Kalimalla gave the Bethesda mission no sign that they would, within weeks, ask Kempe for baptism.[286]

So here we have a version of the past that would have been unpalatable to both Wilhelm Schwarz and Hermann Kempe. One cornerstone of Aranda Lutheranism was Erwein Wurmbrand's revolver. Tekua and Kalimalla had been driven to the mission by Wurmbrand's violence, had chosen their goal before they left the Finke for Bethesda, but were prudently prospecting the route forward before subjecting themselves to Lutheran initiation. Perhaps the lesson the young men took back to the Finke was just this: the way ahead is clear, we have seen the young Dieri take it and survive. But it was only the younger Western Aranda who attended classes who were qualified, under the Lutheran way of doing conversions, to act on the knowledge. Prohibited by their ignorance of the Word, no senior men joined Tekua and Kalimalla in the first baptisms of 1887.

Five years later, in July 1890, Heidenreich may not have known Kempe's letter to Wurmbrand existed. If Kempe supposed that Wurmbrand had not kept his letter and sent it south, he could have had no reason to tell Heidenreich about it. Besley, however, knew what was in his file, and how powerful a weapon it could be. Perhaps it was in his camel pack at Hermannsburg. The Kempe letter, even more than the flogging of the heathen-Christian women, could have closed the mission, since it would have detached from Heidenreich all his religious allies in the south and left the mission exposed to the pastoralists' vengeance. Even if we limit Heidenreich's knowledge to what we know he knew at the time, he faced a delicate situation. There was a German-speaking population, among them men of influence like Friedrich Krichauff, MP, Robert Homburg, MP, and the editors of the *Church messenger* and the

Australische Zeitung, who had read the Schwarz account of the Wurmbrand killings in 1885. Schwarz's report and the reports of his two fellow missionaries attracted unfavourable attention among the southern Lutherans.

"We have many heathen here at present who are determined to remain from fear of the police who are taking harsh action against them on all the neighbouring stations. In recent weeks the police have also made several visits to us. They arrested four Blacks who had fled here. One was freed on our assurance of his future good behaviour while the others were shot. God knows how many apart from these three have been shot to date, and will be in future." To this sentence the editors of the *Church messenger* added a footnote, the first of only two such comments to be found in all the mission's reports published in the *Church messenger*: "Without a hearing, judgement and law? In this way the innocent often have to suffer for the guilty. Where is the basis for such arbitrary action on the part of the police, denying the Aborigines all rights and privileges of British citizenship?" The editors may have been provoked to this exceptional intervention by the manner in which Kempe and Schulze reported the same incident, as part of the mission report compiled by Heidenreich from the individual reports of the three men. Kempe simply ignored Wurmbrand, commenting only that "We have little to fear from the Aborigines resident on our mission. They scarcely try to steal cattle any more. When it has happened recently it has been strangers who have been the ringleaders. ... our Aborigines have understood that it is far better and safer to earn their bread by working than by stealing, and that is a step forward that should not be underestimated." Louis Schulze was published five months later: "Our heathen are now, since the policeman shot three dead, no longer so impertinent. So some good has arisen from that disgraceful act."[287] By this time Heidenreich had settled the disturbance among the southern Germans. "Can I note, concerning the shooting of the three heathen," he wrote in July, "that the editors of the *Australische zeitung* were good enough to send me for comment and further information their three questions to our missionaries, before publication. Because they were so obliging I have done so, and can inform you also that the Protector of Aborigines demanded a detailed report from our missionaries immediately after the event and received it, warts and all." This was so far from the recorded facts of what happened before and after, as I suppose, Schwarz and Jürgens forced from Kempe the letter of April 13th to the Protector, that it must be regarded as a convenient invention. It seems to have worked, however. The *Australische zeitung*, published by Friedrich Basedow, a former Protector of Aborigines, a near neighbour of Heidenreich's from the village of Tanunda, and his local Member of Parliament, printed nothing about the Glen Helen episode.

Bryan Besley's position, had Heidenreich but known, was even more delicate. The revelation of the truth of 1884-5 would not only have damaged his reputation but also put him and his men in jeopardy of criminal prosecutions. If the Glen Helen matter could not be suppressed, it had to be contained and neutralised. So began, on the second day of the enquiry, a curious pantomime in which, according to Heidenreich's account of it, Besley pretended not to know what he knew about the mission's role in 1885, and Heidenreich, and later the two missionaries, pretended it scarcely mattered. Here is Heidenreich's report to his southern constituents:

At this point in the proceedings there arose the old business that Brother Kempe and I had settled with the Minister, so that the Blacks would be better treated. The Inspector had later received a detailed telegram from the Minister, and given the order to all his people. He [Besley] said that he also had a witness with him, Mr Mac Donnald [McDonald] who could provide information on the shooting. But because by this time Mounted Constable Wombram [Wurmbrand] had left the police service and was wandering about in the North, and Schleicher was dead, he asked the Brothers once again, if they wanted to make a criminal matter of the case. If so, he would cross-examine the witness. We all felt that the guilt would fall on Schleicher who can no longer answer for himself. Further, the Brothers were asked if they had been on the spot when they got the news and had seen whether the three had been shot from behind or from the front. At that they had to say that they had not been present in person, rather it was the Colonists Baden and Jürgens, the former having since died and the other moved to New Zealand. So the Inspector said it came down to whether they [the Aboriginal victims] were shot from the front or the back. If they were shot from the back that corroborated the earlier report to the Minister that they had been shot while escaping, because they would not stop when he [Wurmbrand] called on them to do so in the Queen's name, as he has every right to do in such cases. He went on to make clear that he was prepared to take it up if they wished to make a criminal case of it. The Brothers made it clear that they did not want to do that, and so McDonald was not cross-examined on it and the matter was settled.[288]

It seems Heidenreich had forgotten in the course of writing this section of his report the assurance he had received from the Chief Secretary in 1885, that in future Aborigines would only be fired on in self-defence. It seems likely that Besley and McDonald had discussed beforehand their curious interpretation of gunshot wounds to the back as proof that the victims were attempting to escape, and of a lack of murderous intent on the part of the shooter. It is clear enough that if the matter had been dealt with purely on the basis of McDonald's evidence, and in front of Henry Swan, Wurmbrand and his accomplices, including McDonald, would have been found innocent. But Henry Swan's Enquiry was not competent to try murder cases. Presumably for that reason, when Swan reported later that the missionaries' use of violence and restraint was excusable he made no mention of the principal evidence advanced by the missionaries in favour of that conclusion, the Glen Helen killings. In fact the Glen Helen killings were beside the point of the missionaries' violence against their women Aranda-Christians.

Heidenreich was grateful for Swan's understanding of the missionaries' position. "Mr Swan said after the Brothers' explanation that they had imposed punishment on the heathen with good intentions, so that they would not be shot down, and although it was not in accord with the law the missionaries were excused by their good intentions." And Heidenreich added "I must say that Mr Swan has shown himself completely just and independent in his enquiry into the Station, and has helped us to a just outcome more than my helper Mr Taplin."

It was not Heidenreich's purpose to deny the fact of the Glen Helen killings. In fact he thought "It is certain that these three are not the only ones to be shot down. There are people crippled by bullet wounds even on our Station, and that can not be truthfully contradicted by the Northerners [Central Australians] or the police. But without clear proof of the circumstances and the perpetrators there is nothing an earthly court can do about it." Instead, it was for God to judge and punish, and he supposed ex-Mounted Constable Erwein Wurmbrand, now reported in the North West of Western

Australia, to be "a madman wandering about among the savages with a dwarf on his back." To which the editors of the *Church messenger* added their second editorial comment: "(?)".

At Hermannsburg on Monday morning July 21st 1890 before the formal proceedings began the Enquiry party inspected the mission's buildings and that wonder of the Centre, the vegetable garden. From 10.00 am Kempe gave evidence on the claims made by Schwarz in Adelaide and his own claims in the letter published in the Adelaide press. Apart from his own statement we can assume Kempe was questioned by the Enquiry Commissioners, Swan and Taplin, but soon after Louis Schulze began his evidence on the second day the transcript indicates that William Willshire began his cross-examination. It continued for the remainder of the day, until the hearing adjourned at 5.30 p.m. On the Wednesday Kempe was re-called so that Willshire could cross-examine him. Willshire's questioning was aggressive, according to Heidenreich. It succeeded not only in forcing detailed confessions from Schulze and Kempe about their beating of the women, but also in undermining the mission's criticisms of the pastoralists' conduct toward Aborigines.

Firstly there was the question of immorality. Kempe reported the mixed couples he had seen on his occasional trips off the mission, including the Aboriginal women in men's clothes on horseback, but the instances were few since he had not often travelled far from the mission station, and he knew few names. In any case, had he seen what went on under the blankets? Certainly Kempe had sacked Schleicher for cohabiting with an Aboriginal woman, but not until sometime after she had borne him a child. Their worker Docherty was sacked "at once" for a casual relationship. Schulze denied he had reprimanded the Colonist Freiboth in his single days for a similar reason. Yes, the missionaries had encouraged a marriage that broke the Western Aranda's own marriage laws. Between the indefinite nature of their accusations, and the conduct of white men on their own station, the missionaries attack on frontier morality was looking rather thin.

Willshire achieved a similar result on the question of firearms. No doubt the Colonists, like all station workers, wore revolvers when out on the run. But so, it turned out, did missionaries, and sometimes the revolver was in the missionary's hand. They had wanted to dissuade Reingaraka from killing another man with whom he had a quarrel. They did so by going in to the camp and destroying Reingaraka's spears. "I had a revolver in my hand when I went into the camp", Schulze conceded. This was hardly more than prudent behaviour, but it made the missionaries seem no better than the pastoralists.

The Enquiry's focus on Willshire was such that he was able to become *de facto* the leader of the prosecution of the Finke River mission while himself in danger of little more than embarrassment. Even that danger was avoided, since Willshire's lies went unchallenged. On the morning of the third day it is recorded that "At this stage the Missionaries say they have no wish to call against the police or whites any other evidence". Willshire had already pushed Schulze into saying "your being at Boggy Waterhole is no more detriment[al] to our mission than any other white man would be. I have nothing against you." So, before the end of the third day of the hearings the Enquiry was, in effect, over. There was little risk now of embarrassment to police, Minister or Government. Willshire denied the Schwarz charges, without contradiction from Kempe or Schulze. He repeated his own charge that cattle-killers took refuge at the mission, but only one of those he named was at Hermannsburg at the time. "I have always considered those [to be] Mission blacks who were at any time residing on the place." For that reason he was able to include among the "mission blacks" the Owen Springs man Billy Cloud, but he conceded Billy Cloud was now "a reformed character". James McDonald's complaints about the mission's harbouring of cattle killers had the same character. The warring parties now stood back at a distance from each other, their weapons sheathed. The frontier courtesies that had been pushed aside by righteousness and indignation were now restored. The Aboriginal people remained in the bed of the Finke.

After the missionaries and William Willshire had presented their evidence the Enquiry had only to listen to the pastoralists deny any misbehaviour. At Hermannsburg they heard James McDonald, his loquacious cook Ben Rogers, and Frederick Thornton of Tempe Downs. Thornton praised Willshire's native police patrol, claiming that it prevented the shooting of Aborigines by pastoralists. He did not, of course, admit to having shot any himself, nor is there any evidence that he did more than practice dispersal in the first degree. Despite his praise for Willshire's work he had written off 300 head the previous year, but could only report seeing the remains of twenty one beasts. When he complained about the "mission blacks" he was referring to those coming down from the north-west, that is from the west of the mission lease. He claimed that he made it a rule on his station that none of his men should feed an Aboriginal woman, to prevent them keeping mistresses. He had heard of a native girl called his lubra, but on enquiring in the camp found it was a six year-old child sent to him unsolicited by a man to the south of the station. Thus arose the stories of white men's black wives. He employed four or five Aboriginal men and two women. Curiously, one of the women employed in the Tempe Downs kitchen had been attacked by a group of Aboriginal men who thought her "a sort of outlaw" for informing on them, according to Ben Rogers, who had cooked at Tempe Downs before moving to Glen Helen.

There followed a break of four days. The party used this time to inspect Palm Valley. They rode their camels up Palm Creek, along the spring-fed lagoons and among the striking palms, up onto the plateau. Here Besley named two columns of rock "Swan Pillar" and "Taplin Pillar" and the surrounding chaos of stone "Heidenreichs Town". They returned from the other-worldly beauty of the ranges to Hermannsburg before splitting into two parties. One, including Swan and Heidenreich, went up the Finke to the inspect, not Glen Helen Gorge, but the cattle yard, while Schulze accompanied Taplin to the Ellery Creek sheepyard. The mission staff were pleased, according to Heidenreich, to receive advice from the Swan and Taplin on the better breeding of cattle and the yarding of sheep. It left the Enquiry party with a much more favourable impression of the mission as a pastoral station.

The Enquiry resumed its work at Hermannsburg on July 28th to hear more leisurely evidence from William Willshire and Hermann Kempe. Willshire described his modus operandi. He claimed he never made arrests because the cattle-killers on Tempe Downs found it too easy to escape to the hills when he approached. Nevertheless he was able to destroy their weapons and that kept the cattle-killing down for some time. When asked why he did not later arrest those who had escaped when caught in the act, he said it was because the station managers had not taken out warrants against them. Still, if William Willshire and his troopers were in fact leaving corpses all over Tempe Downs it is a puzzle that none of the Western Aranda or Matuntara returning from that district reported it to the missionaries, or, if they did, that the missionaries failed to report it to anyone. After listening to Hermann Kempe and Louis Schulze we can have little confidence that they would have reported such stories to Swan-Taplin, but it is consistent with Kempe's character as we know it that he should have reported incidents of this kind to Heidenreich as further evidence of the damaging consequences of pastoralism, uninhibited by his own role in encouraging police violence. I doubt that Schwarz could have been so brow-beaten by Swan that he remained silent on any incidents of which he had knowledge, but we can have no confidence that Swan would have recorded them if there was no corroboration. In any case, Schwarz had left the Finke shortly after Willshire established himself at Boggy Water in August 1889.

Hermann Kempe, speaking for himself and Louis Schulze, recommended for the first time that government reserves should be established at various points along the Telegraph, with secular management and independent missionaries. It was in essence the proposal that Charles Taplin had published at the end of the previous year. Hermannsburg would continue under its existing constitution, however. The reserves would regulate employment, especially of women, and "The Police should be instructed to send all natives especially children to the reserves." He also recommended that a court of full jurisdiction should be established at Alice Springs. Kempe was by implication declaring the Hermannsburg model of the mission colony inappropriate for Central Australia. He was too compromised by his own conduct to point out that if British law were applied to offences by Aborigines against other Aborigines, such as Latya's murder of the Hermannsburg boys, or the later killing of Mototoka, then he would not have felt the same need to collaborate with Erwein Wurmbrand in delivering their own idea of justice.

By Thursday July 31st the Enquiry had travelled back east to Owen Springs, to hear its overseer, Charles Gall, and his boss and

Mount Burrell's manager, Allen Breaden, who employed seven
Aboriginal men, three boys and seven women. Like McDonald,
Breaden knew the mission and found the missionaries hospitable,
but thought they did not feed or clothe their Aboriginal workers well
enough. Unlike the missionaries, the station managers fed only those
who worked. Charles Gall, a Justice of the Peace, claimed that he had
always accompanied Mounted Constable Wurmbrand on his visits
from 1883, and that "not a black was shot on this run". He attributed
Wurmbrand's immediate and almost total success to "constantly
following up the Natives' tracks". Edward Polhill, a stockman on
Owen Springs, had another plausible reason for the harmony that
had descended on that station by the early 1880s, as we shall see in
chapter 16.

By August 2nd the Enquiry was in Alice Springs, hearing the
Telegraph Station Master Joseph Skinner, and then at Stuart to hear
the local brewer Wesley Turton. Neither knew of mistreatment of
Aborigines or of complaints against the police. Turton, one of the
few men in the Centre living with a white wife, had been a frequent
visitor to the mission (white women went there to give birth) and
thought its Aboriginal people well-treated and happy. It was on one
of those visits that he told the missionaries of seeing Willshire in
Adelaide with his trackers and a girl of fifteen or sixteen years. While
he knew them all and had spoken to them, he had not enquired how
the girl came to be there. "In conversation with the missionaries at
the Mission Station on my return I told them I had seen a lubra with
Willshire in town, I do not think I mentioned that the native trackers
were also there." Further east at Paddy's Hole Swan and Taplin
spoke to the prospector Frank Stacey and the local storekeeper
Joseph Harding. Harding did "not know of any cases of blacks being
shot in my own personal knowledge", but he did know the mission
well as a source of cattle, and had no criticisms of it. Back at
Heavitree Gap on August 10th the Enquiry listened to Edmund Parke
of Henbury Station, who had lived for four or five years within
seven miles of Hermannsburg when his head station was at Ellery's
Creek. He was not asked about the young man Inubauka reportedly
wounded with shot by John Breaden at that station, as Schwarz later
reported in Adelaide, or about Chinkanaka, whose "two wives had
been stolen by a white man" from the same place, according to
Schulze's earlier evidence.

Heidenreich had stayed at Hermannsburg to share for a while the life of his mission. While the Christian community of Hermannsburg was enjoying a feast a Matuntara woman arrived in the camp with a small child whom she killed, according to reports from the Aranda-Christians. The flesh was shared with other women. The missionaries did not make independent enquiries, and while Heidenreich reported the story to the Enquiry later in Adelaide, Henry Swan left this hearsay out of his report too. Before Heidenreich left, Geology Brown arrived from the west. He took some photographs of the mission people assembled but the light was not good enough to get a picture. Heidenreich met up with Swan and Taplin at Mount Burrell on the road south, so missing the evidence taken at Stuart from Wesley Turton, one of the two witnesses called by the missionaries. It did not matter, because Heidenreich had lost interest. He knew what was in Henry Swan's mind. He knew he had already saved the mission. At Mount Burrell, while the other members of the party made a side-trip to Chambers Pillar, Heidenreich stayed to talk one last time with Hermann Kempe. "I therefore had time to discuss this and that with Brother Kempe, and to share with him something of the Enquiry's changed point of view, and to hear his opinion."[289]

On August 19th, before the Enquiry party reached Oodnadatta, John Gordon ceased to be the Minister for the Northern Territory when the Government of John Cockburn fell, to be replaced by a Ministry led by a tough-minded pragmatist, Honest Tom Playford.

Heidenreich had rejoined the Enquiry party by the time it took Frank Gillen's evidence at Oodnadatta on August 23rd 1890. If Heidenreich was present, Gillen was being blunt indeed when he described the missionaries as "conciencious honest men trying to do good according to their lights, but ... I doubt their ability to effect any good. ... I can imagine that the same institution under educated Englishmen might do much good." There is no evidence that Frank Gillen had at this time ever visited Hermannsburg. Gillen, then at Charlotte Waters just inside the southern border of the Northern Territory, had "not known of a single instance of their [Aboriginal people] being ill-treated by whites". He considered the Aborigines "quiet and inoffensive, they kill cattle occasionally but in that they are no worse than some of the whites." Their treatment was "better than in any other part of Australia, and I attribute this to the example set by the Government officials who were strictly instructed to treat the natives with kindness and consideration and never use firearms except in self defence these instructions have been strictly carried out. The natives have been encouraged to camp on our reserves when driven off the surrounding country by the pastoral lessees". He supported setting up reserves at each telegraph station where Aboriginal people might go and be rationed when driven off their country. Despite his fifteen years residence in the Centre, Frank Gillen appeared not to know the Aboriginal people had the legal right to occupy and take their living from the pastoral leases.[290] Gillen's complacency may tell us more about the style of questioning he received from Swan-Taplin than it does of his own convictions. Less than a year later he told the Pastoral Lands Royal Commission meeting in Alice Springs that "They [the pastoralists] have given them [their Aboriginal workers] enough to eat, but [have] not always treated them so well as they should have done. Government should provide rations for the old and infirm, who are in a chronic state of starvation".[291]

In fact, as both Gillen and Mounted Constable South conceded to the Pastoral Lands Commission in April 1891, the pastoralists were resisting protective reserves because they now depended on Aboriginal labour. If it were removed the stations were unprofitable, even in good years. Gillen "did not know what the squatters would have done without the assistance of the natives", and South did "not know how the services of the aborigines could be dispensed with."

Before the end of August 1890 Henry Swan was back in Adelaide writing to John Gordon's successor, David Bews, requesting payment of an additional fifty pounds. Bews was surprised to find his files silent on the terms of Swan's appointment.[292] Bryan Besley got back to Port Augusta at the same time. He wrote immediately to Commissioner Peterswald reporting that "so far as the evidence has been taken there is nothing against the Police."

On September 10th in Adelaide the Enquiry held a torrid twelve-hour session to hear the evidence of Mounted Constable Robert Hillier, pastoralist Billy Benstead and, last of all, Wilhelm Schwarz. Hillier's evidence directly contradicted William Willhshire's on the subject of Willshire's women, as we have seen earlier, and stood up in the face of aggressive questioning from Besley, but neither Taplin nor Heidenreich pressed for it to be taken further. In fact, Heidenreich claimed to have "learned nothing new" in the course of the day. There had been "no other clear proof presented against him [Willshire]", Heidenreich claimed, echoing the Enquiry's official position that Willshire could not be criticised for merely travelling with Aboriginal women.[293]

Hillier thought that he had offended Frederick Thornton by reprimanding him for dispersing Aboriginal people from their waters, but he had not himself seen evidence of cruelty. In fact, he thought those Aboriginal men and women employed at the ruby fields were well-treated, and knew of none leaving their white employers and consorts. Hillier lasted little more than a year at the Heavitree Gap police station. Considering his record of chronic drunkenness, neglect of duty and insubordination it is surprising he continued in the police force for another twenty four years before he was dismissed.

It can hardly have been an accident that Wilhelm Schwarz was the last of the witnesses to be heard. He was in Adelaide when the Enquiry left for the Centre, but was not interviewed then. Schwarz's interview with Swan on September 10th was a vigorous business and lasted until 9.00 pm that night. Schwarz made specific accusations of immoral conduct against Charles Walker for seducing in 1880 Chinkanaka's wife, a mission student at the time, but Walker was now dead. He had seen a stockman called Coulthard riding about with a woman in men's clothes, but Coulthard was still in Central Australia. As was John Breaden who peppererd Inubauka with shot. On the other hand, the Enquiry was able to put to him for confirmation that he had flogged Ereminta for cattle-killing. If Schwarz mentioned Glen Helen Gorge it was not recorded.

Swan had little to do when he left the hearing room that night. Within a week he had signed off his brief report and without waiting for a copyist to produce a fair copy handed it in to his new Minister in his own hand, amendments and all. It was presented to the Legislative Council a week later on September 23rd, although the Minister David Bews was a Member of the lower House. Charles Eaton Taplin had, of course, signed it too. [294]

13

BURYING GHOSTS

If you had been listening to Henry Swan's Enquiry as it progressed around the Centre then nothing in his report would surprise you, especially its omissions and elisions. He assured the members of Parliament and the readers of the Adelaide papers that the Aboriginal people of the Centre "are persuaded to move with little trouble" when the pastoralist wanted them off the waters on his run. On the matter of "a black coming to the mission station covered with shot wounds" Swan asserted that it was "not supported by the evidence of his [Schwarz's] brother officials who were living on the mission station at the same time". If he was referring to the case of Inubauka who had been shot by John Breaden, then he was half right. Neither Kempe nor Schulze had supported the story, but neither had they been asked about it. It was simply not raised in the Central Australian hearings. In any case, Inubauka had fallen to a spear before Swan-Taplin arrived in the Centre. If, on the other hand, Swan was referring to the case of the woman Wodoa then he had failed to check the record of evidence, because Schulze confirmed it. On the Glen Helen killings by Mounted Constable Wurmbrand, Swan reported only that "We were unable to get any direct evidence of what took place... but the whole matter was reported to the Commissioner of Police at the time (about five years ago), and this report we have seen, and it has fully satisfied us there is nothing in the charge". This outrageous lie was buttressed by a less direct one, with Swan claiming that the delegation Heidenreich led to the Chief Secretary in 1885 had "expressed themselves fully satisfied with" Wurmbrand's report. He made no reference to the Police Commissioner's offer to introduce a more restrictive policy on shooting Aborigines, for the obvious reason. The fact that Swan was confident that his lies would not be contradicted speaks loudly of the demoralised state of the Finke River mission.

On the immoral commerce between white men and Aboriginal women, Swan acknowledged the station workers were no angels, but judged that Schwarz's statement on the subject was "calculated to give a wrong impression". He would not have been expected to go into great detail. As far as Willshire's women were concerned, since the charge from Schwarz was more particular, so was Swan's denial: "there is no evidence that he has been guilty of any immorality with the natives". He added: "In regard to M. C. Willshire we are [of the] opinion that while native troopers are required he is the right man for the work ... We are convinced there is no foundation for any charge of his being guilty of shooting down blacks". Still, Swan recommended Willshire's camp be moved a greater distance from the mission. Not that the missionaries wanted it, but, we can conclude, because Willshire needed the disguise that distance can offer.

There were still the generalised charges of indiscriminate killings by pastoralists and police for which the Enquiry had found - or admitted - no evidence, and these Swan disposed of without recrimination. "We think the missionaries have made their statements without careful consideration, and acting upon reports from natives without testing their accuracy." Neither of these charges could be levelled against Swan's Enquiry, but after the embarrassment missionary Flierl had suffered in the Jackey case these further apparently baseless accusations by missionaries were bound to cause aggravation among the pastoralists and their friends, and to weaken the standing of the German missionaries among those who were usually their friends.

The pay-off for Heidenreich was contained in these words:

> ...whilst there is evidence that on one or two occasions they adopted measures showing a lack of judgment on their part (chains were used to detain certain of the native *prisoners* on the station and thrashing was resorted to as a *punishment*), still in no case did their actions towards the blacks amount to cruelty, and we believe them to have been prompted by the kindest motives. [My italics]

The main pay-off to Charles Eaton Taplin for putting his name to this farrago was a strong recommendation in favour of protective reserves. The Enquiry had noted that only the mission thought itself obliged to feed the young, sick and infirm. Swan identified in the gentlest possible terms a problem that became serious and distressing to frontiersmen in drought periods - starvation among the dependents who could no longer stay on their permanent waters or travel about with those who were more capable physically. It was also the perfect inducement to cattle-killing. Swan used the evidence of the long-distance travels of the Aboriginal peoples of the Centre to conclude that they were not narrowly territorial. The plan was to put these reserves every 200 miles, and to bring to them the old people and the children who would anchor the rest. While the charitable motive was paramount in this recommendation, there was also a lash of discipline in its tail; "we submit that unless these reserves are taken in hand by the Government, as we suggest, and not simply leave the natives to do as they like on them ... they would only be an element of evil in the black settlements".

Henry Swan had one more political task to do. He offered Charles Eaton Taplin an introduction into the lower levels of the party of government. On September 29th Swan recommended that Taplin be appointed a Justice of the Peace. He no doubt passed on to the new Minister David Bews the obligations that he had undertaken with Taplin, that the Government would take action on the proposed Aboriginal reserves. Of this we have the evidence of the official correspondence generated by a letter of September 2nd from the owners of Glen Helen, seeking government rations for dependent Aborigines on their station. The file went round in circles without leading to a Cabinet decision because officials were still divided on the relative merits of government protective reserves and ration depots on pastoral stations. The Protector favoured reserves, but claimed he could not spend north of the South Australian border, so that the Minister for the Northern Territory would need to find the money. A few months later David Bews died. However sincerely Bews treated the proposal, there were others in government who had already made their minds up against it. "I know from certain sources that his [Taplin's] plans will not be realised", Heidenreich told his German-reading audience.[295] In the open air of electoral politics there were much more vigorous issues demanding attention. At the end of September 1890 the big news was a continuing strike of waterside workers in Port Adelaide and so the fate of Central Australia's Aboriginal population was pushed aside. Swan and Taplin had here struck the note of the future, although it would have to wait long past Premier Playford's term, past the depression of the 1890s, before a new national government in a new Century took action.[296]

The evidence taken by Swan's Enquiry was never published. It is unlikely it was seen by anyone beyond the Ministers directly concerned. There is some reason to doubt that one of those, Robert Homburg, the Attorney-General, ever saw the document. Six months later he appeared to believe that Aboriginal witnesses had been called. The one copy that survived to be found, admittedly in the Attorney-General's files, is the original, bearing the signatures of the witnesses. In contrast, there were at least three copies of the evidence of Gillen's enquiry into William Willshire.[297] Henry Swan did not have the power to keep his evidence locked up, but the Minister to whom he reported did, and so did his permanent Secretary, unless his Minister wished to take a different position. Charles Eaton Taplin also believed that the evidence that Henry Swan had kept out of his report, and possibly other material that had been kept out of the record of evidence, would be made known within government in support of the recommendation of protective reserves. In June 1891 Taplin wrote this plaintive comment in a letter to the *Register*: "With the weight of evidence that is before them *in one form and another* it is a pity our Government cannot see their way to do something to improve the condition of the blacks in the interior" (my italics). He wrote again on September 12th 1891 directly to the Minister for the Northern Territory enclosing a press clipping from Queensland advocating government reserves. "If your Government would adopt a similar policy, in the event of not being inclined to undertake the actual oversight or responsibility of work among the natives, it would be giving those who feel for their present neglected state an opportunity of undertaking it with a prospect of doing substantial good."[298] Taplin was discovering that his moment of power had passed.

Even so, the equability of Swan's report did not fool anyone. The *Observer*'s leader-writer, while he thought it "reassuring to the public to be informed upon the authority of two competent, and, we believe, thoroughly impartial, judges that the harrowing accounts put in circulation of revolting inhumanity and wholesale immorality are not based upon fact" and that the report gave "reasonable assurance that the natives are not being inhumanely treated in South Australia" still thought the report "whitewashes the accused all round". South Australians could still be confident that they had been spared the "record of atrocities inflicted upon the natives in some parts of Australia".

Kempe and Schulze were left to deal with their own further trials in the Centre, but Heidenreich had to deal with some consequences too. Schwarz was still in a rented house in Tanunda, at the expense of the Mission Committee for this and his modest upkeep but without regular employment. Henry Swan's report had saved the mission but had not polished its reputation. Hermann Kempe wrote directly to the Institute in Germany asking for replacement missionaries to be sent, so ignoring the chain of command and angering Heidenreich. He had also written personal letters to government officials including Inspector Bryan Besley. Heidenreich feared that Kempe had damaged the cause of the mission. The political hazard created by Kempe's attempts to justify himself can be estimated from his complaint to Heidenreich on 16 September 1890 that he and Schulze had been "hoodwinked" ("verblüffen") by the enquiry.[299] Fortunately for Heidenreich and the Government, Kempe did not write to the press. Considering all this the Mission Committee concluded that "the missionaries have lost all joy to continue in their present sphere of action. We cannot consider it advisable to be absolutely opposed to granting their request." But first Germany had to find some willing candidates, and the Mission Committee had to find ways of discharging its obligations for the future of the three current missionaries. It resolved that it would not undertake financial responsibility for missionaries in future.

On October 16th 1890 the *Register* carried this brief report:

THE FINKE MISSION ENQUIRY.-

We are informed on good authority that as a result of the enquiry by Messrs Swan and Taplin as to the treatment of Aboriginals in the Far North, Mr Schwarz, the Lutheran Missionary, who made certain allegations against the whites, has been called upon by the Chairman of the Missionary Society for his resignation.[300]

The story was picked up by the *Australische zeitung* of October 20th, occasioning an outburst of angry letters to Heidenreich, to which Heidenreich responded through his Committee's minutes with shrill indignation but without denying the central claim of the story.

Wilhelm Schwarz refused to return to the Finke, having learned when his personal effects reached Adelaide how deeply his former colleagues detested him. He also refused Heidenreich's perverse demand that he put his reasons in writing. Instead, Heidenreich declared, through his Committee, "We now expect him to tender his resignation and shall induce him to do so." Schwarz was paid until the end of 1890 and offered his resignation orally. On February 12th, 1891, on Heidenreich's insistence, ten days before Ereminta was shot in Walker Creek, Schwarz wrote to Institute Director Harms in Germany, "since my return to the Mission Station in Hermannsburg is not necessary nor advisable, I ask you most sincerely to allow me to accept a call as pastor in this Synod or elsewhere ... since it is highly unlikely at the moment that this Mission could increase its outreach by establishing a new Station."

Wilhelm Schwarz had begun 1890 as a heroic missionary in the eyes of the South Australian Lutherans. Now an official enquiry had declared him a slanderer and his own Superintendent Heidenreich was not going to forgive him for putting at risk both the mission and Heidenreich's reputation. Heidenreich angrily rejected Schwarz's attempts at self-justification, letting him carry the charge of making accusations that could not be proved, but taking no account of the way Heidenreich himself had conspired with Swan and Besley to prevent evidence coming before the Enquiry. In fact, all of Schwarz's particular accusations were true, and the Enquiry or its leading members knew that. Some at least of his generalised accusations were capable of testing, had the Enquiry chosen to pursue the sources of evidence available to them. Schwarz was entitled to feel aggrieved, but appears to have taken his dismissal without public complaint. He was no longer a Hermannsburg missionary, and was just one step away from resigning altogether his commission as an officer in God's expeditionary forces.

When Henry Swan's report was tabled in Parliament, the restive back-bencher, John Gordon, gave notice in the Legislative Council of a motion to discuss it. He huffed like a man who is looking forward to an opportunity to embarrass his opponents. While his motion remained on the Notice Paper as an Order of the Day it was beyond the power of Government to remove it. But on October 15th when its turn came for discussion, after several deferrals, there was no debate. Wiser heads had prevailed.[301]

In the meantime, on October 7th a pastoral delegation led by Charles Chewings had attended Gordon's replacement as Minister, David Bews, requesting passage of the Northern Territory Lands Bill. This legislation, which had already passed the Legislative Council, involved lower rents and longer lease terms. Bews said he was keen to get the Bill through before the end of the year and "he would endeavour as far as possible to meet their [the pastoralists'] wishes" on their outstanding grievances. A year that had started badly for the pastoralists had ended relatively well. If only politics could make rain.[302]

As Henry Swan took possession of his Court in the village of Gawler fifty kilometres north of Adelaide he could also reflect on a busy and successful year. Charles Eaton Taplin, had gone to Central Australia with an empire to win, because Wilhelm Schwarz had come south hoping for his own. But, instead, Henry Swan had succeeded in confirming his title to his own, more modest, fiefdom. He had allied himself with three men, William Peterswald, Bryan Besley and Georg Heidenreich, who all had territories to defend. They were intelligent, experienced and tough-minded and they all knew how to fight in the political arena. In their capacity for dissimulation and manipulation Henry Swan and Bryan Besley were the equals of the leading politicians among the senior Western Aranda men. Charles Eaton Taplin on the other hand had ideals, ambition and hope but no experience of government, and his only ally was Wilhelm Schwarz, who was a brave and passionate man but no politician.

And what of the principal target of Schwarz's attack on January 9th, 1890? William Willshire was riding high at Boggy Water. He had saved more important hides than his own by exposing the missionaries' desperate practices. If you had been forced to make a choice, you would have said that Willshire's menage at Boggy Water would outlast the Finke River mission. Even the Aboriginal people, confined to the bed of the Finke, could read the signals. When Kempe returned from escorting Heidenreich back to rejoin the Enquiry party on the track south "his flesh and skin were pale, withered."[303] The visit of Swan and Taplin had indeed been a trial for Kempe and Schulze and their idea of a mission to the Western Aranda, but William Willshire's turn in the dock was fast approaching.

THE TRIALS OF
WILLIAM WILLSHIRE

1891

14

THE TRIALS OF WILLIAM WILLSHIRE

By any estimation Henry Swan's report was a triumph for William Willshire. He had been found innocent of any offence at all, unlike the missionaries. His standing as an accomplished leader of Aboriginal troopers had been endorsed. The big men of the Centre who may have looked askance at this somehow unmanly frontiersman had been lined up to chorus their endorsement of the work he, and the other police of the Centre, had been doing. A camel train of official visitors had passed through Boggy Water to witness the growth of his domain with its population of resident Aboriginal people, and to be impressed by the style and the horsemanship of his Native Constables. Inside the Enquiry's hearing room at Hermannsburg he had taken on the role of prosecutor of the missionaries as if born to it. Whatever his audience thought of the performance, in William Willshire's eyes it can not have failed to impress. The result was on the record for all to see.

Both Willshire's high morale and the direction taken by the public's sympathies are evidenced in the publication by the *Observer* on December 27th 1890 of Willshire's first essay at popular fiction. Attributed to "A correspondent in the interior", it is a portrayal of a political meeting of Aboriginal men at Running Water on the Finke River. It relies on its readers to find comical the notion that Aboriginal people should attempt an interest in South Australian Parliamentary politics. In truth there were few people in the world outside of South Australia who shared that interest. Willshire employs little but heavy sarcasm to achieve his humorous effect, being more concerned to demonstrate that Willshire himself was on top of metropolitan politics. We meet Mr Illpilla and Mr Illarra (both places on Tempe Downs) and the "chief" Mr Lamerta (Illamurta), "the only man at the meeting that owned a pair of trousers". All the Willshire trademarks are there: the walk-on role for himself, as "Willshire of Black Police notoriety", the Australian Natives

Association, the Aboriginal men who "were as compact as a cake of blacking, and had no more sentiment in them than a bar of soap", and the resort to doggerel to heighten the story's impact on the reader. But when we remove the music-hall Aborigines we are still left with the authentic core of Willshire's affections, "my own country;/ Where dusky virgins live, who are all free from guile...". It refers to the fall of the Cockburn government - which happened in August 1890 - as a recent event, implying that the piece was written shortly after the departure of the Swan-Taplin party from the Finke. It was a small triumph for William Willshire, author, but it was hardly a credit to the *Observer*. In fact Willshire's attempt at humour was too artless even for the weekly gossip and joke newspaper, *Quiz*.[304] Perhaps someone was doing Willshire, the maligned frontier policeman, a favour.

But then, after the burst of public attention, back on the Finke his enemy Ereminta prepared to strike at the centre of Willshire's power and affections. We do not know precisely when it took place, and even the form of Ereminta's taking of Nabarong remains obscure. Nabarong may well have been killed for accepting her new husband, and Willshire's later report that his fictional Chillberta had died on the Finke was based on this hard fact.[305]

We know it was Nabarong whom Ereminta took from Willshire at Boggy Water some time after the departure of the Swan-Taplin party in the middle of 1890. We have this from a man who knew Willshire better, perhaps, than any person alive; Archie/Coognalthika. Archie was with Erwein Wurmbrand on his second expedition to Glen Helen in April 1885. In July of 1886 he was left alone in charge of the police station, and later that year, and in 1887, he made patrols on his own or with another Native Constable to Undoolya, Owen Springs, Hermannsburg, and Bond Springs. In April 1887 he was described as being on patrol "on his own enquiries" to Emily Gap. If there was an Aboriginal man who could be said to have been a Native Constable in a substantive sense, and not just an armed Aboriginal tracker in a uniform, it was Archie.[306] He alone had come from Alice Springs to help Willshire set up his new base at Boggy Water. He later went on to serve with Ernest Cowle at Illamurta Springs. There was still an Archie at Illamurta in 1911, probably the same one. He was a very powerful Aboriginal man, by the standards of Central Australia in the 1880s. Archie also knew what his commanding officer did when no other white man was around.

On the timing of Ereminta's attack the best circumstantial evidence is the manner of Ereminta's death. The ferocity with which Willshire dealt with Ereminta on the morning of February 22nd 1891 suggests he had only recently found that, for all his power, he could be bested by a trouserless black man. The evidence from Willshire's troopers is that they came to Tempe Downs from Glen Helen, and camped on the night of the 21st of February on the 'other' side of Tempe Downs, presumably the western side. This implies, in turn, that they had come down from Glen Helen by the longer western route, rather than the more direct route down the Finke. It is plausible that this entire circuit, from Boggy Water to Glen Helen and down to Tempe Downs, was in pursuit of Ereminta.

Whenever it happened, Ereminta's assault was intolerable. It would also have seemed undignified to Willshire's white peers that a white man should be so unbalanced by the loss of a black woman. Had one of Willshire's constables or another black employee been attacked, then Willshire could have expected his white neighbours to support some punitive action without complaint. Indeed it was the killing of old man Namia reported to Besley one year before that he eventually used as a public pretext for going after Ereminta. The abduction or murder of Nabarong was no such event, and the perpetrator was no 'bush black' but a man well and favourably known to the whites. He had returned to Tempe Downs station and had thereby gained the protection enjoyed by the "civilized black". William Willshire was moving into unmapped country.

When he did act, on February 21st 1891, he did so with a mixture of calculation and rashness. He probably knew that Frederick Thornton, and Charles Chewings, who was up for an extended visit, had left the station on Walker Creek to visit other leases many kilometres to the north and would be away for some time. He knew that Ereminta would not think him imprudent enough to attack at the head station of Tempe Downs and he knew also that the station workers, who lived on the front-line of the power struggle of black and white, were his most loyal allies. All that was in favour of his chosen place and time, but a man less bewitched with his own powers or the passion for revenge might have hesitated to place his fate in the hands of so many strangers, white and black. The principal threat to him was that word would be carried to Hermannsburg by Aboriginal witnesses, especially Nungoolga, whom the missionaries had been pressing to return since she had eloped with Ereminta. According to Kempe he had sent emissaries to Tempe Downs station to persuade her to come back, but without success. Even here Willshire's decision was perhaps better judged than he was later given credit for. He understood where Hermann Kempe stood on the treatment of those among the senior men who encouraged resistance to Christianity, especially those who seduced heathen-Christian women from Hermannsburg. And after the deal Heidenreich had concluded with Inspector Besley at Hermannsburg the previous July, he could conclude with reason that he was safe from direct attack by missionaries Kempe and Schulze.

As Willshire travelled down Walker Creek and across to the Finke, with the cremation fires of Ereminta and Donkey still smoking behind him, his state of mind was unlikely to have been placid, but whatever demons troubled him did not include the fear of detection. Had he seriously contemplated that he would be brought to account for his actions he could have made a detour on the way to Tempe Downs. Charles Gall at Owen Springs station was a Justice of the Peace and was qualified to issue warrants for the arrest of Ereminta and Donkey. To have pursued warrants for cattle-killing would have required the cooperation of Frederick Thornton as the owner of the cattle supposed to have been killed. Thornton would hardly have sought the arrest of two men, one of whom he was at that moment employing, but Willshire himself was competent to ask for warrants against the men accused of murdering old man Namia at his camp in January the previous year. It was Attorney-General Homburg's view that Willshire needed no warrant beyond the fact of Namia's murder.

The best evidence in favour of the rationality of Willshire's action is what happened next. Or, rather, what did not happen, for no outraged protest emerged from Central Australia after Nungoolga and Theeanka found their way back to Hermannsburg. When Hermann Kempe did refer to the matter it was in his quarterly report to Heidenreich written on March 31st 1891:

Naomi who ran away from us has lately returned. She ran away with her husband, who, either because he would not or could not leave off killing bullocks on the Tempe Downs Station, was finally shot dead by Mounted Constable Willshire or by one of his black assistants called Thomas.[307]

On past experience this report, had Heidenreich put it in the *Church messenger*, would not have been a problem for Willshire or the Government, provided it remained in German. This was not to be tested, since on February 26th Willshire himself wrote a report to Bryan Besley. It is a strange document, part incident report, part apology for eighteen months of futile efforts to catch the Tempe Downs cattle-killers, part bombast ("there was one movement of mine they did not see, that was the last one") and part diatribe against Ereminta and Donkey for alleged offences against Tempe Downs' livestock and the killing of Namia. He claimed to have been pursuing Ereminta and Donkey, among others, for cattle-killing, and to have sought their arrest. His trackers Larry/Aremala and Joe - his name for Thomas - had been obliged by the violent resistance of Donkey and Ereminta to shoot them.

In this account of the event Willshire placed himself one hundred yards from the alleged struggles between his troopers and Donkey and Ereminta. "In conclusion, I respectfully beg to state that In no way whatever, have I disregarded the instructions, of the Commissioner of Police, firearms were only used in self defence, and then only to notorious murderers & cattle killing ringleaders whom it was impossible to arrest". Willshire's stress on Ereminta's and Donkey's past murders was continued through to the trial, so it is worth noting that in all Willshire's accounts Ereminta was responsible for throwing the spear that killed Namia, who was Aremala's father, while Donkey is supposed to have killed Thomas's father in earlier feuding. (In fact, according to Thomas's evidence to Gillen, it was Thomas's *brother* who was killed two years previously by Matuntara men, perhaps including Donkey). But on the morning of February 22nd 1891, as all accounts agree, Thomas shot Ereminta, not Donkey, and Aremala killed Donkey. Willshire gave no explanation of this discrepancy and judge Bundey's Court did not seek one, although it was a critical piece of evidence.

As if to dampen Besley's expectations that this bloodshed might see an end to cattle-killing on Tempe Downs Willshire concludes his report of the killings with this disclaimer:

It is to be hoped the precedent set in this case, will have the effect of stopping or checking cattle killing, but I am afraid it wont, because, for 16 years they continued to kill cattle on "Undoolya", the natives are not afraid of death, if they were, those that remained would leave off cattle killing, but from experience, I have seen on many stations, that their depredations continue.

Willshire was telling his superior officer that death is the penalty for those suspected of cattle-killing on his part of the Central Australian frontier, and that even such extreme measures were without effect. Even for Willshire this was bold talk. There was no reference to burning bodies, or to warrants, and there was no signature.[308]

Willshire saw no need for haste in reporting the incident at Tempe Downs. Unlike his earlier reports of the excitement at Anna's Reservoir he posted rather than wired his report. It was March 23rd before Inspector Besley read it and passed it on to Commissioner Peterswald "for perusal". Besley also requested his Commissioner to pass Willshire's report to the Protector before returning it to him. As an afterthought, sandwiched between the text of his note and his signature, Besley inserts: "M. C. Willshire & Trackers appear to me to have only done their duty." Peterswald forwarded it without comment to J. G. Jenkins, Willshire's new Minister, who marked it "Seen and Returned". It then was passed to Protector Hamilton who could see no need to say more than "Seen and returned". The matter would have ended there, but for Willshire's inability to leave well enough alone.

On March 4th he wrote again to Besley, this time seeking warrants for the arrest of other cattle-killers on Tempe Downs. Perhaps he wanted to build a reputation for procedural nicety, just as a precaution. This caused Minister Jenkins to send the file to Attorney-General Homburg, on April 8th, 1891. Homburg could see no need to involve himself in the issuing of warrants for cattle-killing. Willshire need only have Frederick Thornton, as the person responsible for the property that had been stolen, make a complaint and he, Willshire, could pursue the alleged perpetrators. We know, as Homburg did not, why Willshire did not wish to follow that course, apart from his long-established habit of not seeking arrests. But Homburg had not forgotten the Swan-Taplin report, and the version of events in the Centre he had heard through Heidenreich, and he had just finished eleven days acting in the office of Chief Secretary, the Minister responsible for the police. Homburg smelled a rat. With Jenkins' approval he took action, and Homburg's Secretary Charles Cornish was instructed on April 11th to wire the Special Magistrate at Alice Springs, Frank Gillen, with an instruction to Willshire that he should leave Boggy Water and report to Alice Springs.[309]

At this stage of his career, Homburg was not, if ever he had been, disposed to rash political interventions. According to the Observer's political commentator, "When he first went into Parliament he appeared to be fickle, and to keep his feelings always at the boil; so that upon the least blaze of excitement off came the cover, and Mr. Homburg frothed over... From an extreme of volatility Mr. Homburg has gone a little beyond the boundary mark of caution. ... Pessimism is his little weakness; but it never becomes cowardice or even trepidation. ... These qualities unite with absolute fairness and complete conscientiousness to make our Attorney-General one of the most thoroughly appreciated men in the South Australian Parliament."[310] Robert Homburg had joined the party of government long since, and was a leading supporter of his Premier, Tom Playford. But he now had the power to act quietly, within government, and he had not forgotten justice.

In the few days it would take for Robert Homburg's instruction to reach Boggy Water and Willshire to travel to Alice Springs Homburg had some important questions to answer. Who in the Centre could conduct an enquiry in a way appropriate to the serious issues that Homburg suspected were involved, and what form would the enquiry take? Homburg asked that Gillen, who, with his Special Magistrate's hat on was Homburg's agent, to find out when two of Homburg's fellow Parliamentarians, then in the Centre as members of the Pastoral Lands Royal Commission, were arriving at Alice Springs. These two men, Robert Caldwell and Frederick Holder (the latter was later Premier of South Australia) were Homburg's best bet. Neither was a lawyer, but both were middle-aged men of wide experience in the life and politics of South Australia. When they arrived at Alice Springs, however, they were unwilling to spend longer in the Centre. When they wired this disappointing news to Homburg, on April 15th, they also asked whether he wanted a full inquest, which would have involved sending a jury up to the Centre, and a doctor to examine the bodies all assumed to be buried at Tempe Downs. The alternative was to appoint an individual to enquire by taking evidence on oath. Another Henry Swan, perhaps.

Homburg judged the tolerance of his Cabinet colleagues for expenditure on this remote matter would not have run to a formal inquest. He asked Holder and Caldwell to advise him if there were a person in the Centre, not associated with the pastoral interest, who could act in the role of Coroner. And so Frank Gillen, then acting in the job of Alice Springs Station Master, was chosen for a public role on the stage of South Australian politics. It was timely, from Gillen's point of view. Automatic repeaters had been installed at the Alice Springs Telegraph Station, greatly reducing the labour formerly done by Gillen's telegraphists, and his burden of supervision, but it would be years before the number of his staff was reduced.[311] He was the supervisor of all the telegraph stations along the central run of the line, the magistrate and senior representative of government in the Centre, and its physician and surgeon. He was thirty-five years old and had already spent fifteen years on the Line. He was an intelligent and congenial man, a popular official whose interests already included the language and culture of the Centre's Aboriginal peoples. Soon he would be the host for South Australia's Governor, the Earl of Kintore, who was at that moment travelling down the Line from Darwin in the company of Edward Stirling, the Director of the South Australian Museum. Frank Gillen was well-qualified to enter the junior ranks of the party of government, and he was about to be married, to Inspector Bryan Besley's niece. [312]

Frank Gillen, as a loyal son of Irish parents and a supporter of Home Rule for Ireland, was also attracted to the cause of truth and justice for the oppressed Irish. Simpson Newland – pastoralist, politician and writer – reported in 1887 on his visit to South Australia's far north. He commented that "as the wrongs of Ireland are to Charlotte Waters [where Frank Gillen was Master at the time] so is the totalizator to Alice Springs."[313] How far the tolerance of some English British subjects of South Australia embraced Frank Gillen's advocacy of Irish freedom is open to question, but Gillen was as British as the next South Australian and like most Irish-South Australians found no difficulty in reconciling the two loyalties. For the many South Australians who shared the general belief in it, Britishness implied a special kind of justice that grew from good institutions operated by good men. But the kind of justice that Homburg now placed into Gillen's hands was of the inquisitorial kind, a powerful instrument, well-suited to digging out the truth, but it was not compatible with the higher forms of British justice that would later come into play.

When Messrs Holder and Caldwell took Frank Gillen's evidence on pastoral conditions they were impressed by the man. Perhaps it was in part because Gillen spoke more frankly of the position of the Aboriginal peoples of the Centre than did the pastoralists that he came to mind when Homburg asked their advice. In truth there were few other candidates. It gave Frank Gillen the opportunity to be something more than a manager of a telegraph station-and Gillen seized it with both hands. He agreed, too readily perhaps, that a jury inquest was not practicable, and on April 19th, one week after Homburg's first telegram, Gillen swore Willliam Willshire and began taking his evidence.

It was not the first time Willshire had told his story. Homburg had asked Holder and Caldwell to enquire generally while they were in the Centre, and especially to discover whether the Aboriginal men "shot and agst [against] whom the charge of murder is made by Mr Willshire were present at any time at Finke Mission Enquiry". On the track south from Alice Springs, at Ooraminna, they met William Willshire and three of his Native Constables coming the other way. They interviewed Willshire and the constables, giving them the opportunity to present for the first time the tale Willshire had concocted to justify the killings at Tempe Downs.[314]

It is curious that Thomas was not at Boggy Water when Willshire received the summons from Homburg. According to Gillen, Thomas did not see Willshire between that time and the time, one week later, when Gillen arrived at Boggy Water, having just interviewed the other four members of the Willshire troop at Alice Springs. It was the almost-fatal hole in Willshire's defence. The most obvious explanation for Thomas's absence is that he had business elsewhere. But if he had gone away, he was certainly back at Boggy Water when Gillen called on April 21st, one week later. The other possibility, that Thomas was having problems with his conscience, can not be dismissed. Thomas did not join Willshire, Billy Abbott, Kwalba and Coognalthika for the laborious business of burning the bodies of Ereminta and Donkey. He was never again to be under Willshire's authority. It should also be remembered that Willshire had obliged him to shoot a man against whom Thomas had no grievance under Western Aranda custom.

The story Willshire told Holder and Caldwell they simply recorded and repeated in a report to Homburg, scrawled on a single sheet of paper. Willshire needed to make one important addition to the version he had sent to Besley. In that earlier report he had not mentioned the disposal of the bodies. This measure was intended to destroy evidence, but now that an official enquiry was likely to visit Tempe Downs it created the need for an innocent explanation of the evidence that Gillen would soon find. This was not an easy task. Willshire chose to say that he had been asked by 'enemies' of Ereminta and Donkey for their bodies, and the enemies had then, despite Willshire's remonstration, burned the bodies according to a local custom of which Willshire had not previously written, and which no-one has written of since.

The other significant change Willshire made also demands explanation. In this account of the mechanics of the murders he places himself, not one hundred yards to the rear, but face-to-face with Donkey, handicapped by handcuffs while trying to effect an arrest. In this story Donkey resisted arrest, striking Willshire with a yamstick and injuring his thumbnail (Willshire later showed Gillen an injury), causing Aremala to shoot Donkey dead. If this decoration has any purpose beyond making Willshire out to be braver than he had been, we should look to the fact that it placed him 150 metres away from the scene of Ereminta's killing at the time it was happening. Willshire's invention here adds weight to the conclusion that he had something to hide in the circumstances of Ereminta's death.[315]

Willshire's story was supported in its main points by the three Native Constables he took with him on to Alice Springs. In the story as told to Frank Gillen on April 19th 1891 the murder of old man Namia had been promoted from a supplement to the case against Ereminta and Donkey to the main reason. He had indeed been pursuing cattle-killers and in that way came across the tracks of the two men "for whom we had warrants on a charge of murder." In response to Gillen's questioning Willshire added that his Native Constables had told Ereminta and Donkey that they were to be arrested for Namia's murder. In fact, none of the Constables spoke the language of their victims, as Gillen carefully established by questioning them. And before Donkey injured his thumbnail with a yamstick, Willshire continued, he himself had said to Donkey "you killed Larry's father & I am going to handcuff you, If you run away you might be shot". Willshire also claimed he had promised his trackers a trip to Port Augusta if they succeeded in capturing Ereminta and Donkey alive. To Gillen's final question Willshire responded ingenuously "Neither of the deceased natives were witnesses at the late Finke River Enquiry Commission", although he knew, as Gillen did not, that the Enquiry, during its hearings on the Finke, heard no Aboriginal witnesses at all.

While Willshire's constables agreed on those matters critical to Willshire's motives and intentions in the killing of Ereminta and Donkey, there were numerous inconsistencies in the details. Aremala, who had shot Donkey, claimed to have seen four bullet holes in Ereminta's body, including one in the chest and one in the head. Coognalthika and Kwalba were equally positive that there were no bullet wounds to his head or chest, and only two in total. Aremala also denied that Willshire had offered him a trip to Port Augusta as a reward for taking Donkey alive. Such blatant inconsistencies told Gillen that he was hearing a fabrication, but did not tell him what had really happened.

Gillen was fired with a sense of urgency. The next day he was at Owen Springs with Willshire and the constables, hearing Charles Gall's denial that he had issued, or even been asked for, warrants for the arrest of Ereminta and Donkey. Willshire had never applied to him for warrants against anyone, ever. The next day, April 21st, the inquest arrived at Boggy Water to find Billy Abbott in residence. "I did not hear who shot Donkey and Roger. I refused to listen to the lubra [Chinchewarra] as I did not want to know anything about it." He did, however, see the bodies "in the distance".

And now, at Boggy Water, it was Thomas's turn. On Gillen's questioning he refuted every exculpatory element of Willshire's story. They had not seen any cattle killed. They had seen many tracks, but not those of Ereminta and Donkey. Willshire's commands were simple; he "been yabber want to killem". In all respects Thomas's story was consistent with the version Gillen heard from the women two days later at Tempe Downs.

Willshire now volunteered, on oath, that he remembered that he had only *intended* to get Charles Gall to sign his warrant. When he had been at Owen Springs, distracted by other business, he had forgotten to do so. In support of the new story he handed in to Gillen a warrant form completed but unsigned.

Gillen rode on, down the Finke and across the sand ridges, up Walker Creek to Tempe Downs station. On April 23rd he began proceedings by interviewing the white station workers. They were all as unobservant, cloth-eared and incurious as Billy Abbott claimed to be. All agreed that Ereminta and Donkey were bad characters. None mentioned that Donkey was also employed by Frederick Thornton. According to later evidence from the stockman Charles Tucker, Ereminta was at that time working on the station with a group of well-sinkers, who could have arrested him at any time. None mentioned that Ereminta had been employed on Tempe Downs, on and off, over at least the past five years.[316]

Gillen, however, found the evidence of the Aboriginal women Illingia - Donkey's wife - and Chinchewarra, more informative. Three Aboriginal men employed on the station, Mallakie, also known as Peter, Numbucki/Jimmy and Thinarrie, Chinchewarra's proper husband, all supported the women's account of the burning of the bodies.

None of the witnesses, black or white, mentioned strange "enemies" of the shot men emerging from the bush to claim the bodies.

Finally Gillen spoke to Frederick Thornton, who had returned to the station the previous night. He conceded that Donkey and Ereminta were known to him as cattle-killers "but not during the last twelve months", although "they may have killed cattle without my knowledge... When I left the Station on 18th February Donkey was in my employ as a temporary hand. I did not consider Donkey & Roger dangerous natives. I was not informed of the shooting on my return to the Station". This was as far as Thornton would go to back Willshire's story. It was not enough to satisfy Willshire. In 1895 he still burned with resentment, and wrote of "a gentleman who managed a station in the Northern Territory for years. He was exceedingly kind to the natives; he went dead against other white men who abused them; he believed their stories, and made his station a home for them he would not credit it that they were killing his cattle wholesale; but now he knows it to his sorrow; he is a poor man, the run he had is abandoned, and the buildings left for the swarthy tribes to admire in undreamed of solitude." Willshire was being too kind to Thornton, but those who were not Willshire's supporters were his enemies, and he did not forget.[317]

After one day's hard travelling up the Finke, Gillen was at Hermannsuburg on April 25th interviewing Nungoolga and Theeanka. Hermann Kempe translated for Nungoolga, while Gillen made what sense he could of the boy Friday's translation into pidgin English of the Loritja Matuntara language spoken by Theeanka. While it is unlikely these two women had spoken with the women remaining on Tempe Downs between the day of the shootings and the day they gave evidence to Gillen, still their evidence was entirely consistent with the accounts Gillen had heard from the other women two days before.

Two things struck Gillen and the policeman who accompanied him, Mounted Constable William South. In the first place these killings had taken place as close as one hundred yards to the head station of Tempe Downs. A frontiersman could not have failed to hear of violent acts, even frontiersmen like Gillen and South, against whom no accusation of violence can be made. Some frontiersmen boasted of it, but would even such men have failed to recognise that murderous violence, like sex, requires distance or disguise? Then there was the cutting of Ereminta's throat.

We rely mostly on Chinchewarra's evidence, supplemented by circumstantial evidence, for this most brutal aspect of the events on the morning of February 22nd. The transcript of evidence taken at Gillen's hearings, like Swan-Taplin's evidence, records answers to questions that are not themselves recorded. This is made clear to us in some cases by annotations that record the fact that someone other than the enquiry commissioners was questioning the witness. In other cases we can infer it from the staccato character of the statements attributed to the witness, the lack of a narrative or logical thread between them. In the case of Gillen's Aboriginal witnesses, who knew at best the pidgin English in use at the time, we can assume that in many cases the statements attributed to a witness are not simply answers to questions, but summaries of several answers to a series of questions lead by Gillen, and possibly South, or those who interpreted for the witness. These answers would then have been edited in their recording to provide the context, the sequence of events, the qualifications, built from simple, one-clause answers that are often in themselves ambiguous or misleading. Gillen had been talking to Aboriginal people for fifteen years and knew well the protocols of courtesy that led them to follow the lead of leading questions from high-status people like himself. If a high-status person seems to be looking for confirmation of an assertion he has turned into a question, it will be given to him. The interviewee may then make a statement of his own that contradicts the version he has just assented to. The capacity for scholarship Gillen later demonstrated in his collaboration with Professor Baldwin Spencer gives us confidence that his questioning of Chinchewarra on this critical matter did not generate her answer. In any case, it is unlikely on Gillen's own evidence to Swan-Taplin the previous year, and to the Pastoral Lands Commission a few weeks earlier, that he would even have guessed Willshire capable of such an act.

The record of Chinchewarra's evidence on this point is brief. "Me been seeem blackfellow Policeman shootem Roger, then him tumble down and no bin singout, then nother blackfellow policeman more shoot him, me been see Willshire cutem Roger neck longa big fellow knife, then him bin takem longa Camel." Gillen asked subsequent witnesses directly whether or not they had noticed anything about Ereminta's body. None had. This was not conclusively against Chinchewarra's account, since all of these other witnesses had only seen the body well after Ereminta died, and after it had been moved from the place he died. Chinchewarra's evidence convinced Mounted Constable South. Back in Alice Springs by April 27th, having left Gillen to travel alone to Hermannsburg, South wired his Commissioner in Adelaide. "Evidence against Willshire appalling..." he introduced his summary, "have brought Willshire in under strict guard". A sense of panic began to spread through official Adelaide. It caught up with Homburg, who wired Gillen the same day: "What is the result of the enquiry... Reports of a serious nature circulated here".

Later, at the trial, Kwalba, who admitted firing a shot into Ereminta's leg, gave clear testimony that Ereminta had no wounds to the chest or head, that is, no fatal wounds, and that he was still alive when Willshire instructed Kwalba to go up to the kitchen for breakfast. It seems likely that Thomas and Kwalba were acting on instruction to leave Ereminta disabled but alive, for the cruel ceremony of triumph that Willshire was about to perform.

When Gillen arrived back in Alice Springs on Monday April 27th he wired Homburg: "just returned. Ridden 330 miles since noon Monday". As one who suffered chronically from haemorrhoids Gillen must have felt every mile. Later that day he reported again at length, "Case most serious and revolting police should be instructed arrest Willshire who is here at once". His favoured version of events was the evidence of Thomas "who had not seen Willshire since he received your instructions [to come to Alice Springs]" He omitted the crucial detail of Willshire's work with the butcher's knife, but the doom hanging over Willshire was perceived by his constables. "Archie now wishes to be re-examined" Gillen reported to his Minister the same day, "shall I re-examine Archie and other tracker who wishes to amend his statement". "Re-examine all witnesses and keep every witness at the [telegraph] station" Homburg responded. Archie and Kwalba gave new evidence to Gillen, supporting Thomas's version of events. At some later time Aremala/Larry made a revised statement to Mounted Constable South.[318] Before the day was over Commissioner Peterswald had wired Inspector Besley in Port Augusta; "Instruct South to arrest Willshire ... and bring him before Mr Gillen".

The next day, April 28th 1891, Gillen reported to Homburg that his work was done. He had re-examined two of the recanting constables, in Willshire's presence, allowing Willshire the opportunity to cross-examine, and would send the depositions down by the mail leaving the next week, with a copy to South for the police. Homburg had assured him that "the Government greatly appreciates your efforts", no doubt expressing sincerely his own opinion. On the basis of his good work, Gillen wrote to Homburg two days later recommending the Boggy Water police patrol be wound up and offering to serve as a sub-Protector of Aborigines.[319] Both matters were beyond Homburg's powers. Willshire was in the lock-up he had helped build at Heavitree Gap. It was of log construction and scarcely larger than a country privy; accommodation for blackfellows. His future now lay in the south, where he was soon to be taken in chains, and where Ministers and judges presided over events. He was gone before the Earl of Kintore came down the Line from the north.

Frank Gillen had tried William Willshire according to his best judgement of the evidence of the witnesses and found him as guilty as sin. It was the only such test Willshire was to suffer. Gillen was supported in his verdict by Willshire's police colleague Mounted Constable William South. Even Bryan Besley and William Peterswald seemed, in the early days after Gillen's enquiry, to have abandoned Willshire. After he received South's panicky telegram of April 27th, Besley wired Peterswald that he was "astonished" by it. He could hardly say that it came as no surprise. In a more considered statement made in the form of a letter he wrote to Besley on May 1st, South further distanced himself from Willshire.

> *I have the honor to inform you that I have doubts of M.C. Willshire's sanity. I have known him for nearly 14 years, & have always considered him eccentric, with an inordinate love of Notoriety.*
> *He has a peculiar habit of introducing things foreign to the subject of conversation.*
> *Until now I did not regard his peculiarities seriously, but think his conduct in the unfortunate shooting case at Tempe Downs most unaccountable, unless the result of insanity...*[320]

Can we take South's letter seriously as diagnosis, or was it more a cop-out for South and the South Australian police force. If we take South's information at face value, it is hard to know whether it could serve to lessen Willshire's responsibility, or increase that of his superior officers. It was, after all, only *after* the alleged events at Tempe Downs that South had begun, he claimed, to "regard his [Willshire's] peculiarities seriously". Hardly a convincing case for Willshire's insanity. Instead it was a reason to seek some more persuasive motive for the act at Tempe Downs. And if Willshire's peculiarities were severe enough to lessen his responsibility for his actions, and evident before Tempe Downs, what on earth were

Besley and Peterswald doing promoting him? And why had his colleagues protected him? The police force's protection of Willshire had resumed by July 23rd 1891 when William South gave evidence at the trial.

In May 1891, however, South's clear message to Besley was that Willshire's position was indefensible. The letter was in Commissioner Peterswald's hands on May 19th. Perhaps Peterswald would have gone to his Minister, the Chief Secretary, three weeks earlier and lobbied against arresting Willshire, but Homburg allowed him no time to do so. However, the game was not over.

Earlier, on April 30th, by which time accounts of Willshire's report to Besley had already appeared in the Adelaide press, Heidenreich wrote from Adelaide to Homburg. He quoted Kempe's account of Naomi's return, reported earlier in this chapter, and then told Homburg that "as Mr Kempe's report does not say enough I have asked him [Mr Schwarz] to provide me with more details about recent events." This is the first indication that Heidenreich's accommodation with the police at the time of the Swan-Taplin enquiry was temporary, unlike Hermann Kempe's. Schwarz's report, quoted verbatim by Heidenreich, told Homburg the story of Ereminta's former wife, who had been stolen by Willshire, and that Ereminta was (when Schwarz had left the Centre in the middle of 1889) Thornton's "best and most trusty blackboy" who had been provoked to cattle-killing and violence by Willshire's action. He explained how Willshire used the enmities between the Western Aranda and the Matuntara. "Willshire knew well that the two tribes were at enmity and took delight in acts of violence against each other ... in this way ... the poor savages are shot down like wild dogs." Schwarz thought the money spent on Native Police should be used instead to extend the work of the mission. Heidenreich concluded his letter with this endorsement of Schwarz's claims. "I have myself seen Ereminta's former wife in Willshire's hut, and she appeared from her behaviour to be 'master' of the house. Our blind Martha, also makes serious charges against Willshire for molesting her with immoral intentions, which of course has not happened before witnesses." Martha could herself have been a witness at the Swan-Taplin enquiry, had she been called. As a Christian she could also have been sworn. It was late in the day for Heidenreich to come to the aid of earthly justice for the Aboriginal people of Central Australia, but better late than never.

This was the first time Homburg was given the key to the motive for the Tempe Downs killings, but it was not complete. His informants did not mention, and probably did not know of, the abduction or murder of Nabarong. That conclusive fact remained behind the curtains, to be exposed at the trial.

On April 28th, according to Commissioner Peterswald's telegram to Inspector Besley, Willshire was "to be sent down *to Adelaide* as soon as possible" (my italics)[321], but just one day later William South in Alice Springs was informing Besley that Willshire had been committed to *Port Augusta*, where judge Henry Bundey of the Supreme Court was to preside at a session of the Circuit Court in July. There were practical difficulties in arranging Willshire's escort to the south, related in part to the approach of Governor Kintore, but the arrangements had yet to be finalised when South sent his telegram on April 29th. In fact the decision to commit Willshire was Frank Gillen's, acting as the Centre's sole Magistrate. Gillen made that decision on April 28th. when Peterswald still believed Adelaide would be the venue for the trial. When Besley passed on to Peterswald the news of Willshire's committal to Port Augusta, on April 30th, he made no mention of the Adelaide Court. Instead he asked, "should he not have been committed to Palmerston". Palmerston, now Darwin, was indeed the local Court for the Centre, although located 1300 kilometres to the north of Alice Springs, but Besley's point seems contrived. He had countenanced the sending of at least two prisoners from the Centre to the Port Augusta Court since the Palmerston Court had been established several years before.[322] The judges of the South Australian Supreme Court had found the practice acceptable, and in the end it was a matter for them to decide. Besley's motives need not detain us. He was no fool. He knew Palmerston, a town right on the frontier, would provide a jury more sympathetic to Willshire than would Adelaide. But what can lie behind Peterswald's reply to Besley on this question of venue, when he wired back on the same day that "committal to Port Augusta matter of arrangement"? Whose arrangement, we do not know, but it seems unlikely that Gillen's decision on April 28th was made without instruction from Adelaide, and certain that the source of that instruction did not involve, on April 28th, the Commissioner of Police.

The choice of Port Augusta as the location of the trial had some weighty consequences for the justice of Willshire's trial. Port Augusta was the entrepot for the Central Australian frontier, over-shadowed by the metropolis of Adelaide since the extension north of the railway, but unchanged in its dependence on pastoralism. The prospect of finding from among its adult population a jury of men who could with an easy conscience convict a frontier policeman, someone whose whole purpose was to secure the lives and property of the pastoralist, was poor indeed. If, on the other hand, Frank Gillen had shown his face in Port Augusta at this time he might have found a hanging party standing on every street corner. Every judge of the Supreme Court had the power to direct that a trial be moved from its local court but Bundey chose not to take the trial to Adelaide. It would have occasioned further delay, but so what? Willshire was bailed shortly after he arrived in Port Augusta, on June 1st, and awaited justice with his parents in Adelaide. Willshire's lawyers were both in Adelaide, too. The cost of the time his barrister Sir John Downer spent in travelling between the two cities would have kept a South Australian family for a year.

Willshire did not travel alone south from Alice Springs. A caravan of witnesses travelled too, most of them Aboriginal. One of the witnesses was Billy Abbott, who was fortunate that he too was not in chains. On April 30th Peterswald instructed Besley to have South take Abbott's evidence "carefully [but] not on oath". South was also "to take out [a] warrant for Abbott quietly as accessory but do not execute it unless he attempts leaving district and shows that he will not be willing to give evidence as witness." The documents on file do not explain why someone thought to have been an accessory to murder should have been excused from his own charge provided he gave evidence in the trial of the principal to the murder. Frank Gillen was not asked to serve as a witness, and neither was Frederick Thornton.

As the bewigged and gowned Henry Bundey walked the short distance from his hotel to the Port Augusta Courthouse on July 23rd 1891, accompanied by two mounted police on foot with swords drawn, he needed no convincing of the weight of the British justice he represented.[323] It was the flower of a British civilization that had schooled him from penniless childhood to great social distinction. The rules and procedures by which Bundey was to work this day were as elaborate as Gillen's procedures had been simple. There was of course the black-letter law made by the Parliaments of Great Britain and South Australia but, in any area of law as important, and well-exercised, as that applying to the crime of murder, those rules were embedded in the rules the judges themselves made in their courts, in conversation with their peers the senior barristers. Like Willshire's defence counsel, Sir John Downer, Bundey had served as a government Minister, but he had graduated from representative politics to a higher plane of government, the judiciary. Downer's talent and reputation were such that he could hardly afford the enormous losses he would have suffered in moving from the floor of the court to the bench. Above all this reigned the simple fact that the purpose of Bundey's court was not to find out the truth, as Gillen had sought to do, but to manage the conflict between accuser and accused while preserving the procedural standards that were the heart of British justice. And, one might add, the dignity and self-regard of the presiding judge.

Bundey was, at 53 years of age, in the prime of his professional life. He had been elected to the House of Assembly twenty years before, as a young lawyer, defeating Friedrich Krichauff in the process. Within three years he was Minister for Justice and Education. Politics had not delayed his progress in the law. He was made Queen's Counsel in 1878, the first of three years he served in the office of Attorney-General. Three years after that he was made a judge of the South Australian Supreme Court, a position superior in status and salary to any government Minister. It is not surprising to find his biographer describing him as a handsome, affable and courteous man, but there was part of Bundey's temperament that did not quite fit the job description for the positions he had held. He was also an exceptionally sensitive man. In 1875, the second year of his first Ministerial appointment, he had suffered a breakdown ascribed to overwork. Strange as it may seem he was particularly sensitive to argument, and on one occasion fainted when an angry argument took place in the corridor outside his office. Bundey was a political liberal. He favoured the education of girls, the role of trade unions and the arbitration of industrial disputes, and opposed capital punishment. Here at his threshold to the Port Augusta court stood no hanging judge.

Perhaps as he considered the business before him that day Bundey reflected that in 1866, one year after he had been admitted to legal practice, two of his clients were sentenced to fourteen years in prison for a crime of which they were later found to be innocent. "Such a startling experience as this at the threshold of a professional career seldom falls to the lot of a young barrister. As may be supposed, it made an indelible impression on me". It was the leading example Bundey gave in a pamphlet he wrote later, in 1900, under the title *Conviction of innocent men*. He concluded "justice does sometimes miscarry in times of public excitement", but all the examples he gave were cases of wrongful conviction. It was not his concern to give examples of prisoners dubiously discharged in times of public excitement, and he made no mention of the Willshire trial, surely the most famous trial over which he had presided. [324]

Before entering the Port Augusta court Bundey had read the depositions Gillen had taken from the witnesses, including those witnesses who had not been brought south. They had, in any case, been summarised in the *Observer* on May 2nd that year. We do not know which version of the evidence Bundey saw. Most likely it was Gillen II, since that version was also sent to Adelaide from Besley in Port Augusta and was a clean copy, all in one copyist's hand, unlike Gillen I. If Bundey had refrained from reading the *Observer*'s summary on May 2nd he may have been ignorant of one important fact that the *Observer*'s readers knew: When Gillen had re-heard the recanting native constables, Willshire had been present and had cross-examined them. This vital information had been omitted from Gillen II.

The Port Augusta court house was a young building in 1891, square in shape and modest in scale and only one-storey high. Today it is an incongruous island of late Victorian architecture in a waste of car-parking behind Port Augusta's retail centre. Its facade carries too much detail for its size but here form represents many functional distinctions. Henry Bundey entered the court house by the porticoed judges' door. It was just one of six entrances, but by far the most pretentious, a cramped attempt at grandeur. On the opposite side of the building to Bundey's door was the public entrance which led to an island of spectators' seating. Here one hundred people could, and no doubt did on this day, sit facing directly the judge on his raised podium, the court's highest floor level.

All the other players in this judicial performance also had their own entrances, and all led, like Bundey's entrance, into ante-rooms reserved for them, and from which internal doors led in turn into the theatre of justice itself, the court room. The witnesses entered their door beside the public entrance. Their room is a tiny parlour holding no more than four people, with a fireplace and iron grate in one corner. On the third side of the building the jury's door led to a more spacious parlor, also provided with a fire-place and a simple table around which the members could meet to talk or eat. On the fourth side is the door for the court officials and the prisoner. The prisoner, William Willshire, was led in here, to a small slate-floored cell that had no fire to take the winter chill from the stone. His cell connected through a door directly to the prisoner's dock on the right of Bundey's podium at the front of the court.

The atmosphere of the court room, while the colours are the sombre tones of varnished wood and slate, is intimate. On July 23rd it buzzed with anticipation and a subdued anger. The crowded public gallery, rising up before the players like bleachers at a sporting event favoured strongly the prisoner, as it would later show. Among the spectators were reporters for the Adelaide papers and the *Port Augusta Dispatch*, and even a writer designated to write local 'colour' under the by-line of *The Sketcher*. James Willshire was there, of course, with Billy Abbott's father, W H Abbott, and his employer, Sir Charles Todd, the South Australian Post-Master General and director of the Telegraph. Under their gaze, when Bundey had taken his central place on the judge's podium, Willshire was brought in to his dock, a narrow gallery on the right hand wall. This prisoner's gallery is a stage in itself. The twelve men of the jury were led into their protective enclosure opposite him. Willshire faced directly the most important audience of his life, with Bundey off to his left and the public to his right. He stood on the same level as the judge, above all other players.

When the first witness, Native Constable Kwalba, was called a strange and significant feature of this particular judicial theatre became evident. He took his place in the witness box, placing him directly in front of his master Willshire, just one and a half metres away, and a good fifteen centimetres lower. While Kwalba faced directly the public gallery, with Bundey behind him and Willshire to his right, Willshire could easily have leaned over and placed his hand on his trooper's head. The architect of the Port Augusta Court house might well have designed it for William Willshire to exert his influence upon his Native Constables.[325]

Below judge Bundey, prisoner Willshire and the jury were the lawyers, the main players in this drama of justice. Sir John Downer and Thomas Gepp, the solicitor assisting him, represented Willshire. Like Bundey, John Downer had been South Australia's Attorney-General, but he had also been its Premier, and was to be Premier again the next year. He was paramount among South Australia's lawyers, the top dog. He earned from his legal wits each year more than most rich men earned from their large capital, and several times more than Henry Bundey. People were pleased to pay him his fees because he had to an extraordinary degree the talent to speak the public language of the time, to charm, to persuade, to bully, to scorn, and to dissect his opponents in the theatre of the court. Square-faced and portly, he was only forty-eight years old but had already been a Knight for four years. His was a commanding presence in this small country court-room. In his proxy duel with his accusers, William Willshire had an artillery piece. Like any competent advocate Downer picked up the sense of indignation, outrage even, in the gallery and the jury box. To it he added the weight of his gravitas. Like any capable barrister he shared with the revenge killers of Central Australia the ability to attack without pity.

The Crown Prosecutor James Stuart had sole responsibility for the case against the prisoner. It was against Downer, not Willshire, that the prosecution had to direct its weapons, and those weapons were Aboriginal men and women from Central Australia dressed in the hand-me-down clothes in which they had been sleeping, in the open, at the edge of town.[326] They knew little English and what they knew they had learned from the lowest order of South Australian workers. They spoke a language that was, to native English-speakers, a crude pidgin that was based on English but had its own register of associations that were foreign to most of their audience. It accepted as ordinary words and expressions some that were regarded in the south as rude, vulgar, brutal or childish. To make one example stand for many, Thomas told the court "Me shootum Roger; knock um heels over head". This expression would normally be read by his audience as implying, at the least, callousness, but to Thomas it may have been the expression generally used in the Centre to mean 'I shot him down'.[327]

The Aboriginal witnesses had been taught to defer to senior men, but had no experience of court-room procedures. Henry Bundey in his shoulder-length wig was, to one of the women, the most imposing "flour-bag whitefellow boss" she had ever seen. It was an unequal contest, distressing to those who dislike the sight of the strong wounding the weak or the sound of a crowd baying for the victim's blood. While this was going on down in the court's pit, while the partisan crowd looked on, to Henry Bundey fell the task of keeping the peace. It was not the job for a man who could not bear conflict.

Crown Prosecutor Stuart was a public servant who had previously been a magistrate in the Adelaide local court. His office adjoined that of Attorney-General Homburg and perhaps for this reason the records show nothing of the communication between them. There is also no record of any communication he had with Premier Tom Playford, or with any other Minister of his Government. We can only consider that he was the sole author of the way he conducted his case against William Willshire, and draw our own conclusions about some of its features that seem remarkable to us, a century later.

James Stuart, not a barrister of note in South Australia, chose to lead the prosecution himself, yet two days before the Willshire trial Stuart had employed Sir John Downer to prosecute several cases of less weight in the Gladstone Circuit Court. Perhaps the Willshire side had engaged Downer before Stuart was ready to do so, but Downer was not the only barrister in South Australia better qualified than James Stuart.[328]

In the first place, Stuart chose to lead his case with the evidence of the four Native Constables, who were implicated as, at least, accessories to the murders of Ereminta and Donkey and at risk of further incriminating themselves by their evidence in Port Augusta. Homburg had recognised this problem, when the Protector, at Besley's suggestion, drew it to his attention, but chose not to appoint legal representation for them. Instead, their interests were put into the hands of the Crown Prosecutor Stuart, a peculiar position reflecting, once again, the reluctance of government to spend large sums of money on Aborigines. Every word the Native Constables said against Willshire was liable to be discounted for their self-interest.

It was not that Stuart lacked alternatives. Of the women witnesses none was implicated in the crime although two were married to the victims. One of the women, Chinchewarra, had no personal interest in the events at all, and was a fluent and confident speaker of Central Australian pidgin English. There were also the black station workers who had been unanimous in their account of the circumstances of the cremations. It is telling that when he interviewed witnesses on July 20th, two days before the trial, Bryan Besley chose to speak only to the civilians, ignoring the four Native Constables who were his subordinates.[329]

Having chosen to begin with the Native Constables, Stuart chose as his first witness Kwalba/Jack.[330] We do not know why he did so. Kwalba was one of the three Native Constables who fired shots into one or other of the victims; only Archie had shot no-one. But, considering the prosecution's case that Willshire "instigated" the killings, Stuart's strongest witness was Thomas. Thomas had not lied to Holder and Caldwell or Gillen. He was also a Christian, and that meant he could give evidence on oath, as no other Aboriginal witness but Nungoolga could. Bundey simply records "Aboriginal natives to be taken without oath", implying that Stuart did not tell him about Thomas and Nungoolga. Stuart, of course, may not have known, but he could easily have found out.

The performance of the four Native Constables under cross-examination by John Downer was predictable. All were made to contradict their revised evidence to Gillen, mostly in answering leading questions. Since they had told two contradictory stories to Gillen it was not always clear which one they were assenting to, and which they were denying. As far as Downer was concerned it hardly mattered; any confusion was good confusion. In Thomas's case his apparent self-contradiction had a different character.

Thomas had to this point given only one version of events at Tempe Downs on February 22nd 1891. Nevertheless, he was led into saying that Willshire told him he wanted Ereminta and Donkey "taken". Whoever introduced that word into the court's proceedings it was interpreted by one newspaper report as a synonym for "arrested". Bundey's notes do not make that leap of interpretation, nor did the reporter for the *Register*. His report was sent by telegraph and therefore at a great expense that favoured brevity. He reported Thomas saying "that Willshire said he wanted them to shoot Roger and Donkey, but added that Willshire said he wanted them taken *for this purpose*" (my italics), providing the most direct support in the trial evidence for Willshire's intent to take personal responsibility for the death of one, or both, of his victims. This highly suggestive evidence was not pursued.[331]

John Downer, in cross-examining Thomas, went straight to the question of motive. In response to his question, Thomas is recorded in Bundey's notes as saying "Donkey & Roger kill my brother". It appears that the facts were otherwise. In an earlier statement to Gillen, Thomas was cross-examined carefully on this point by Willshire. This is what he answered (Willshire's questions are not recorded). "The Tempe Downs Blacks killed my brother. ... I once speared a black in the head after the Tempe Downs Blacks killed my brother, He was a Tempe Downs Blackfellow. Donkey was one of the Blacks who killed my brother." No mention of Ereminta. We should bear in mind, however, that the protocols of revenge-killing did not demand precise selection of victims; a form of group responsibility might be applied.[332]

It was immediately after Thomas's cross-examination that Bundey fed John Downer a fall-back position. "I ask if this Court has any jurisdiction to try this case" he recorded in his notes. Despite prosecutor Stuart's advice that all was in order, and a reminder of Bundey's own powers as a Supreme Court judge to decide on venue, Bundey recorded "I reserve to Sir Jno Downer the right to move as he may be advised that this Court has no jurisdiction to try the prisoner, inasmuch as the alleged offence occurred within the boundaries of the Northern Territory."[333]

When it was Native Constable Archie's turn to sit below Willshire's gaze in the witness box there occurred one of those scarifying moments when everyone is struck by a revelation that changes everything but cannot be named. That it should come from Archie is intriguing, because Archie, having repeated his own version of events at Tempe Downs reverted, under cross-examination by John Downer, to William Willshire's fictional account more thoroughly and convincingly than his three colleagues.

In this way his evidence aided significantly in Willshire's defence. But before he had been questioned into this position he gave the court the key to Willshire's motive. In Bundey's transcription Archie said "me take em rifle & revolver to shoot Roger, & Donkey, because they took away Mr Willshires Lubra her name [Nabarong]- that's why we shot Roger & Donkey".[334]

If motive is the key to conduct in real life, and essential to sustaining a charge of wilful murder, in Henry Bundey's court it was of no account, at least not when it supported the prosecution's case. We can understand that John Downer did not refer to this aspect of Archie's evidence in his cross-examination, but it is harder to understand why prosecutor Stuart, or even Bundey, left Archie's revelation hanging in the middle of the Port Augusta court-room, surely the object of the attention of every observer on that day. We can imagine the deepened silence in the court as all minds except those of the main players turned inwards to digest this stunning news. No-one said another word on the subject. The next witness, Aremala/Larry, whose English was the best of all the Aboriginal witnesses brought south, was not asked to confirm it. Aremala did say, under cross-examination, that it was Donkey, not Ereminta who killed Namia his father, contradicting earlier evidence from Willshire's reports to Besley. He had said the same to Gillen. The discrepancy was not noticed by the court, but the supposed fact was, and, according to Bundey's notes, was developed through questioning. In Aremala's case the question of motive was not overlooked.

The existence of Nabarong and her fate were critical to evaluating Chinchewarra's evidence of Willshire's work with the butcher's knife. Besley certainly knew of it, because he had questioned Chinchewarra himself three days before. Her blunt statement "me been see Willshire cutem Roger neck longa big fellow knife" occurs in both Gillen I and Gillen II and therefore it is reasonable to assume that Bundey had seen it too. And yet the court was not allowed to hear it. When the first of the Aboriginal women, Nungoolga, was called to give evidence someone, presumably prosecutor Stuart, decided her evidence should be interpreted. Had the evidence of all the Aboriginal witnesses been interpreted the court would have been well served. However, there is no obvious reason why Nungoolga/Naomi should have been singled out for translation. Her evidence to Gillen was translated by Hermann Kempe, largely because it was taken at Hermannsburg and translation was available. When Bryan Besley spoke to her in Port Augusta he noted no particular difficulty in understanding her, as he did in the case of Theeanka, a Matuntara woman. Nevertheless, the police interpreter, Native Constable Chickyllia, who had been brought south, was called into the court. John Downer objected immediately, on the grounds that Chickyllia "had been a tracker under Willshire" according to the *Port Augusta Dispatch,* and Chickyllia was discharged. The *Observer* put it slightly differently: he was "a native discharged from the employ of accused." The inference was clear; this man was likely to be biased against Willshire. There is no basis in the circumstances of Chickyllia's career with the police in Central Australia to support that assertion. Chickyllia, also known as Wilkie, was employed in the Centre, mostly working from Alice Springs, from the beginning of 1886, at the latest, until the beginning of 1889, when Willshire left for Port Augusta, Adelaide and then Boggy Water. While based at Alice Springs Chickyllia worked also for any other policeman who needed his assistance. He may well have spent time with Willshire at Boggy Water and may have chosen to leave Willshire to return to Alice Springs, but there is no evidence of any misbehaviour on his part, and at the time of the trial he was still a Native Constable, a fact not reported to the court but evident from a photograph taken at the time. If anything, Willshire regarded Chickyllia more highly than the other Native Constables at Alice Springs. The writer for the *Port Augusta dispatch* who described the 1888 photograph of Willshire, Wurmbrand and their Aboriginal assistants records Chickyllia as "Corporal of Native Police", and shows him as Willshire's leading assistant. Chickyllia's rank was not recognised by the police service, but may reflect what Willshire thought of him in 1888.

Having ruled Chickyllia out as an interpreter, the court could have proceeded as it had with the Native Constables. Instead it was decided that Nungoolga's evidence would not be taken, and, more remarkably, that the evidence of *none* of the other civilian Aboriginal witnesses waiting outside the court would be taken. It appears prosecutor Stuart did not even request it. Here is an absence as striking as the presence of Nabarong, and just as neglected by Henry Bundey in his record of the proceedings. Bundey simply recorded "Nung-wool-Ka - witness - no evidence".[335] It seems that, for whatever reason, Henry Bundey did not wish to use the wide discretion the law of South Australia had given him in the presentation of Aboriginal evidence. His court allowed the evidence that was taken from Aboriginal witnesses to be turned into a circus act by the manner in which it was taken. It would have been difficult to avoid this outcome without limiting the freedom of Willshire's lawyer to cross-examine. But where he did have discretion, Bundey allowed evidence he knew to be important to be kept out of his court.

We can accept that any fastidious judge might feel distressed when the witnesses before his court appeared to contradict themselves so radically as the four Native Constables did on July 23rd 1891. In Henry Bundey's defence, we can imagine that his distaste and impatience grew during the course of the day until he felt impelled to call an end to the whole business. And yet Bundey's court allowed the prisoner, William Willshire, to address questions to witnesses in some language other than English, and to translate their replies to the court. This is recorded in the newspaper accounts, but not in Bundey's notes. He also allowed Bryan Besley, another interested party, to question one witness, and possibly more. Against that standard it is hard to see his rejection of Chickyllia's involvement as the decision of an impartial judge. At the very least, Bundey was determined to bring the trial to an end, despite the weight of the evidence he knew was waiting to be heard.

Having excluded the Tempe Downs women from giving evidence in person, Bundey was surely obliged to do as the Aboriginal Witnesses Act allowed, and have their formal depositions read to the court. There were not only the depositions taken from the Aboriginal witnesses by Gillen in the Centre, but also Bryan Besley's records of his interviews with them two days before the trial, although these were unsigned. Shortly after neglecting to do this, Bundey's court was allowed to hear a statement ("diary") of Willshire's, prepared under much less demanding conditions. As the accused, Willshire was not permitted by the law of the time to give evidence.[336]

Deprived of his further Aboriginal witnesses prosecutor Stuart had only two white witnesses to produce. It is hard to understand why he did so. Billy Abbott simply repeated his denial that he had anything to do with the burning of the bodies, and was not questioned in detail about the circumstances of their burning, which he could hardly claim not to have noticed. We know that the stockman Charles Tucker and the cook Denis White had been brought south to Port Augusta, because Bryan Besley interviewed them three days previously. At that time Tucker had told Besley that Ereminta was employed with some well-sinkers on the station while at the same time, he claimed, actively engaged in cattle-killing. White now reported that he had woken when Ereminta and Donkey were shot. This was not surprising as it was daylight and White slept outside under a verandah, but he thought the noise was rocks rolling down the nearby hillside and went back to sleep. In his earlier evidence to Gillen, White clearly recalled hearing gunfire after Willshire's arrival at the station. Chinchewarra had told him that the police had shot two Aborigines but he had not enquired further, even when Willshire came to the kitchen. Neither man had noticed the cremation fires. We can imagine the sport a barrister like John Downer would have had with these prevaricators. Prosecutor Stuart, it seems, wished only to spare them the bother.

William South, on the other hand, Stuart called as a witness for the prosecution but allowed to serve as a witness for the defence. "He [Willshire] is an able officer", South assured the court, "& I believe he gives very general satisfaction".[337]. South presented to the court Willshire's "diary" of the events at Tempe Downs. This was read out to the court, to the applause of the gallery. South also put on the record the conclusion of Holder and Caldwell, arrived at after no more enquiry than listening to Willshire's story, that "we are of [the] opinion that no blame attaches to Mounted Constable Willshire", although that conclusion can not be found in Holder and Caldwell's report to Homburg.[338] When South had been stood down, prosecutor Stuart provided the jury with no summary of the prosecution's case, another matter which Bundey failed to note.

The case for the defence, on the other hand, was presented twice. John Downer thundered for forty-five minutes. The case was

one of the most disgraceful that had ever been brought into the Court. Here was a man of high character and responsible position performing arduous and dangerous duties, practically carrying his life in his hand, an officer of noted energy, integrity and ability, brought down from the far interior, hurled into gaol, and put in the dock to answer on peril of his life a charge of murder because he had thoroughly done the difficult work entrusted to him. The extraordinary character of the evidence brought forward by the Crown almost made one at times look upon the case in a humorous light but for the fact that a man's life was at stake. ... [Willshire] was put to the risk of being hanged on the testimony of two self-convicted murderers, whose statements were of the most extraordinarily contradictory character.

The only point of Downer's that Bundey noted in his notebook was in error: "Gillens enquiry - accused not present". Downer's language was more colourful. Gillen's enquiry, he said, "was carried out in the good old Star Chamber style in the absence of the accused".

Judge Bundey's summary of the evidence provided a more telling defence. It was, according to the *Port Augusta dispatch*, "particularly in favour of the prisoner". He balanced the claims of the Aboriginal victims of the shooting to protection from arbitrary murder against the need to support the police in their work. He read through his notes of the evidence, concluding that had the evidence of the Native Constables been that of white men he would not have sent the case to the jury, but since the question of Willshire's influence on them had been raised he was leaving the matter to the jury to decide. In the course of his summary, according to the *Observer*'s report, John Downer "asked His Honor to point out that each of the two blacks shot the particular man against whom he had a blood feud. This His Honor did", so confirming the second major point of misinformation promulgated through this trial. The report of the *Port Augusta Dispatch* adds a further and more damaging declaration from Bundey, that "in British law a man could not be convicted upon the evidence of an accomplice". Coming from the judge who had prevented the hearing of evidence from witnesses who were not "accomplices", this declaration has a particularly unsavoury odour. There was no mention of Nabarong.

Given that the swell of sentiment in favour of the prisoner was now universal, and included the prosecution, it is not surprising that a Port Augusta jury needed only fifteen minutes to reach its conclusion. By 5.00 pm it could report to Bundey that there was "not a tittle of evidence incriminating the prisoner". William Willshire walked out of the court a free man. The cheering crowd accompanied him to his hotel, where his family and friends may have experienced a sense of relief rather than jubilation. Having survived the capital charge of wilful murder, Willshire was now immune to any of the lesser charges he richly deserved. His troopers had, by implication, been found guilty of murdering Ereminta and Donkey, but no further action was taken against them. At least three of them, Archie, Larry and Kwalba, continued in the police service. Aboriginal men, it seemed, could not only be killed by police with impunity, they could also kill each other.

While Henry Bundey's justice exonerated Willshire, official South Australia drew a different conclusion. The police of the Centre were reminded of their duty not to fire on Aboriginal people except in self-defence. Willshire's Native Constables were dispersed as trackers and the Boggy Water police camp closed. Later, in 1893, two policemen were stationed at Illamurta Springs near the eastern boundary of Tempe Downs run. William Willshire applied for the posting, for which he was well-qualified, but was refused it. In December 1891 procedures for paying Native Constables were tightened to require that payments be witnessed.[339] When Frank Gillen was made a sub-Protector of Aborigines in November 1891 he was especially instructed that "Any circumstance of a pressing or extraordinary character that may occur in relation to the aborigines you will report to the Minister [for Education and the Northern Territory] without delay."[340]

It is not difficult to derive from the evidence available to Henry Bundey's court - which is still all the evidence there is - a better understanding of what happened than emerged on July 23rd 1891. We can all come to our own conclusions. The people of Port Augusta were not willing to condemn the frontier policeman, but from one of them, who confessed he might be in the minority, came an editorial essay on July 31st that expressed most clearly and sanely what had gone wrong in Central Australia.

If no attempt is to be made to alter the conditions which now obtain, it would seem as though the protection of our aborigines might be regarded as a mere cant term.... we have a police officer appointed to take charge of a corps of native trackers away in the interior. The former has absolute control - in fact his rule is despotic. The men whom he governs are ... by custom and heredity prone to kill. They are, moreover, armed with the most deadly and destructive firearms, and have every means to hand for committing crime secretively in regions far removed from centres of civilization. In the event of a crime being committed, to say that either the one or the other can be brought to justice is simply ridiculous, after hearing the Court case of last week..... On the other hand supposing the native police to be capable - and everything points to the feasibility of the supposition - of shooting down the Rogers and Donkeys of the interior whenever they saw fit or tribal custom demanded it, who are we to bring to book for the crime? Not the native offenders, seemingly, otherwise we presume the murders of the two blacks at Tempe Downs would have been avenged.[341]

The anonymous author went on to advocate the formation of Aboriginal protective reserves.

There were those, of course, who agreed with Tom C. Fowler, a friend of the Willshires, who gave heartfelt thanks that "there are men in the land who will do justice to a white man". For now, however, I will leave you to share for a moment the grief of a British gentleman who had attended the trial, knew "many persons from the North" and "was in the North soon after the murders took place" (meaning, perhaps, soon after they became public knowledge). He wrote in the *Observer* under the name of "Justitia", although he sent the Editor his card, and was, most probably, Charles Chewings. If he was, it would make some kind of dramatic dénouement to the trial, since Charles Chewings was, as much as any man, the reason Willshire's police force had been established. How could he have foreseen this brutal consequence of his enterprises, not so much the death of two black men as the wounding of British justice?

I have expected to see some letter appear in your columns taking an opposite view in the Willshire case to that of your late correspondents, for after the trial so many persons from the North expressed their dissatisfaction at the way in which it was conducted. I was present, and never heard a more entirely one-sided affair. Surely when so many witnesses were brought such a long distance at the public expense it would have been only right in the public interest to examine them? The Crown

Prosecutor refused to do this .... No one who watched the countenances of the four black trackers could doubt that they spoke the truth at the trial, and if the other black witnesses had been produced and their evidence taken it would no doubt have put a very different aspect on the business. Everyone was determined that Willshire should be acquitted, and the speech of the counsel for the prosecution might certainly have been that for the defence. As several people remarked, Sir John Downer's services were quite unnecessary. ... Now, it appears to me that no individual ought to be entrusted with the autocratic power Willshire possessed over the lives and properties of these comparatively defenceless people. ... No man should be left very long in the position Willshire occupied, for his character and perception of right and wrong must inevitably deteriorate. One of the trackers in his examination said he "was ordered to kill Donkey and Roger, because they took away Willshire's lubra". No questions were asked on this point, though it might have been the clue to the whole affair....

Willshire's acquittal had also saved his accomplice Billy Abbott from prosecution. The day after embracing Willshire emotionally outside the Port Augusta court room, W H Abbott, Billy Abbott's father, still in Port Augusta, suffered a heart attack. He was taken to his hotel room, but by the time his friend Charles Todd had rushed to see him Abbott was already dead, at 62 years of age, another of William Willshire's casualties.[342]

Frank Gillen was now confirmed in his position as master of the Alice Springs Telegraph Station and of the central section of the Line, a sub-Protector of Aborigines and a newly-married man whose career seemed to be progressing well. There is no evidence that the people of the Central Australian frontier thought any the worse of him for convicting Willshire. To the Aranda peoples he seemed a strong friend, and has since been given the whole credit for the fact that Willshire was called to account for his crime. The policeman himself did not forgive Gillen. He wrote five years later:

In 1891 a forensic gentleman, notorious for his ignorance of magisterial duties, made a faux-pas by not taking my measure correctly. I'll give him this much credit, that he succeeded in making me most infernally uncomfortable for the time being in his impetuosity to sheet home an offence to someone. He waxed vehement, boisterous, fierce, turbulent, angry, and frantic, and transported himself from place to place in a most unseemly fashion to interview a migratory clan of sore-eyed gins, and mobilize them to give evidence against a "white man." ... I never meddled with long-haired Rose at Charlotte Waters, and I have to this day failed to comprehend why he displayed such venom, and thus comported himself... He frothed, he foamed, like an unchained sleuth-hound. May be his zeal and passionate ardour carried him away to spiteful regions. Had he worked as diligently for his own interest as he worked against mine, he would have become a wealthy man in a short time.[343]

As Gillen's scholarly reputation and his children grew throughout the 1890s he hoped, reasonably enough, for promotion to a metropolitan position. He thought of the North Adelaide Post Office but Post-Master General, Charles Todd, never allowed Gillen closer to Adelaide than Port Pirie, two hundred kilometres to the north of the metropolis in which he might have found respect among the educated elite. He died in 1912 at the age of 57.

William Willshire returned from Port Augusta to Adelaide "very ill owing to the terrible mental strain to which he has been subjected", according to a supporter. Whether he was suffering from some kind of mental breakdown or merely from alcohol poisoning we do not know. But he was to bounce back. It is an advantage of needing to seem a hero to yourself before others that the means of success are in your own hands. Even his savings were not entirely consumed. His solicitor, Thomas Gepp, dunned Robert Homburg for the full cost of his and Sir John Downer's legal services, £277/-/7, but was offered only £110, leaving Willshire with £177 to pay for his one-day trial, less whatever had been raised for this purpose among his friends. He later claimed the expenses had ruined him financially, but that is unlikely.[344] And he was still a Mounted Constable, First Class, in the South Australian police force.

As a result of his actions William Willshire was forced to leave behind on the Finke perhaps the only women who had ever loved him as he needed to be loved, with uncritical admiration. He also left behind his infant daughter Ruby, and possibly other children, whom he may have loved as a durable reflection of himself. He was never to see any of them again.

Frank Gillen, a South Australian British Irishman, was master of the Central Australian section of the Overland Telegraph line in 1891 when Robert Homburg commissioned him to try his fellow frontiersman, William Willshire. He pursued the truth vigorously, perhaps too vigorously for some in government. Ten years later, when this photograph was taken, he had established his reputation as a leading field anthropologist in a partnership with Professor Baldwin Spencer (MV XP14540).

Robert Homburg, South Australian Attorney-General, who pursued William Willshire after the Tempe Downs killings, but was unable to hold South Australian justice to the challenge of convicting him (*CSA I;248*).

Aboriginal witnesses' accommodation, 1891, and judges' entrance, Port Augusta Court, 2002. Protector Hamilton asked Bryan Besley to have the witnesses recorded as examples of a dying race (*RGSSA*).

Justice (William) Henry Bundey, who presided at William Willshire's trial for murder, July 21st, 1891, was fond of lecturing on justice, but made no comment on the lessons to be drawn from the Willshire trial (*SLSA B11219*).

Sir John Downer (left), top-gun lawyer, sometime Attorney-General and head of government in South Australia. Here shown with future Australian Prime Minister Edmund Barton (centre) in 1897 helping draft the constitution for the new nation. As Willshire's defence barrister he was more legal fire-power than was needed (*NAA: A1200, L16929*).

15

WHO KILLED EREMINTA? A RETRIAL

Judgement by hindsight is the cruelty historians practise on their subjects, many of whom are better people than their accusers. It should have been clear from the beginning of this account that I consider the evidence for Willshire's guilt conclusive. Should judge Bundey and his justice be allowed to escape re-trial for coming to the opposite conclusion? It seems to me there was enough wrong with the Willshire trial to justify the attention of armchair critics located in the lofty heights of the early twenty-first century. As we have seen in chapter six, British law was adapted to the fact of Aboriginal difference more than a generation before Bundey presided at Willshire's trial. British judges, however, had not adapted their practices to make sure Aboriginal evidence could play its due part. Bundey could have moved his trial to Adelaide, he could have insisted on interpreters, he could himself have taken more prominent role in questioning or designated some experienced person who could do it for him, he could have constrained the aggression of John Downer, he could have tried to whip the prosecutor into doing his duty and he should have so far resisted the pressure of the crowd in his court on that day as to ensure all important witnesses were heard. Some of the important circumstances of the Tempe Downs story could have been established beyond reasonable doubt if the neglected witnesses, black and white, had been called, since those circumstances were not in dispute.

To do all of these things might have required Bundey to go beyond the precedents set by his fellow judges, and beyond the limits of the identity he had developed for himself as a public figure within Adelaide society. At the time of writing this, courts are only beginning to rein in the defence barristers who have to date intimidated child victims of sexual abuse. Judges are now taking a more leading role in family law matters, where adversarial justice has contributed much to human unhappiness. Henry Bundey, like some of his present-day counterparts faced with difficult circumstances, was more comfortable working for the defence than for truth.

The most grotesque failing of the Willshire trial was beyond Bundey's direct control. The prosecution ran dead, sacrificed some of its important witnesses and sometimes led evidence for the defence. Why and how did this happen? It seems the process was under way as early as April 28th, the day after Willshire's arrest but we do not know who was driving it. If Homburg was being pushed the obvious culprit was Premier Tom Playford, a man with a simple utilitarian view of the role of government and the bulldozer qualities for the job. Cabinet government operates on consensus, and it needed only one senior figure to express serious reservations about the direction they were being taken by Homburg's pursuit of truth and justice. James Stuart who prosecuted for the government, a much more obscure figure, must also carry a substantial share of the responsibility for what he did, and failed to do, at the trial of William Willshire. Did it all happen from an emerging consensus that South Australia could not afford to hang a policeman, or was there an active conspiracy? There is always the permanent conspiracy of the public servants against the rashness of their Ministers. Whatever Homburg's permanent Secretary Charles Cornish did it certainly did not retard his career, since he rose to the top of the South Australian public service. And what of Robert Homburg, the instigator of justice in this matter? He continued in office as Attorney-General for a total of more than two years, a good tally for the time, and ended his life and career as a judge of the Supreme Court of South Australia, but of his views on the trial or its outcome we know nothing. We are unlikely ever to know, unless some personal papers of one of the leading players should emerge into the public domain in future. Homburg's inherent caution may have combined with worry about the reputation of German-South Australians, evident in his letter of April 1890 to Pastor Dorsch. Secret whitefellow business.

All of the officials considered above, except the public servants, came in to the story only after the deaths of Ereminta and Donkey. The police were there at the moment, and before.

Is William Willshire's responsibility for Ereminta's death diminished by the "insanity" that William South claimed to have diagnosed in him in 1891? It should be clear from Willshire's career that he was not mad. No person suffering from a major affliction such as schizophrenia or bipolar disorder or major depression could have done what Willshire did. It is true that he exhibited a high degree of vanity, that contemplating himself, whether in photographs or in print, was to him a source of great satisfaction, that he could allow no other person to stand between him and the hallucinatory mirror in which he saw a heroic image, and that he considered himself, on the flimsiest of grounds, entitled to the approbation of South Austalians generally. To consider these characteristics to be madness would over-fill the asylums, however many of them were built, and many of Willshire's companions in bedlam would come from the highest levels of government. Alfred Deakin, a prominent political leader of William Willshire's generation wrote this of Henry Parkes, one of the most successful politicians of James Willshire's generation.[345]

No actor ever more carefully posed for effect. ... He had always in his mind's eye his own portrait, as that of a great man, and constantly adjusted himself to it."

On first appreciation that might be said of Willshire, but these further observations of Deakin's could not:

"A far-away expression of the eyes, intended to convey his remoteness from the earthly sphere, often associated with melancholy treble cadences of voice in which he implied a vast and inexpressible weariness, constituted his favourite and at last his almost invariable exterior. Movements, gestures, inflexions, attitudes harmonized, not simply because they were intentionally adopted, but because there was in him the substance of the man he dressed himself to appear.

Those two characteristics - the harmony of substance and presentation, and the knowledge of the codes of behaviour and thought by which other people are persuaded of the truth of the person we represent ourselves to be, even to a more every-day degree, were what Willshire entirely lacked. There was no art in Willshire's attempts at self-aggrandisement because, it is clear, he had no grasp of the materials from which good reputation is crafted.

Willshire never cracked the code. In 1894, partly from desperation and partly from opportunism, Commissioner Peterswald decided to send him to the Top End. Willshire tried to re-create the dream that inhabited him during his time at Boggy Water. Placed again in charge of Aboriginal trackers and sent to the outside stations of the north, particularly on the Victoria River, Willshire behaved more murderously than in the Centre, if oral history is any guide. He spent much of his time writing the book that integrated more successfully than his three previous attempts, the different strands of his ambition. *The land of the dawning* is more explicitly violent and sexual than *The Aborigines of Central Australia*, less scatalogical than *A thrilling tale*, a journalism of the self that is more late-twentieth than late-nineteenth Century. It addresses not the metropolitan audience he pursued in his earlier works, but a bush audience, the combos, the drinkers and those who read authors, like Ernest Favenc, who painted the bush life in unnaturally vivid colours. It did not work. As he acknowledged himself: "I find it very difficult to write a book of travels. I am compelled to record scenes and instances through the medium of myself" and that self was altogether too explicit and full of itself to win general respect at that time. For his trouble the *Northern Territory times* dismissed the booklet as "a brochure of unmitigated rubbish and vulgarity". Recalled to the south he appealed, like his nemesis Frank Gillen, for a metropolitan posting, but he also was kept a safe distance from Adelaide. [346]

In 1896, when he was 44, Willshire married a twenty year old woman. It was not a close marriage, but produced three children for Willshire to dote on, at least until the two surviving children reached adolescence. In 1908 he left the police force in order to come finally to Adelaide where he became night-watchman at the Adelaide abattoir at Gepp's Cross. In this position he was provided with another uniform in which he could pose for the camera, perhaps for the last time, seeing himself as no-one else would.

Perhaps the timidity he demonstrated by staying in the police service in the south, long after it ceased to confer lordship, demonstrates to us that he recognised his limits, and was determined to hang on to the status of the small town policeman rather than take the risk of striving for prominence among the crowd of ordinary citizens of South Australia. In the end he did achieve a kind of fame through the exaggerated accounts of his depredations which have fed into white and black mythologies of the Centre. It was not the kind of fame Willshire wanted at first, but, in the end, better than being ignored.

How does this bear on Willshire's culpability? When away from the frontier he seems to have been responsible for little more than insubordination and occasional eccentricity, apart from the domestic disfunctions we may only guess at. His superior officers, Bryan Besley and William Peterswald, while they recognised the nature of the man, kept him on the frontier where isolation and an excess of power over the Aboriginal peoples of the Centre provided a fertile ground for this eccentricity to flower into acts of outright evil. For Willshire, no doubt, his deeds were products of a kind of necessity, but his commanders had choices. They chose to send him to live for months at a stretch among weaker strangers, to depend for survival on the power of his weapons and the practices of those he was supposed to rule, and to discover, like Joseph Conrad's character Mr Kurtz, the darkness in his own heart, that "strange commingling of desire and hate".[347] For that reason Besley and Peterswald should share responsibility for the deaths of Ereminta and Donkey, among other probable Willshire victims who remain nameless. And, incidentally, for Erwein Wurmbrand's attested murders.[348]

In their turn, the police were the agents of government, which gave them the task of protecting life and property with too few resources. Central Australian pastoralism was no gold rush. It is common now, as it was then, to call all pastoralists "squatters", but there were no squatters in Central Australia; they were all rent-paying lessees of the South Australian government. It was a policy of government that embodied the dominant utilitarian faith demanding the capitalisation of the Waste-Lands. Successive governments were careless of the frontier anarchy that expansion would unleash. Government's fault was not that it sought the economic development of Central Australia and the civilization of its peoples. Its fault was that it cared too little about civilization to invest in enough government. Central Australia was a frontier not because the Aranda peoples' countervailing power prevented the establishment of government, the imbalance of fire-power saw to that, but because South Australia was not prepared pay the costs of bringing Central

Australia's peoples within the rule of its law, a rule that might have lowered the Aboriginal rate of death from violence as their death-rate from disease was, inevitably, increasing.

The governments of South Australia were, as we have seen, the creatures of their electorate. The electorate was always under-informed about events in Central Australia. Sometimes it was actively misinformed. Sometimes it demanded retribution rather than justice and when it demanded justice, through the public voices we can read, there were not the means to give effect on the frontier to that demand. However much a metropolitan Government might be embarrassed by the failures of government on the frontier the constituency for justice was never strong enough, or pervasive enough, to make justice for Aboriginal peoples the issue on which governments were formed or broken. In the end, the electorate was indifferent to these remote, strange peoples, always few in number, and the indifference of others is all that the bad people need to get their way. For this reason the South Australian electorate must join a now crowded prisoners' dock in my court of hindsight, charged with an accessory's contribution to Ereminta's death.

By now Henry Bundey would think the prisoners' gallery at Port Augusta Court House unconscionably crowded, but there were two others he had himself, by implication, identified as culprits: Thomas and Aremala/Larry. Granted that Aremala fired the bullet that killed Donkey, and the shot from Thomas's rifle caused Ereminta a wound that would have proved fatal in Central Australia, had Willshire allowed it time, where do they fit in the queue to the door of the prisoners' gallery? Granted also that Willshire instigated the killings, should we regard Thomas and Aremala as willing accomplices rather than victims of a violent man's threats? As far as Aremala is concerned, let him take his place in the dock. The morning of February 23rd 1891 at Tempe Downs head station were neither the time nor the place he would have chosen for a revenge killing had he not been armed and instigated by William Willshire, but, eventually, he would have killed Donkey. Willshire's revenge served his purpose. By the way, it is unlikely that anyone in Willshire's party had clearly identified Donkey and Ereminta as the particular killers of old man Namia, Aremala's father. The attack probably took place while Willshire's troopers were absent. Revenge parties planned their business to avoid surviving witnesses and took great pains to avoid leaving tracks. But Donkey was on the agenda for Aremala's revenge, and Ereminta, as a leading Matuntara man, may have been lower down that list.

In Thomas's case there is more reason to doubt his motive. The Matuntara had killed his brother, as he had killed Loritja, but the missionaries had shown him a world-view that did not demand that he continue the process, and his employment with Willshire provided him with protection from both his enemies and his offended friends should he choose to walk away from his obligations to revenge. Thomas's behaviour after the killings, the way he distanced himself from Willshire, gives us good reason to accept that he acted under pressure when he shot Ereminta. As we let him out of the cell we might also spare a thought for Hermann Kempe and Louis Schulze, soon to be driven from the Finke by hardships even they could not bear. Their complicity with police violence had emboldened William Willshire; perhaps it had even tipped him into the extravagant pursuit of revenge that his colleagues thought insane. But in Thomas, Hermann Kempe's favourite Aranda Christian, who had become a puzzle to them, their teaching had made its impact. In a sense, it was Kempe, Schwarz and Schulze who had put William Willshire in the dock at Port Augusta by instilling in Thomas a new *tjurunga*, part of which was a rudimentary Protestant conscience.

To reinforce this last point we should move forward in time and see what became of the nascent Western Aranda Lutheranism of 1891 by following some of the people we have met. Before we do, it is time to return all the other occupants of my prisoners' gallery to their graves, and Henry Bundey to his. In the end, retrospective justice is no justice at all; understanding the past is a goal high enough for hindsight.

EPILOGUE

16

CONSEQUENCES

"memory has become ignorant"
Nathanael/Rauwiraka [349]

No-one knows how many Western Aranda there were in 1877. In 1880 Hermann Kempe estimated a population of 500, but it could have been little better than a guess. It was one of the unscripted tasks of Swan-Taplin to count the Aboriginal people on the stations. They did this, even collecting a list of names. They also asked the opinions of the white men they interviewed. Most said the population had little changed, others that it had reduced significantly. Few of them had enough evidence for a firm opinion, but if we take them at face value the differences in their estimates may reflect real local differences in the impact of disease, social disruption and violence. The missionaries at Hermannsburg conceded to Swan-Taplin that there were no fewer Aboriginal people in their vicinity than there were at the beginning, although it weakened their charge that pastoralists were engaging in large-scale murdering.[350] Heidenreich reported that the Enquiry had recorded the names of 112 Aboriginal people on the mission station, although the list found with the Enquiry's evidence comprises only 38 names. Of all the Arandic-speaking people on the stations visited by the Enquiry, Heidenreich tells us that the names of 1,000 persons were recorded.[351] Wilhelm Schwarz, interviewed separately in Adelaide, estimated about 300 people on the stations within Western Aranda territory in 1890. The missionaries recorded the deaths of Western Aranda people from new diseases, especially influenza, measles, tuberculosis and syphilis, but attempted no quantitative estimates. When Louis Schulze wrote his paper on the Western Aranda for the Royal Society of South Australia he canvassed causes of death. While he did not explicitly rank them, his list is headed by revenge-killing, followed by disease and then white violence.[352]

Towards the end of their time the missionaries reported that the Western Aranda were peculiarly susceptible to epidemic infections, being flattened by diseases that were shrugged off by the whites. A decade or two later Carl Strehlow was observing how little troubled were the Western Aranda by infectious diseases, although in 1899 measles carried off 16% of Hermannsburg's resident Aborigines and 17% of those remaining were blind or partially-sighted.[353] No doubt droughts greatly increased the power of infections to kill those people who pursued their hunter-gatherer lifestyle, but even those settled on stations could at times be susceptible to high death rates from infection. It seems such incidents were poorly reported and recorded. When Swan-Taplin visited Owen Springs station, the oldest in the Centre, Edward Polhill, a stockman, volunteered a detailed report on an outbreak of disease that killed "fully one hundred" one summer in about 1882. It affected only the Aboriginal people, and killed those employed on the station as well as those living independently.

It attacked both men women and children. Myself and a mate were starting for the Alice Springs races and in the morning we gave our clothes to two lubras to wash. About 4p.m. we sung out for them to bring our clothes yet altho' they had washed & hung them out to dry they were both dead then. The Lubras were both well in the morning.

Henry Swan did not note this event in his report. Allen Breaden, the manager of Mount Burrell and Owen Springs, supported Polhill's evidence when he said the Aboriginal people were "nothing near as numerous as they were when I first came into the country". No such general outbreak of fatalities was recorded by the missionaries, supporting their estimate that the population of Western Aranda was little changed in 1890. The general complacency about the Aboriginal population that the Swan-Taplin enquiry members brought back from their white witnesses may have had more influence on the policy-makers in Adelaide than the quarrels about alleged misbehaviour by missionaries, police and pastoralists. We should not forget, however, the missionaries' pessimistic projections about the future of the Western Aranda shortly before Swan-Taplin visited them. Kempe predicted "all men capable of reproducing will be gone by 1900", and Schulze's forecast was equally dire; "These folk surely have no future, they decline in leaps and bounds and the mission can only serve as the grave-digger. We have often wondered that so many young couples have no children; on the other hand there are many deaths, from natural and unnatural causes".[354] It was clear by 1912, in Carl Strehlow's time, that these predictions were far too pessimistic, at least as far as the Western Aranda living on the mission were concerned, with births rising well above deaths.[355]

The Western Aranda experience of high mortality did not stop in the 1890s. It was not until communications improved after 1945 that the physical and political isolation of the Western Aranda finally ended, and with it their liability to die unnoticed in large numbers. Today there are perhaps 1500 speakers of Arandic languages in Central Australia. Many of them are dwellers on the fringe of modern Australian society, with low rates of participation in education and employment and below-average life-expectancy. But many descendants of the Western Aranda and the Loritja peoples also own large slabs of that fringe, including the former mission lease and Tempe Downs station, and choose to live there.

The trial of William Willshire and the flight to the south of Hermann Kempe and Louis Schulze mark a transition in Central Australian affairs, but there were as many continuing threads as there were new ways of doing things. Coognalthika/Archie, Kwalba/Jack and Aremala/Larry continued in the police service, while at some point Thomas/Tekua returned to life on the Finke River mission station. While policing of Aboriginal cattle-killing continued to be based in part on policemen dispensing illegal punishment by flogging, it was no longer acceptable conduct to kill alleged cattle-killers or to carry out arbitrary reprisals against groups of Aborigines, dispersal in the third degree. Such activity, if it continued, was forced underground, and became much riskier for anyone who did it.[356]

None of the missionaries ever returned home, to Germany or to Central Australia. Only Schulze found steady employment, as a Pastor in Western Victoria. Kempe and Schwarz moved frequently, as "clapped-out missionaries" between congregations until they retired, not without respect, but appearing more and more archaic as Lutherans of the old school among their Australian flocks.

Hermann Kempe did offer to return to the Finke, provided he was paid £140 a year for it, but the station passed out of the hands of his Lutheran Synod before the sincerity of the offer could be tested. As we have seen, he had already conceded any claim to exercise worldly power on the Finke when Swan and Taplin came calling, and the option of using state power to create reserves ring-fenced by law was not pursued at that time. We may assume that Kempe had resiled from the Antinomianism that had infected him on the frontier when he collaborated with murderous policemen, just as we may assume that in the settled south of South Australia no senior men of other faiths were murdering his catechumens as the recalcitrant Western Aranda men, like Latya, had done in the 1880s.

We must conclude that Kempe had not changed his views after March 1891 when he reflected on one terrible possibility that the doctrine of Sin and Grace, as he understood them, gave rise to:

> *With all children of nature who lack any kind of written history, we cannot know what sins their forefathers were guilty of; we cannot know either if God has already extended to them the hand of Grace before the present day, one or more times, and if they through deliberate, disdainful obduracy have rejected it.*[357]

And so would the Old Testament's curse on the children of Ham be extended, through the Gospel of the New Testament, to explain the continuing misery of the Western Aranda. Perhaps a people could fall from God's Grace so deeply that they could never again rise. This was not the prospect Kempe had brought with him from the Hermannsburg Mission Institute.

The real loser in the eventual sale of the mission to the other Lutheran synod, the Immanuel Synod, was Georg Heidenreich. His creation now belonged to someone else, and all he could do was salvage the value of the mission's improvements and livestock for his *alma mater*, the Hermannsburg Mission Institute in Germany. More than that, his congregation continued sending money to the Finke River mission despite its association with unorthodox doctrines, and this further offended his colleagues in the Evangelical Lutheran Synod. In 1902 he was obliged to choose where his loyalty lay. He left his Synod and formed a rival Evangelical Lutheran Synod On the Old Basis, taking his Bethany congregation with him.

This terrible conflict among the South Australian Lutherans could have been avoided if the South Australian governments of 1892-4 had done their job correctly. The assets and improvements of the Finke River mission station belonged to the government of South Australia, not the Hermannsburg Mission Institute and not to any private citizen of South Australia, Lutheran or otherwise. The mission had never had a formal lease, just a letter of permission from a Minister of government, and that meant the mission's occupation conferred no ownership rights at all, not even ownership of the improvements built up on the mission station through the capital invested by its sponsors and through the sweat of its black and white residents. It seems no government Minister in 1894 was prepared to tell Heidenreich this, and who can blame them. It is unlikely Heidenreich himself would have been so timid had *he* been the Minister concerned. Having ensured the value of the mission's assets went back to Germany Heidenreich later showed that his love and loyalty for the Finke mission itself were above doctrine and church politics. When he contrived with Kempe and Besley to keep Wurmbrand's murders secret it was only, he might tell us, for the greater good that the Finke River mission would achieve.[358]

Did the missionaries ever re-consider the nature of the faith they tried to transplant on the Finke? There is no evidence that they did. Wilhelm Schwarz was ready to continue as ruler and preacher, but his reputation had been destroyed. His capacity for sympathy leaves us to suppose he might have made some of the pragmatic changes that Lutheran missionaries made in their missionising later on, much later on.

Of the relationship between the three ex-missionaries we can know this much. Some time after 1891 they all came together for a group photographic portrait. The two principals, Kempe and Schwarz are seated in front, still solid, square men, with Schulze standing behind. Whatever residue of anger remained, they have signed the truce of veterans, veterans of a hard campaign, and perhaps they have accepted each other. Schwarz died suddenly in 1920 aged 78 years, but had been chopping his own wood until a fortnight before. Kempe spoke at his funeral. His words were not recorded, but in his *Lebenslauf* Kempe makes no comment on Schwarz while remembering clearly his resentment of Heidenreich. Heidenreich may well have exaggerated the intensity of the animosity between the missionaries, significant as it was, in order to justify his recall of Schwarz, and to explain why the Word appeared unable to hold the Aranda-Christians in the new way. Schulz died in Victoria in 1924, the youngest of them at 73 years of age, a good age for a man whom the Prussian army had judged too delicate for military service. Kempe himself died four years later, in March 1928, aged 84, a relic of a kind of Lutheranism, narrow and German-speaking, that was already part of South Australia's history. He had outlived three wives, including the first whom he had buried on the Finke a week before his final, desperate flight from a typhoid epidemic in November 1891.

These three men are respected in the Lutheran histories for what they endured. They are given less credit than they deserve for what they achieved simply because the station was abandoned, by missionaries if not by the Colonists, for the years 1891-4. But, like a fire in a coal seam, the faith of the Aranda Lutherans burned on, even if later missionaries sometimes saw only smoke. Those baptised in the late 1880s were the foundation of all that followed. Hermann Kempe, Wilhelm Schwarz and Louis Schulze were the missionary founders of Aranda Lutheranism, not the more famous Carl Strehlow. In another sense Aranda Lutheranism was formed by the Western Aranda themselves from the exotic materials brought to the Finke by the missionaries. At the fore-front of the Western Aranda who crafted the new faith were Andreas, Thomas and Moses, who all remained on the Finke long after the first missionaries had gone.

In 1894, when the Finke River mission had been sold to the Immanuel Synod, the young missionary Carl Strehlow took charge. Strehlow had already spent two years with the Dieri at Bethesda and so was the only missionary in the mission's first fifty years to arrive with some preparation for his work. He was a talented linguist, not afraid of power, and his fellow-missionaries never challenged his authority. When he had settled in he did something remarkable for a man who thought the old Western Aranda ways were the work of the Devil; he sat down with four senior men, not all of them Christian, and recorded faithfully what they told him about their life and beliefs. Thomas was one of his informants. The result is one of the treasures of Australian anthropology, *Die Aranda- und Loritja-Stämme*. It was published in German before the first World War but has long been out of print. It has never been published in English. To date, plans to remedy this outrage have been defeated, originally by cost, now by the politics of ethnicity. Among Carl Strehlow's stalwart Western Aranda helpers was Moses Tjalkabota who also taught the Western Aranda language to the next missionary, Friedrich Albrecht, after Carl Strehlow died in office in 1922. When Carl Strehlow's son, T G H Strehlow returned to the Centre as a young scholar in 1932, many of the old men who told him about the inner lives of the Western Aranda were also graduates of the catechism classes of Kempe, Schwarz and Schulze. Moses Tjalkabota was first among them, but Nathanael/Rauwiraka and Thomas played a role. Thomas, like Moses, was by now a missionary himself, travelling to the camps and settlements beyond Hermannsburg to spread the Gospel. Thomas became the Western Aranda stalwart that Andreas had been in 1888. We know from Bruce Plowman, who visited between 1915 and 1917, that by then Thomas spoke fluent English, and a number of the Western Aranda were literate in their own language.

Who knows how much of the ceremonial songs and personal stories recorded by Strehlow junior is made up of refractions through the prism of Western Aranda thinking of the religion of these first Lutherans, who taught in a crude pidgin of Western Aranda, German and English? In the realm of ideas and faith the missionaries too left behind on the Finke hybrid children with the vigour to survive.

Even at the end of his twenty-eight years at Hermannsburg the missionary Carl Strehlow did not like the look of these hybrids. By this time the Western Aranda Lutherans were hearing the voices and seeing the visions of the Christian cosmology. Strehlow reported:

About 3 months ago some of our christian blacks had dreams and visions in which they saw angels and heard heavenly music, which they taught the others; on some evenings they sang for hours and hours and closed these exercises with prayers. One man ... who is attending the baptismal instruction brought me a hymn of 21 verses describing the last judgment which shows that he has closely followed the religions instructions on Sundays and he told me in the evening that he was very joyful, because he had seen angels and heard heavenly music. ... Some days later Rebecka, an old christian woman ... came and told me that she had seen the angel Gabriel. ... She writes: "I saw the heaven near. I was not sleeping but awake. I saw the heaven opening and a fire flame coming down. I wondered what this was. Then I saw an angel with a small child. He said to me: Do you know me? I then said: Yes, thou art the angel Gabriel, standing before me.

He said: Yes, how do you know me:

I said: I don't know; tell it to me, so that I may know it.

Gabriel showed Rebecka a child who had died recently, and three of her own children who had died long before, and they called her to join them in heaven. She then saw angels descending a ladder from heaven, singing "and I sang also and they commanded me to teach this song to all." The theology was impeccable, but Strehlow was not impressed by this intimacy with the Christian spirits. "The song, Rebecka wrote down, is very poor" he reported dismissively; its words were limited and its music monotonous. Another man had a vision too, and yet another brought Strehlow two hymns "whose contents were good."

Despite his reservations, Strehlow came to a position that seems to have lasted into the present. He told his Aranda Christians, "Visions are alright if they are in accordance with the revelations of the Bible and to show one's faith in good works, especially to fulfill one's calling properly". He also noted something that would not have surprised Kempe, Schwarz and Schulze in 1889. "It is very remarkable, that the most of these visions were granted to christians, who showed great faults in their life; ... The blacks concede this, but the[y] say, that these visions had the purpose to rouse them up and convert them from their sins to a better life. If this purpose would be

fulfilled the visions would not have been in vain granted to them."
The content of the visions had changed over the thirty years since
Andreas reported his to Louis Schulze, but their inspiration had
not.[359]

The nature of Aranda Lutheranism has been characterised in
this way: "Central to this process [of Christianising] was a focal
indigenous idea; that people's being is realized through a law
understood in terms of right practice in a place." That focal idea is
called by the Western Aranda themselves "pepe", a transcription of
the English word "paper", but a much bigger idea than the English
word connotes. Pepe, or, as the early missionaries might have said,
the Word, covers not just that central Christian sacred object, the
Bible, and its contents, but the liturgy, songs and practices of
Lutheranism and Lutherans on the Finke. In effect, the Western
Aranda have turned Lutheranism into a new *tjurunga*, one
universally available to man, woman and child. It is today open to
argument which system of belief now conserves more authentically
the spirit of the earlier Aranda faith and practices, modern Aranda
Lutheranism or modern Aranda traditionalism.[360] It is not an
argument that would interest many Western Aranda.

Of the fate of Nathanael's mother and Ereminta's widow,
Naomi/Nungoolga, I know nothing.

We must not think that all of the Western Aranda and Loritja
people became Christian. Chinchewarra returned from Port Augusta
to Tempe Downs to other husbands and a life of influence among the
Aboriginal people of her region. She worked for the white man and
occasionally helped to kill his cattle. She could magic her Aboriginal
enemies and won respect for it. She found white admirers including
the man who managed Tempe Downs in the 1930s, Bryan Bowman,
and the Freudian anthropologist Geza Roheim, who listened
attentively to her at Hermannsburg mission in 1929. While Roheim's
business was just to record her dreams and run them through his
psychoanalytical biscuit-cutter, in the process he also recorded the
important elements of the story of her life, as she wanted it to be
told. She walked out of her brief stay at Hermannsburg with the
memorable words "Too much soup! Too much Jesus!" She appears
not to have left the Centre again after 1891 and died childless in 1964
at Tempe Downs new station, a few kilometres from where she was
born.

Of her one hundred years - give or take a few - she spent about the first twenty entirely within traditional Aboriginal life, and for the next seventy five remained within the isolated world created by pastoralism and Aboriginal culture as they evolved together in the western James Ranges, neglected by the rest of a world in even greater turmoil. Now, after 140 years, she is among the few whose story will survive among those who bother to dig Central Australia's past. She has an entry in the Northern Territory's published dictionary of biography. Through others, like Geza Roheim in 1929 and, just the most recent, the present author, she has crafted her own repute. No small achievement.

She was not the only one to hold fast to the old ways. The Loritja Matuntara man Arabi, leader of a group of cattle-killers active on Tempe Downs, and whom Willshire claimed he was keen to deal with, survived another thirty-five years, including two compulsory trips to Port Augusta's school of Aboriginal assimilation, the prison. He split his time in the Centre between tracking for the police and cattle-killing. Missionary Friedrich Albrecht was told by Moses Tjalkabota in 1926 that Arabi, with "several of the old tjurunga bosses were doing their utmost to restore the tjurunga cult to its former importance by holding monster corrobborees with all the blacks assembled there [at Jay Creek near Alice Springs]."[361] Arabi also proselytised at Hermannsburg before Albrecht's arrival, and it disappointed the new missionary that his Christians were not strong enough simply to reject him. Arabi, like the senior men of 1880, refused to respond to missionary questioning.[362]

When missionary Friedrich Albrecht arrived at Hermannsburg in 1926 he noted the presence on the station of an old Christian man. He refers occasionally to "old Andreas" who, like the other Christians, had Christian visions. Albrecht once asked Andreas whether he regretted having been for so long a Christian, "But he didn't want to hear anything about that." On the 23rd of August 1926 Albrecht recorded: "At midday old Andreas was called home. One could see in him no sign that he feared death. When we came to carry him out old Beata [Andreas's wife] castigated those Christians standing around for no longer visiting him, and especially that they had not sung with him on Sunday afternoon." It was precisely fifty years since Heidenreich and Kempe had first visited the mission lease, and the mission committee from Adelaide was paying a visit to mark the occasion. During their celebrations they did nothing to mark the passing of Andreas, the Western Aranda instigator of Aranda Lutheranism. On this point, as on most of the mental, moral and physical struggles of the first years of Aranda-Lutheranism, the memory of the southern Lutherans had become ignorant.[363]

Chinchewarra in late 1963 or early 1964, within a few months her death at Tempe Downs new station. Having outlasted all of her contemporaries, and still with a sense of style at about 100 years of age, Chinchewarra was childless (*Mrs S. Crogan/Mr P O'Brien*).

Narcissus with a much-reduced mirror. After the limitless possibilities of the frontier, William Willshire was confined by country village, household and subordination. The fear and laughter of his Aboriginal audience had departed. Even a promise to resign could not persuade Commissioner Peterswald to transfer him to Adelaide. He was obliged to resign first, in 1908, and accept the costume of a night-watchman. First photograph, 1892-9, second 1899-1907, third, after 1907 (*Mrs P Cole/Hesperian Press*).

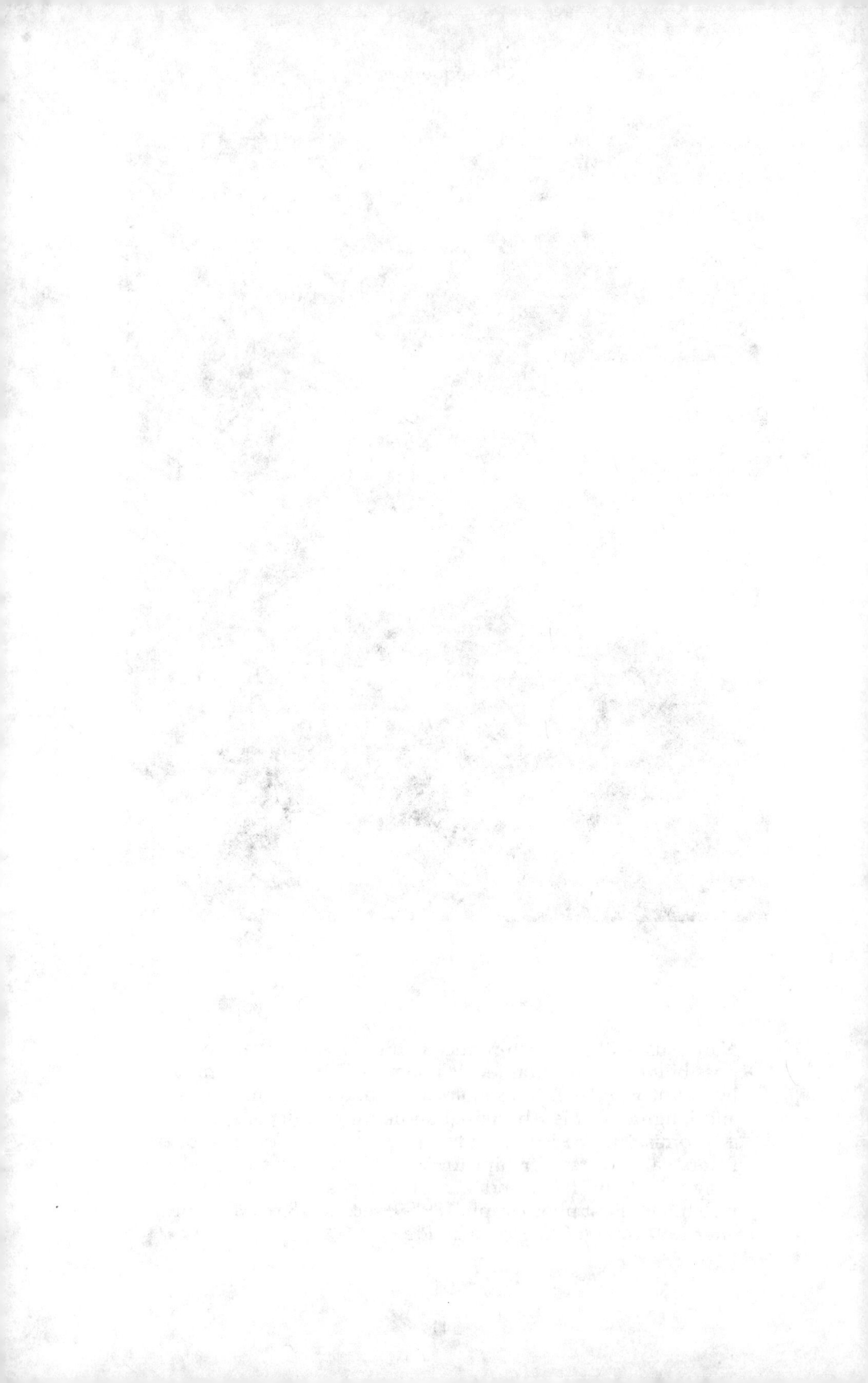

SELECT LIST OF PERSONS

Andreas/Kalimalla. Western Aranda boy, friend of Thomas, with whom he broke from the senior men to seek baptism as a Christian.

Aremala/Larry. One of Willshire's constables at the time of the Tempe Downs killings.

Besley, Bryan. Inspector of Police in Port Augusta, responsible for the police in Central Australia.

Bundey, (William) Henry. Lawyer, politician, judge at Willshire's trial.

Chantoonga. Woman from Emily Gap near Alice Springs. One of Willshire's common-law wives.

Chillberta. Young woman celebrated in Willshire's *A thrilling tale...* Probably the alias of Nabarong.

Chickyllia/Wilkie. Native Constable in Alice Springs.

Chinchewarra. Loritja Matuntara woman, born on Tempe Downs. Witnessed the Killing of Ereminta in February 1891.

Chinkanaka. Senior Western Aranda man, and boss of the Ntaria camp in 1877, who lost his wives and later his life to the impact of pastoralism.

Coognalthicka/Archie. Long-term Native Constable in Alice Springs and Boggy Water, and loyal associate of William Willshire.

Donkey. Matuntara man, associate of Ereminta's and a fellow-victim of Willshire and his constables.

Downer, John. Leading barrister, politician and occasional head of government in South Australia. Defended Willshire at his trial.

Ereminta. Matuntara man from Tempe Downs. Husband of Naomi/Nungoolga. Willshire's rival for Nabarong, and later victim of Willshire's revenge.

Gall, Charles, JP. Manager of Owen Springs pastoral station during the Swan-Taplin enquiry and the Tempe Downs killings.

Gillen, Francis. Telegraph station master in Central Australia, and the Special Magistrate who investigated the Tempe Downs shootings in 1891.

Gordon, John Hannah. Presbyterian, pastoralist, businessman,
	Mayor and Member of Parliament. The Minister responsible
	for setting up the Swan-Taplin enquiry.
Hanna. Wife of Thomas, by inheritance.
Harms, Ludwig (Louis), Theodor and Egmont. Successively founder
	and directors of the Hermannsburg Mission Institute near
	Hamburg in Germany.
Heidenreich, Georg Adam. Lutheran Pastor at Bethany near
	Adelaide and Superintendent, on behalf of the
	Hermannsburg Mission Institute, of the Finke River mission.
Homburg, Robert. Member of Parliament and Attorney-General at
	the time of the Tempe Downs killings. Later a judge.
Inubauka. Young Western Aranda man, driven from the Ellery
	Creek lagoon by shot-gun.
Jürgens, Heinrich Georg. Lay-worker (Colonist) on the Finke River
	mission, 1877-1889.
Kempe, (Friedrich Adolf) Hermann. Missionary of the
	Hermannsburg Mission Institute and head of the Finke River
	mission, 1887-1891.
Macdonald, James. Manager of Glen Helen station at the time of the
	Wurmbrand killings and during the Swan-Taplin enquiry.
Maria/Adilka. Early baptisand. Married to Andreas through lack of
	alternative Christian women, against Western Aranda
	custom and her family's wishes.
Moses/Tjalkabota. A Western Aranda boy born around the time of
	the missionaries' arrival on the Finke. One of the first
	converts and later a missionary of Aranda-Lutheranism.
Nabarong/Naparoon. Woman from west of Tempe Downs, probably
	Loritja Matuntara. Promised wife of Ereminta and common-
	law wife of Willshire.
Naomi/Nungoolga. Born Matuntara, widow of Western Aranda
	man, baptized Christian and wife of Ereminta. Mother of
	Nathanael.
Nathanael/Rauwiraka. Son of Nungoolga, Ereminta's widow. One of
	the first Aranda-Lutherans and an important source of
	information for T.G.H. Strehlow in the 1930s.
Peterswald, William John. Police Commissioner in Adelaide in the
	period covered by this story.

Select list of persons

Schulze, Louis. Missionary of the Hermannsburg Mission Institute, served on the Finke River mission from 1878 to 1891.

Schwarz, Wilhelm Friedrich. Missionary of the Hermannsburg Mission Institute, worked on the Finke River mission 1877-1889. His accusations against police and pastoralists led to the Swan-Taplin enquiry in 1890.

Strehlow, Carl. Took control of the Finke River mission in 1894 after the departure of Kempe, Schwarz and Schulze. Author of the major ethnography of the Western Aranda and Loritja peoples.

Strehlow, T. G. H. Son of Carl, researcher and translator among the Aranda in the 1930s and 1940s.

Swan, Henry Charles. Businessman and associate of the Downers who accepted the SA Government's commission to enquire into the accusations against the police, pastoralists and missionaries in 1890.

Taplin, Charles Eaton. Activist for the Aborigines Friends Association, commissioned, along with Henry Swan, to enquire into events on the upper Finke River.

Thomas/Tekua. Western Aranda boy, initiated in the early 1880s and among the first baptized in 1887. Later a trooper for Willshire and afterwards a stalwart of the mission.

Thornton, (Richard) Frederick. Manager of Tempe Downs at the time of the 1891 killings.

Todd, Sir Charles. Scientist and South Australia's Post-Master General, 1870-1906. Architect, builder and operator of the Overland Telegraph.

Willshire, William Henry. Mounted Constable, Central Australia, 1882-1891.

Wodoa. Woman fatally wounded during a dispersal under the leadership of Mounted Constable Daer, early 1880s.

Wurmbrand, Erwein. Mounted Constable in Central Australia who shot prisoners in Glen Helen Gorge in 1884.

Illustrations are reproduced courtesy of the sources indicated by abbreviations in the captions, and listed below. Those illustrations unattributed are the author's.

ACKNOWLEDGMENTS

Emeritus Professor John Mulvaney encouraged me to
continue with this enquiry, when his good sense must have been
sounding the alarm, and introduced me to Mr Dick Kimber in Alice
Springs who shared his local knowledge. My consultant Lutherans
in Adelaide, Pastor Paul Albrecht and Dr Maurice Schild hid their
perplexity with my amateur theology under unfailing courtesy and a
willingness to read large parts of the draft. None has any
responsibility for the directions I have taken.

The anonymous staffs of Public Records South Australia, the
Australian Archives, the Mitchell Library and the National Library of
Australia were always professional and helpful. Mr Lyall Kupke and
Dr Myra Oster of the Lutheran Archives in Adelaide seemed never
to tire of my demands. Dr Barry Cundy and the staff of the
Australian Institute of Aboriginal and Torres Straits Islanders
Studies shared their gem of a library, and Dr Philip Jones and Ms
Lea Gardam of the South Australian Museum helped me visit their
photographs. Mr Jim Sykes and Mr Alan Peters of the South
Australian Police Historical Society made the work of their members
available, and Françoise Barr of the Northern Territory Archives
guided me where indexers have yet to tread. The entire staff of the
Strehlow Research Centre in Alice Springs were hospitable,
especially Jane Bowland the Librarian and Shane Hersey when he
was Acting Research Director, and later Michael Cawthorne. In Port
Augusta the Sheriff Mr Peter Manuel and Mr Robert McSporran and
Mr Mick Tomalin, Sheriff's Officers, gave me access to the
courthouse at no notice at all. Mr Trevor Blowes, Deputy Clerk, SA
Legislative Council, dug out the manuscript of the Swan-Taplin
report from his files. Mr Bruce Greenhalgh allowed me access to the
archive of the Supreme Court of South Australia. Mrs Sandy Crogan
and Mrs Philippa Cole made available material in their possession
and Mr P J Bridge of Hesperian Press was generous in his advice. Dr
Mike Smith of the National Museum of Australia shared his deep

knowledge of the country of Willshire's Central Australian dreams. Mr Sid Coulthard of the Ukaka community permitted access to Tempe Downs, but my truck fell apart before it was reached. Mr Chris Walsh of the Ngurratjuta Corporation helped with arrangements and commiserated. Mr Frank Williams gave me use of his amazing Flinders Ranges database. Pastor David Gogoll showed me Georg Heidenreich's still-thriving church and his home, and allowed me to copy the church's photograph of his predecessor. Janet Wilson helped with editing and Laura Vallee advised on image processing.

My politico-legal advisers, The Hon. Christopher J Sumner and The Hon. John Bannon were chosen more for their hospitality than their expertise but they also provided the latter, Sumner having occupied the office of South Australian Attorney-General a century after Robert Homburg and Bannon having sat in Tom Playford's chair and, after that, researched South Australian history of this period.

UNPUBLISHED SOURCES

Albrecht, Friedrich Wilhelm. *Mein Missionstagebuch*, 1926-7. Typescript of original manuscript. Lutheran Archives.

Australian Archives/National Archives of Australia (AA/NAA). The source of records of Naturalization, some of the records of land leasing and of police business in the Alice Springs area, including the period of South Australian administration before 1911. Sources used in particular matters are referred to by end-note where they were judged significant.

Basedow, Herbert. Papers. Includes typed transcriptions of the telegrams between Adelaide and Barrow Creek during and after the 1874 attack. Mitchell Library, MSS 161/7.

Gillen, Frank. Evidence taken on instruction from Attorney-General Homburg between April 20th and April 27th , 1891 at Tempe Downs, Boggy Water, Hermannsburg and Alice Springs. The original of the evidence with the signatures of the witnesses has disappeared (with one exception noted later), but two copies, which confirm each other in all essentials and most detail and therefore indicate a common source, are in the South Australian Public Records Office.

Gillen I

The first set of transcripts, which I have labelled "Gillen I", comes from the police files (GRG 52/92) and includes the core of the evidence, supplemented by interviews with the Aboriginal witnesses by Inspector Besley in Port Augusta on 21st July 1891, i.e. two days before the trial. This direct evidence is supported by what appear to be incomplete attempts to produce abbreviations for other official purposes. These versions add little but some of it is significant; nor do they show obvious signs of deliberate deletions. The entire set has been folio-numbered sometime after it was lodged in the archives. This set lacks page 1 and part of page 2 (Willshire's evidence) but includes at folios 33 and 34 two pages of evidence signed by Gillen personally. This is the evidence of Native Constalble Kwalba/Jack, is reported in pidgin like most of the Aboriginal evidence. The version of this in "Gillen evidence II" has been substantially re-written into standard English. There is no docket or cover sheet for *Gillen evidence I*, and therefore no information about which officials saw it. It is probably based on the copy of the original material made in Alice Springs for South to send to Besley.

Gillen II

The second set, designated "Gillen II" is a good copyist's copy of the core of the Gillen evidence, apparently written and numbered as one document, and came from the Attorney-General's files. It includes the first page absent from Gillen evidence I and was misfiled, I think deliberately, at GRG/1/2/554, although the reason for the misfiling may be the transcript of the Swan Taplin evidence with which it was bundled. There are few significant differences from *Gillen I*, but these include the absence of the record of Besley's interviews of the Aboriginal witnesses at Port Augusta, and a failure to record that Willshire cross-examined the recanting Native Constables in Alice Springs on April 27th, 1891. This version of the evidence was sent from Besley to Commissioner Peterswald on 14th May 1891, and from Charles Cornish (Homburg's Secretary) to the Crown Solicitor on May 19th. There is no record of Homburg's having seen it.

The signed originals of the Gillen evidence may well have been those Gillen sent to Homburg at the end of April 1891. It seems likely that both prosecution and defence lawyers at the trial depended on *Gillen II.*, although the police were familiar with *Gillen I*.

Hartwig, Mervyn C. *The progress of white settlement in the Alice Springs district and its effects upon the Aboriginal inhabitants, 1860-1894.* PhD thesis. University of Adelaide, 1965.

Mission Committee. Translated extracts of the minute book of the Mission Committee, 1876-93, translated by Werner Hebart. 51pp. Lutheran Archives.

Lutheran Church of Australia. Archives (LA) (Adelaide, South Australia). Source of a bound set of the *Church messenger (Lutherische kirchenbote für Australien)*, the minutes of the Mission Committee and microform copies of some of the relevant correspondence from the archives of the Hermannsburg Mission Institute in Hermannsburg, Germany, and other key documents. Other significant items are end-noted.

Northern Territory Archives (NTA). Those of the official records of the South Australian administration of the Northern Territory that were not held in Adelaide, or trapped in Canberra after the Northern

Territory was granted self-government in 1978 were passed on to this archive. Other official records of the period of South Australian rule are held in other NT government agencies, particularly records relating to land.

Public Records South Australia (PRSA)/State Records South Australia (SRSA). Various series were consulted, of which those of the police, the Minister for Education and the Northern Territory, the Attorney-General and the Protector of Aborigines were the most useful. Significant items are referred to in end notes.

Swan-Taplin. Evidence taken in July-September 1890 by H. C. Swan, SM and Charles Eaton Taplin as Commissioners appointed by the South Australian Government to enquire into allegations by and against the Hermannsburg missionaries at the Finke River mission. Swan and Taplin produced a written report to the Government and this was printed as Parliamentary Paper no. 148 of 1890. The evidence, along with a number of other important documents generated by Homburg's dealings with Gillen and Heidenreich, was misfiled in GRG 1/2/554 of 1891, a file established for a much smaller purpose, some time after the trial of Willshire in 1891. My candidates for the burial of this material, still politically incendiary after the trial, are Homburg himself or his Secretary, Charles C. Cornish who was astute enough politically to be promoted by 1899 to the top official position of Secretary to the South Australian Premier (i.e. Prime Minister).

PUBLISHED SOURCES

Albrecht, F. W. "Fifty years of mission work in Hermannsburg Central Australia". In P. G. E. Albrecht, *From mission to church, 1877-2002, Finke River Mission*.

Albrecht, P. G. E. *From mission to Church, 1877-2002, Finke River Mission*. Finke River Mission, 2002.

Albrecht, P. G. E. *Hermannsburg, a meeting place of cultures, personal reflections*. Nungalinya Occasional Bulletin, no. 14. [Darwin], Nungalinya Publications, 1981.

Albrecht, P. G. E. *Social change and the Aboriginal Australians of Central Australia, a study of factors inhibiting social change and of policies and methods which can stimulate social change*. 120pp. Privately printed, 1970, 1998.

Albrecht, P. G. E. *The nature of Aboriginal identity*. Magill, SA, PGE Albrecht, 1997.

Altmann, Max. *The silver-miner's son, the history of Louis Gustav Schulze, missionary, details of his ancestors and family descendants of the past 200 years*. Mt Barker, SA, M Altmann, 1980.

Attwood, Bain. *A life together, a life apart, a history of relations between Europeans and Aborigines*. Melbourne University Press, 1994.

Austin, Tony. *Simply the survival of the fittest, Aboriginal administration in South Australia's Northern Territory 1863-1910*. Darwin, Historical Society of the Northern Territory, 1992

Austin-Broos, D. "The meaning of Pepe, God's law and the Western Arrernte". In *Journal of religious history*, October 2003, 27(3);311-28.

Australian dictionary of biography. Melbourne University Press.
  Downer, John William. Volume 8, 1891-1939;330-2.
  Chewings, Charles. Volume 7, 1891-1939;634-5
  Gillen, Francis. Volume 9, 1891-1939;6-7.
  Heidenreich, Georg Adam. Volume 4, 1851-1890;373-374.
  Homburg, Robert. Volume 9, 1891-1939;355-6
  Willshire, William Henry. Volume 12, 1891-1939;515

Australian Natives Association. *History of the Australian Natives Association, 1871 to 1921*. ANA, 1921.

Avramis, Stathis. *A guide and index to South Australian electoral rolls on microfilm*. Adelaide, School of Library and Information Management.

Barzun, Jacques. *From dawn to decadence, 1500 to the present, 500 years of Western cultural life*. Perennial, 2001.

Begbie, Richard. "The pedal radio of the Great Outback". In *Antique radio classifed*, vol 16, no 7, July 1999. Taken from the Web, http://www.antiqueradio.com/traeger_pedal_07-99.html

Bell, Diane. *Daughters of the dreaming*. Sydney, Allen & Unwin, 1993.

Biographical register of the South Australian Parliament, 1857-1957. Howard Coxon, John Playford and Robert Reid. Wakefield Press, 1985.

Blaess, F. H. J. *The Evangelical Lutheran Synod in Australia, Inc., and mission work amongst the Australian natives in connection with the Dresden (Leipzig) Lutheran Mission Society and the Hermannsburg Mission Institute, 1838-1900*. BD thesis, unpublished, 1941.

Bowman, Bryan. *A history of Central Australia, 1930-1980*. 3 v. Alice Springs, Bryan Bowman (Colemans Printing), nd. Available from Big Kangaroo Books, Alice Springs (www.bigkangaroobooks.com).

Bowman, Bryan. *The Glen Helen story*. Bryan Bowman (Colemans Printing), 1989. Available from Big Kangaroo Books, Alice Springs.

Buchanan, Gordon. Packhorse and waterhole. Angus and Robertson, 1933.

Breen, Gavan. The Ingkarte's ear. (Paper presented to the Strehlow Conference, September 2002.

Breen, Gavin. *Introductory dictionary of Western Arrernte*. Alice Springs, IAD, 2000.

Bundey, W[illiam] H[enry]. *Some suggestions on land reform*. Adelaide, printed by Webb Vardon & Pritchard, 1872.

Bundey, W[illiam] H[enry]. *The conviction of innocent men*. Adelaide, Wigg, 1900.

Bundey, W[illiam] H[enry]. *Some thoughts on the administration of the criminal law in South Australia*. Vardon & Pritchard, 1891.

Campbell, Judy. *Invisible invaders, smallpox and other diseases in Aboriginal Australia, 1780-1880*. Melbourne University Press, 2002.

Castles, Alex C and Michael C Harris. *Lawmakers and wayward whigs, government and law in South Australia, 1836-1936*. Adelaide, Wakefield Press, 1987.

Castles, Alex C. *An Australian legal history*. Sydney, Law Book, 1982.

Chewings, Charles. *Back in the stone age, the natives of Central Australia*. Sydney, Angus and Robertson, 1936.

Chewings, Charles. *Beiträge zur Kenntnis der Geologie Sud- und Central-Australien*. Heidelberg, Universitats-Buchdruckerei von J. Horning, 1894.

Chewings, Charles. *Extracts from a report on the Tempe Downs Station*. [Adelaide, 1891].

Chewings, Charles. *The sources of the Finke River. Reprinted from the Adelaide* Observer. Adelaide, W K Thomas, 1886.

Church messenger, i.e. *Die Lutherische Kirchenbote für Australiens*.

Clarke, Keith M. *Busy wires, the telegraph and South Australia*. Waramanga, ACT, K M & G Clarke, 1991.

Cleland, J. Burton and Brian Maegraith. "Notes on the pathological lesions and vital statistics of Australian natives in Central Australia". In *Medical journal of Australia*, 19 July 1930, 17;80-3.

Cleland, J. Burton and H. Kenneth Fry. "Outbreak of scurvy with joint lesions in Australian Aborigines in Central Australia". In *Medical journal of Australia*, 29 March 1930, 17;412.

Clyne, Robert. *Colonial blue, a history of the South Australian police force, 1836-1916*. Adelaide, Wakefield Press, 1987.

Cockburn, Rodney. *Pastoral pioneers of south Australia*. Blackwood, SA, Lynton Publications, [1974]. Facsimile.

Combe, Gordon D. *Responsible government in South Australia*. Adelaide, Government Printer, 1957.

Coulthard, William. *Diary of William Coulthard, 1903. An account of his journey from South Australia to the Winnecke's Depot goldfield, and his subsequent activities on a Central Australian station, between February and August 1903*. Transcribed and annotated by Kate Holmes. 1988. Photocopy held in the Northern Territory Library.

Coxon, Howard, John Playford and Robert Reid. *Biographical register of the South Australian Parliament, 1857-1957*. Adelaide, Wakefield Press, 1985.

Crowley, F K. *South Australian history, a survey for research students.* Libraries Board of South Australia, 1966.

Cyclopedia of South Australia in two volumes: an historical and commercial review, descriptive and biographical, facts, figures, and illustrations: an epitome of progress. Edited by H.T. Burgess. Adelaide, 1907-9.

Die Lutherische Kirchenbote für Australiens [Church messenger]. Tanunda, South Australia.

Elder, Bruce. *Blood on the wattle, massacres and maltreatment of Australian Aborigines since 1788.* 3rd ed. New Holland, 2003. (First edition, Child & Associates, 1988).

Evans, Raymond and Bill Thorpe. "Indigenocide and the massacre of Aboriginal history". In *Overland*, 163, Winter 2001;21-39.

Favenc, Ernest. *Tales of the Austral tropics.* London, Osgood, McIlvaine, 1894.

Favenc, Ernest. *The last of six.* Sydney, the Bulletin, 1893.

Favenc, Ernest. *The secret of the Australian desert.* 1896.

Fels, Marie H. *Good men and true, the Aboriginal police of the Port Phillip district, 1837-1853.* Melbourne University Press, 1988.

Finlayson, H H. *The red centre, man and beast in the heart of Australia.* Libraries Board of South Australia, 1979. Facsimile.

Fitzpatrick, Brian. *A history of the Australian Natives Association, 1871-1961.* Melbourne, ANA, 1961.

Foster, Robert. "Rations, coexistence, and the colonisation of Aboriginal labour in the South Australian pastoral industry, 1860-1911". In *Aboriginal history*, volume 24, 2000;1-26.

Foster, Robert. "Logic's unexpected celebrity". In *Fatal collisions, the South Australian frontier and the violence of memory.* Edited by Robert Foster, Rick Hosking and Amanda Nettelbeck. Adelaide, Wakefield Press, 2001.

Frazer, J G. "Notes on the Aborigines of Australia". In *Journal of the Anthropological Institute of Great Britain and Ireland*, vol 24, 1895;158-185.

Gillen, F. J. *Gillen's diary, the camp jottings of F. J. Gillen on the Spencer and Gillen Expedition across Australia, 1901-1902.* Adelaide, Libraries Board of South Australia, 1968.

Gooley, M J. *Some early telegraph procedures in South Australia.* Adelaide, Australian Telecomunicaitons Commission, 1976.

Gribble, E. R. B. *Forty years with the Aborigines*. Sydney, Angus & Robertson, 1930.

Griffiths, Tom. "The social and intellectual context of the 1890s". In *Exploring Central Australia, society, the environment and the 1894 Horn Expedition*. Edited by S. R. Morton and D. J. Mulvaney. Sydney, Surrey Beatty, 1996.

Haccius, Georg. *Hannoversche missionsgeschichte, dritter Teil, erster Hälfte*. Hermannsburg, Missionshandlung, 1914.

Haccius, Georg. *Hannoversche missionsgeschichte, zweiter Teil*. Hermannsburg, Missionshandlung, 1910.

Halse, Christine. *A terribly wild man*. Allen & Unwin, 2002. [A life of J B Gribble]

Hardy, Jane, J.V.S. Megaw, and M. Ruth Megaw. *The heritage of Namatjira, the watercolourists of Central Australia*. Melbourne, Heinemann, 1992.

Hassold, F. "Pastor W. F. Schwarz". In *The Australian Lutheran*, May 26, 1920;82-6.

Healy, J. J. "The Lemurian Nineties". In *Australian literary studies*, May 1978, 8(3);307-316.

Hebart, Th. *The United Evangelical Lutheran Church in Australia (UELCA) its history, activities and characteristics, 1838-1938*. Edited by J. J. Stolz. Adelaide, Lutheran Book Depot, 1938.

Hill, Barry. "Through Larapinta Land, Baldwin Spencer's glass case". In Morton and Mulvaney, *Exploring Central Australia*.

Hill, Ernestine. *The Territory*. Sydney, Angus and Robertson, 1951.

Hirst, John B. *Adelaide and the country, 1870-1917*. Melbourne University Press, 1973.

Horn Scientific Exploring Expedition. *Report on the work of the Horn Scientific Expedition to Central Australia*. 4 volumes. Facsimile edition. Bundaberg, Queenlsand, Corkwood Press, 1994.

Howell, Peter. "Saints or scoundrels? A re-appraisal of some notable South Australians, with reflections on related issues". In *Journal of the Historical Society of South Australia*, 7, 1980;3-23.

Jaensch, Dean. *Election statistics of colonial South Australia*. Bedford Park, SA, the author, 1974.

Jaensch, Dean. *The Flinders history of South Australia, political history*. Adelaide, Wakefield, 1986.

Jones, Philip. "Traveller between two worlds". In Jane Hardy, and others, eds., *The heritage of Namatjira, the watercolourists of Central Australia*. Melbourne, Heinemann, 1992.

Kempe, [Friedrich Adolf] Hermann. Plants indigenous to the neighbourhood of Hermannsburg, on the River Finke, Central Australia, collected by the Rev. H. Kempe, Corr. Memb. (Named by Baron F. von Mueller, ...Hon Fellow) (Read February 7, 1882). In *Transactions and proceedings and report of the Royal Society of South Australia*, vol 5 (for 1881-82) Issued December, 1882;19ff.

Kempe, [Friedrich Adolf] Hermann. "From joiner's bench to pulpit". Edited and introduced by P. A. Scherer. *Yearbook of the Lutheran Church of Australia*, 1973;22-50.

Kimber, R G. *Man from Arltunga, Walter Smith, Australian bushman*. Arltunga Hotel and Bush Resort and Hesperian Press, 1996.

Kimber, R. G. "Genocide or not? The situation in Central Australia, 1860-1895". In *Genocide perspectives I, essays in comparative genocide*. Sydney, Centre for Comparative Genocide Studies, 1997.

Kimber, R. G. *The end of the bad old days, European settlement in Central Australia, 1871-1894*. (Occasional Paper no. 25). State Library of the Northern Territory, 1991.

Krichauff, Friedrich E. H. W. Further notes on the "Aldolinga," or "Mbenderinga" tribe of Aborigines. In *Proceedings of the Royal Geographical Society of Australasia, South Australian Branch*. Sessions 1886-7 and 1887-8, vol 2. Adelaide, Government Printer, 1890; 77-80.

Krichauff, Friedrich E. H. W. The customs, religious ceremonies, etc., of the "Aldolinga' or "Mbenderinga" Tribe of Aborigines in Krichauff Ranges, South Australia. Read August 30th, 1886. In *Proceedings of the Royal Geographical Society of Australasia, South Australian Branch*. Sessions 1886-7 and 1887-8, vol 2. Adelaide, Government Printer, 1890; 33-7.

Kwalba, known as Policeman Jack. Strehlow Research Foundation, *Newsletter*, 1983, 6(1,2) and 1984, 7(2).

Leske, Everard, editor. *Hermannsburg, a vision and a mission*. Adelaide, Lutheran Publishing House, 1977.

Maddock, Kenneth. *The Australian Aborigines, a portrait of their society*. London, Allen Lane, 1973.

McCorquodale, John. *Aborigines and the law, a digest*. Canberra, Aboriginal Studies Press, 1987.

Morton, S. R. and D. J. Mulvaney, *eds. Exploring Central Australia; society, the environment and the 1894 Horn Expedition*. Surrey Beatty, 1996.

Mulvaney, D. J. "A Northern Territory Case Study". In, B. Attwood and S. Foster (eds), *Frontier Conflict the Australian Experience*. Canberra, National Museum of Australia, 2002.

Mulvaney, D. J. *The purpose of a good translation : T.G.H. Strehlow and the oral history of Barrow Creek*. 2002. Strehlow Research Centre. In preparation. http://www.strehlow.com.au/cdsca/strehlow/John%20Mulvaney.pdf

Mulvaney, D. J. "'A splendid lot of fellows', achievements and consequences of the Horn Expedition." In *Exploring Central Australia, society, the environment and the 1894 Horn Expedition*. Edited by S. R. Morton and J. D. Mulvaney. Chipping Norton, Surrey Beatty, 1996.

Mulvaney, D. J. "Anthropology along the Overland Telegraph line.", "Central Australia, 'Land of the Dawning'.", "Sacred storehouses, Illamurta's role." and "Hermannsburg". *In Encounters in place, outsiders and Aboriginal Australians, 1606-1985*. University of Queensland Press, 1989.

Mulvaney, D. J. and J. Golson. *Aboriginal man and environment in Australia*. Australian National University Press, 1971.

Mulvaney, D. J. *From the frontier, outback letters to Baldwin Spencer*. Sydney, Allen & Unwin, 2000.

Mulvaney, D. J. *So much that is new, Baldwin Spencer, 1860-1929, a biography*. Melbourne University Press, 1985.

Murdoch, Walter. *Alfred Deakin, a sketch*. London, Constable, 1923.

Northern Territory dictionary of biography, volume two. Edited by David Carment and Barbara James. NTU Press, 1992.

Pike, Douglas. *Paradise of dissent, South Australia 1829-1857*. Melbourne University Press, 1957.

Quiz [and *the Lantern*]. Weekly. Adelaide.

Reid, Gordon. *A picnic with the natives, Aboriginal-European relations in the Northern Territory to 1910*. Melbourne University Press, 1990.

Roheim, Geza. *Australian totemism, a psycho-analytic study in anthropology*. London, Frank Cass, 1971.

Roheim, Geza. Tjintji-Wara a woman of distinction. In *Children of the desert II, myths and dreams of the Aborigines of Central Australia*. Edited by John Morton and Werner Muensterberger. Oceania Ethnographies, 1988.

Rowse, Tim. "Rationing's moral economy". In *Connection and disconnection, encounters between settlers and indigenous people in the Northern Territory*. Edited by Tony Austin and Suzanne Parry. Darwin, NTU Press, 1998.

Rowse, Tim. *White flour, white power, from rations to citizenship in Central Australia*. Melbourne, Cambridge University Press, 1998.

Scherer, P. A. *Venture of faith, an epic in Australian missionary history*. Second edition. Lutheran Press, 1970.

Shepherd, Shirley. "The significance of the Overland Telegraph line, 1872-1901". In *Journal of Northern Territory history*, vol 7, 1996;41-6.

Smith, M A. "Prehistory and human ecology in central Australia, an archaeological perspective". In *Exploring Central Australia; society, the environment and the 1894 Horn Expedition*. Edited by S R Morton and D J Mulvaney. Surrey Beatty, 1996.

Smith, M. A. *'Peopling' the Cleland Hills, Aboriginal history in western Central Australia, 1850-1980*. (Aboriginal History Monograph 12.) Canberra, Aboriginal History Inc., 2005.

South Australia. Public Records Office. *Guide to records relating to Aboriginal people*. 5 v. 1988-91.

South Australia. Public Service Commission. Eighth report of the Public Service Commission, from October 10th 1888, to July 30th 1891. (Parliamentary Paper 30). 1891.

South Australian legal records. Edited by Robert Foster. 5 v. Adelaide Law Review Association, 1996.

Sowden, William J. *The Northern Territory as it is, a narrative of the South Australian Parliamentary Party's trip...* Adelaide, W K Thomas, 1882.

Stevens, Christine. *White man's dreaming*. Melbourne, Oxford University Press, 1994.

Stone, Sharman N. *Aborigines in white Australia, a documentary history of the attitudes affecting official policy and the Australian Aborigine, 1697-1973*. Heinemann Educational Books, 1974.

Strehlow, Carl. *Die Aranda und Loritja Stamme in Zentral Australiens*. Manuscript translation by Charles Chewings of the book of the same title published Frankfort, 1907.

Strehlow, Carl. [Report of 28 December 1921]. *Lutheran herald;*103-5.

Strehlow, T. [G. H]. "Central Australian man-making ceremonies, with special reference to Hermannsburg, Northern Territory". In *The Lutheran*, April 10, 1978;150-5.

Strehlow, T. G. H. "Agencies of social control in Central Australian Aboriginal societies". In, Strehlow Research Centre. *Occasional paper no. 1*, October 1997.

Strehlow, T. G. H. "Australia's Aborigines, Professor Strehlow examines the Bishops' Statement". In *News weekly*, September 27, 1978;8-10.

Strehlow, T. G. H. *An Australian viewpoint*. Hawthorn Press, 1950.

Strehlow, T. G. H. *Aranda traditions*. New York, Johnson Reprint, [1968].

Strehlow, T. G. H. *Comments on the journals of John McDouall Stuart*. Adelaide, Libraries Board of South Australia, 1967.

Strehlow, T. G. H. *Journey to Horseshoe Bend*. Sydney, Angus & Robertson, 1969.

Strehlow, T. G. H. *Nomads in no man's land*. Aborigines Advancement League of South Australia, Inc., 1961.

Strehlow, T. G. H. *Songs of Central Australia*. Angus & Robertson, 1971.

Swain, Tony and Deborah Bird Rose, eds. *Aboriginal Australians and Christian missions, ethnographic and historical studies*. Bedford Park, SA, Australian Association for the Study of Religions, 1988.

Taplin, Charles Eaton. In *The cyclopedia of South Australia*, vol 1. Edited by H T Burgess. The Cyclopedia Company, 1907.

Telegraphy in South Australia. Adelaide, Telegraphy Museum, 1987.

The Australian Lutheran. Evangelical Lutheran Synod of Australia. Succeeded *Die Lutherische Kirchenbote* from 1913.

The Wakefield companion to South Australian history. Edited by Wilfrid Prest. Adelaide, Wakefield Press, 2001.

Tietkens, W H. "Lake Amadeus and the vicinity". Read August 30th, 1886. In *Proceedings of the Royal Geographical Society of Australasia, South Australian Branch*. Sessions 1886-7 and 1887-8, vol 2. Adelaide, Government Printer, 1890; 38-42.

Tjalkabota, Moses. [Moses's story]. In Paul Albrecht, *From mission to church, 1877-2002, Finke River mission*. Alice Springs, Finke River Mission, 2002. pp. 237-300.

Tjintji-Wara [Chinchewarra] by R G Kimber. In *Northern Territory dictionary of biography*, vol 2. Darwin, NTU Press, 1992;212-3.

van Gent, Jacqueline. "Changing concepts of embodiment". In *Journal of religious history*, October 2003, 27(3);329-347.

Walther, C. F. W. "Why do we call ourselves Lutherans?" In *The Australian Lutheran*, vol 8, nos 3-9, February 4, 1920 – April 28, 1920, *passim*.

Watts. Bronte. "James Taylor, collotypist of Adelaide, 1846-1917." In *Newsletter*, Australian Cartophilic Society, December 1982;4.

Willshire, W. H. *The Aborigines of Central Australia, with vocabularies of the dialects spoken by the natives of Lake Amadeus and of the western territory of Central Australia*. By W.H. Willshire, Officer in Charge of the Interior Police Patrol Party. Adelaide, By Authority C E Bristow, Government Printer, 1891.

Willshire, W. H. *The Aborigines of Central Autralia, with a vocabulary of the dialect of the Alice Springs natives*. Port Augusta, D Drysdale, Printer, 1888.

Willshire, W. H. *The land of the dawning, being facts gleaned from cannibals in the Australian stone age*. Adelaide, W K Thomas Printers, 1896.

Wilson, Bill. "Police trackers, myth and reality". In *Connection and disconnection, encounters between settlers and indigenous people in the Northern Territory*. Edited by Tony Austin and Suzanne Parry. Darwin, NTU Press, 1998.

Wilson, Bill. "The establishment of, and operations by the Northern Territory native police between 1884 and 1891". In *Journal of Northern Territory history*, vol 7, 1996;65-73.

Winnecke, Charles. *Journal of the Horn Scientific Exploring Expedition, 1894*. Adelaide, [South Australian] Government Printer, 1897. Facsimile edition. Bundaberg, Queensland, Corkwood Press, 1995.

Worms, E. A. and Helmut Petri. *Australian Aboriginal religions.* Sydney, Nelen Yubu Missiological Unit, 1998.

NOTES

Me and all-about big-fellow cry

[1] This account of the Tempe Downs killings is based on the evidence taken by Frank Gillen. *See* Unpublished sources.

[2] "Donkey" may be an anglicised form of the name that Donkey was given by his parents.

[3] "Ereminta, known as Roger...". There was more than one Ereminta in the district at the time. We know nothing of the other one, except that he was taller (Swan-Taplin;23). Tekua was also a name used more than once about this time, but the identification of both men is clear from circumstantial evidence, at least as far as the incidents recounted here are concerned. For Ereminta's earlier association with Chewings, see *Sources of the Finke River*;14-16.

[4] Thornton's departure on February 18th. Gillen II;23. Chewings dates the beginning of their tour of inspection as February 20th. Chewings, *Extracts*;[4].

[5] "...the Policemen are shooting". Gillen I;23.

[6] "Come on Nimi..." Gillen I;17. Nimi, Naemi and Naomi are other names for Nungoolga. The pidgin of the evidence has been modified slightly.

[7] "Wow, wow". Spencer and Gillen recorded Aboriginal men shouting "wha! wha! " at points of high excitement in ceremonies. "The noise was deafening" (*Native tribes of Central Australia*;293). Carl Strehlow's informants tell us of raiders shouting wildly "wai, wai, wai" as they attack their sleeping victims (*Die Aranda*;1304-5).

[8] "Me and all about big fellow cry." Gillen I;17

[9] ...Abbott's sometime employer Willshire... Willshire had employed Abbott at Boggy Water in the second half of 1889 and early in 1890. Abbott was at Boggy Water again when Frank Gillen came calling on his enquiry. It is possible that Abbott helped Willshire to plan his attack by providing intelligence on Ereminta's movements, and also acted as a scout immediately before the attack.

[10] "literally thousands" of Willshire victims. Bruce Elder;169 (first edition), 235 (third edition). These figures appear to relate to Willshire's first period of less than one year in the Top End.

[11] "unofficial policy of genocide". An unofficial policy is both oxymoronic and impracticable; a secret policy slightly less so. Barry Hill, *Broken song*;52.

Prophets to the desert

[12] "a man is justified by faith...". Romans;3 21&28.

[13] "I have never found another spot like this." Heidenreich to T. Harms, 5 August 1876, cited in Albrecht, *From mission to church*;313.

[14] "the clothes were a different skin." Tjalkabota;243.

[15] "Schwarz was an ... unhappy young man...". Hassold.

[16] "We were morally blameless". T. G. H. Strehlow, *Songs of Central Australia*;343-4.

[17] "they do not know the Lord Jesus..." Louis Schulze, cited by Blaess;104 from the *Church Messenger*, January 1879;6. South Australian Lutherans, at least, in the 1920s still regarded Darwinian evolution as anti-Christian, going by the regular preaching against it in the *Lutheran herald*, successor to the *Church messenger*.

[18] "Schwarz and Kempe were not discouraged ... by such scientistic assumptions." A nice expression of this view can be found in a letter to the *Church Messenger* by missionary Louis Schulze in December 1878, shortly after he arrived on the Finke to join Kempe and Schwarz (1879:1;6. Cited by Blaess;104).

[19] "...without an admission of guilt." *Church messenger*, 1887;105.

[20] "... a German village." In 1891 Kempe ascribed the failure of their converts to hold to the straight and narrow to, in part, the fact that "The land offers them no opportunity for agriculture, which is the basis of all culture." *Church messenger*, 1891;108.

[21] "Country can get wild too." Heather McDonald;23.

[22] Lutheranism. The reference shelves of libraries groan with encyclopedias and other works from which you can take an introduction to the Lutheran reformation. Barzun, in *From dawn to decadence*, gives weight to Luther the man, and his religious and historical context, as well as to Lutheranism (p. 4-64). Beginning on

February 4th, 1920, *The Australian Lutheran* republished sections of a work titled "Why do we call ourselves Lutherans?", first published in 1844, by the Reverend Professor C F W Walther, DD, justifying the separate identity of Lutheranism within evangelical Protestantism. It was surely archaic in 1920 Adelaide, but its conviction makes it instructive. Kempe and Schwarz would, I think, have found little to disagree with. (Vol 8, nos 3–9, February 24 – April 28, 1920).

[23] The curriculum of the Hermannsburg Mission Institute. Haccius vol. 3, 1st half;550-1.

[24] "...Lutheran conversion to Christianity..." The Hermannsburg missionaries on the Finke did baptise infant children of baptised adults. English was not taught at the Finke River mission's school until 1887.

[25] "...faithfulness in instructing." *Church Messenger*, no 7, 1885;109. Cited by Blaess;47.

There is no government among them

[26] "... without clear rules...". Georg Heidenreich to Theodor Harms, 22 August 1881. Haccius;376.

[27] "The Lutherans worked earnestly to deal with the practical issues....". Haccius, vol. 3, first half, and Blaess, chapters 2 and 7-9.

[28] "the Directorate in Hermannsburg has the overall leadership". This history of the founding of the Finke River mission is from Haccius, vol. 3, first half;354ff.

[29] "Heidenreich was the sole signatory...". GRS 4/1890/574.

[30] This account of the trek north is taken from, Scherer, *From joiner's bench to pulpit.*, and *Venture of faith.*

Women and children first

[31] "I longed for the important songs." Tjalkabota;252.

[32] "I want my very own tjurunga." Tjalkabota;259.

[33] "...no child had been struck by an adult." *Church messenger*, 1887;105.

[34] "Friedrich Albrecht repeated Schulze's experience". *Mein missionstagebuch*;46,62.

[35] "...children can not be trained..." Blaess;61, 64.

[36] "... somewhat excitable." Schwarz's words: "fast regen".

[37] "... devils, hob-goblins, spirits of malicious intent". *Agencies of social control*, unpublished version.

[38] Researcher Jenny Green presented at a meeting in September 2002 an unpublished paper based on discussions with Aranda people in the Alice Springs area covering these concepts, and much more. Speaking at the same meeting, *Traditions in the midst of change*, a non-Aranda man who speaks Aranda and knows the Aranda people well reported that most Aranda-speakers remain convinced that disease, and especially premature death, are the result of sorcery.

[39] According to Carl Strehlow's informants, the goal of a punitive raid was the same, whether its cause was a dispute with a neighbouring camp or the inferred sorcery of a more distant people. The goal was to wipe out all members of the targeted camp, men, women and children. The method was surprise attack in the morning twilight, and there were songs and chants specific to the preparations for the attack and its execution. While such massacres were the ideal form of the Western Aranda response to hostile magic there is persuasive evidence of only one such event taking place in or near Western Aranda country, the Irbmangkara massacre that took place in about 1875-80. TGH Strehlow (Journey to Horseshoe Bend;34-49) is the only source to claim the victims had behaved sacrilegiously, and dates the event 1875. Tjalkabota's account places it closer to 1880 (Tjalkabota;242). There is ample evidence of more selective killings of individuals and small groups, often taking place in series, as reprisal followed reprisal, perhaps for generations.

[40] "don't throw stones at hollow logs". Tjalkabota;240. The Western Aranda lived with two particular continuing enmities, both with people they called Luritja: the northern Luritja or Kukatja people whose territory bounded that of the Western Aranda to the west along Missionary Plain, and the southern Luritja or Matuntara, the people whose lands were to the south-west within the lease of the Tempe Downs Pastoral Company. Although they also shared family and religious connections with them it did nothing to reduce the

constant anxiety the Western Aranda felt about their western neighbours. They felt themselves to be constantly surrounded by the Enemy, whose hand was always waiting to strike. If the Enemy did not injure in his own interests he was available to do the work of devils. In 1884 Wilhelm Schwarz saw how, in the person of the Enemy, the natural and supernatural faces of evil were combined. In a period of calm air, loud explosions, like canon fire, had been heard near the station. The Western Aranda attributed the sounds to the snapping jaws of a hungry devil that devoured men. Of course, no people were seen to be taken by these devils. "If the devil cannot catch a man in this way, he incites their enemies against them instead, so that one or more are killed by them." (*Church messenger*, March 1884.)

[41] Chinchewarra's going in to Tempe Downs. Roheim;20-1.

[42] "Children, you must not look...". Tjalkabota;256.

[43] "iliara". From Chewings' translation of Carl Strehlow;1130.

[44] "Every person he met could be given a family relationship...". These quasi-family relationships were based on the Aranda "class" system that divided all people into four or eight sections. While it served to limit genetically close marriages, it went far beyond that, and balanced the isolated life of the food-gathering clans by a much broader-ranging set of obligations and claims on people, very useful in times of localised drought. See Spencer and Gillen, *The native tribes of Central Australia*, chapter 2.

[45] "We who are fathers and sons." T G H Strehlow, *Agencies of social control*;12. Carl Strehlow (1201) lists 183 relationship names, of which many are homophones defined by context.

[46] "They shared creator spirits...". T G H Strehlow, Agencies of social control;4,8.

[47] "It soon brought also rewards." Stanner, *Religion*;(240, 265-6).

[48] "I want my very own tjurunga." Tjalkabota;259.

[49] "Most of the calories consumed...were gathered by the women." This weighting of the economic role of women may have been a recent development, on the time-scale of Aboriginal occupation of Australia, perhaps within the previous one thousand years, as population increase forced a greater reliance on the labour-intensive

gathering and processing of plant foods (see Smith, *Prehistory and human ecology*;68-70).

[50] "...women are expected to find the daily food." Blaess;65.

[51] "A senior man with three wives lived in luxury". On the other hand, it has been observed that it is by no means certain that a man with four wives is better off than a woman with one quarter of a husband.

[52] "So normal was the man's beating...". Hersey;5, quoting Carl Strehlow.

[53] "... a husband was about fourteen years older than his first wife". Spencer and Gillen. *The native tribes of Central Australia*. Chapter 17.

[54] "An initiate was entitled to marry", according to Spencer and Gillen, after sub-incision. T G H Strehlow, in *Agencies of social control*, claims that young men did not take wives until their mid- to late-twenties. Carl Strehlow, advised by four men including Tekua, delays the entitlement to marry until after the *Ngkura* ceremony, when the youth is called *iliara*, provided he has grown a beard. Before this stage, a youth who had sex with his intended wife or another woman would have been killed and his body burned (Carl Strehlow;1250). It was no offence for an initiated man to have sexual relations with a woman of the correct class, although it may have been an offence against another man's property in that woman. One of the Western Aranda terms for adulterer was translatable as "vagina-thief", and a wronged man's feelings might better be described as a sense of injustice rather than jealousy.

[55] "The absence of ceremony marking marriage..." I have followed Spencer and Gillen in this. T. G. H. Strehlow reports an elaborate marriage ritual involving his Western Aranda informant Rauwiraka, but this account may have been contaminated by Christian ceremony since Rauwiraka was a baptised Christian (recorded by the first missionaries as Rauauka or Raueraka), with the baptismal name Nathanael, and had witnessed many Lutheran ceremonies, including marriages of his contemporaries. Strehlow does not report this fact in his paper. Carl Strehlow has a more credible account of a simple ceremony before the man takes charge of his wife, and she assumes her task of feeding him (1238-1241).

[56] "The husband took on family obligations at his initiation". See Bell for an account of how, a century later, Aboriginal women played an

active role in the initiation of their sons, and so influenced the web of reciprocal obligations within which they lived (pp. 209-10). Bell also provides a corrective to the biased perspective that comes from the male sources of my mostly male sources.

[57] "William Willshire's trackers each had at least one wife...". Swan-Taplin;70.

[58] "Chinchewarra's experience..." In an episode both marvellous and horrible, the anthropologist Geza Roheim visited Hermannsburg in 1929 to gather grist from Aboriginal dreams for his Freudian mill that ground coarse but exceedingly uniform. That is the horrible part, although it is well within a long tradition continued by Marxists to this day, of fitting Aboriginal experience within imported theoretical strait-jackets. The marvellous part is that he spoke to Chinchewarra at length and recorded her account of her past as well as of her dreams. The result is all too brief, but much better than we have for most of the other Aboriginal characters in this enquiry. It forms, with a bit of romancing, the basis for a very decent biography of Chinchewarra in the *Northern Territory dictionary of biography* (vol 2;212-3).

[59] "Chinkanaka's two wives had been stolen by a white man". Swan-Taplin;11. We know from Schwarz (Swan-Taplin;78) that Charlie Walker of Henbury station 'stole' one of Chinkanaka's wives. Walker accompanied Charles Chewings on his exploration of the Tempe Downs leases, and left his name on the creek on which the first Tempe Downs homestead was built. See also Hartwig;306. From Carl Strehlow's informants we know that Chinkanaka was boss of the Ntaria camp when the missionaries arrived. His inability to challenge Charlie Walker or to persuade his wives to return is therefore telling. Instead he fell to a spear before Swan-Taplin arrived. Chinkanaka is one possible member of the two-man delegation that made first contact with Kempe and Schwarz in August 1877.

[60] "young men and boys found they had services to offer the white men" The preference of the colonists for the young and the female is confirmed in accounts by contemporaries: "The women are good but the men are bad" (Willshire, *Land of the dawning*;6); "To make useful helpers the natives, of both sexes, require to be taken in hand young, the younger the better" (Chewings, *Back in the stone age*;46); "the boys

who were useful were fairly treated, but the men were maltreated" (Schwarz, *Register*, January 10, 1890).

[61] "demonstrate openly their atrocious character." *Church messenger*, September, 1889;138.

[62] "They don't knock you about". *Observer*, 1 August 1891, 41/243-42/234. Actual words: "'Me whitefellow's lubra ... Me likeum whitefellow ; him no knock about; him gib it plenty tucker.'" It seems likely from the circumstantial evidence that the speaker was Chinchewarra herself.

[63] "When Kempe dismissed Theodor Schleicher...". *Hermannsburg chronicle*;7. Schwarz in the *Church messenger*, 1889;107.

[64] "And I did go." Tjalkabota;244. I have used Tjalkabota's story as a proxy for the experience of the other children. This unique record is the gift of Tjalkabota himself and of the Albrechts, father and son; the father, F W Albrecht transcribed the memoir in Aranda, probably in the 1930s and the son, Paul Albrecht, translated it in his book published in 2002. I have checked Tjalkabota's memory against the contemporary written record of two particular events, the return of the Kempes from their furlough in 1886 and the visit of the Swan-Taplin Enquiry in 1890, and found it after 40 years faultless in its detail (*Church Messenger*, January 1887;6-7, and April 1891;60-1.) TGH Strehlow in *Songs of Central Australia*, quotes from a memoir by Tjalkabota that appears to be distinct from the Albrechts' version, since he ascribes its creation to 1948, but that version, now in the Strehlow Research Centre, is only a shadow of the Albrecht version which is more likely the source used by TGH Strehlow.

[65] "...the mission's methods of schooling..." Schwarz to Heidenreich, 1880 (the first year of schooling), Blaess;165.

[66] "...none of the privileges of Aboriginal manhood." The costs to young Aborigines seeking to progress into white society are well illustrated by this account by Frank Gillen in 1899. "A boy was taken from the interior eight or ten years ago and brought down the country. [i.e. to Adelaide or the agricultural south of the Colony.] ...He was away for ten or twelve years, and when he got back to Charlotte Waters again he had almost forgotten his own language, and he could speak perfect English. One day he came to me and said, ' I think I will go and get cut'...and I said, 'Look here, Jim, you are a fool to submit to that.' He said in reply. 'Well, I can't put up with the

cheek of the women and children. They will not let me have a lubra, and the old men will not let me know anything about my countrymen.' " (Stone;120)

[67] "..in understanding they are children." *Church Messenger*, 1885;54.

[68] "Why don't you ask the children?" Blaess;115-6.
There were of course, and are, Western Aranda words meaning "happy". (Breen, *Introductory dictionary*.) If the missionaries were trying to get across another main sense of the German word "glücklich", i.e. "fortunate", there may be another and simpler explanation for the incomprehension of the Western Aranda; they did not believe in luck.

[69] "Then they went to dig in the garden." Tjalkabota;247. For "Iliara" see Spencer and Gillen's "Urliara", meaning men who have passed through the final stage of initiation, *Engwura/ngkura*, involving months of totemic ceremonies, with the intended result of completing the educating and civilising of the young men (*The native tribes*;271-). According to Carl Strehlow (1115) the *ngkura* candidate had not fully graduated until he had exhibited to the women and children the designs of his personal *tjurunga*, perhaps the only occasion in a man's life when this was done, and he passed to the first stage of full manhood, named *nitia*. In other words, he was now entitled to be called a man, atua, for the first time, and to take his intended wife. The young men's anger needs no further explanation, and their inability to act on it, according to Tjalkabota's account, is telling.

[70] "We have been Christians for a long time ..." Tjalkabota;258. (Spencer and Gillen, Chapter 9;273).

[71] "The older men now asserted themselves". While the missionaries were all distracted by the Swan-Taplin enquiry in July 1890 the older men took all the baptised Christian boys away from the station for initiation.

[72] "they will become devils...". Tjalkabota;275. This "social initiation" was a continuing theme in the life of Western Aranda on the Finke River Mission. Paul Albrecht, born on the mission in 1932 and himself a missionary, records that in the time his father headed the mission, 1926-51, "I do not know of one Aboriginal Christian or non-Christian who was not initiated..." although his father's policy was that Christians should not submit to initiation. (Paul Albrecht,

Hermannsburg). There is also a social use of *tjurunga*, for example in supporting claims to land.

[73] Mototoka's death. *Church messenger,* 1888;103. Leske (20) puts it differently. He was killed for criticising a corrobboree, and "because he was responsible for the death of an Aboriginal he had never seen or known." i.e. for a revenge killing or, less likely, attributed with a killing by magic. Leske gives no source for the claim.

[74] "But the native does not forget injuries easily..." T G H Strehlow. *Aranda traditions*;62,83.

[75] "there were stories and songs..." A worker with the Ernabella community of the Pitjatjantjara in northern South Australia, the Reverend Bill Edwards was so impressed by the way song accompanied all activities that he concluded Descartes' dictum, "Cogito, ergo sum" – I think, therefore I am – should be put into Aboriginal form as "Canto, ergo sum", - I sing, therefore I am (discussion in Alice Springs, September 2002).

[76] "God's great love makes so little impression". Kempe in the *Church messenger,* 1889;108.

[77] "...their thoughtlessness leaves them easily contented" Blaess;61.

[78] "'Spare the rod and spoil the child'". *Church messenger,* August 1889;124.

[79] "the young people deliberately deserted their own people". T.G.H. Strehlow, *The Aborigines*;9.

Animal spirits and the waste-lands of the Crown

[80] "SA [South Australia] smokes big for very little fire." Ernest Cowle to Baldwin Spencer, January 1903. Mulvaney, *From the frontier*;168.

[81] "cattle herds increased at a rate of 25%". Hartwig;312-3.

[82] "without regard to any territorial claims...". Castles and Harris, *Lawmakers and wayward Whigs*;5, 22.

[83] "some strong words in the pastoral leases protecting their rights". Robert Foster;12-13. " The leases gave Aboriginal people unimpeded access to pastoral lands, including 'springs and surface waters'. It ensured their 'unobstructed right' to 'use occupy dwell on and obtain food and water' as well as to 'make and erect such wurlies and other dwellings as they have heretofore been accustomed to make

and erect and to take and use food birds and animals ferae naturae in such a manner as they would have been entitled to do if this demise had not been made.'" "In essence, these provisions guaranteed those Aboriginal people whose country was occupied by pastoral leases, the right to continue living on their land 'in such a manner as they would have been entitled to do' if the lease had not been granted, provided they did not interfere with stock or property."

[84] Western Aranda property in land. Carl Strehlow, *Die Aranda*;1283.

[85] "he established friendly relations...' Chewings, *Back in the stone age*;vi-xviii.

[86] "... numerous Coulthards". See Kate Holmes.

[87] "Mrs Soandso". *Swan-Taplin*;30.

[88] "I passed the remark that it [the child] was mine". Swan-Taplin;29.

[89] "The station managers were the government". We know next to nothing of life on the pastoral stations of this period, much less than we do about the mission. Even our knowledge of the life of the Aboriginal people is better, thanks to missionaries and anthropologists, or we can believe it is.

[90] "...enormous costs of transport.." In a letter of 16th April 1890 Heidenreich reports to Kempe and Schulze that of the £200 received for their wool clip, Chewings had deducted all but £67 for bringing it south. Cattle, on the other hand, could walk themselves to market.

[91] "...about twelve." Daer to Besley, 11 August 1887, SAPHS;475/1887.

[92] Bowman, *History*, 25, writing of the 1930s, when the technology of pastoralism had changed little since the 1890s.

[93] "... the cattle had been run about." *Register*;31 August 1888, in PRSA GRS 5/49/1889.

[94] "absurd to sell...". National Library of Australia; J H Symon's papers MS 1736/1/letterbook 2; 67

[95] "...not on one particular run." Swan Taplin, Evidence;30.

[96] "...not convincing evidence [on cattle-killing]..." According to James Gall, JP, manager of the Owen Springs sub-station of Mount Burrell, "In the beginning of 1884 Mr Gilbert one of the owners wrote to me asking if I would advise him to clear the cattle away & desert the country as the losses were so great, but in consequence as I have said before the effect of the Native Trackers was to almost entirely do away with cattle killing and we have had peace since, except an odd

poddy now and then. This was an outside station at the time..."
(Swan-Taplin Evidence;50.

97 "...bailed up in a gorge..." Swan Taplin Evidence;26.

98 The missionaries' description of cattle killing, as expressed by Carl Strehlow, was identical to the accounts of other station managers, and their responses differed only in the mission's policy after 1884 of not using police. (Hill;64-5)

99 "Krichauff represented the mission and introduced the delegation". *Register*, 31 August 1888, in PRSA GRS 5/49/1889.

100 "The heathen ... have given up completely stealing and killing cattle." *Church messenger*, 1884;38.

101 "Kempe's letter of May 1884...". PRSA, GRG 52/1/1885/150.

102 "...harrassed more than they killed..." Bryan Bowman claimed on the basis of his experience managing Tempe Downs in the 1930s that Aboriginal cattle-killing at that time produced a loss of condition recognisable to southern buyers as "nigger-shock" (Bowman, *History*;26).

103 Stock losses to white thieves. In September 1888 Robert Benstead and Willie Curtis were fined £30 each for stealing six of Elder's colts, probably from Owen Springs (NTA, F 255; September 14 & 16). Kimber reports that at about the same time Joe Harding duffed 800 head of cattle in the Centre, and was not caught (*Man from Arltunga*;9).

104 "The police from the Alice were out the other day". Information on police movements at this time is taken from the Alice Springs police journal, NTA F255.

105 "Mr Thornton was much pleased." PRSA, GRS5/49/1889.

106 "...rations to the pastoral stations". Foster thinks the practice of rationing through pastoralists "probably responsible for ensuring the preservation of coexistent rights on pastoral leases [in South Australia]." *Aboriginal labour and the SA pastoral industry*;25.

107 "...the reserves would not work..." By 1936, adequate time for reflection, Chewings had changed his mind. "To restrict their liberty in any way would be a cruel wrong" he wrote in his reflections on the Aborigines of Central Australia, shortly before he died. *Back in the stone age*;150.

Law or war?

[108] "the law of the land...".Ernest Cowle on 10 June 1899 (Mulvaney, *From the frontier*;128).
[109] Stannard. *Aboriginal history*, vol 1, no.1
[110] Clyne; 46
[111] "...strict adherence to legal forms and quibbles." Pike;294.
[112] "the case is hardly one of 'law' ...". Hartwig;420-1.
[113] "... northern frontier attitudes." Reid;99.
[114] "call upon the natives thrice in the Queen's name..." James Foster Smith, claiming to quote Foelsche, *Observer*, 5 December 1885;14/1068.
[115] "Frank Gillen was appointed a Special Magistrate." This made it possible in the 1890s for Aboriginal cattle-killers to be tried in Alice Springs, provided that the charge was of 'larceny of beef', a lesser offence than cattle-killing and within the remit of a Special Magistrate.
[116] "The use of the pistol ought to be discouraged". *Register*, 31 August 1888.
[117] "Inabauka...failed to move quickly enough..." Swan-Taplin;78.
[118] "'Mr Dare, Mr Dare, Mr Dare'". Swan-Taplin;77
[119] "...indiscriminate killing." The Anna's Reservoir reprisals, like those following the attack at Barrow Creek ten years before, are documented in official reports (Mounted Constable Willshire's report to Inspector Besley is SAPHS 2/2/43, items 12 and 13) that make clear enough for any rational reader the indiscriminate nature of the killing engendered by the use of the "Queensland rush", but not the scale of it. Kimber, in *The end of the bad old days*, and *Genocide or not?* has attempted to estimate the number of victims using sources not available to other researchers. Mulvaney in *A Northern Territory Case Study* has shown that neighbouring clans were caught up in the dragnet. The best review of the application of law and of policing in the Centre in this period is still Hartwig's (387-440).
[120] "We fired about thirty rounds amongst them." *Observer*, October 4, 1884.
[121] " the officer in charge will be held strictly responsible." Reid;113-115.

[122] "Police presence on most stations was a rare event." The movement of the Mounted Constables based in Alice Springs, or passing through it, can be traced in the Alice Springs Police Journal for the period from the beginning of 1886 to the beginning of 1889 (NTA, F255, labelled incorrectly 1883-9).

[123] "The recipe for success..." See Fels on the Victorian Aboriginal police force; e.g. page 6: "The description of traitors and murderers does not fit the evidence discovered for Port Phillip in the 1840s, which suggests that the men who joined the police extended their cultural repertoire... And that they made a distinction between government business and tribal business." "...moving with remarkable ease across cultural boundaries, managing to do the European job well, while governing the play, so to speak, in the world of Aboriginal action that continued to exist below the surface of the European takeover" The mixture of black and white motives in police killings on the frontier deserves more work and less prejudice. On the Queensland force see most of the massacre literature, including the work of Reynolds, notably *Black pioneers/With the white man*, chapter 3.

[124] "W D'arcy Uhr..." See Reynolds, *Dispossession*, p. 52, citing an anonymous correspondent in the *Port Denison times*, of June 4, 1868. That weekly paper was not published on June 4 1868, so I assume the account appeared on another day. I should, however, report that the historians Evans and Thorpe (p. 29) were able to find and cite the same non-issue of the *Port Denison times*. Uhr himself refers in a published letter to his reputation as no friend of the Aborigines, and the drover Gordon Buchanan writing in 1933 refers with approval to Uhr taking the lead in dispersing Aborgines in the Top End after the murder of a white man; "his name was enough to inspire terror among those blacks for many years." (Buchanan;80).

[125] "...the men often killed the blacks without cause..." *Observer*, 13 September 1884;34.

[126] "One of the men [Theodor Schleicher]...". The evidence of Schleicher's involvement comes to us from Willshire's first report of the incident, not from Swan-Taplin (*Observer*, 4 October 1884).

[127] "the group dynamics of the *ngkura* would have favoured conflict." Hartwig concludes that Aboriginal attack or resistance to dispersal was more likely when large groups had gathered (pp. 253-5). The

known incident of attack and retaliation at Anna's Reservoir and the putative one near Owen Springs both involved unusually large groups. A large group meant an important ceremony with much that was secret and sacred going on.

[128]"with the intention of burning down the place". Charles Eaton Taplin, letter to the Editor, *Register*, 25 June 1891, Hartwig;399, Kimber, *End of the bad old days*;15. From Ben Rogers' evidence to Swan-Taplin (35) he was involved in an identical incident, but according to his own account he was not at Glen Helen, or even in the Centre, at this time.

[129] "but the bodies were laying on one heap'. Kempe to Protector Hamilton, 13 April 1885 (GRG 52/1/1885/150). It seems that Kempe wrote "we" on behalf of the Colonists Baden and Jürgens, who reported these events to him later, but was not himself at the sheep-camp. This issue is explored further in *Listening in order not to hear*.

Communication, command and constituency

[130] "The accountability of officials was exacting..." In contrast to Inspector Paul Foelsche, whose command of the police based on Darwin at the top of the Northern Territory was subject to little direct involvement by Adelaide in his day-to-day administration.

[131] " a visit to the south after three years' service." Charles Todd in evidence to the South Australian Public Service Commission, *Eighth report*, 1890, p. iii.

[132] "...the Overland Telegraph was strung across the Centre in order to by-pass it." Hartwig, *Progress*;189-240. By about 1890 automatic repeaters had been installed. For those private citizens who had to pay the high cost of each telegraphed word, a succinctness was encouraged that suited better the bushman's reticence than the over-stated style of Victorian public prose. Frank Gillen got this private telegram from his drinking-companion Mounted Constable Cowle who had just returned from leave in 1897: "Penniless sober sorry". Mulvaney, *From the frontier*;41. For a summary of the building and impact of the Telegraph, see Shepherd.

[133] Protector of Aborigines, E L Hamilton was still in office in 1907. *Cyclopedia of South Australia*;398.

134 This practice mirrors the way the South Australian Colonial Governors, before self-government in 1857, were required to forward all correspondence to the Colonial Secretary in London with their advice on the action to be taken. The Governor's advice was usually followed. Within the government of South Australia, any proposal for new expenditure needed the Minister's approval, and in the recurrent economic recessions the Minister's attention to proposals was very close indeed.

135 Bowman, *History*;30

136 Begbie, *The pedal radio...*

137 Joe Breaden reported to Bruce Plowman thirty years later a visit to the mission in the early 1880s, when the three missionary couples shared the one large room, separated only by screens. Hermann Kempe offered Breaden a bed in this dormitory, but the young Breaden preferred the relative privacy of the wagon-shed (Plowman;83).

138 "I believe in the community of the saints!" Haccius, (third part, first half);367.

139 "Some vigilante killers wrote personal recollections..." For the area of this study, and nearby areas, Kimber in *The end of the bad old days* cites two personal recollections of this kind, but neither is available for public scrutiny.

140 "South Australians were entitled to vote." In fact, only Queensland and Western Australia denied Aboriginal men the vote when they granted manhood suffrage. (Australian Electoral Commission. *History of the indigenous vote*. No date; Page 4. http://www.aec.gov.au/_content/how/education/indig_Vote4.pdf)

141 "... a warning to be on their guard." Mulvaney, *The purpose of a good translation*;[3]

142 "... among them Billy Abbott" Ernestine Hill, The Territory;133, reporting a meeting with Abbott.

143 "... he [Stapleton] was unable to comply with them." Gillen, *Gillen's diary*;108.

144 "...a dispersal by Telegraph staff..." (PRSA, GRG 154/6, vol. 1).

145 "close adherence to legal forms..." The quoted words are Clyne's;172.

[146] Newspaper reports of the Barrow Creek events. *Advertiser*, 28 February 1874;1. *Register*, 24 February 1874;5/384, 25 February 1874;5/405, 5 March 1874;7/463.

[147] "... a campaign of dispersal in the third degree." Mulvaney, *A Northern Territory Case Study*, and *The purpose of a good translation*.

[148] "All this was changed by the coming of the pastoralists..." Reid, *A picnic with the natives*; 85-6.

[149] Logic's story is nicely told in Foster, "Logic's unexpected celebrity."

[150] "Logic was soon pardoned." *Observer*, 12 December 1885;28/1130, 19 December 1885;35/1175. Foster, "Logic's unexpected celebrity"; 127, 131.

[151] " the missionaries of Point Pearce and Point McLeay Aboriginal reserves had organised a corroboree". The demonstration corroboree in Adelaide followed a series of such events held previously at country centres, including Milang near Raukkan. These involved several hundred Aborigines from various parts of the State, including the Eyre Peninsula. While they were probably organised by the missionaries they may reflect a growing consciousness among Aboriginal peoples themselves of what they had in common. Unfortunately the Adelaide event was followed by a general brawl among the Aboriginal participants, caused by some provocative whites supplying grog. (*Australischer Zeitung*, 20 May 1885;1, 27 May 1885, and 23 June 1885;4.

[152] "executing justice on the spot". Quoted in Reid;106.

[153] "It was government itself that was now in disarray." *Observer*, 13 September 1884, 6 June 1885;39, 14 November 1885;14, 31, 21 November 1885;13,24-5,37,

[154] "a most capable and painstaking officer" South Australia. Public Service Commission. *Eighth report, 1891*;xii.

[155] "The Chief Secretary asked us if we wished to make it a criminal case". Swan-Taplin evidence;1.

The weight of the Word

[156] "... a joy mixed with trepidation." Kempe, *Church messenger*, 1888;138.

157 "... his principal financiers". The Hermannsburg Mission Institute's last financial contribution arrived in 1886. It had always been a small part of the mission's income.

158 "... it shall not return unto me void". Isaiah, 55:11, *Church Messenger*, January 1885;9.

159 "...they did not worship him". Haccius;372. Twenty five years later, in Carl Strehlow's time, the dead were sent to an island to the north.

160 "The lay Colonists ... were pressing to be allowed to run their own cattle." Haccius;376.

161 "...examine earnestly how far you are responsible". Haccius;375-6.

162 "... hungry and thirsty for righteousness". *Church messenger*, 1887;137.

163 "Tekua and Kalimalla had helped persuade the boys to submit to initiation." It is possible that this contested initiation - *ngkura* - is the same incident remembered by Tjalkabota (see chapter 4).

164 "... a net made of human hair." *Church messenger*, 1889;88. Carl Strehlow's advisers told him that a cord of dead man's hair, a *gururkna*, was tied around the neck as a protective device when men set out on raids (volume 6;1297).

165 "They had lost their fear of magic and witchdoctors". Blaess;120.

166 "Tekua had been speared and mortally wounded...". Tjalkabota supposed that Tekua had been attacked in error, mistaken for a native constable in the service of Mounted Constable Willshire in Alice Springs. In this, as in most that he says, Tjalkabota was probably right. An entry in the Alice Springs police journal for August 26th 1886 records the news, from telegraph station master Flint, who had been inspecting the line south of Alice Springs accompanied by native constable Wilkie, that "two notorious outlaws 'Billy Cloud, & Melon Charlie' for whom several warrants are out were at Owen Springs ... had stated their intention of killing N C Wilkie & asking M C Willshire to be at Owen Springs on Saturday" ,i.e. August 28th, to arrest them. Kempe got the news of Tekua's spearing on August 29th. Another of the 1887 baptisands, Penneboka/Jakobus, was also serving with Willshire at this time, although he was only about 14 years of age, and may have been selected as a substitute target, for whom Tekua was mistaken. Payback was a rough art, not a science.

All other details of Kempe's journey are from the *Church messenger*, December 1886;182-4, and January 1887;4-7. Baptism details are taken from a facsimile copy of the Hermannsburg register of baptisms held in the Strehlow Research Centre. These differ in some details from the published accounts.

[167] 'Some boys and girls have not left the station.' *Church messenger*, 1887;104.

[168] "nine became candidates for baptism". Kempe in the *Church messenger*, 1888;51.

[169] "... weak in body but strong in sprit." *Church messenger*, 1887;137. In 1929 Maria was diagnosed by Dr J B Cleland as suffering from teritary yaws, a disfiguring infection whose bacterial agent is related to the syphilis bacterium, and normally contracted in childhood (*Medical journal of Australia*, July 19, 1930;80).

[170] "They need... to come to their own understanding...". *Church messenger*, 1887;137.

[171] "Many evil sprits have already been laid aside." *Church messenger*, 1887;105.

[172] "the northern neighbours of the Hermannsburg clans". Probably Western Aranda living north of the Macdonnell Ranges, on the Glen Helen lease, but possibly Unmatjera-Aranda people even further north, where there were ceremonial connections with people around Hermannsburg, as in Rauwiraka/Nathanael's case.

[173] "general slaughter of a biblical savagery." Carl Strehlow recorded from his Western Aranda informants a detailed account of attacks aimed at the total destruction of other camps, whether justified as responses for actual offences by the leaders of a neighbouring camp or for supposed magical assaults from further afield (*Die Aranda und Loritja stämme*;1296-1305, 1334-1347). TGH Strehlow uses this information in his more accessible account of the Irbmangkara massacre dated at about 1875, in *Journey to Horseshoe Bend (37-40)*. Neither makes pleasant reading.

[174] "Others, particularly fathers, stood before the door of God's kingdom and knocked." *Church messenger*, July 1888;102-3.

[175] "He was the first to give witness". Hermann Kempe, *Church messenger*, September 1888;138.

[176] "He keeps his eyes open and tells of offences". Church messenger, April 1888;52.

[177] "not at all such good-natured people". *Church messenger*, June 1889;88.

[178] "she took the name of Hanna." Wilhelm Schwarz, *Church messenger*, no.9, 1887;136. We do not know how far south Thomas went with Koch and Jürgens. It remains possible he went all the way to the Barossa Valley.

[179] " when her husband returns". *Church messenger*, April 1888;52.

[180] Schwarz's report on Hanna's adultery. *Church messenger*, July 1889;107.

[181] "This is the case with our Andreas." *Church messenger*, June 1889;89.

[182] "they enjoy talking about marriage very much ". Louis Schulze, *Church messenger*, April 1888;53. Carl Strehlow's informants told him that pederasty was normal between young initiated, unmarried men and uninitiated boys (vol. 6;1267-8). There is no evidence that the earlier missionaries were aware of it, unless it lies behind this statement of Schulze's.

[183] "a hindrance to a proper family life". *Church messenger*, June 1889;89.

[184] "The married couple lived sometimes unhappily...". Swan-Taplin;10.

[185] "our hearts have been troubled for some months." *Church messenger*, July 1889;106.

[186] "They must pray for God's forgiveness". *Church messenger*, July 1889;107.

[187] "the toxic wind". *Giftwind*.

[188] "Ereminta was noticed favourably". Chewings, *Sources of the Finke River*; 14-6. For Schwarz's flogging of Ereminta, Swan-Taplin;14. James McDonald and Ereminta, Swan-Taplin;27. Alice Springs Police Station Journal.

[189] "We have heard and seen nothing of her." Church messenger, May 1890;43.

[190] "But they can't give them up completely, especially the women." *Church messenger*, September 1889;138.

[191] "Schwarz received a letter from the south." Tjalkabota;257. Kempe told Swan-Taplin (p. 21) that Schwarz had gone south for the sake of his health. In his letter of resignation from the Finke River Mission at

the end of 1890, Schwarz referred to two episodes of heat-stroke, but both of these can be dated, to 1884 and 1886.

[192] Kempe's "very feeble" defence of his management. *Minute book*;16-17.

[193] "and depict us as a flogging mission". *Church messenger*, August, 1889;124.

[194] "Schwarz had chosen the best sites for his new stations." *Church messenger*, September 1877;137.

Frolic on the frontier

[195] "I blow my pipes..." Hugh McCrae;25. "I write as I have felt". Willshire, *Land of the dawning*;23.

[197] The Australian Natives Association. See Brian Fitzpatrick, and *History of the Australian Natives Association.*

[198] "*The heart of all Australia bleeds for you.*" Stapleton;2. Stapleton gives no provenance for this poem, but claims that it was "his first exercise of many in verse while in the territory", implying it was written close to 1883, but it may have been written later.

[199] "the author and a boy native". The photograph was published in Willshire's 1896 booklet, *The land of the dawning*, but may have been taken before.

[200] "Jack Harrison's" death and the Emily Gap incident. W H Willshire, *The Aborigines of Central Australia* (1888);5,10,12. There are more florid examples from *A thrilling tale*, and *Land of the dawning*. See, for example, the "fumigation" of an Aboriginal man (*A Thrilling tale*;[10-11]) and his terrifying of an overfed man at the Top End - "...I for fun ran after him with a shotgun. He was so frightened that he got along as fast as he could. He rolled and wobbled from side to side like a cask in a heavy sea, finally fell down the bank into a large waterhole, and floated powerless, like an inflated diver in distress", (*Land of the dawning*;57).

[201] "the women were later killed for their transgression..." R G Kimber, personal communication, citing the late Walter Smith.

[202] "Willshire's pleasure in the death of Aboriginal men". See *A thrilling tale ...*, probably a distillation of a number of his trips and

people he controlled, and the nearest Willshire's vanity would allow him to approach fiction.

203 "[the settlers] must do something to protect themselves". Clyne;183.

204 Anna's Reservoir raid and reprisals. Willshire's report, 17 September 1884, SAPHS 2/2/43, items 12, 13. *Observer*, September 20, 1884. The *Observer* reports Besley receiving Willshire's telegram on 16 September, the day before the date on his written report. The latter is probably a tidied-up version of what Willshire gave to the telelgraph operators at Alice Springs.

205 The Wild West as theatre. As illustration, in December 1890 the steep ticket price of two shillings did not deter a "large crowd" from attending a display by American cowboys at the Old Exhibition Grounds in Adelaide. *Observer*, 27 December 1890;26.

206 "four copper miners on the Daly River had been killed". Gordon Reid, chapter 8.

207 "The Blacks for Alice Spgs should be classed as Native Police". Peterswald to Besley, SAPHS, COP file 2/4/17, 1884, 830/84-1006/84.

208 "the work von Mueller based on Kempe's collecting..." Kempe, *Plants indigenous.....*

209 'he very much doubted if they can be regarded as the productions of the untutored Aboriginal" Royal Society of South Australia. *Transactions...*, vol 3;xxiv.

210 "...a survey conducted by J G Frazer..." Frazer, "Notes on the Aborigines of Australia";183-5.

211 "It encouraged Willshire 'to persevere in his researches...'" *The Aborigines of Central Australia*, 1888;4.

212 "Willshire's higher pay rate was going to leave him poorer". GRS 1/1890/680.

213 "he begins to want money". *Aborigines of Central Australia*, 1891;38.

214 "we have no other records" Port Augusta Police Station Journal, GRG 5, inserted sheet between pages for April 13 and 14, 1889.

215 Commissioner Roth's findings in the north-west of Western Australia. Stone;125-9. When Willshire was on trial in 1891, four other women witnesses were waiting in Port Augusta to give evidence in a case involving some white cattle-killers.

216 The cost of transporting prisoners in the Centre. In 1902, Mounted Constables Cowle and Williams recorded costs of £68/1/8 for

transferring prisoners from Hermannsburg to Port Augusta, comprising mostly meal allowances (Mulvaney, *From the frontier*;271-3.

[217] "South was able to lend them enough of his own horses..." Winnecke (Horn, vol 1);44.

[218] "There were other ways to accumulate capital". Mission Committee, 27 May 1886;10.

[219] *Second report on the MacDonnell Range country.* AA, A1640/1, 1888/1074.

[220] "the gold and rubies of the Centre". The 'rubies' were in fact garnet, of very little value.

[221] Willshire recorded his finances, probably accidentally, on a memo sheet covering Gillen Evidence II.

[222] Willshire's appeal for funds for an Aboriginal reserve. *Land of the dawning*;66-9.

[223] "his valuation of £300...he performed a marriage ceremony". The Aborigines of Central Australia, 1891;28,38.

[224] "they would have to camp away from the man in charge...". Willshire, *Land of the dawning*;85.

[225] "This large store was built by Billy Abbott." PRSA. GRS/1/1889/857.

[226] "no subsidy should be paid to them". PRSA, GRG 52/1/34/1890.

[227] Willshire's unapproved holiday in Adelaide, 1888. Swan-Taplin, Turton;53-4 and Hillier;70-1. "two trips to the Musgrave Ranges". GRG 5/2/1890/359

[228] "Venereal disease was general". It is likely that the missionaries and most others failed to distinguish venereal Syphilis, imported by the Europeans, from its endemic cousin, non-venereal Syphilis. There were later diagnoses of the related disease Yaws at Hermannsburg.

[229] "A light-hearted girl". Willshire, *A thrilling tale*;[i].

[230] "Ernest Favenc, whose work Willshire read". *Land of the dawning*;22.

[231] Ernest Favenc. *The last of six.*

[232] "as sometimes I am about the locality of Lake Amadeus". GRS 1/1890/610.

[233] " if that officer is aware nothing is now paid for scalps". Correspondence between Willshire, Besley and the Minister for

Education and the Northern Territory about expenditures for Willshire's Patrol is in PRSA file series GRS 4 and GRS 1 for 1889-1891.

234 "Willshire lined up his men in full dress uniform". From Heidenreich's description, and the photograph of Willshire's Native Constables in Port Augusta in July 1891, it is clear that Willshire provided his men with both everyday uniform (dark coats) and dress uniform (white coats with red stripes). *Church messenger*, April, 1891;60.

235 "for which the South Australian public were paying about £1 000 per year". One official estimated in 1887 that the Patrol would cost £1 200. He was told there was only £900 authorised (SAPHS, COP file 569/1887).

236 'I will not offend the missionaries". Willshire to Besley, SAPHS, Commissioner of Police file, 260/1890.

The law of desire

237 "He also asked for a letter to the Policeman". *Church messenger*, January 1890;8.

238 "Dear Mr Willshire...". SAPHS, Willshire file, COP 260/1890.

239 "Thomas seemed to me very peculiar". *Church messenger*, May 1890;44.

240 "the poor savages are shot down like wild dogs". Heidenreich to Homburg, 30 April 1891. PRSA GRG 1/2/554, 1891.

241 "on a murdering expedition against people to Hermannsburg's west". *Church messenger*, May 1890;44. The expression Schulze used, "Mordzug" has been translated literally. It was also applied to revenge raids by Aborigines against Aborigines.

242 "I did not flog Martha the blind lubra". Swan-Taplin;12-16.

243"she appeared from her deportment to be "master" of the house." PRSA GRG 1/2/554, 1891. Our sources on Willshire's women include TGH Strehlow's informants (of whom Moses Tjalkabota was a principal) recorded in his index of Aboriginal persons held in the Strehlow Research Centre, the missionaries' informants, and Willshire's longest-serving Aboriginal Constable in the Centre, Archie/Coognalthicka, speaking at Willshire's trial.

244 Thornton's "best & most trusty blackboy." Schwarz cited in Heidenreich to Homburg, PRSA GRG 1/2/554, 1891.

245" Those signed by you are informal". PRSA GRS 4/1890/86. After Willshire's departure, Mounted Constable South was instructed to provide monthly paysheets countersigned by another Officer. PRSA GRS 4/1891/748, September 29th 1891. In December of the same year *witnessed* acquittal of payments to the Native Constables was required (item 843). By this time South had authority to appoint up to twelve Constables.

God's imperialists and the party of government

246 "... a man who shunned public attention". Schwarz provided botanical specimens to Australia's great plant taxonomist, von Mueller, but resisted von Mueller's wish to name a genus of plants (Schwarzonia) after him (*see* Hassold). Von Mueller went ahead anyway.

247 Friedrich Krichauff. A "permanent backbencher, dogged, humourless and highly successful". South Australia's "chief campaigner for trees". (Hirst, *Adelaide and the country;*53). He signed, as a Justice of the Peace, the applications for naturalization Kempe and Schwarz made three weeks after their arrival in Adelaide, and presented Hermannsburg's annual report to the Minister responsible for funding the mission (e.g. *Observer*, 1 February 1890). He possibly edited the drafts as well.

248 "...the Colonial enterprise as a whole never felt threatened..." Settlement on the Eyre Peninsula in the Colony's far west was delayed for a time by conflict with the Aboriginal peoples of that area.

249 "...innocent natives may not be confounded" ...: *Observer*, 18 October 1884;31.

250 Wilhelm Schwarz's address at the YMCA. *Observer*, 11 January 1890;31/79.

251 "John Hannah Gordon was the natural target". Hartwig;330

252 John Gordon had written six years before... (SAPHS, Commissioner's files;2/4/17;828.

253 "Chewings had formed the ambition to grow blood stock." Chewings, *Extracts*; [4]. "Nothing but pedigreed Hereford bulls bought from the Hon. J. H. Angas and Werocata Station have been used, and the herd show very distinctly the marks of good breeding."

254 "...not, of course, paying its way." According to a report by J Lancelot Stirling in the *Register* in 1891, in a two-and-a-half-year period the railway's operating result was: expenses £23,789; returns £7,200. The recorded "profit" of the South Australian railways in general, £602 000, was based on its working costs only, i.e. ignoring their capital cost of £11 160 299, and all interest payments since inception (*Blue book*, 1891;25). The Telegraph, by 1891, was paying 3% on capital, but only after writing off losses of £282 000 (Public Service Commission, *Eighth report*;iii). No wonder South Australia's public debt had grown, since the Telegraph went through and the rail line was pushed north of Port Augusta, from £17/1/9 for each person to £59/5/10 (1876-1886, Combe;119), and to £67/18/- in 1891 (SA Parliamentary Paper no. 9, 1891;19), since revenue per person increased little.

255 "...no more money..." By July of that year, when the Enquiry convened at Hermannsburg, Willshire had his two extra native troopers at Boggy Water (Swan Taplin evidence;37), authorised as a result of the killing of the Aboriginal man, Namia/Peter, at Boggy Water on January 9th, 1890.

256 "'Something must be done...'" Reprimand from Commissioner Hamilton to Inspector Besley, 16th July 1880, *Clyne*;183.

257 Ereminta's attack on Willshire's camp. In his Swan-Taplin evidence, Willshire gives both "about four months ago" i.e. March 1890, and November 1889, as the time of the attack. I can see no reason Willshire should have invented the January 9th 1890 date on the report he sent Besley, or delayed reporting an attack on the earlier date until the later date, but it is possible. It is also possible that the Matuntara made more than one attack on Willshire's camp at Boggy Water (Swan-Taplin;37-8).

258 "...with his demonstrated bluntness..." Schwarz had already offended his northern neighbour, James McDonald, manager of Glen Helen station, by his un-Christian (from McDonald's perspective) attitude. "When I came to the Mission Station in 1885" McDonald

reported to the Enquiry in July 1890, "I asked Mr Schwarz to relieve me of all the old and helpless blacks when he placed his hands on my shoulders and replied, 'we will take all the young women from your station' and you can keep the old people. On my telling him that I would apply for native rations from the Government, he told me I might do so but I would not get them". The police and pastoralists expected missionaries to be a combination of Sunday school teacher and Florence Nightingale (the Florence sainted by publicity, not the real one).

259 Willshire was not in the Centre in December 1884. Willshire asserted this without contradiction, but a telegram to Besley shows him still in Alice Springs when Wurmbrand was on his Glen Helen excursion. He was no doubt preparing to leave for the north, and may not have heard of the outcome until much later.

260 "...naturally uncouth." Willshire to Besley, 10 March 1890 (two letters), PRSA, GRG5/2/1890/260.

261 "the version of Willshire's defence Peterswald fed to the press." *Register*, 6 May 1890;5.

262 'I will not offend the missionaries". Willshire to Besley, SAPHS, Commissioner of Police file, 260/1890.

263 "[the missions] were doing more harm than good." *Register*, February 20, 1890.

264 " a letter from Kempe and Schulze dated March 13th, 1890". *Advertiser*, April 1, 1890.

265 Taplin's letters to the *Observer* defending the missionaries' complaints, 22 February and 1 March 1890.

266 The story of Jackey's treatment is taken from cuttings in PRSA, GRG 52/1/383/1889.

267 Schwarz's addresses to the Mission Festivals. *Church messenger*, June 1890;59-61.

268 'It is probable that the Government will order an enquiry". *Register*, 6 May 1890;5.

269 "The publication of their Willshire letter was accompanied by an editorial." *Register*, 6 May 1890;4-5.

270 "Heidenreich wrote immediately to Homburg for advice." *Church messenger*, April 1891;58.

271 "I will close the mission". This and other aspects of the negotiations between Heidenreich and Gordon come from the

Church messenger (April 1891;58-9, in this instance) or the *Minutes* of the Mission Committee.

272 "On May 8th Henry Charles Swan wrote to the government". PRSA GRG 1/4/1890/466.

273 " Henry Swan owned the Angorichina pastoral station in the arid northern Flinders Ranges " Flinders Ranges Research [consultancy] (Nic Klaassen) http://members.ozemail.com.au/~fliranre/blinman.htm

274 Henry Swan's pursuit of public office is documented in South Australian *Parliamentary Paper* 92 of 1890, and in Dean Jaensch, *Election statistics of colonial South Australia*;184.

275 "He thought the task of preventing cattle-killing hopeless". PRSA GRG1/2/1866/128. NB II;7.

276 "I could leave at a weeks notice if necessary". PRSA GRG 35/1/1870/229.

277 "the political associations of Swan and the Downers". *Observer*, 2 August 1890;26, 38, 40.

278 "I don't know if I can save the missionaries." Heidenreich to Harms, 19 May 1890, LA, Hermannsburg microfiche H2/13+/58.

279 "Gordon's letter commissioning Swan and Taplin". PRSA GRS4/1890/p177.

280 'Heidenreich's report of the journey". *Church messenger*, April 1891;59-61. "Tatsch [?Haj] Jemmidar" is Heidenreich's phonetisation in German of the Warrina cameleer's name. The English version doubtless is different.

Listening in order not to hear

281 "Eriakura". Beyond reasonable doubt the same Charlie Cooper who, according to Kimber (unpublished talk, September 2002, after consulting the T. G. H. Strehlow papers) was born about 1860 and whose public Aboriginal name was Irriakurra. He was one of the younger leaders at the 1896 *ngkura* organised at Alice Springs for Spencer and Gillen (*The native tribes*;320), served as Spencer's main informant in 1923 for his 1926 book, *The Arunta* (according to T. G. H. Strehlow, *Songs*;xxix) and lived to become in the 1930s a source for T. G. H. Strehlow also.

---

[282] "... with black cockatoo feathers stuck in his hat". This account of the circumstances of the Enquiry is based on Heidenreich's report in the *Church Messenger*, 1891;60-1, and Tjalkabota's memoir;262-3. Despite the different perspectives of the leading Lutheran Pastor and the young Western Aranda boy, and the forty years separating their writing, the two accounts are entirely consistent in their recording of days, places and people.

[283] "I shall bring white men & black men forward as witnesses." Willshire to Besley, May 5, 1890. Manuscript copy made for the Attorney-General's files.

[284] "Martha and Maria told me something". Swan-Taplin;12.

[285] Wurmbrand's translation of Kempe. 'Ein Nest auszunehmen' - 'to clean out a nest' - is as much a figure of speech in German as in English. My own translation of "Sie aber durch Ihr hiersein die Schwarzen aber an Glen Helen keineswegs zur Ruhe gebracht haben, sondern dieselben noch ... die Gegend unsicher machen, indem dieselben sich jetzt auf unserm Lande herumtreiben und zwischen der Vieh wirthschuften..." would be "Your time on Glen Helen failed completely to pacify the blacks, the same people are continuing to make the district unsafe and to roam about currently on our country where they work away at the cattle as if they owned them". No dictionary available to me gives the compound 'wirthschuften', but its components are clear enough.

[286] "More powerful lessons than could be found in the Lutheran catechism." *Deutsche Kirchen und Missions-Zeitung,* 22 October 1885;162-3, 26 December 1885;202, 26 March 1886;42 and 7 June 1886;83.

[287] "Our heathen are no longer so impertinent". Schwarz and Kempe, *Church messenger*, March 1885;53-4, Schulze, July 1885;110.

[288] "the matter of the Glen Helen killings was settled". *Church messenger*, April 1891;61.

[289] "I therefore had time to discuss this and that with Brother Kempe". *Church messenger*, May 1891;76.

[290] "conciencious honest men trying to do good". Swan-Taplin;67-9.

[291] "They have not always treated them so well as they should have done". South Australia. Parliament. *Parliamentary paper* 33, 1891;xli.

[292] David Bews and the terms of Henry Swan's appointment. PRSA, GRS/1/1890/581.

[293] "Heidenreich claimed to have learned nothing new about Willshire's women". *Church messenger*, May 1891;74.

[294] Henry Swan's manuscript report is held as Parliamentary Paper no. 148 of 1890 in the files of the Legislative Council.

Burying ghosts

[295] "his plans will not be realised". *Church messenger*, May 1891;76.

[296] The Hermannsburg lease, AA, A1640/1 [18]90/696, and Swan's proposal of Taplin as a JP, PRSA GRG 1/4/1890/974. Under Section 117 of the *Crown Lands Act* of 1888 South Australian governments could at their own initiative grant leases of up to 100 square miles for use as Aboriginal reserves.

[297] "the weight of evidence that is before them". *Register*, 25 June 1890.

[298] Taplin's request for funds for reserves. PRSA, GRS1/1891/629.

[299] Kempe and Schulze had been hoodwinked by the enquiry. Hartwig Harms, *Traüme und tränen*;270, fn107.

[300] The demand for Schwarz's resignation. *Register*, 16 October 1890;5. Other details from Mission Committee;31.

[301] "When Henry Swan's report was tabled in Parliament". South Australia. Legislative Council. *Votes and proceedings*, 1890;89 passim.

[302] Bews and the Pastoral Lands Bill, 1890. *Observer*, October 7, 1890.

[303] "his flesh and skin were pale..." Tjalkabota;263.

The trials of William Willshire

[304] Willshire's first essay at popular writing. *Observer*, 27 December 1890;26.

[305] Nabarong is listed as Nap-a-roon and Nap-er-roon in Willshire's 1891 and 1895 booklets.

[306] "a Native Constable in a substantive sense". NTA, Alice Springs Police Journal, 1886-9, and PRSA GRG52/1/1885/150. His presence at Illamurta in 1911, McLaren, *The Northern Territory and its police forces*;344

[307] Kempe's report on the Tempe Downs shootings. Heidenreich to Homburg, 30 April 1891, PRSA, GRG/1/2/554 (secreted material).

[308] Willshire's report on his Tempe Downs shootings. PRSA, GRS 1/1891/254. Presumably it was this document, along with another attributed to Willshire and dated February 23rd, the day after the murders, that were read to the jury at the end of the trial. This is taken from Bundey's notebook. The documents, which may have been confected from the Willshire report in the archive, have not survived. They were property of the Supreme Court and later, I assume, destroyed by the Court.

[309] "Homburg smelled a rat". Copies of Homburg's telegraphic exchanges with Gillen, Holder and Caldwell, along with other documents relating to Homburg's role at this critical time, were with the other secreted material on PRSA, GRG/1/2/554. Homburg's short period as Chief Secretary, PRSA, GRG 24/1891, e.g. docket 149.

[310] "a little beyond the boundary mark of caution". *Observer*, July 25, 1891;41/185.

[311] Automatic repeaters at Alice Springs Telegraph Station. Their use in 1891 is evidenced in a visitor's report, *Observer*, 25 July 1891;33/177.

[312] "Frank Gillen was about to be married". His fiancee was Bryan Besley's niece. The best account of Frank Gillen's life is in Mulvaney, *My dear Spencer*, pp. 1-22.

[313] Newland, Simpson. *The far north country*. Adelaide, 1887;18

[314] Holder and Caldwell's report of their interviews with Willshire and his troopers was written on April 17th. PRSA, secreted material (GRG 1/2/554 of 1891).

[315] The injury to Willshire's thumb. In January the previous year Willshire had claimed £5/-/6 for medical treatment of an injured hand. PRSA, GRS 4/27 of 1890.

[316] "later evidence from the stockman Charles Tucker". Gillen I;39, taken by Besley.

[317] "a gentleman who managed a station". Willshire, *Land of the dawning*;27.

[318] Aremala made a revised statement to South. This is found in the second version of the evidence in Gillen I;86.

[319] Gillen's offer to serve as sub-Protector. PRSA, GRG 1/2/524 of 1891.

[320] "I have doubts of M.C. Willshire's sanity". PRSA, GRG 5/2/264 of 1891, filed at GRG 5/2/418 of 1891.

[321] "Willshire was scheduled for trial before the Supreme Court in Adelaide". Telegram Peterswald to Besley, 28 April 1891.

[322] Central Australian prisoners tried at Port Augusta. Toombana and Nitrinitrinia were convicted for assault on the manager of Erldunda in 1888. Hartwig;614.

[323] Henry Bundy's trial of Willshire. There is no official report of the trial, but detailed reports were carried in the *Register* and the *Port Augusta Dispatch* on July 24th, and the *Observer*, on July 25th 1891. Henry Bundey recorded the trial in his judge's *Notebook* covering 1891.

[324] Bundey, *Conviction of innocent men*;5, 16.

[325] "Willshire could easily have placed his hand on his trooper's head". In Sydney's St James Courthouse, also built in the late nineteenth Century, the prisoner sits behind counsel, facing the judge, and on the court's lowest level. Here the witness occupies the position to the judge's right that Willshire occupied in the Port Augusta courtroom.

[326] "men and women in hand-me-down clothes". Thanks to Protector Hamilton, a Port Augusta photographer was sent by Bryan Besley to their camp in sand dunes on the edge of the town to take a group portrait. Hamilton was not concerned for the welfare of these people from another world. He wanted them recorded as specimens of Central Australian Aborigines while there were still specimens to record.

[327] "Me shootum Roger; knock um heels over head" *Observer*, 1 August 1891;41/233-42/234.

[328] "James Stuart chose to lead the prosecution". *Observer*, 25 July 1891;21.

[329] "Bryan Besley spoke only to the civilians". Gillen I;38-52.

[330] "Stuart chose as his first witness Kwalba/Jack". The sequence of witnesses is taken from Bundey's notebook, which differs in some respects from the newspaper reports.

[331] Willshire wanted Ereminta and Donkey "taken for this purpose". *Register*, July 24 1891;5/165. Note there is also a fuller report of the trial, identical to the *Observer*'s, on p. 4.

[332] Thomas's statements on the killing of his brother. Gillen I records (p. 83) without date what must be a second version of Thomas's

evidence (p. 65), possibly taken when the recanting constables were heard again, on April 27th. This is not found in Gillen II.

333 The jurisdiction of the Port Augusta Court. Bundey, *Notebook*;155-6, and Section 7, South Australia, *Act of Parliament no. 6 of 1868-9*.

334 "That's why we shoot Roger and Donkey." *Port Augusta dispatch*, 24 July 1891;[341]. Also in the *Observer*, 25 July 1891;176.

335 "Nung-wool-Ka - witness - no evidence". Bundey, *Notebook*;164. The way Aboriginal evidence was moulded by courtesy was widely understood at the time, and continues to be a factor among Aboriginal peoples following traditional lifestyles today. T. G. H. Strehlow writing after the Second World War notes "the natives' desire to please their questioners - a desire that vitiates much of their evidence when given in a court of law". (*Songs*;xxx). He also points out that Aboriginal translators played an active role in questioning and compiling the replies of the people they were translating for (*Songs*;xxviii), but bear in mind that 'interpreting' pidgin English involved English-speaking questioners in the same kind of interventions.

336 The Aboriginal Witnesses Act, and the admissibility of the written depositions of Aborigines. *Aboriginal Witnesses Act 1848*, 11 and 12 Vic. No 3, Sections 3-5. McCorquodale;65. "Depositions of every Aboriginal giving unsworn testimony to a preliminary enquiry shall be reduced to writing and verified by signature of the justice. Upon trial or hearing, such deposition shall be admissible in circumstances where the written affidavit or deposition upon oath of any person might be lawfully read or received."

337 "Willshire gives very general satisfaction". Bundey notebook;165.

338 "no blame attaches to Mounted Constable Willshire". The report Holder and Caldwell sent to Robert Homburg (located with the other secreted material) came to no such conclusion, although they may have said it elsewhere. Holder and Caldwell were so casual in their enquiries that they exchanged Archie with Kwalba in the events of February 22nd 1891, and concluded one of the victims, Ereminta, "had a bad character" on no evidence at all except Willshire's assertion.

339 William Willshire was refused the Illamurta posting in 1893. PRSA, GRG 5/304 of 1893. Procedures for payment of Constables tightened, PRSA, GRS 4/843 of 1891.

[340] "Any circumstance of a pressing or extraordinary character". PRSA GRS/789-90 of 1891.

[341] The anonymous editorial writer in the *Port Augusta dispatch*. July 31, 1891.

[342] W H Abbott's death. *Observer*, 25 July 1891;32/176.

[343] "a forensic gentleman notorious for his ignorance". Willshire, *Land of the dawning*;90-1.

[344] Tom C Fowler, Justitia and A Colonist of 1844 wrote to the *Observer* on August 15, 1891. Willshire's legal expenses. PRSA, GRG 1/1/966 of 1891.

Who killed Ereminta?

[345] Alfred Deakin on Henry Parkes. Murdoch, *Alfred Deakin*;148-9. The careers of Deakin and Parkes overlapped, and both were leaders of the push to federate the Australian colonies.

[346] "a brochure of unmitigated rubbish and vulgarity". *Northern Territory times*, 24 July 1896;2

[347] Joseph Conrad. *Heart of darkness*. Penguin Classics, 1995; 113.

[348] On William Willshire's sanity. The most plausible medical description I have found for Willshire's malignant vanity is Narcissistic Personality Disorder. The symptoms fit him like a glove, as they no doubt fit many others who have killed no-one. Willshire's abrupt shifts of attention probably had another cause altogether. A form of epilepsy is one possibility.

Consequences

[349] "memory has become ignorant'. Rauwiraka, the last of T G H Strehlow's informants to die, in 1952. *Songs*;677.

[350] There were "no fewer" Aboriginal people on the Finke. *Church messenger*, April 1891;61.

[351] Swan-Taplin's listing of Aboriginal persons, according to Heidenreich. *Church messenger*, May 1891;75. The list of Aborigines present at Hermannsburg at the time; Swan-Taplin;21 & [21A]. No other lists were found with the evidence, but this Domesday Book of Aranda Australians in 1890 is worth pursuing further.

---

[352] "No-one knows how many Western Aranda there were". The early figures are from Hartwig;25-32. Schwarz's 1890 estimate is from Swan-Taplin;79. Polhill's evidence is at Swan-Taplin;49.

[353] "in 1899 measles carried off 16%". Carl Strehlow, *Die Aranda* ...;1362.

[354] "They decline in leaps and bounds". *Church messenger*, 1890;8,44.

[355] Carl Strehlow's data on Western Aranda population. Preface to *Die Aranda...* The most likely cause of sterility among the Western Aranda was gonorrhoea, less symptomatic than syphilis but more chronic and sterilising. The non-venereal syphilis endemic on the Finke provided no immunity against gonorrhoea, as it did for the imported syphilis. (Judy Campbell, *Invisible invaders*;20). Campbell also points out the main cause of mortality among the mainland Aboriginal peoples was smallpox, but there was no smallpox epidemic on the upper Finke after the 1860s. Cowle's letters to Spencer contain a number of direct observations of the impact of disease (Mulvaney, *From the frontier*;335), and report Aboriginal thinking about the causes of these new whitefellow diseases (124, 133) raising the possibility that new diseases created many new causes of revenge killing.

[356] "Aremala continued in the police service". Mulvaney, *From the frontier*;37,124. Aremala assisted the Horn Expedition in 1894. Kwalba's story, Strehlow Research Foundation, *Newsletter*, vol. 6, no. 1, Jan 1983;1-2. Kwalba was one of Spencer and Gillen's main informants in 1896. In 1894 the Horn Expedition also had the assistance of a Thomas (Hill; "Through Larapinta land";39). Much later, in 1928, came the egregious Coniston killings.

[357] "we cannot know what sins their fore-fathers were guilty of". *Church messenger*, 1891;108.

[358] Heidenreich's loyalty to the Finke River mission. Blaess;150-1.

[359] The visions of the Western Aranda in Carl Strehlow's time. *Lutheran herald*, March 27 1922;194. Here we have evidence of more historical treasures: original literary works by Aboriginal Australians in their own language.

[360] "a focal indigenous idea". Austin-Broos, *The meaning of Pepe*;312.

[361] Arabi's career. Van Gent;342, 362, *Lutheran herald*, 1 March 1926;76, Mulvaney, *From the frontier*;34-6, etc, especially endnote 15, p. 291.

362 "Arabi refused to respond to Albrecht's questioning". F W Albrecht, *Mission diary*;6.

363 "old Andreas was called home". Friedrich Albrecht, *Mission diary*;76. Missionary forgetfulness may have also had its advantages for Andreas. His marriage to Beata we may assume to have been a Christian one, from her name and his standing as a Christian on the mission, but it appears that his first and undesired Christian wife Maria/Adilka was still alive at the time. (Cleland, "Notes...";80.)

Index